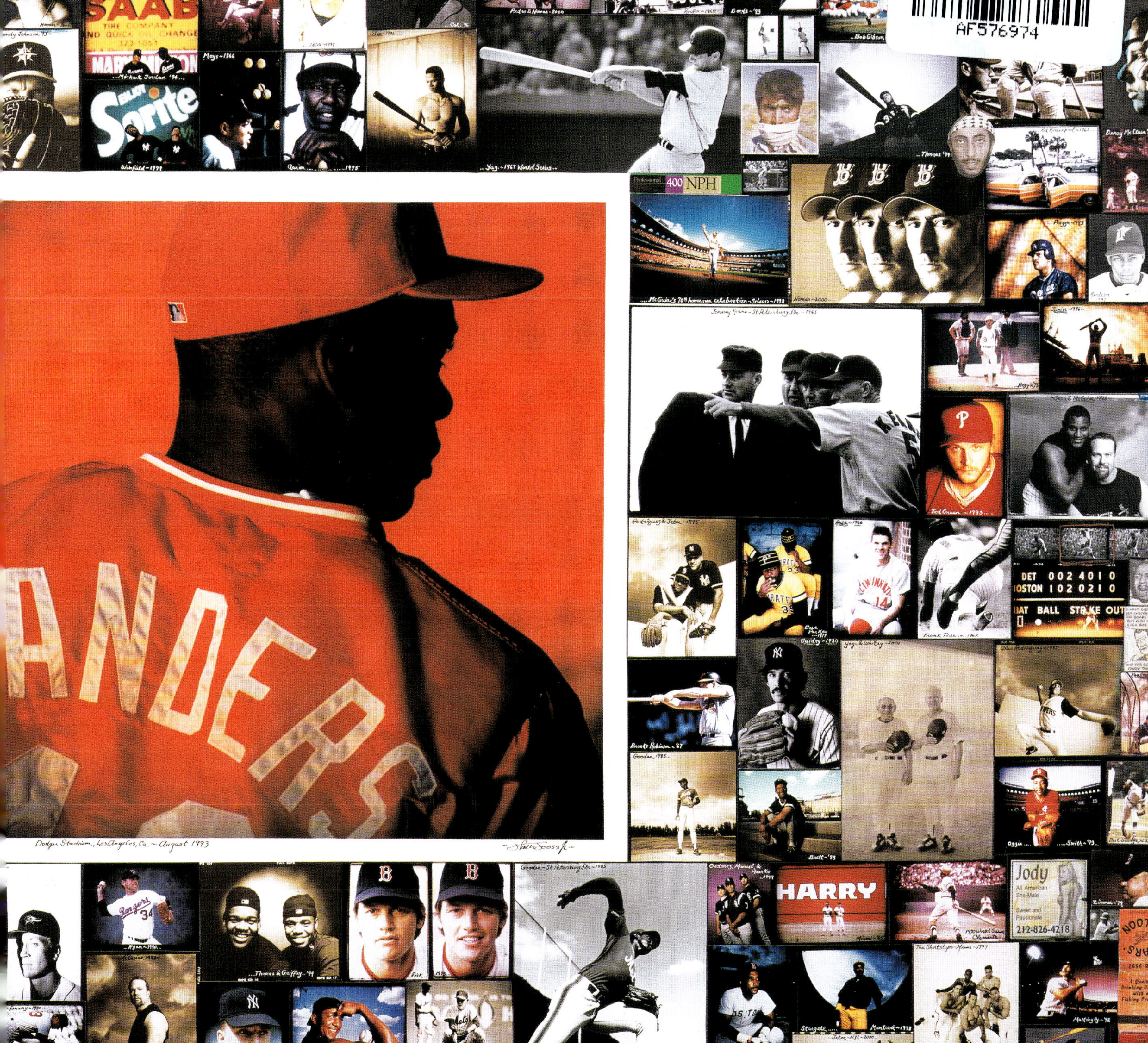

SAAB
TWINS
Martínez Wins
NPH
ANDERS
Dodger Stadium, Los Angeles, Ca ~ August 1993
Yaz - 1967 World Series
DET 002 401 0
BOSTON 102 021 0
BAT BALL STRIKE OUT
HARRY
Jody
All American
She-Male
Sweet and Passionate
212-826-4218
Bonds blasts HR No. 599
On Sept. 11, the 90's ended.
Sunday, July 28, 2002

CLASSIC BASEBALL

CLASSIC

TEXT BY DAVE ANDERSON

THE PHOTOGRAPHS OF WALTER IOOSS JR

BASEBALL

HARRY N. ABRAMS, INC., PUBLISHERS

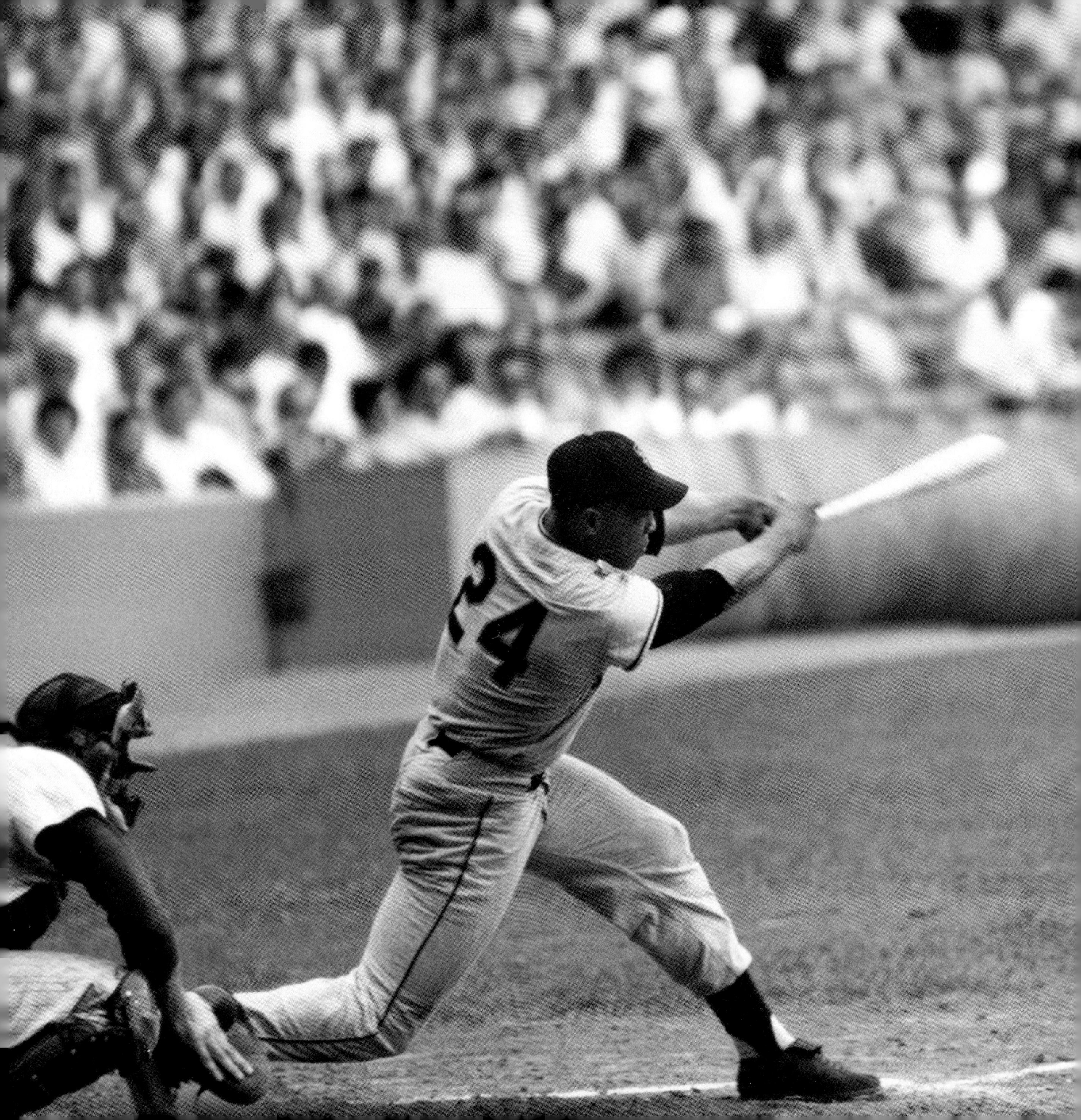

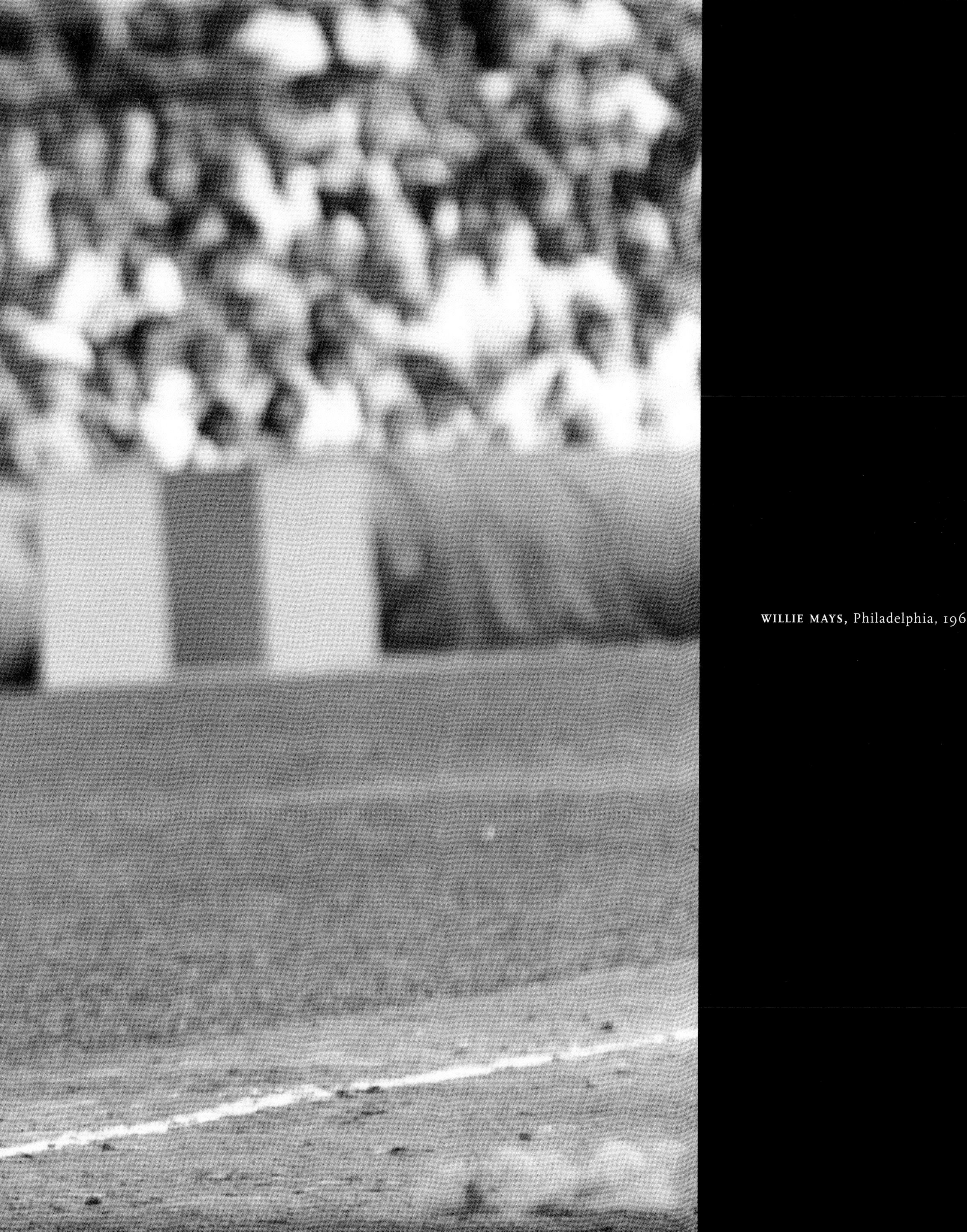

WILLIE MAYS, Philadelphia, 1963

HNNY KEANE, St. Louis manager, Al Lang Field,
St. Petersburg, Florida, 1964

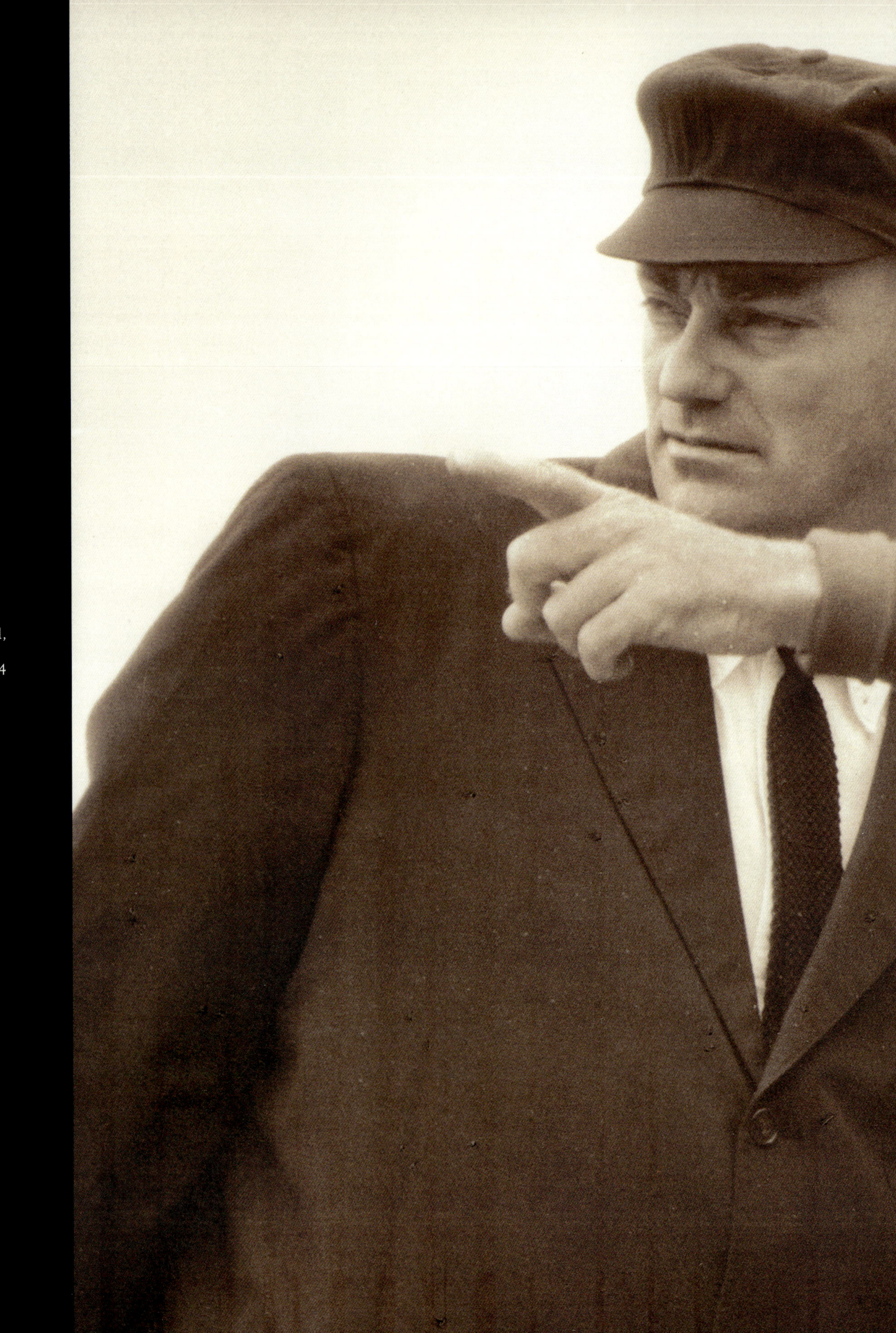

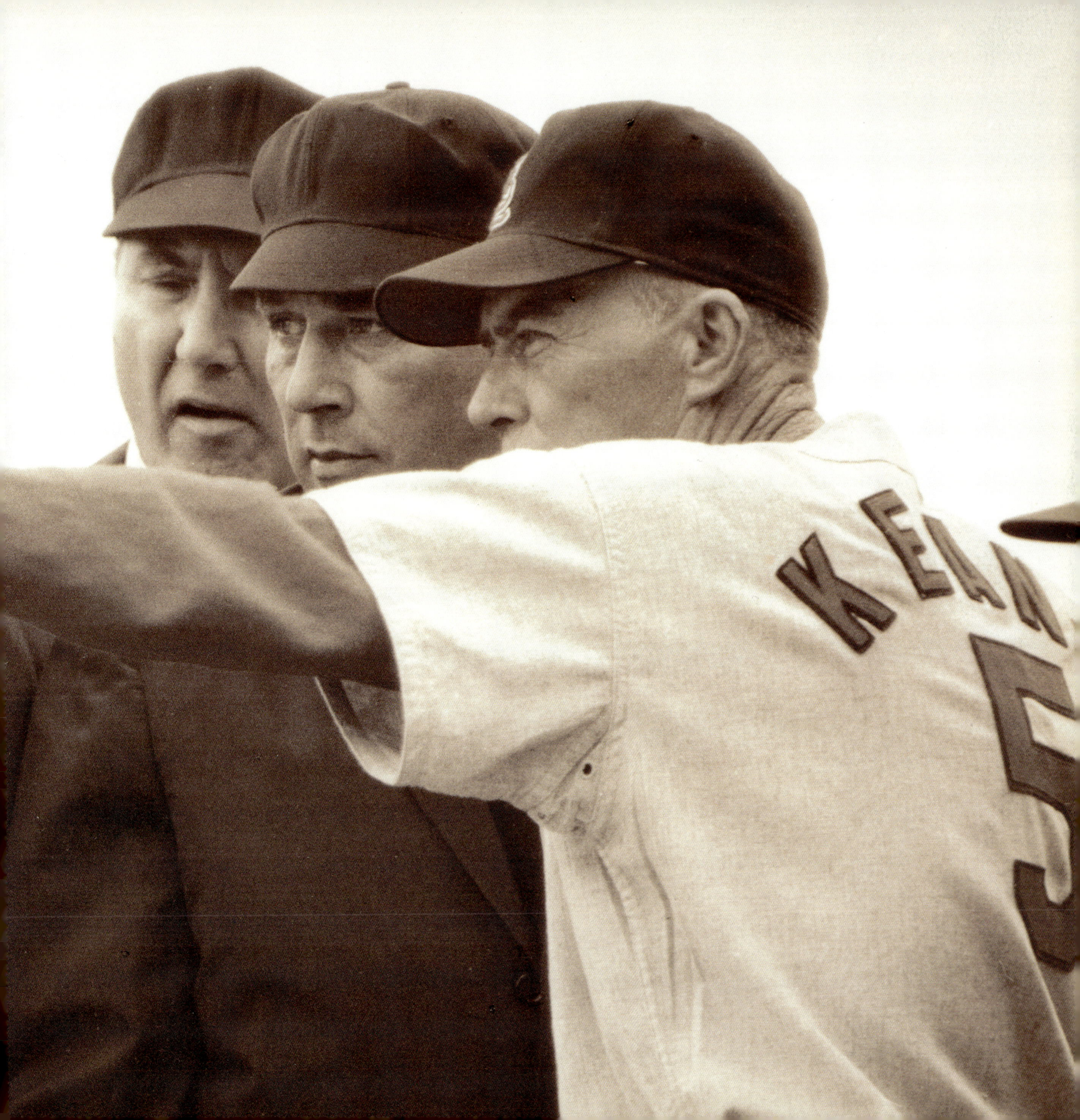

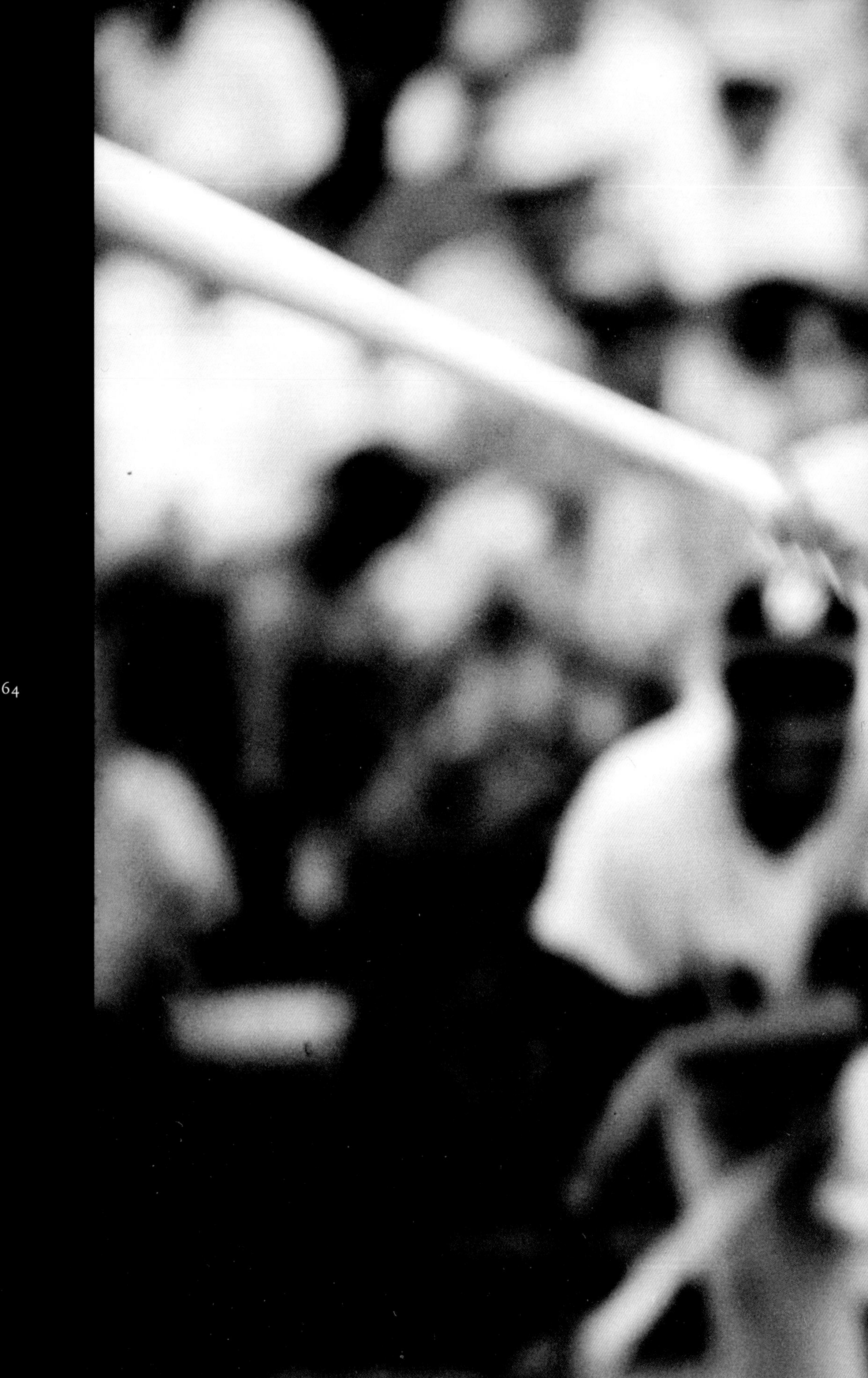

MICKEY MANTLE, Pompano Beach, Florida, 1964

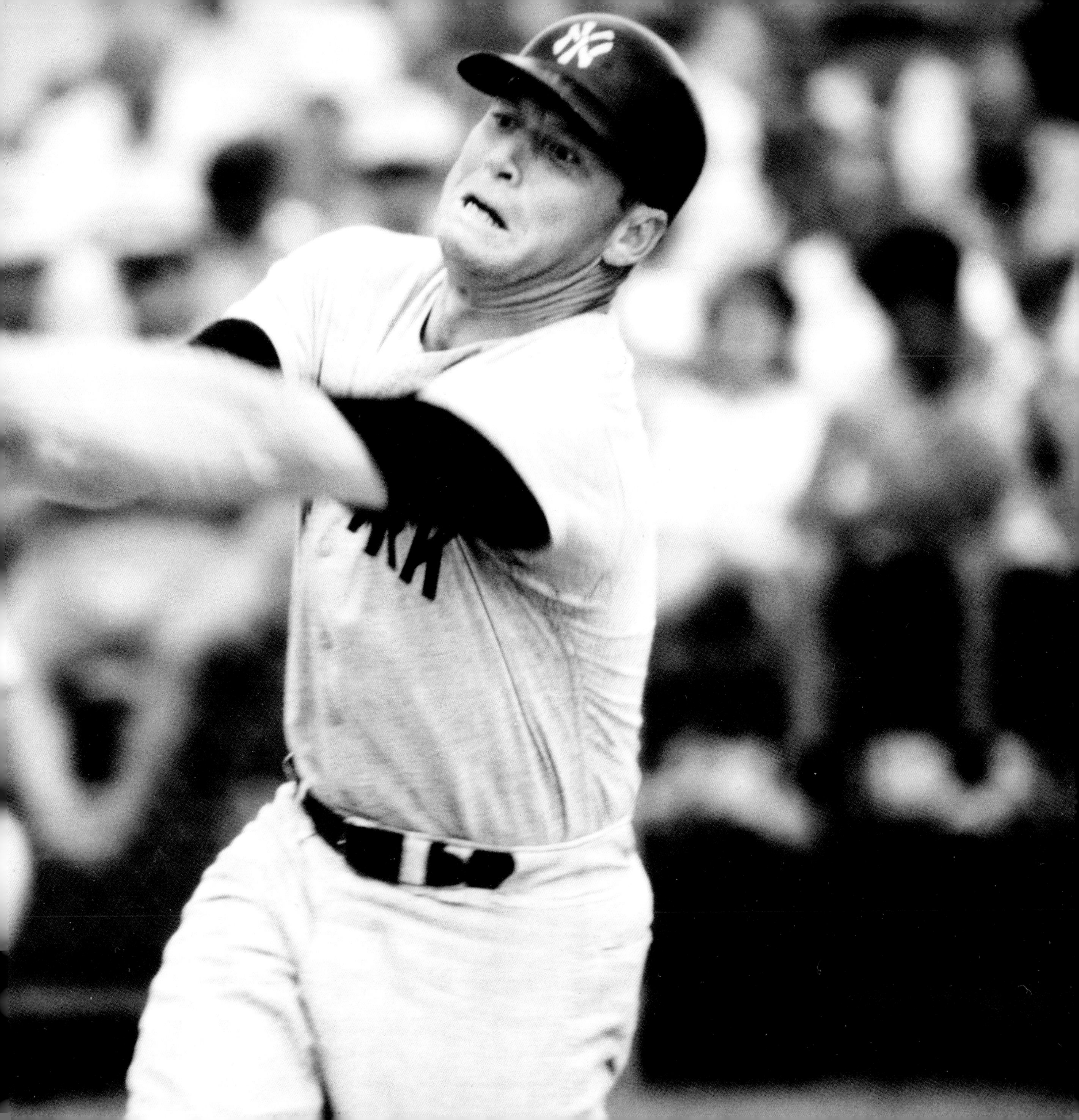

CLASSIC BASEBALL CONTENTS

14

PREFACE | WALTER IOOSS JR.

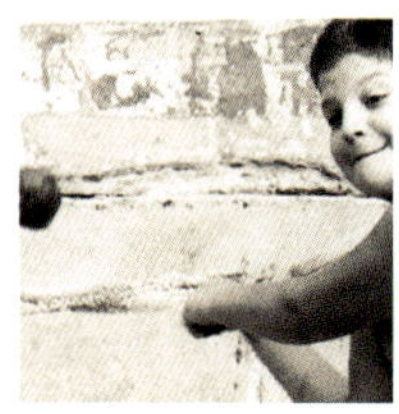

22

INTRODUCTION

DAVE ANDERSON

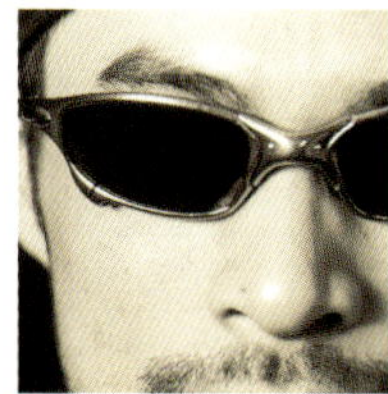

32

FACES

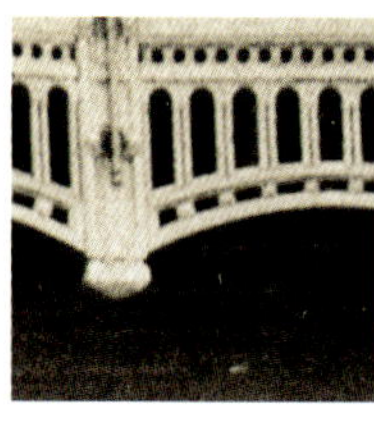

60

BALLPARKS

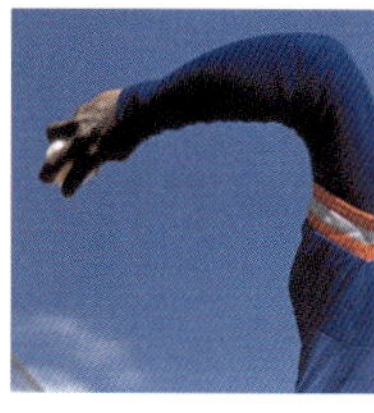

92

PITCHERS

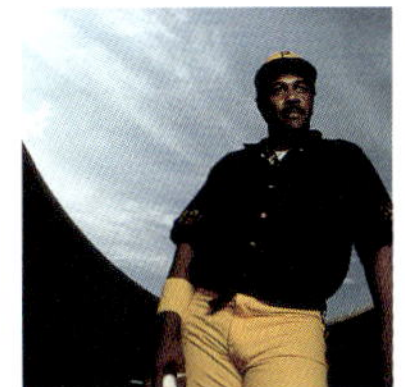

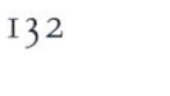

132

HITTERS

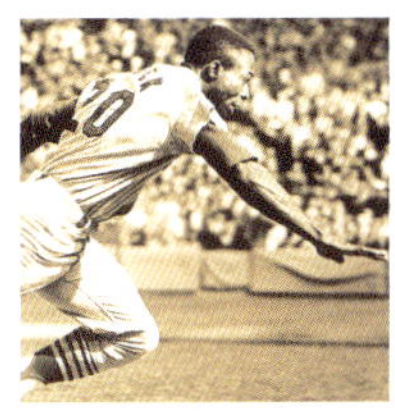

160

BASE RUNNERS

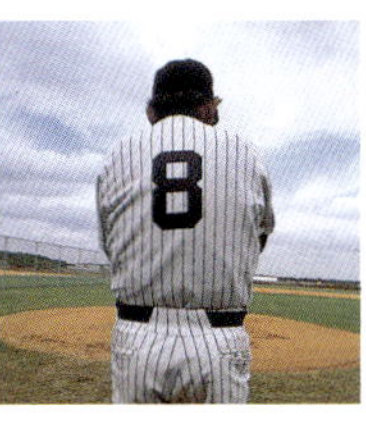

178

MANAGERS

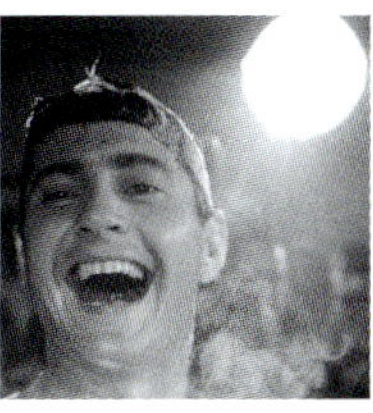

194

CELEBRATIONS

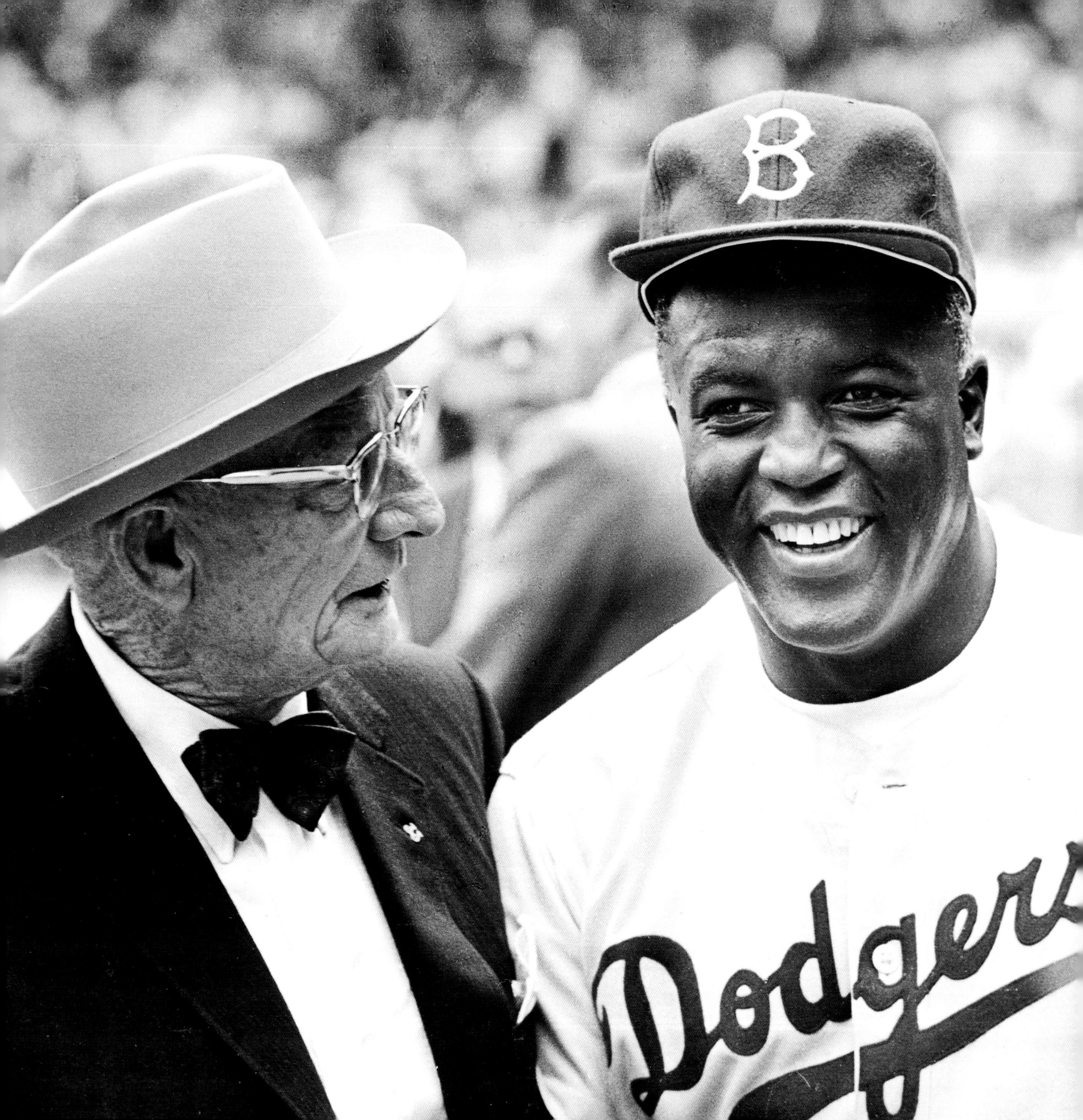
B
Dodgers

JACKIE ROBINSON AND CLYDE SUKEFORTH, Dodgers manager in 1947, Old-Timers Day, Polo Grounds, New York, 1962

ACKNOWLEDGMENTS

I've been fortunate to know many wonderful and amusing baseball people who shared their time and friendship with me, especially:

Art Mahaffey, John Callison, Willie Stargell, Dick Allen, Pat Corrales, Junior Griffey, Derek Jeter, Keith Hernandez, Tim McCarver, Orlando Cepeda, Dave Parker, Dock Ellis, Tom Seaver, Reggie Jackson, Earl Weaver, Casey Stengel, Cal Ripken Jr., Darryl Strawberry, Davey Johnson, the '64 Phillies, the '79 Pirates, the '86 Mets.

And to my beautiful wife, Eva, my sons, Christian and Bjorn, my mother and my late father, thanks to all of you for making my life so wonderful.

WALTER IOOSS JR

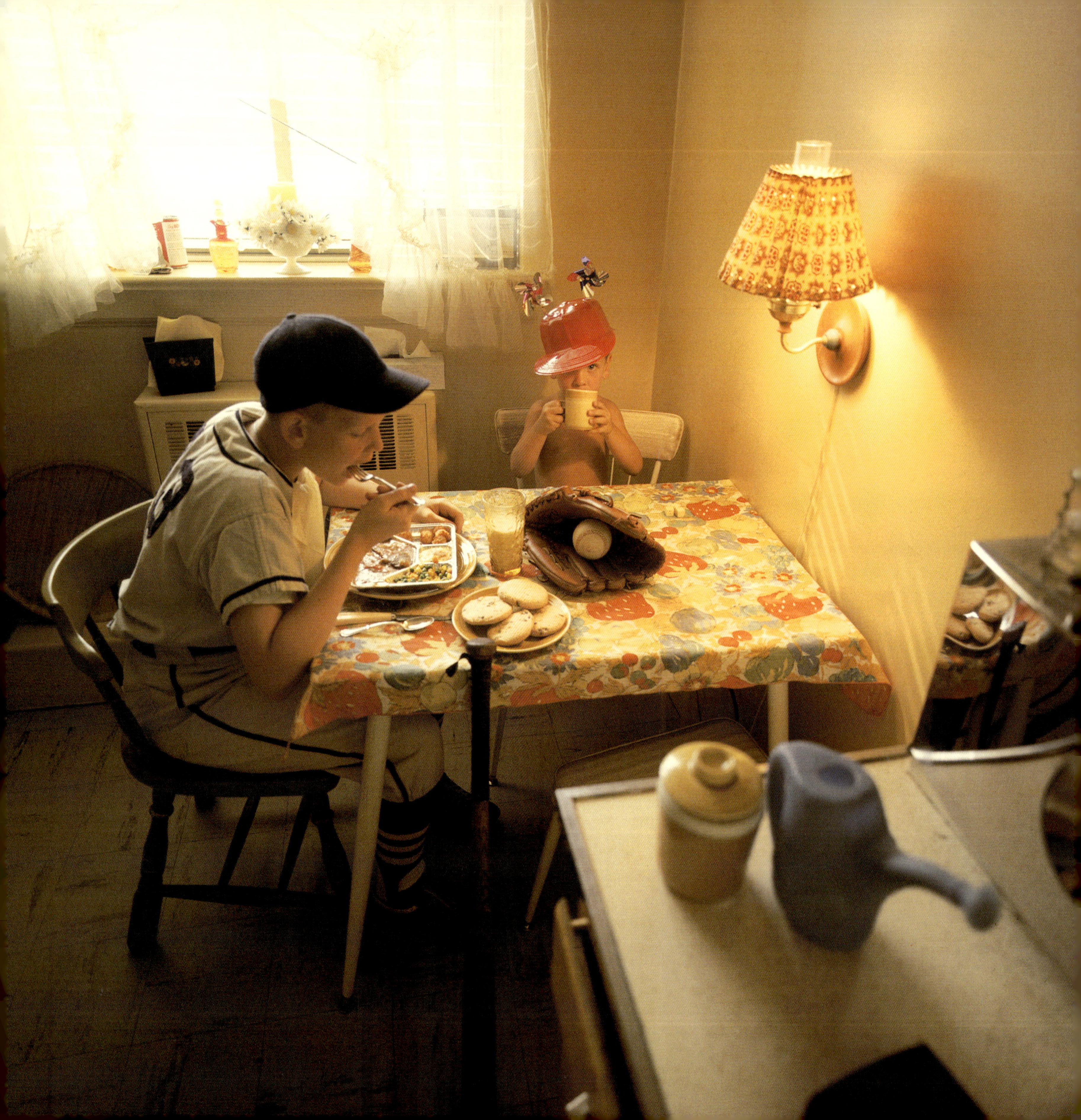

PREFACE by Walter Iooss Jr.

LITTLE LEAGUER, Orange, New Jersey, July 1965

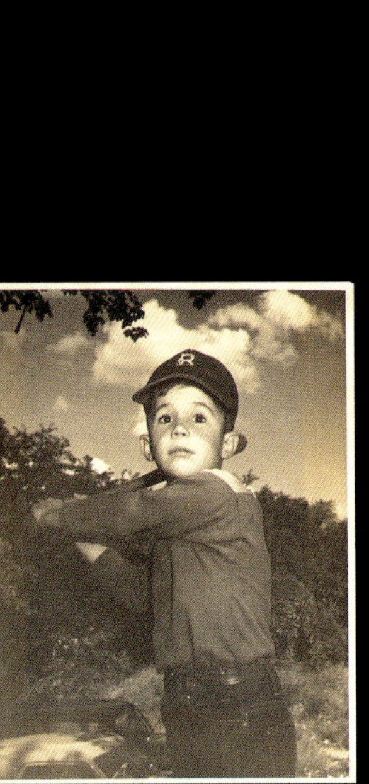

ONE OF MY EARLIEST MEMORIES is posing for a photograph taken by my father in the backyard of my East Orange, New Jersey, home. Me in my Brooklyn Dodgers uniform, standing on a stool, as I now realize, so my father could make the background less cluttered. The date was October 1948. I was five years old. Somehow that moment remains in my fading memory. Decades have passed since I last saw that photograph, but the memory lingers. Why? Was it my childhood love of the Dodgers? Or was it because that was the moment that baseball and photography came into my life: Walter Iooss Jr. photographed by Walter Iooss Sr. I never thought about that photo until more than half a century later, when I was looking through old baseball photographs for this book. This only makes it more of a mystery, but I think that moment was the genesis of my career as a photographer as well as of my love of the slow, enticing game called baseball. It's a game of sporadic bursts. Just when you think you're about to be lulled to sleep, something happens that's breathtaking. The center fielder has been standing out there for several innings, for example, but suddenly he has to run and leap to make a catch against the fence. In 1959, eleven years after that fateful day of that backyard photo, my

WALTER IOOSS JR., age 5, East Orange, New Jersey. Photograph by Walter Iooss Sr.

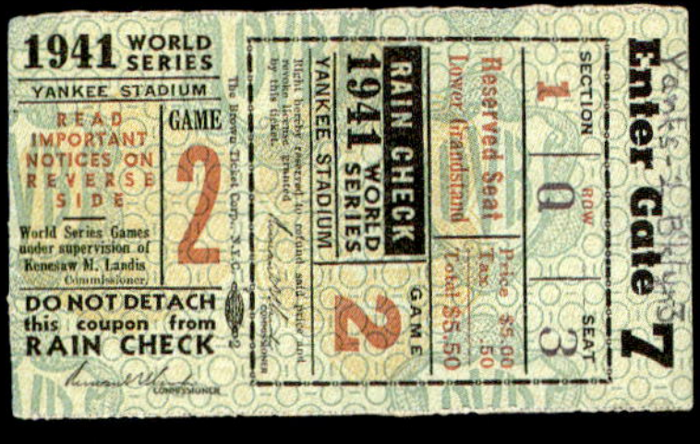

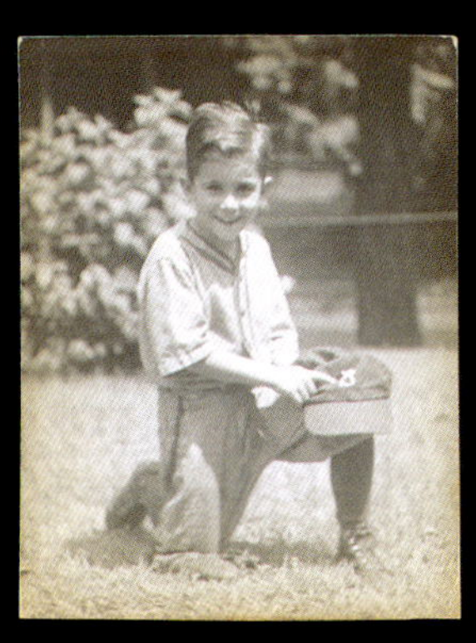

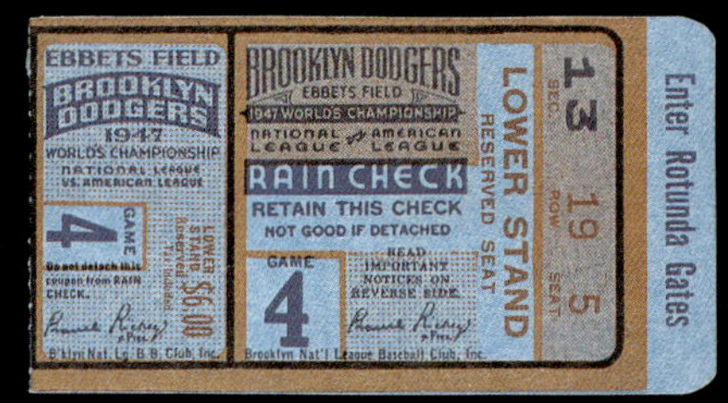

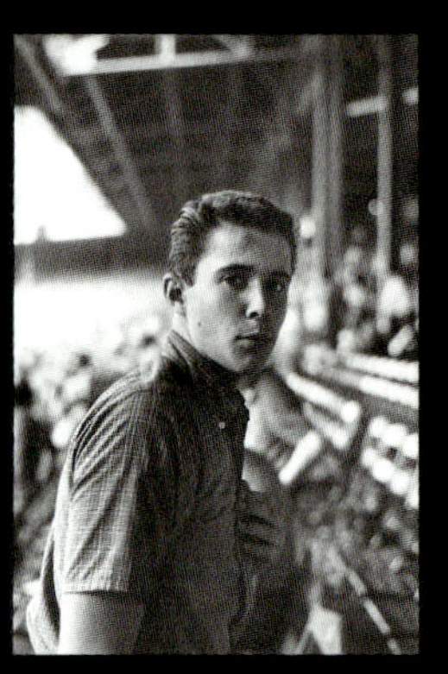

SNAPSHOTS OF YOUNG WALTER with baseball tickets used by Walter Iooss Sr.

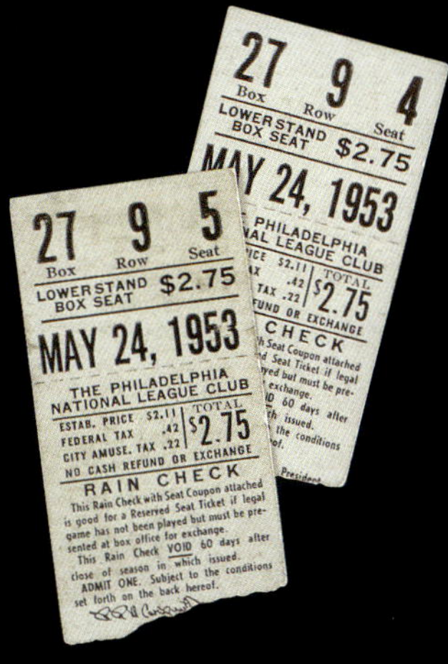

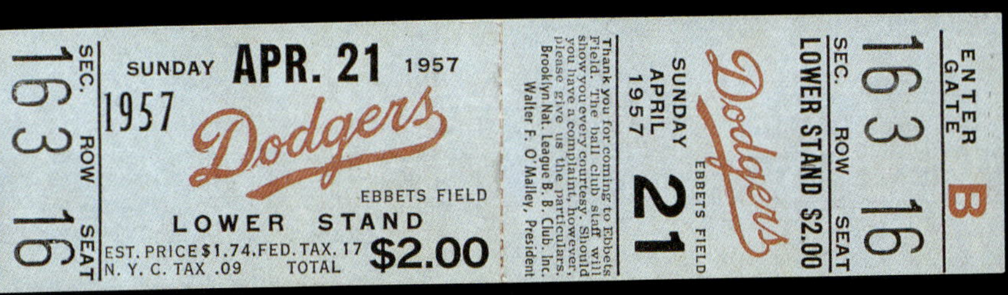

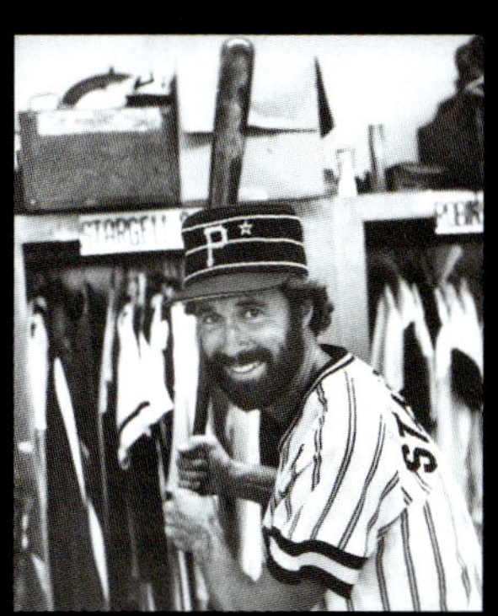

WALTER IOOSS JR. at Pittsburgh Pirates spring training, 1978 (FAR RIGHT). Photograph by Willie Stargell.

father's early love of photography was rekindled. He would buy tickets to sports events and we both began shooting pictures from the stands at Yankee Stadium and at Connie Mack Stadium in Philadelphia.

Those were the ballparks where my career as a sports photographer began. And I have continued shooting baseball every year since then, not wanting to interrupt the connection from season to season. No matter that my career sidestepped from journalism into advertising in the late 1980s and '90s, the number stands at forty-three years and counting.

My love for the game really blossomed in those fanatical boyhood summer days when I played stickball from daybreak to nightfall, my pitching arm so dead I could hardly lift my fork for dinner. In time, that love traveled to many places:

To Connie Mack Stadium, for example, where I was often younger than any of the Phillies' players; to the Polo Grounds, the first home of the New York Mets, where I learned how charming Casey Stengel could be and how mean-spirited some of the New York press photographers could be. To the Bronx House of Detention, a.k.a. Yankee Stadium, where I was once removed from the seat I had purchased by an usher who told me I had to leave the ballpark because no one was allowed to take pictures from the stands. I thought he was kidding, but I learned that there is no kidding in Yankee Stadium. As I stood to leave the stadium that day, I looked over at the New York press photographers who were all smiling. Welcome to Yankee Stadium, home of endless regulations and rude behavior.

Eventually my love for baseball took me to Florida for my first assignment to cover spring training for *Sports Illustrated* in 1963. I traveled with writer Frank Deford, who was just out of Princeton. To me, spring training showed the true beauty of baseball: players and fans mingling, almost like a family picnic. In the 1970s, I realized that one ballpark in Florida seemed to encapsulate all of this: McKechnie Field in Bradenton, where the Pittsburgh Pirates trained. In the bullpen, a rope separated fans from players. Kids hung over the right-field fence. You could almost smell the ghosts of all the Hall of Famers who had passed through there in Grapefruit League games.

Connie Mack, the Polo Grounds, Ebbets Field are long gone now, of course. The only intimate fan-friendly major-league ballparks that remain are Wrigley Field in Chicago and Fenway Park in Boston.

But there's hope. Camden Yards in Baltimore may be the best ballpark in baseball. And today's players rank with the best I've seen over fifty years. Griffey Jr., Big Mac, Sosa, Jeter, A-Rod, Maddux are comparable to Koufax—well, maybe not Sandy—Mantle, Mays, Aaron, Spahn, Marichal.

But it's really not fair to compare eras in any sport. Today's baseball players are under a much more powerful magnifying glass than players of other eras were. The news media that often ignored or covered up the abuses and problems of players now hide little from their readers or viewers. And the number of press and broadcast people at any event has so exploded over the years that it's difficult for the players to give us all the attention we want. Even though baseball is more media friendly than most sports—players and reporters mingle in the dugout, around the batting cage, and in the clubhouse—today we all get less from the players.

With all that said, I only ask you to look at these photographs with memories of warm summer days and nights, of a game where so many of its beautiful moments occur when nothing is occurring. This is my vision and some of my own memories of baseball. And of fathers and sons.

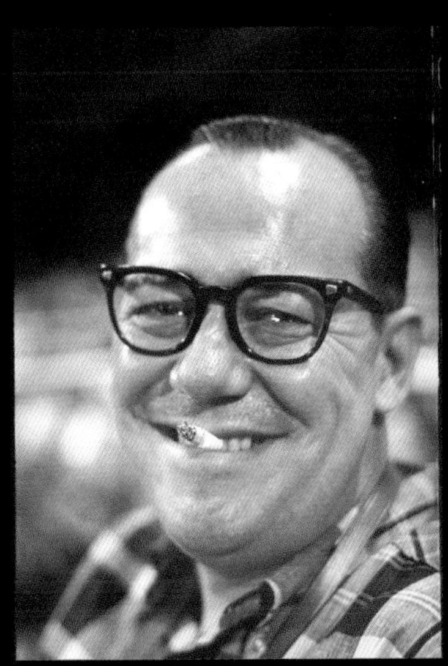

WALTER IOOSS SR. photographed by Walter Iooss Jr.

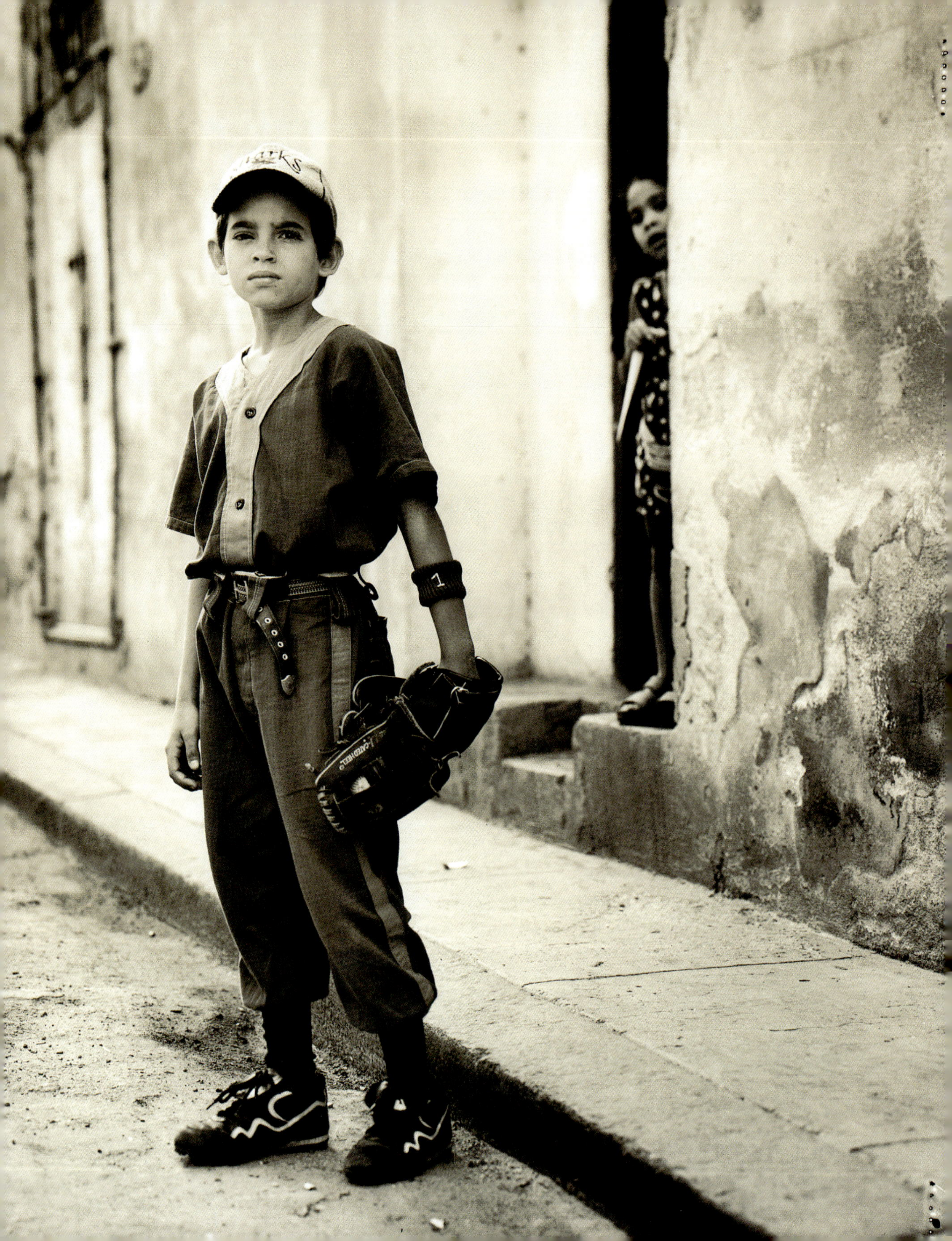

INTRODUCTION by Dave Anderson

HAVANA, Cuba, 1999

OTHER PHOTOGRAPHERS might not have noticed it, but Walter Iooss Jr.'s gift is seeing what others don't. On a *Sports Illustrated* assignment in 1999 in Cuba, Walter was riding through the shabby streets of Old Havana when he noticed youngsters playing the game he had played at their age in Brooklyn and East Orange, New Jersey—stickball. The batter, thicker through the middle than the others, was wearing only shorts and sandals. Behind him, three boys perched on black iron bars across a shuttered window above the street corner. On the cracked sidewalk, five boys and two girls were serious spectators. Another boy crouched, holding a small dog. And as the pitcher threw what appeared to be a raggedy tennis ball, all their eyes were on that ball.

"The beauty of this whole book," Iooss says now, "is in that picture."

So is the beauty of Walter Iooss Jr. as a photographer. Seeing those kids playing stickball was what he calls a "decisive moment," especially in Cuba where the light, for a photographer, is so different.

"The best light in Cuba is reflected off these faded pastel-toned walls," he says. "It might be amber, it might be pink. Even with black-and-white film, it's perfect. The light looks like somebody set it up in a studio."

For youngsters anywhere in Cuba, the year-round warm weather lets them play baseball or stickball virtually every day.

"I like to photograph kids, because I guess I still dream the way kids do," he says. "Those years playing those games were some of the best times of my life. When I see kids doing it now, I just want to jump into their shoes. Photographing them is the closest I can come to it."

For Iooss, that street-corner scene in Old Havana and a little kid all dressed up to play baseball represent a time warp to the 1950s, when he was growing up. Much of this book is a time warp too.

"I was a stickball fanatic," he says. "We didn't use the Spalding ball, what people called the Spaldeen, the pink rubber ball. It got bent out of shape too easily. We used a Wilson tennis ball and threw it hard. When school closed for the summer, we played twelve hours a day. All morning, all afternoon, went home for dinner, then played after dinner."

Those stickball games evolved into baseball games on high-school diamonds where Walter was a first baseman. "I wore my baseball pants tight around my leg like Mickey Mantle," he says. "I thought that looked so cool."

WALTER IOOSS HAS TAKEN PRIZEWINNING PHOTOS OF every sport, as well as of the beauties in many of *Sports Illustrated*'s annual swimsuit issues, but baseball has been his favorite ever since he began going to major-league games with his father. He has Brooklyn roots. His grandfather, Augustus Iooss, was a ragtime piano player known as "The Pride of Brooklyn." Walter Sr.

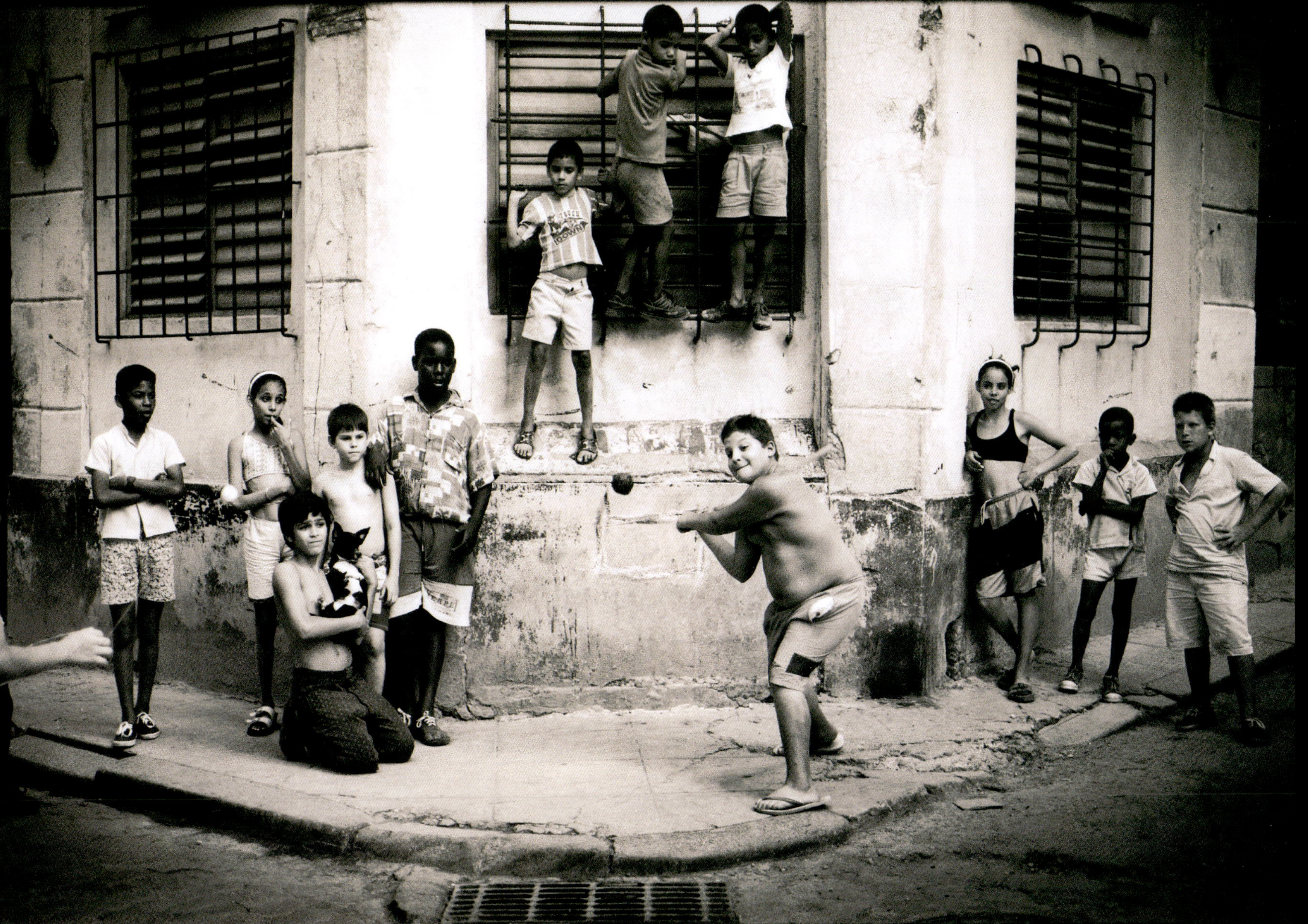

also was a musician, a jazz bass player with Benny Goodman's band. Although his parents divorced when he was four, Walter often visited his father, who lived at 50 Lefferts Avenue in Brooklyn. From there, they could walk to Ebbets Field, the home of the Brooklyn Dodgers through the 1957 season.

"If there was a sellout, we'd stand on Bedford Avenue waiting for somebody to hit a home run over the screen in right field," he says. "But usually we sat behind the Schaefer beer sign in left field. I particularly remember seeing Karl Spooner strike out fifteen in his Dodgers debut."

That's a baseball fan. Iooss had turned eleven the week before but he remembered Spooner, a left-hander with a flaming fastball who had just joined the Dodgers from the minor leagues late in that 1954 season. In his next start, Spooner struck out 12 for a 2–0 record with 27 strikeouts. His potential appeared unlimited. But he hurt his arm, had an 8–6 record in 1955, and disappeared into obscurity.

Iooss soon was going to Yankee Stadium, the Polo Grounds, and even taking the train down to Connie Mack Stadium in Philadelphia with his father.

"My father had a 35mm single-lens reflex as well as what was an avant-garde lens for that day, a 300mm f/4.0 lens that he bought in 1960," he recalls. "It's important that the first lens I ever used was that 300mm telephoto. I was never playing around, even from the start. Life looked better to me through that 300mm lens."

His images looked better too. He liked them so much that in 1959, he phoned the *Sports Illustrated* offices in New York. After the switchboard operator plugged his call into the photo editor George Bloodgood's extension, he asked if he might stop by with his portfolio.

"Do you have any nudes?" Bloodgood asked.

Nudes? The high-school junior laughed. "I didn't even know what nudes were," he recalls. "I was sixteen years old. I had braces on my teeth." He was just hoping for a freelance assignment from *Sports Illustrated*, then as now a weekly museum of photographic art. When no assignment developed, he wangled a photo credential that gave him a free pass for two Princeton football games in exchange for his pictures. Afterward, he delivered a set of his photos to *Sports Illustrated*.

"When they used one of fullback Cosmo Iacavazzi in a goal-line plunge," he remembers with a smile, "I got $150 for it. $150!"

More importantly, Walter Iooss Jr. had his name in a *Sports Illustrated* credit line at sixteen, and after a few more of his photos appeared, the magazine's legendary managing editor, Andre Laguerre, had a question.

"Who is this I-ossis?" he asked.

Laguerre learned that the Flemish name is pronounced "Yohss," as in dose. Not that many other people bothered to learn how to pronounce it. Or spell it. They were too busy admiring Walter's photos, many of which were taken from the stands at major-league baseball games. As a kid freelancer who was still in high school, he often was barred from the photographer's box at ballparks; he's always wondered if the older photographers, even some on *Sports Illustrated*, just didn't want him around. But their resentment may have been a blessing.

"I learned to stay away from the photographers' box," he says. "If you stay with all the other photographers, you get the same pictures they do."

Working on his own whenever he had the time during his last years in high school, Iooss sold many of his early photos to other magazines, notably Dell's sports magazines, for $25 each, sometimes $50.

"Big money," he says with a laugh, "for a high-school kid then."

Walter would be accepted to study photography at Rochester Institute of Technology in upstate New York, but he never enrolled. Just after his graduation from East Orange High School, he was assigned by *Sports Illustrated* to go to Groton, Connecticut, to photograph an octogenarian sailor. Three months later, when he had just turned eighteen, he was among several *SI* photographers covering Roger Maris's attempt to break Babe Ruth's home-run record in the 1961 season finale against the Boston Red Sox at Yankee Stadium.

"They stuck me in the stands in right field with a 400mm lens," he recalls. "The plan was for me to get Maris hitting the ball for the home run. I then had to get the ball as it went into the stands, but I didn't even have a motor drive. Just a handheld camera."

Iooss got Maris's follow-through after the Yankee slugger had connected with Tracy Stallard's pitch, but as he turned to shoot the scene in the stands where the ball landed, he couldn't find the fan, Sal Durante, who caught the ball. *SI* didn't use his photo of Maris's swing; the editors preferred another photographer's shot from the mezzanine in right field, but Iooss got a freelancer's day's pay: $100.

"My buddies couldn't believe it," he remembers. "One of them said, 'You mean they buy you a seat, you watch the game, and even if they don't buy any of your pictures, they pay you $100.'"

By 1962, at the age of nineteen, Walter Iooss Jr. was a name on the *Sports Illustrated* masthead. Even so, whenever he picked up his photo credential at the press window at a sports event, his name was invariably misspelled. If his credential was at the venue at all. Even when he insisted that he was covering the event for *SI*, he often heard, "*Sports Illustrated* wouldn't hire someone like you." Someone so young. Someone surely so inexperienced.

But in 1963, he and another baby-faced photographer, Neil Leifer, were assigned by *SI* to cover the Yankees–Los Angeles Dodgers World Series.

"Neil was twenty-one, I had just turned twenty," he says. "We looked like we were kids and we were. We were also archrivals in the sense that each of us was hoping to get the cover of the magazine. We were different, too. Neil thought about pictures twenty-four hours a day—always talking about them, always thinking, always planning, always an idea. I adapted to the moment."

And he has adapted so well to so many moments.

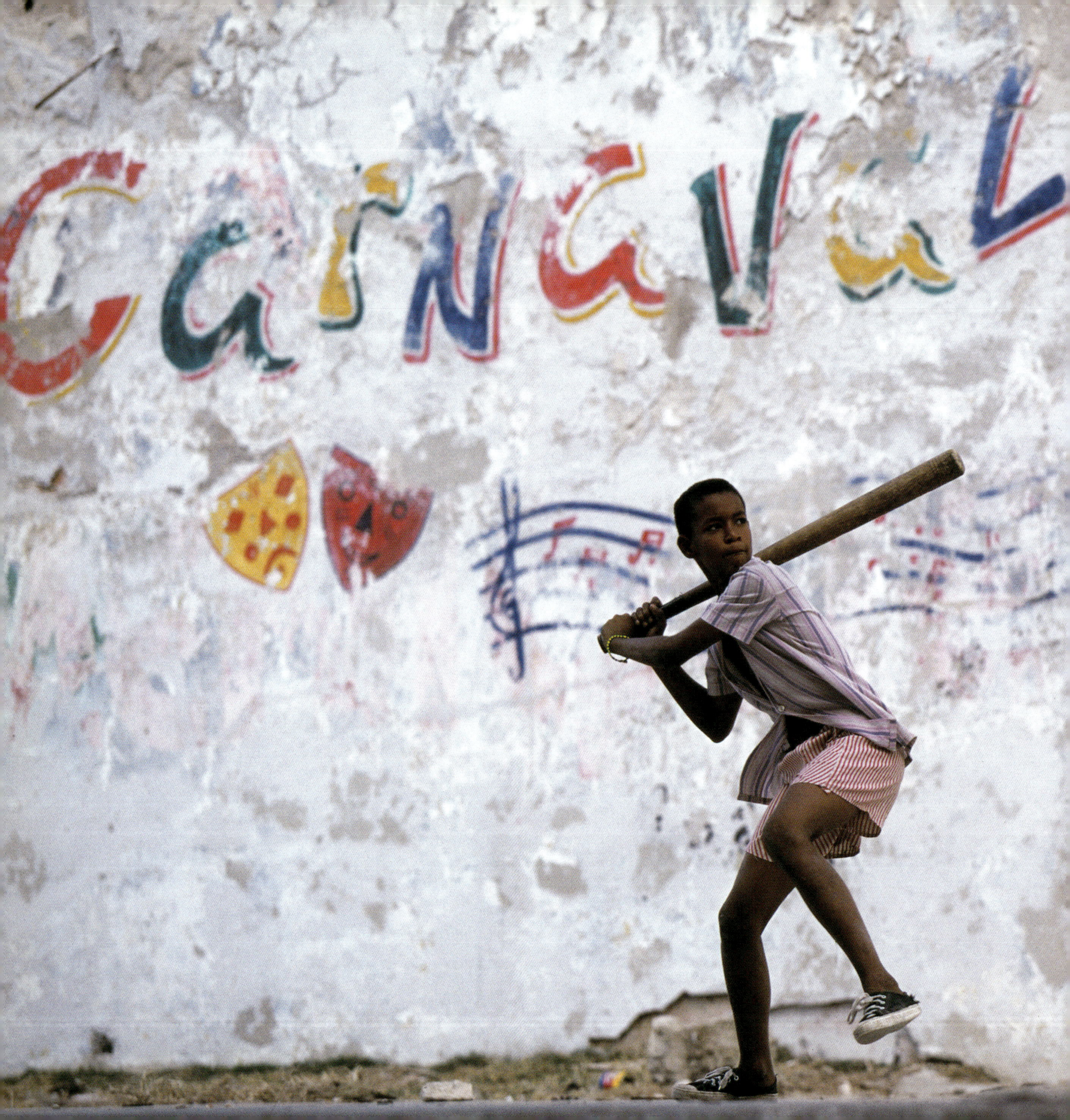
Carnaval

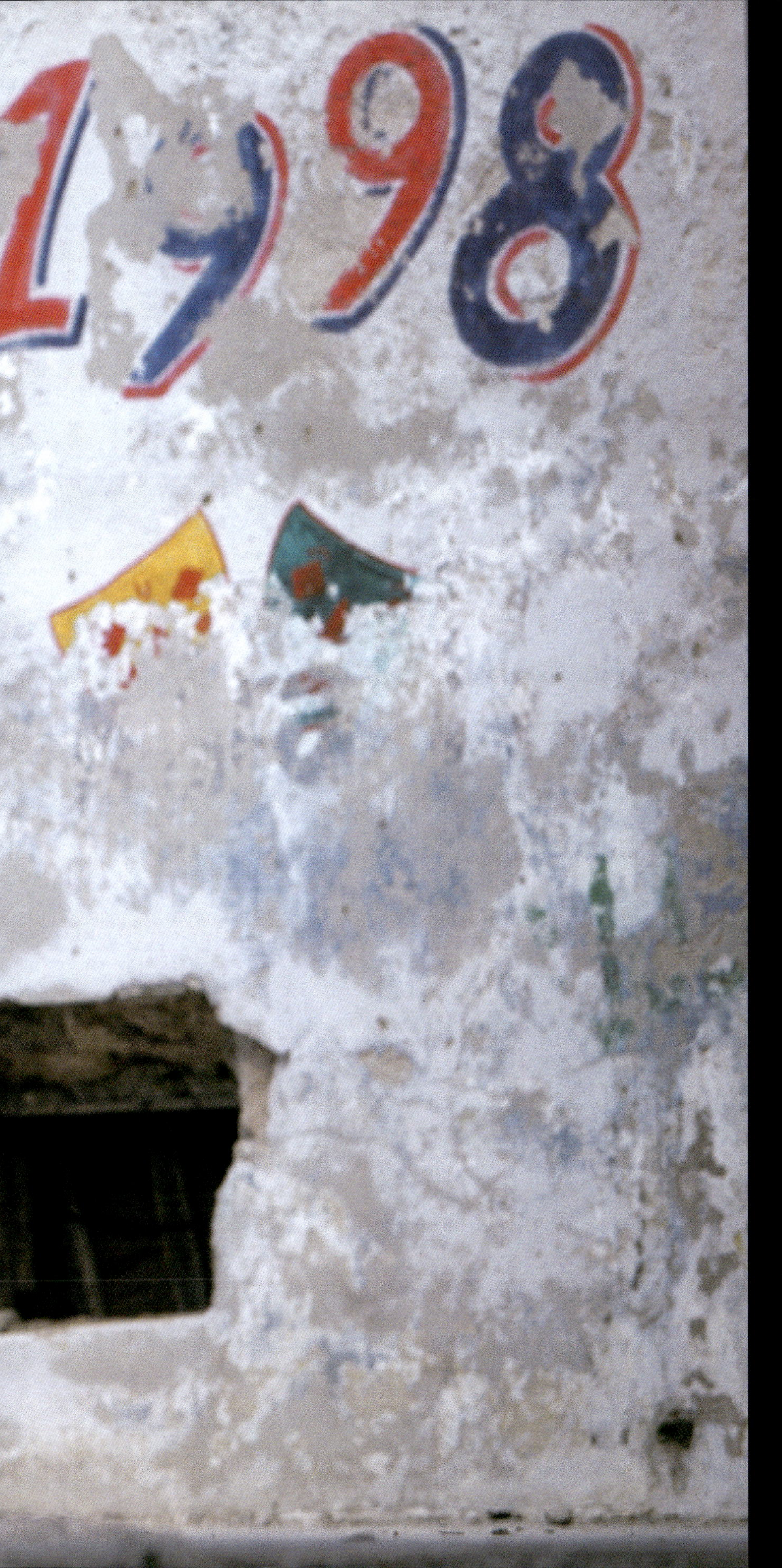

HAVANA, Cuba, 19

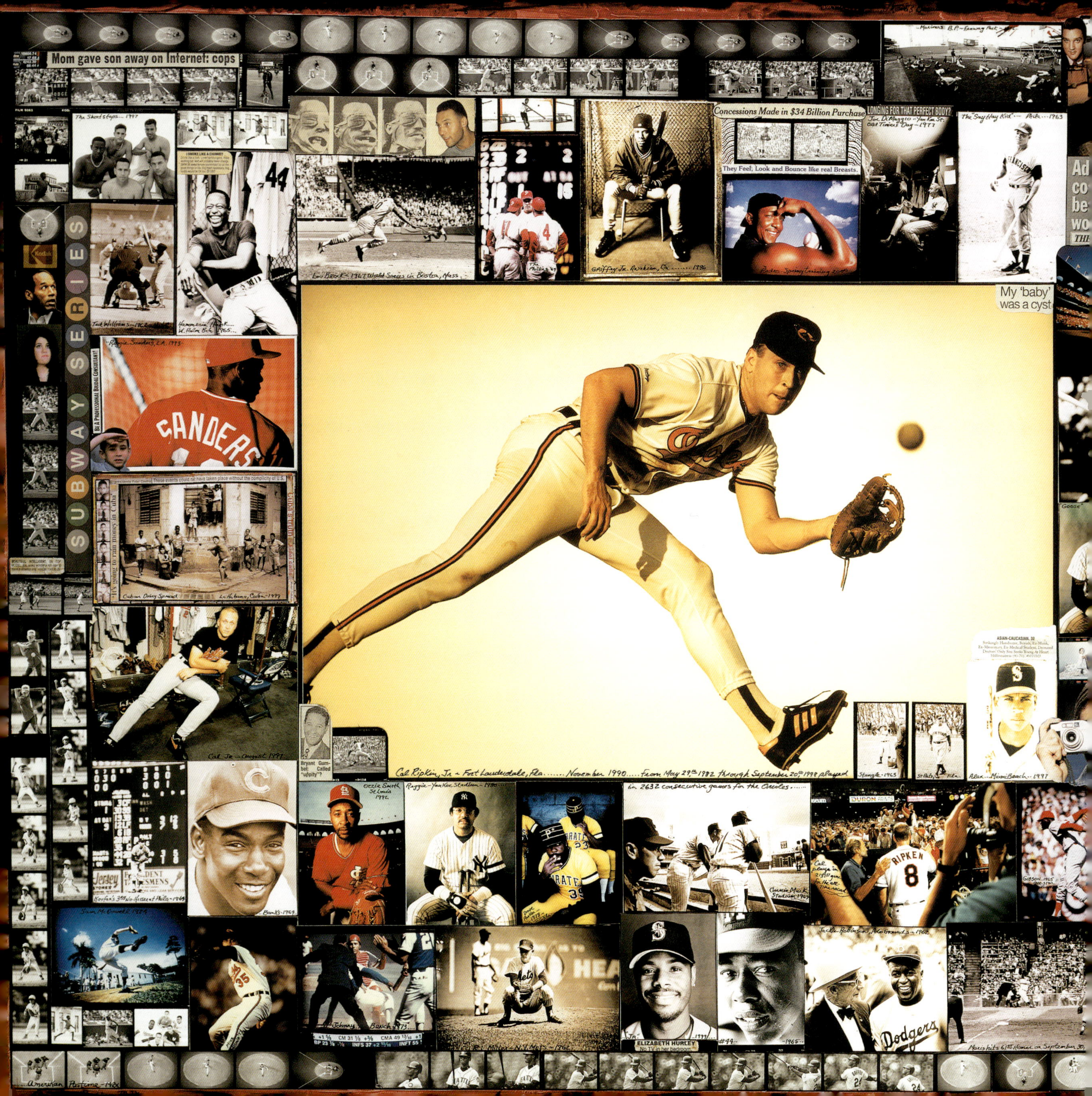
Mom gave son away on Internet: cops
Concessions Made in $34 Billion Purchase
They Feel, Look and Bounce like real Breasts.
LONGING FOR THAT PERFECT BODY?
My 'baby' was a cyst
SUBWAY SERIES
SANDERS
RIPKEN
8
Dodgers
ELIZABETH HURLEY
No TV in her bedroom
Cal Ripkin, Jr. • Fort Lauderdale, Fla. ...... November 1990 ..... from May 29th 1982 through September 20th 1998 played in 2632 consecutive games for the Orioles.....

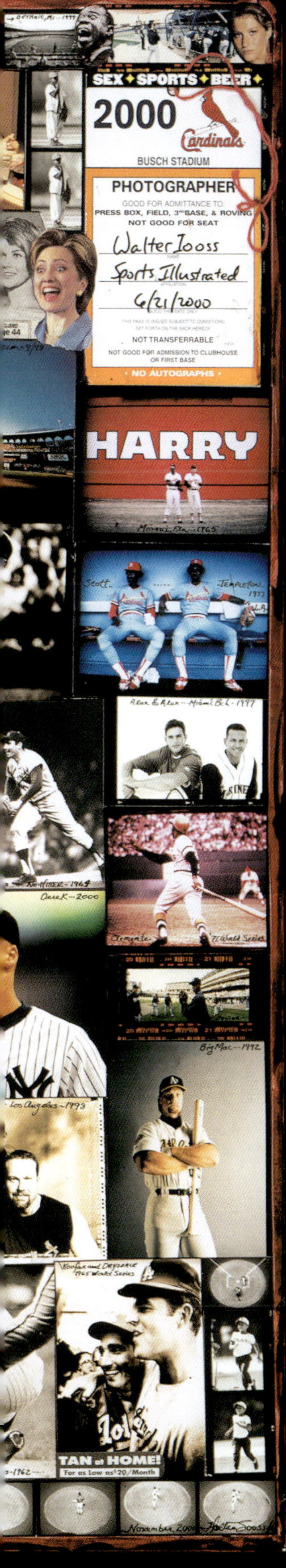

A **CAL RIPKEN JR.** collage

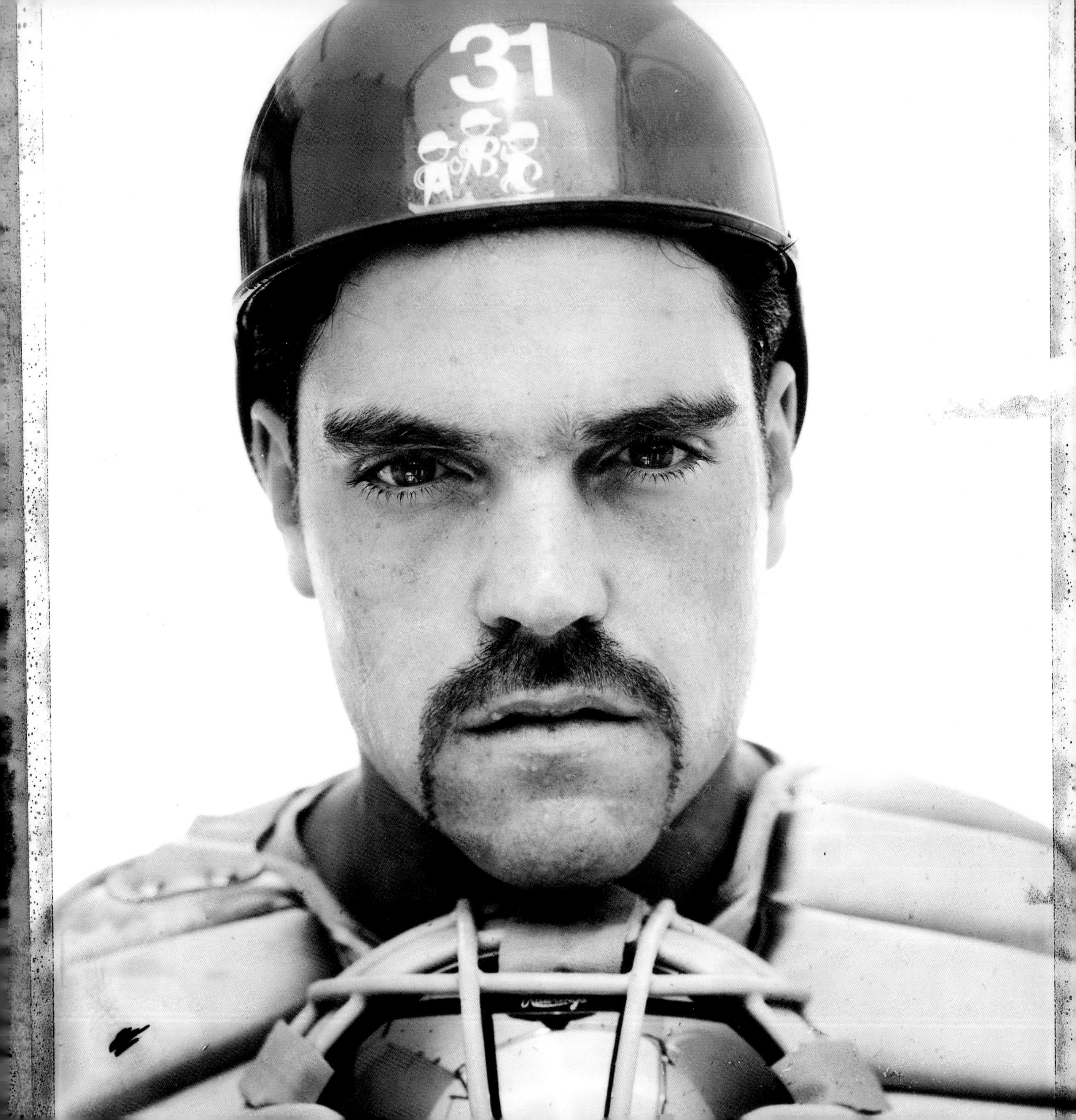
31

FACES

MIKE PIAZZA, Miami Beach, Florida, 1999

DON'T JUST LOOK AT WALTER IOOSS JR.'S PORTRAITS. Examine them. Explore them. Analyze them. "These aren't accidents," he says. "I love to photograph athletes, but the games don't do it for me. It's not just sports action I'm after; it's people in their environment. Let me pose 'em the way I want. I look for backgrounds, setups, lighting, composition. Every millimeter in that frame is important. I want everything to be perfect. Controlling a picture is what the art of photography is all about because most of our lives are out of control. If you can put a person in the position where you want him, with the light just right, it's yours. It's no one else's." Especially when the photographer's angle is just right. "You have to believe that the angle you shoot is the best angle, the only angle," he says. "There are no other angles."

His angle is not accidental. He searches for his angle. "I think every photographer ought to take two weeks to go to sports events with no cameras and just walk around looking," he says. "You don't see the game when you've got a camera. You see isolated plays. It's hard to break away from the game, but when you do, there's a whole separate game on the bench or somewhere else in the ballpark."

Getting any famous ballplayer to take the time to do a photo shoot during the off-season is difficult enough. But when Iooss asked Cal Ripken Jr. to leave his Baltimore home and fly to Fort Lauderdale, Florida, where the light was better, for *Sports Illustrated*'s layout on "Living Legends" in 1991, the Orioles shortstop was there. On time and without complaint.

"When Cal makes a commitment, he's there," Iooss says. "If you tell him, 'one o'clock Thursday,' he'll take out his little date book, turn to that Thursday, and write '*SI*, one o'clock.'"

That day in Fort Lauderdale Stadium, Ripken put on his Orioles uniform, went out to shortstop, loosened up, and then fielded ground balls for nearly an hour as Iooss clicked away. When the photo session ended, Ripken went into an otherwise empty clubhouse, took off his soggy uniform, and strolled toward the shower room.

"Sorry," he was told. "No water. They don't turn the water on until it's time for spring training."

Ripken smiled, found a stray towel, dried himself off as best he could, put on his clothes, returned to the Fort Lauderdale airport, and flew home to Baltimore. Without complaint.

When Mark McGwire and Sammy Sosa were hitting 70 and 66 homers, respectively, in 1998, Iooss was assigned to shoot them together.

"That year," he says, "is the only year that rivaled baseball in my childhood. I just loved Sammy Sosa. I knew he would smile, that he would enjoy being photographed, but I was concerned about McGwire. He was usually so tense, so tight. I needed him to lighten

BOB FELLER, Lakeland, Florida, 2001

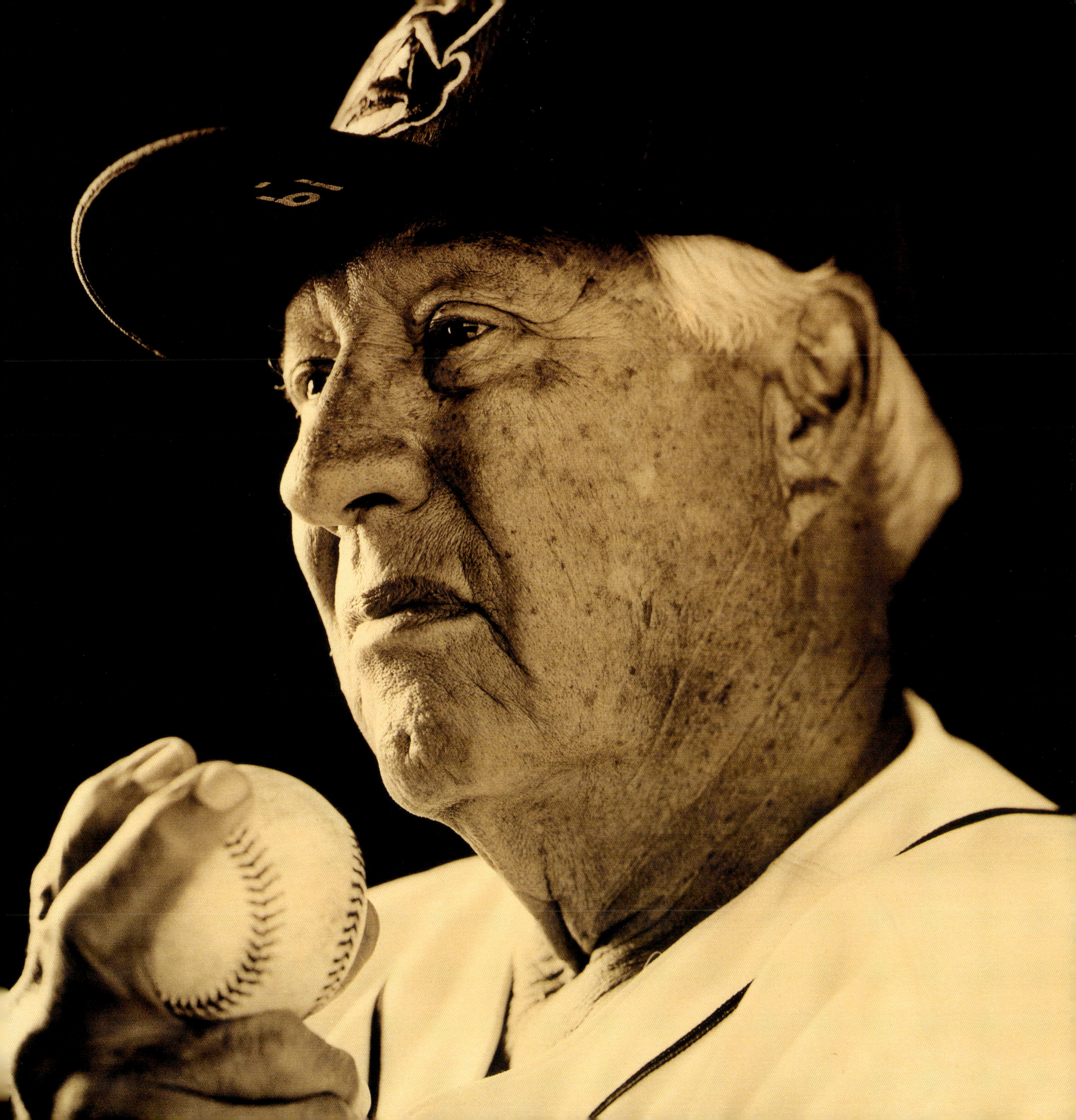

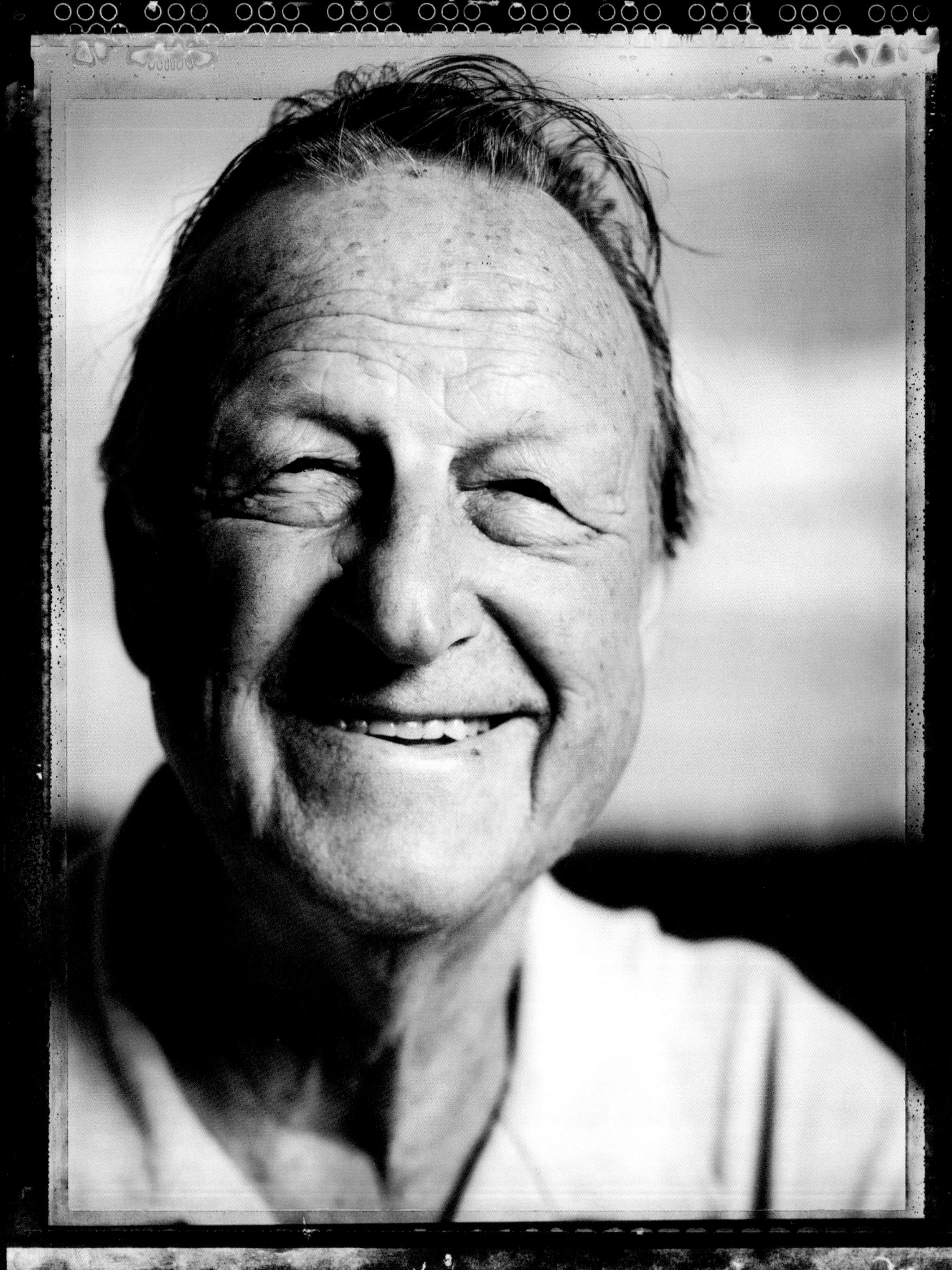

up and he did. It's the only photo of him I've seen where he was happy."

Ken Griffey Jr. seldom appears happy.

"He's got everything—the arm, the range, the sweetest swing," Iooss says, "but he's the worst-conditioned superstar I've ever been around. He never runs, never lifts weights, never stretches. When his Mariner teammates were stretching one day in Fenway Park, he was standing by himself and I heard him tell some of his teammates, 'When you make $10 million, you don't have to stretch.' When I asked him why he wasn't better conditioned, he said, 'I don't want anything to interfere with my swing.'"

One day, on a visit to the Atlanta Braves clubhouse, Iooss found Hank Aaron playing cards with the legendary Satchel Paige.

"A little kid was there too," he recalls. "So was an empty Coke bottle with a baseball on top. What a prop."

Iooss shot Satch's well-traveled face, then caught Aaron in a rare hearty laugh during that card game, but when he posed Aaron for a portrait on another occasion, the man who hit a record 755 home runs never cracked a smile, never seemed to enjoy the moment.

"He was surly," Iooss says. "When I later read about all the horrible hate mail he received before and after he broke Babe Ruth's record, I understood why he was that way. I felt so terrible."

For about a decade before Joe DiMaggio died in 1998, he would be asked to throw out the first ball for the Yankees' annual Old-Timers Day game at Yankee Stadium. On those occasions, he usually wore a white shirt, patterned tie, blue blazer, gray slacks, and glossy black shoes. But in earlier years, for Old-Timers Day, he always went to a locker in the clubhouse and changed into his pinstriped uniform with the number 5 on the back.

"Just the way he sat at his locker there, he had the mystique," Iooss says. "You knew he was a star."

The old Willie Mays had that same majesty about him. When some youngsters hanging around Pacific Bell Park in San Francisco learned that Iooss was expecting Mays to turn up for a photograph, one was so awed, he said, "Willie Mays is going to be *here*." And soon he was, arriving at the head of a parade of admirers. But when Iooss posed him, he kept squinting.

"He couldn't take my bright lights," Iooss recalls. "His eyes are very sensitive."

Those same eyes had told Mays to swing at the pitches he hit for 660 homers, second to Aaron on the career list. But now those eyes were older. Iooss softened the glare of his lights. When that photo session ended, Mays was asked and agreed to pose with his godson, Barry Bonds, there for a Giants game that day. Would the slugger who would hit a record 73 homers in 2001 take a few minutes for a few photos?

"Only if it's for the cover," Bonds sneered.

Walter Iooss Jr. couldn't guarantee the *Sports Illustrated* cover, but even if he could have guaranteed it, he would not have. Not for anybody that arrogant.

STAN MUSIAL, Jupiter, Florida, 2001

JOE DI MAGGIO, Yankee Stadium, Old-Timers Day, 1980

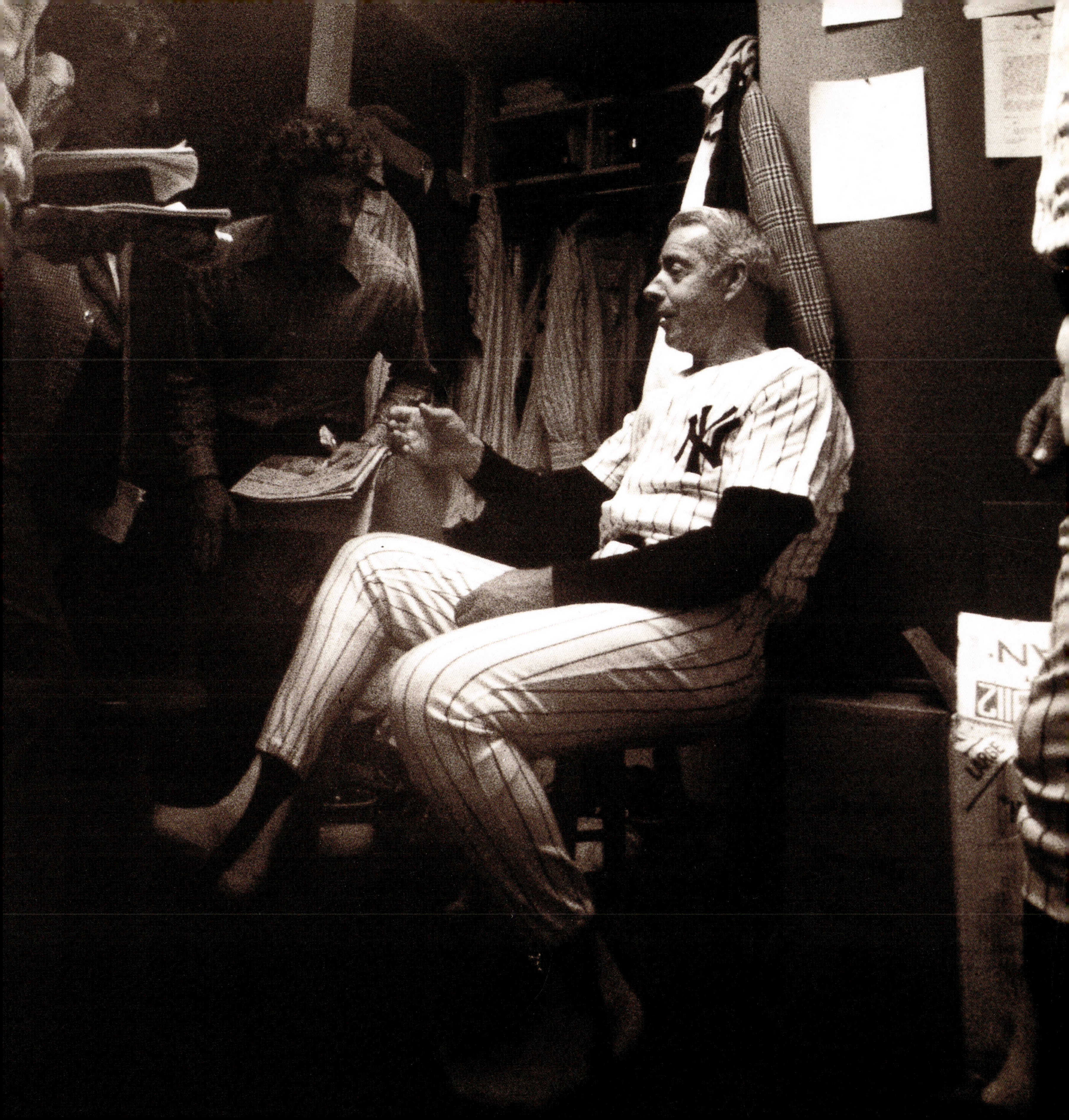

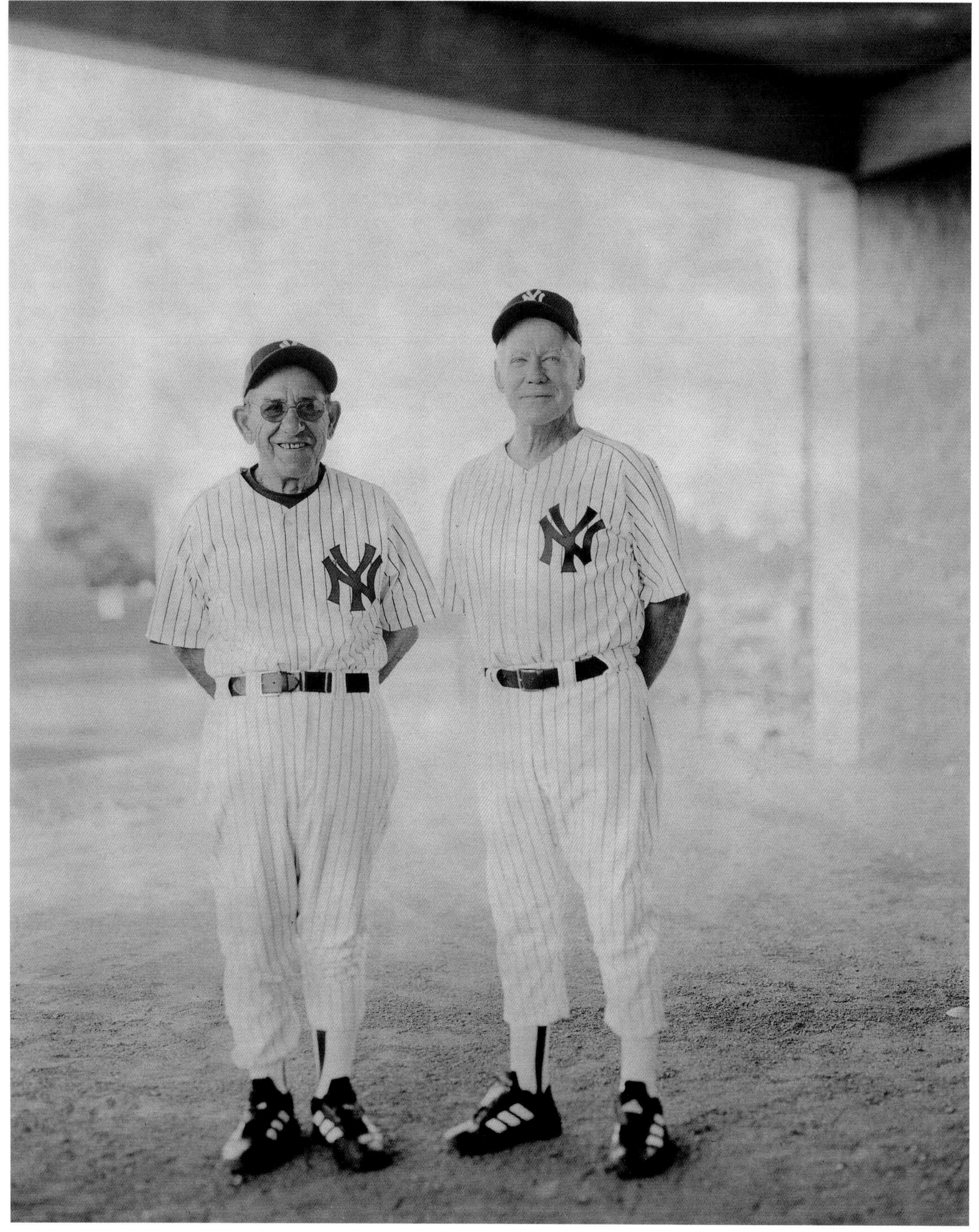

YOGI BERRA AND WHITEY FORD, Legends Field, Tampa, Florida, 2001

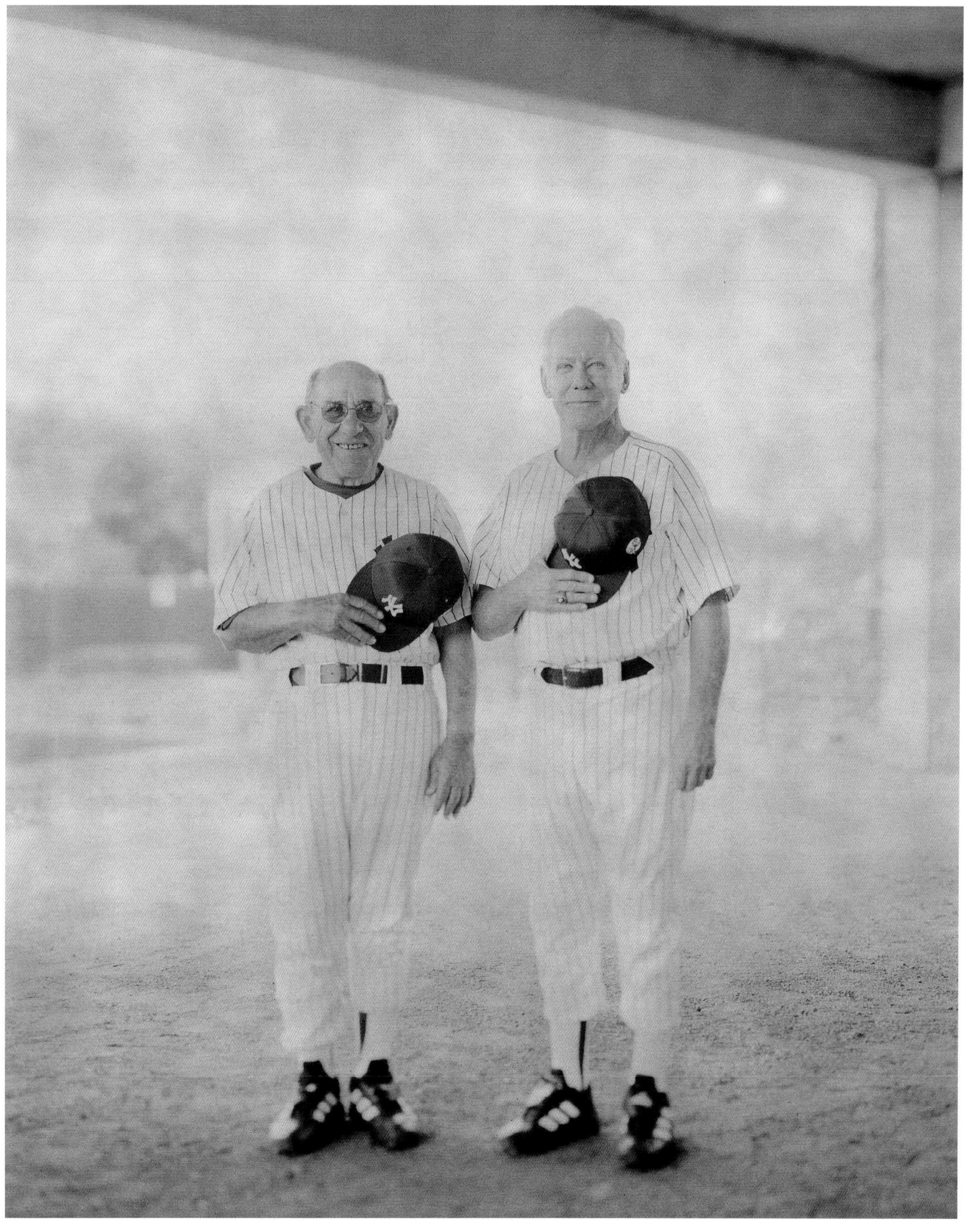

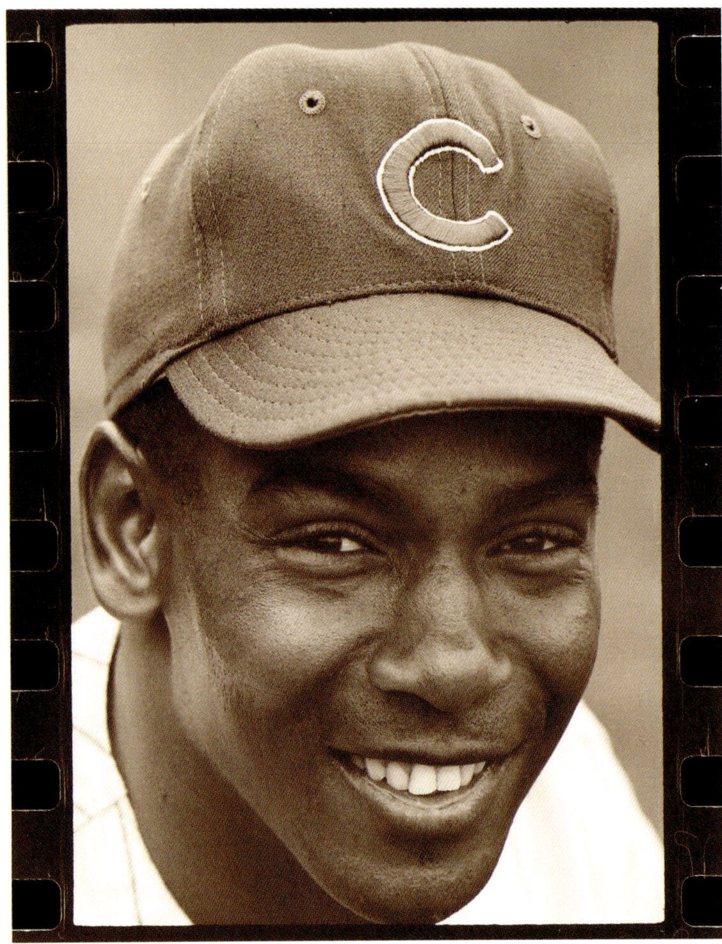

ERNIE BANKS, Scottsdale, Arizona, 1964 (ABOVE),
and at Wrigley Field, Chicago, 2001 (RIGHT)

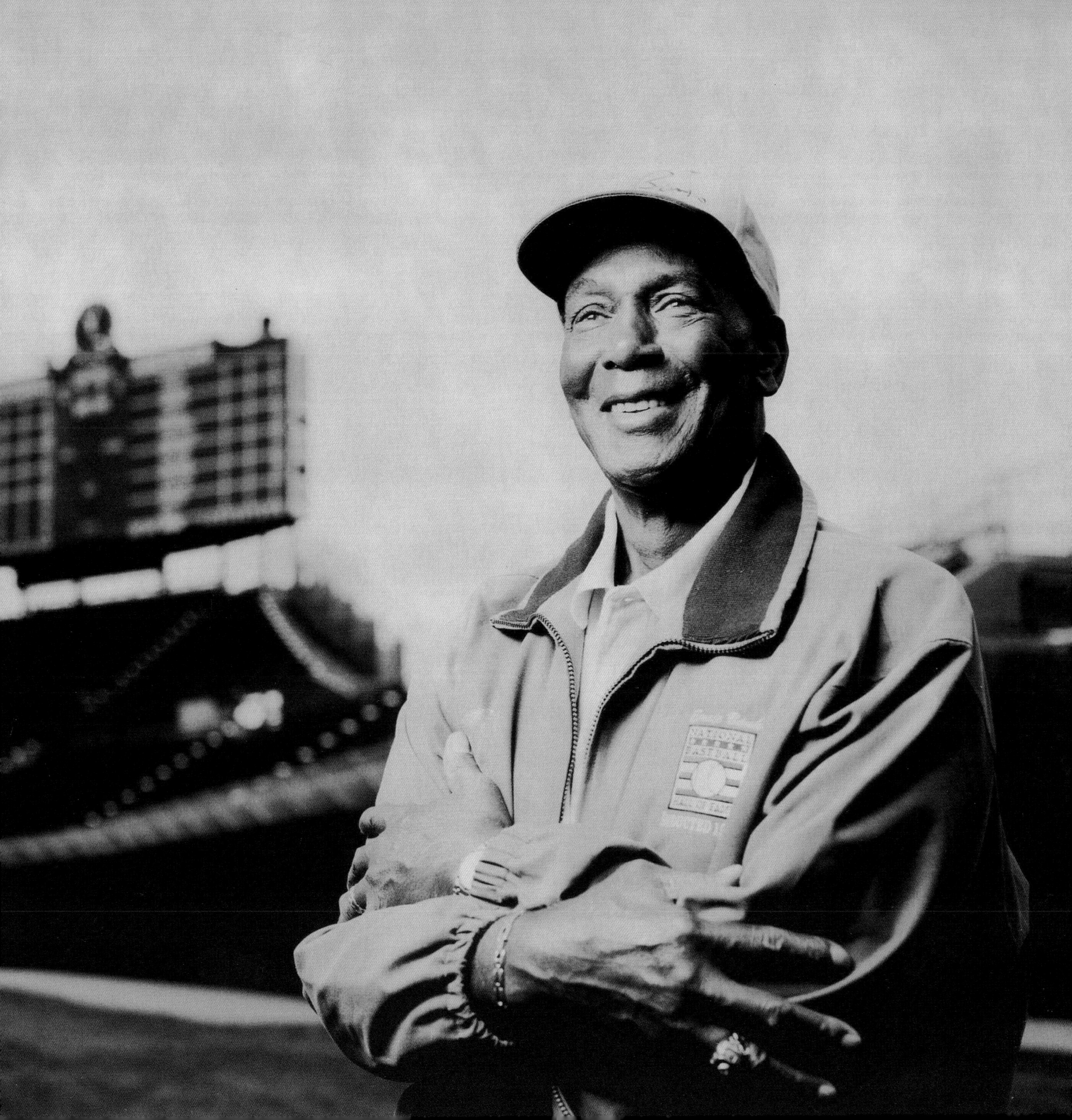
NATIONAL
BASEBALL
HALL OF FAME

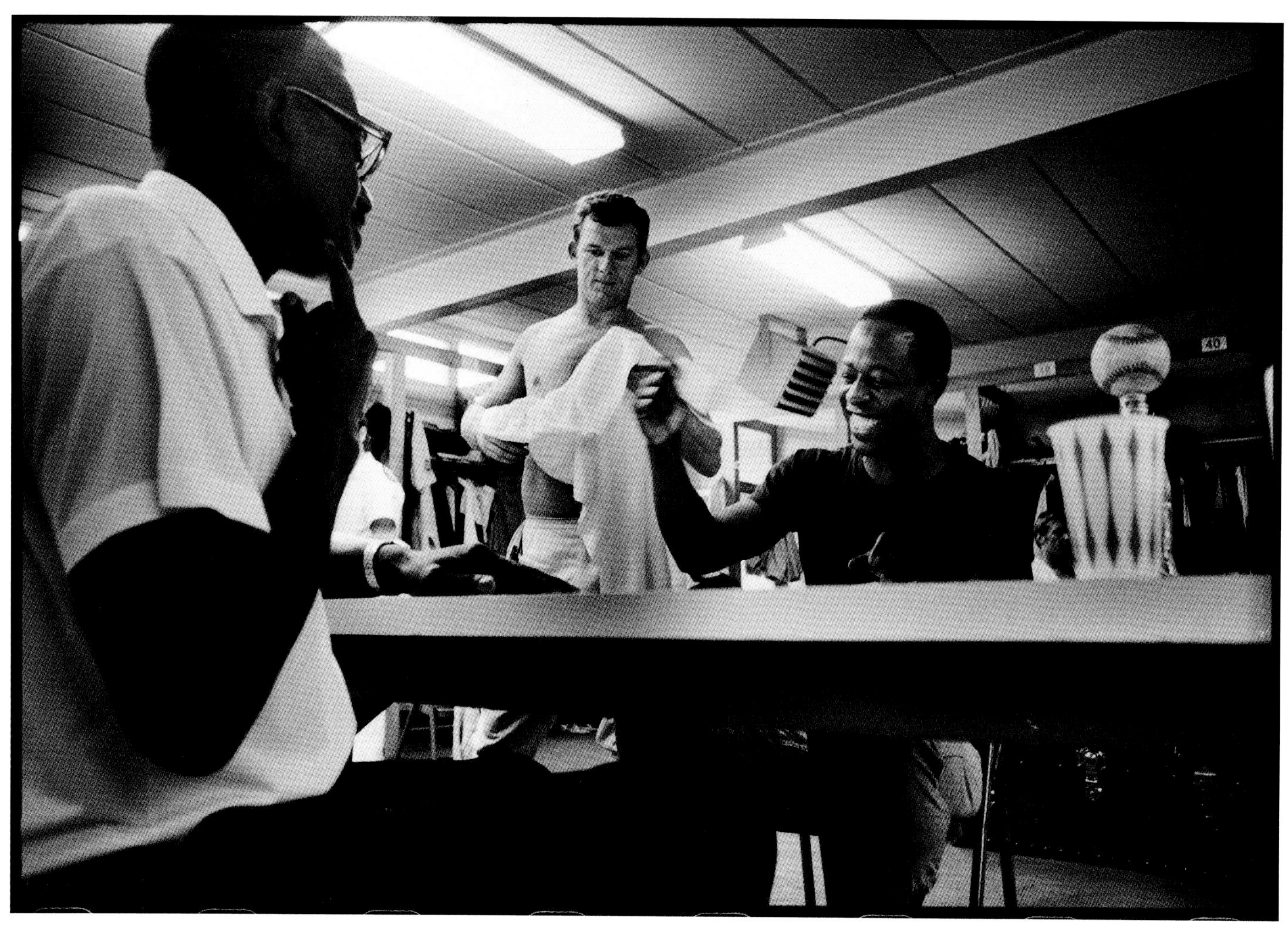

SATCHEL PAIGE, PAT JARVIS, HANK AARON, Montreal, 1969

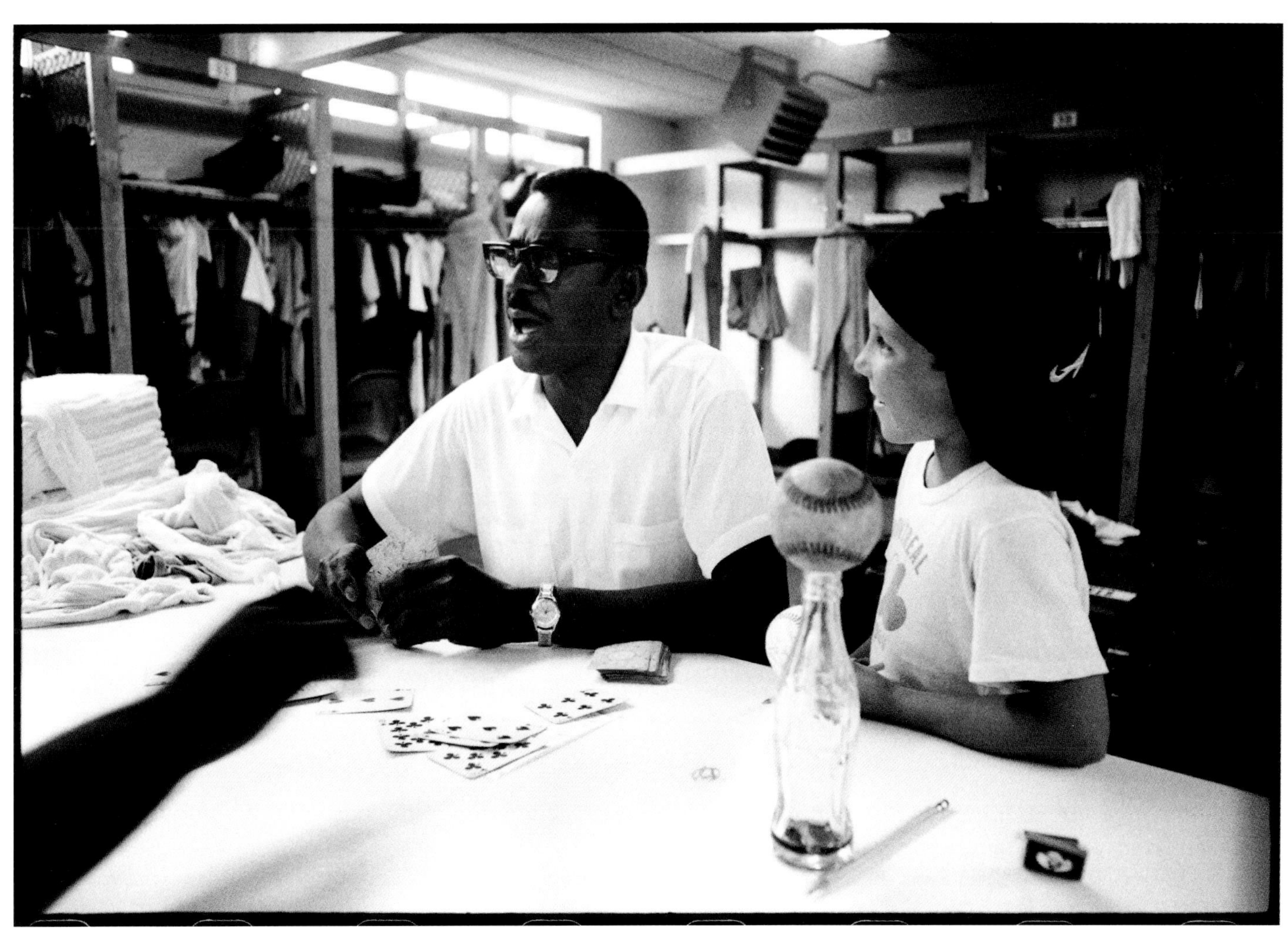

SATCHEL PAIGE, Montreal, 1969

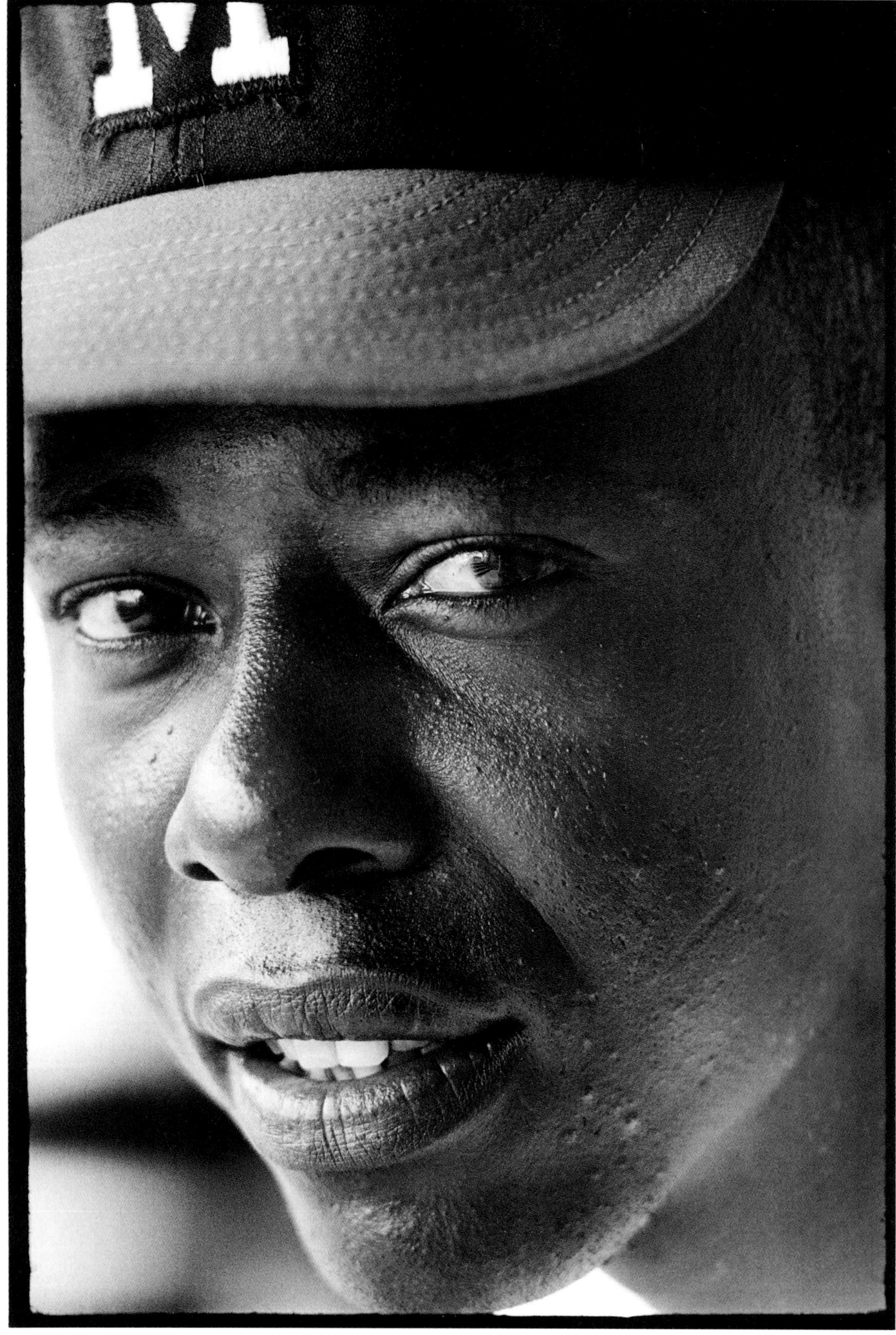

HANK AARON, West Palm Beach, Florida, 1969 (ABOVE), and at Montreal, 1969 (RIGHT)

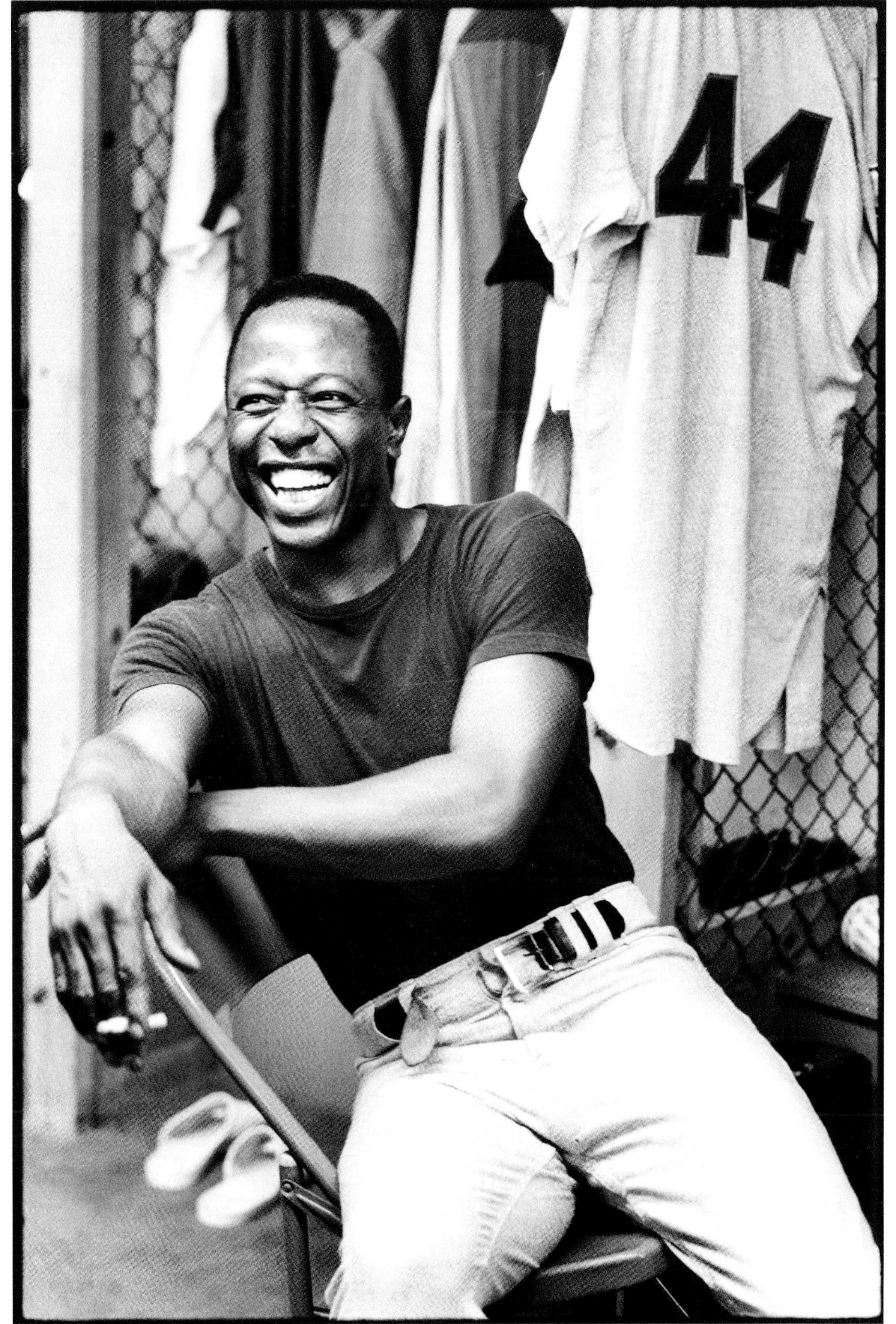
44

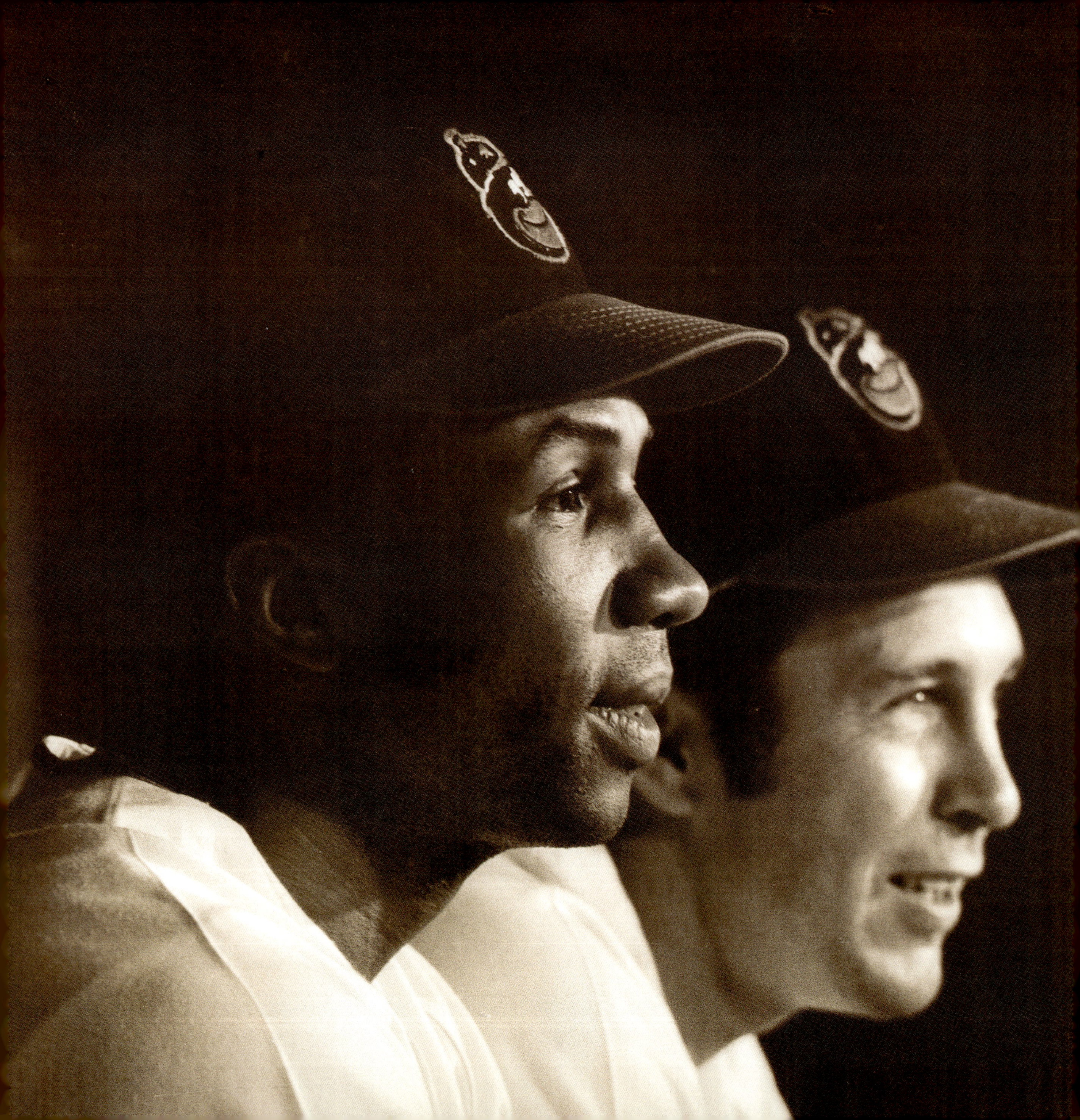

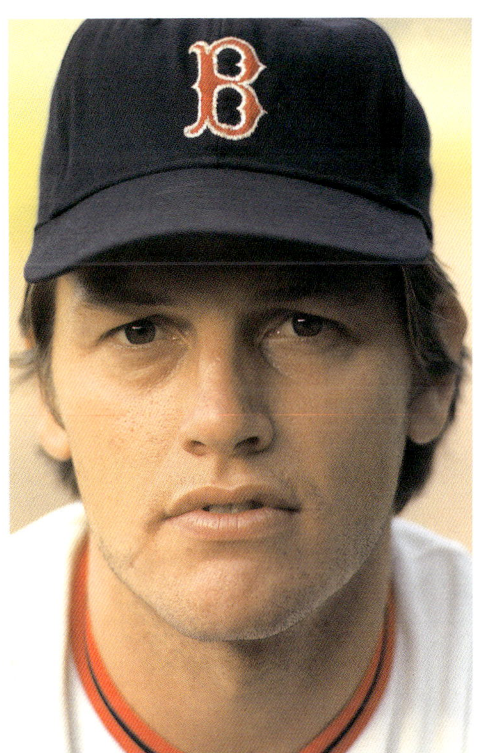

FRANK ROBINSON AND BROOKS ROBINSON, Baltimore, 1970

CARLTON FISK, Boston, 1973

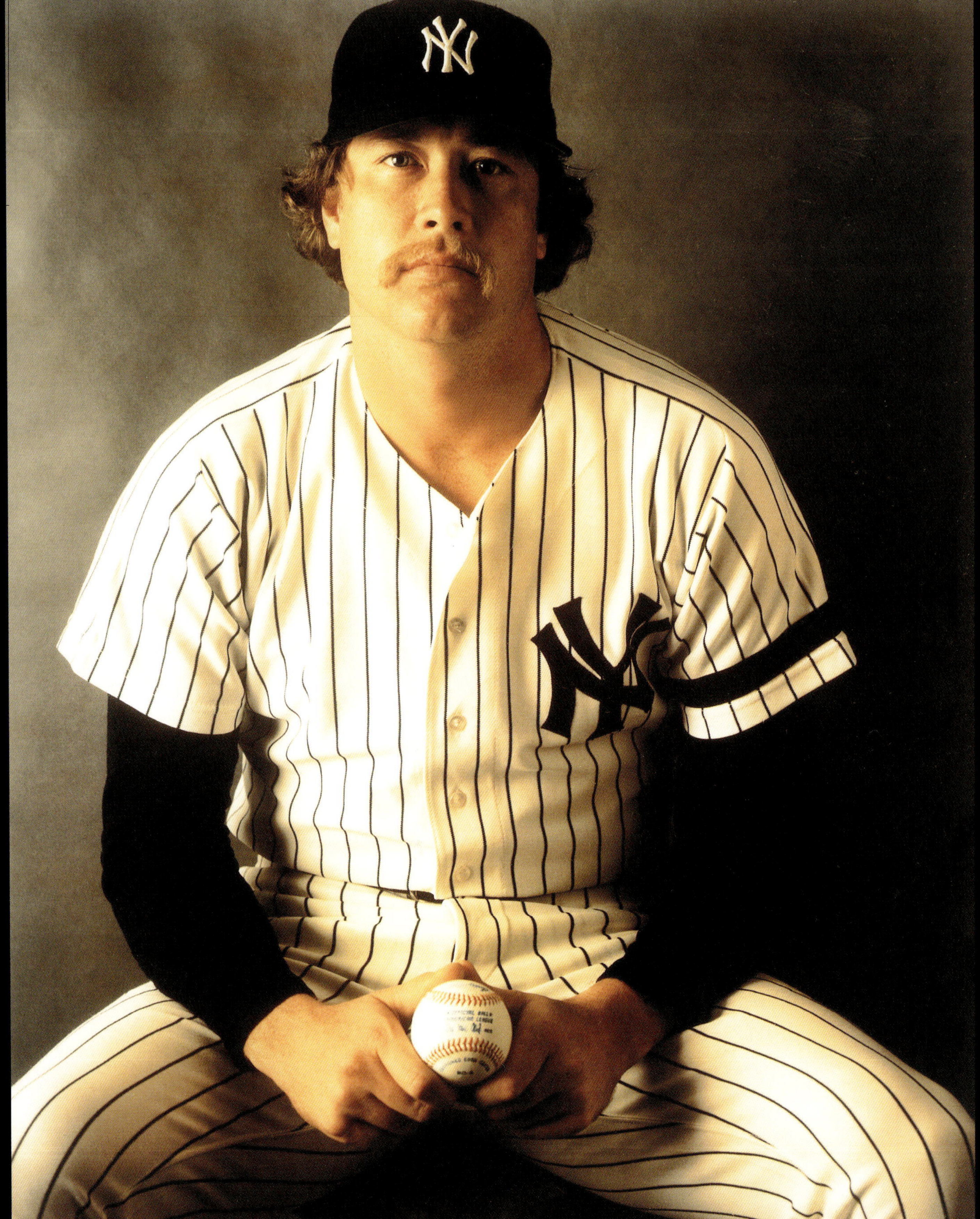

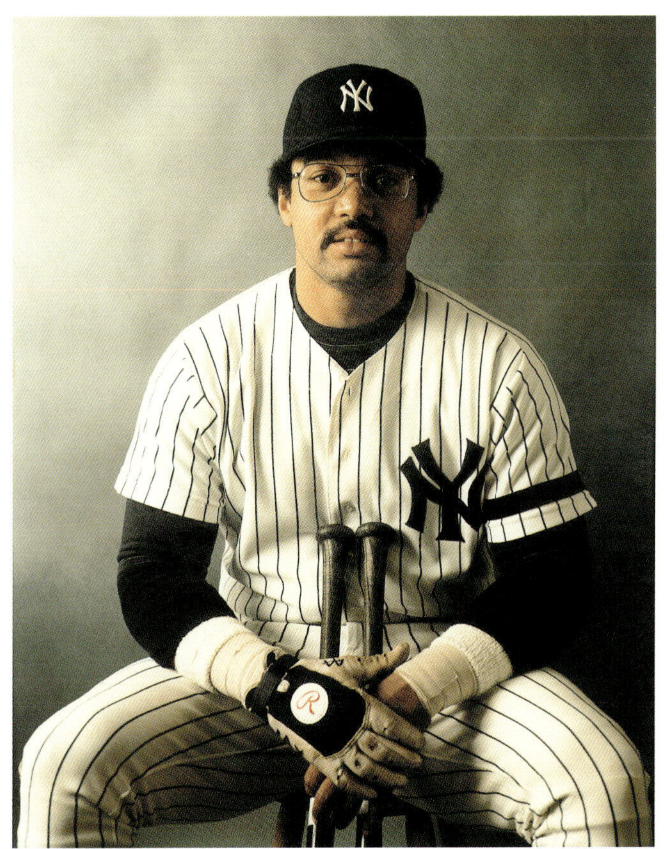

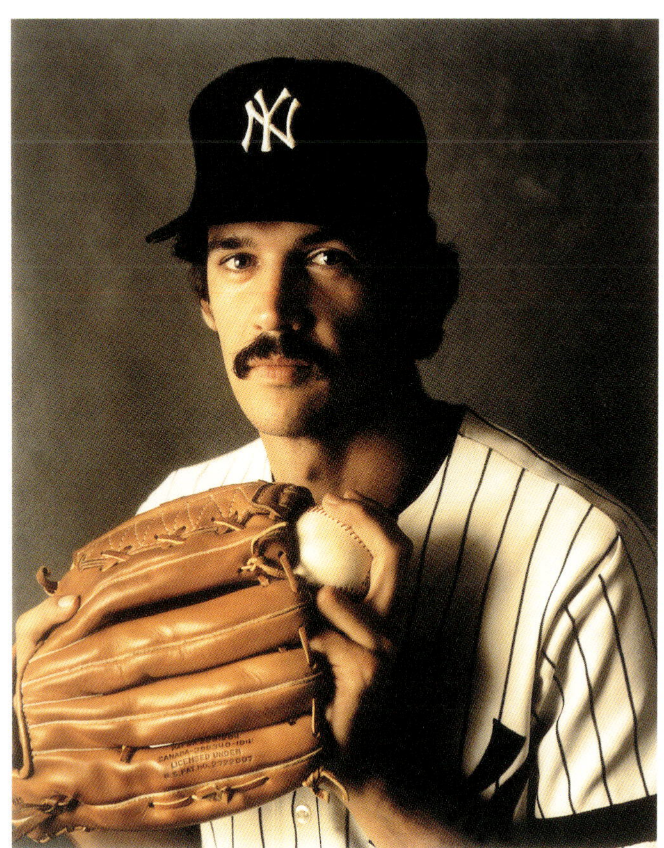

GOOSE GOSSAGE, REGGIE JACKSON, RON GUIDRY, Yankee Stadium, 1980

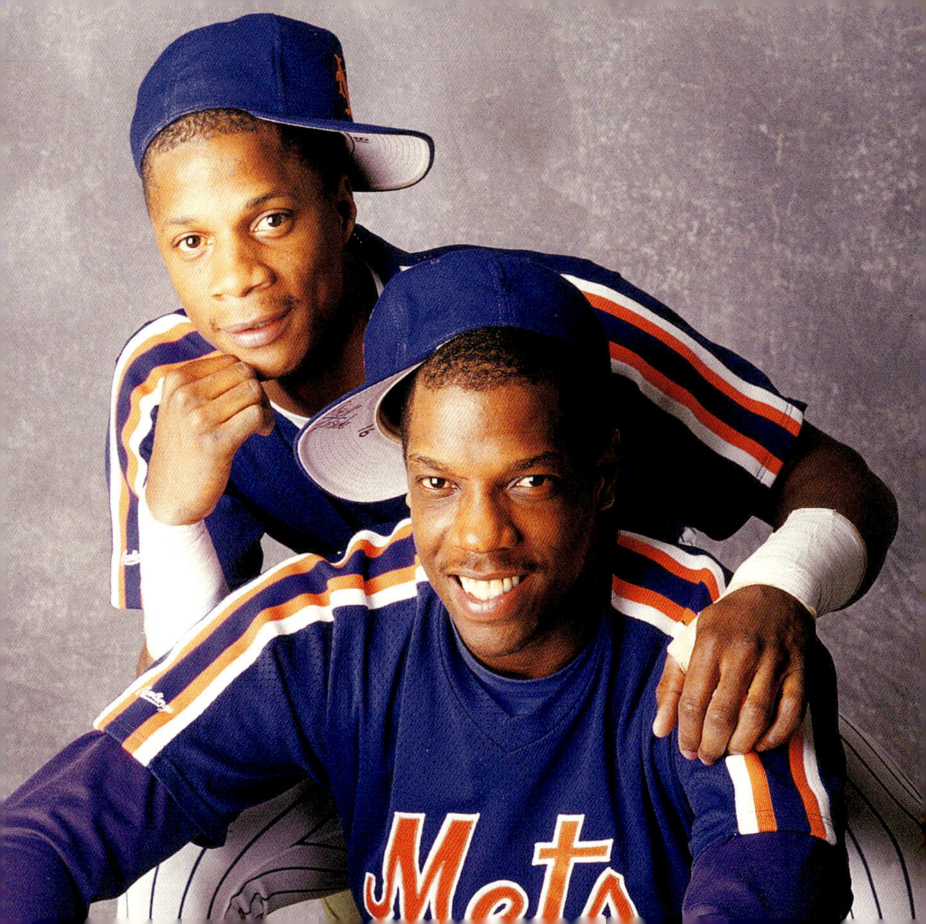
Mets

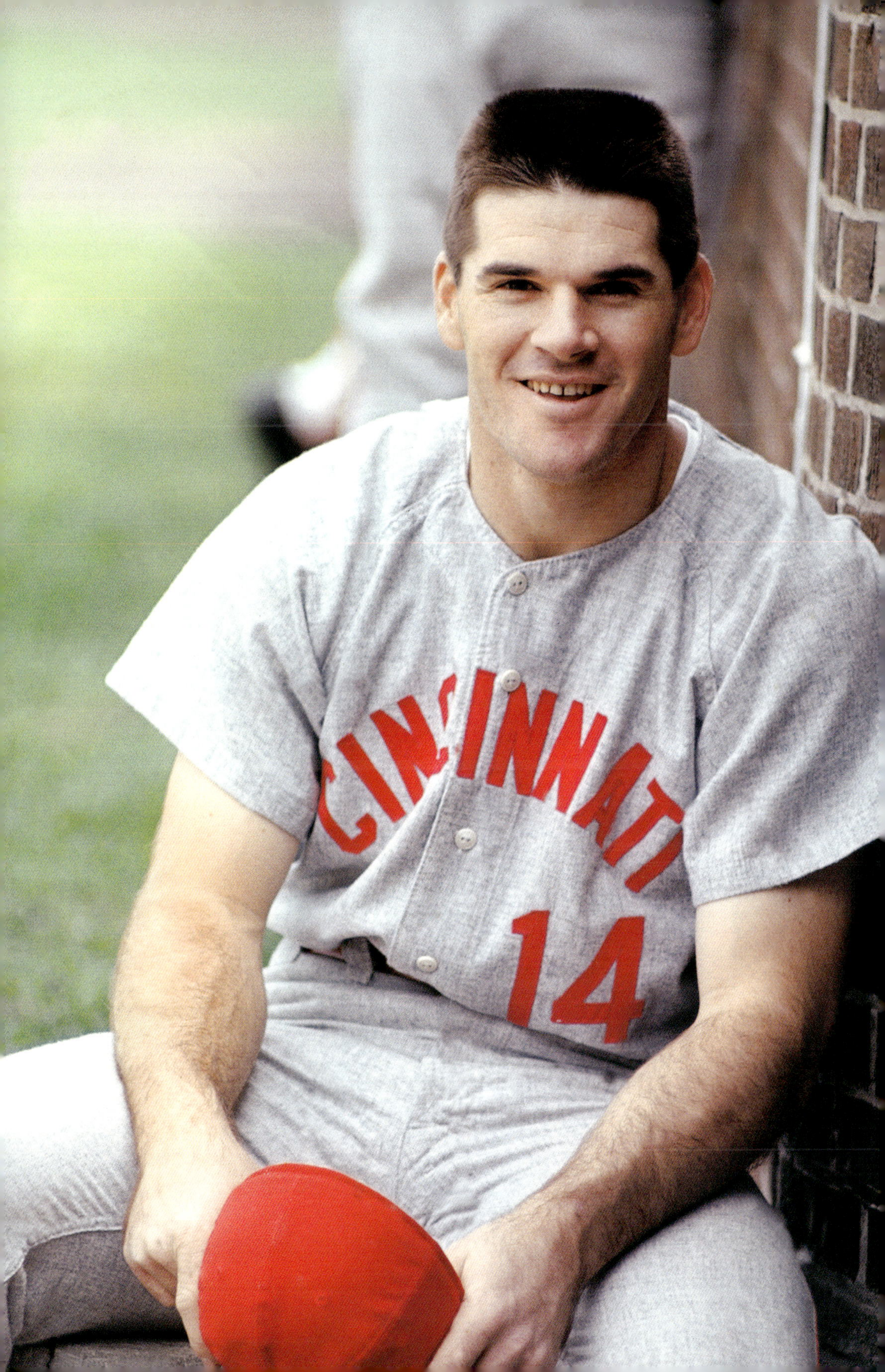
CINCINNATI
14

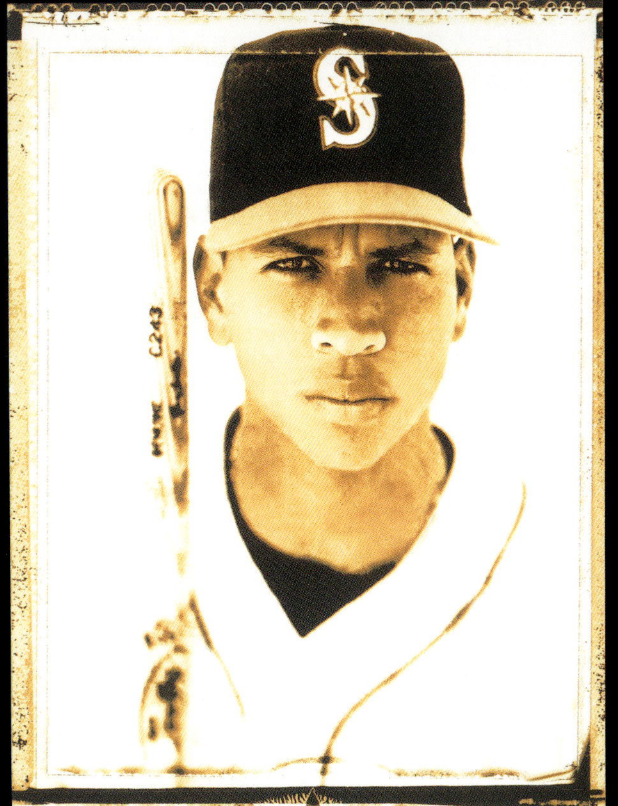

DRIGUEZ, Miami Beach, Florida, 1997 **KEN GRIFFEY JR.**, Anaheim, Califo

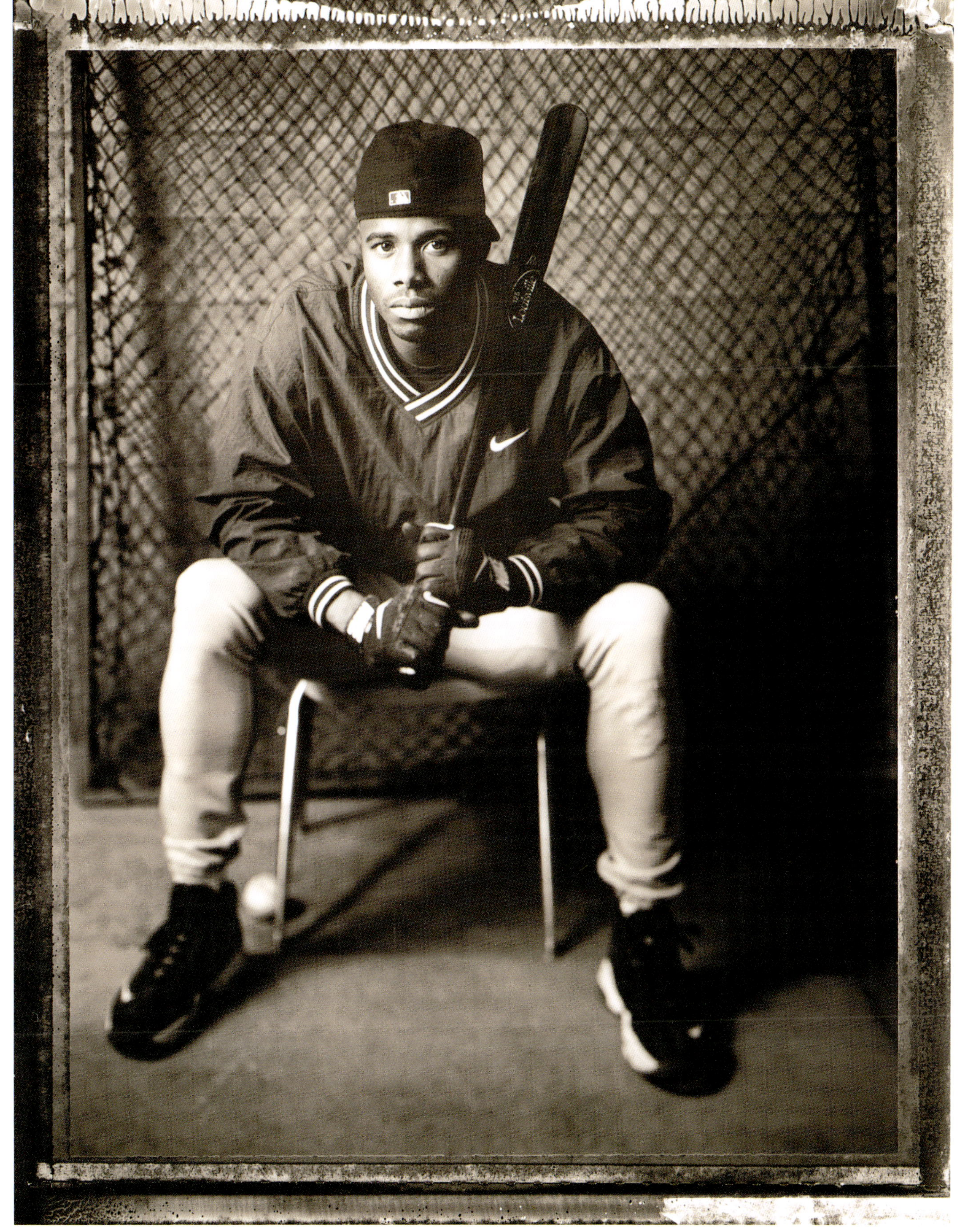

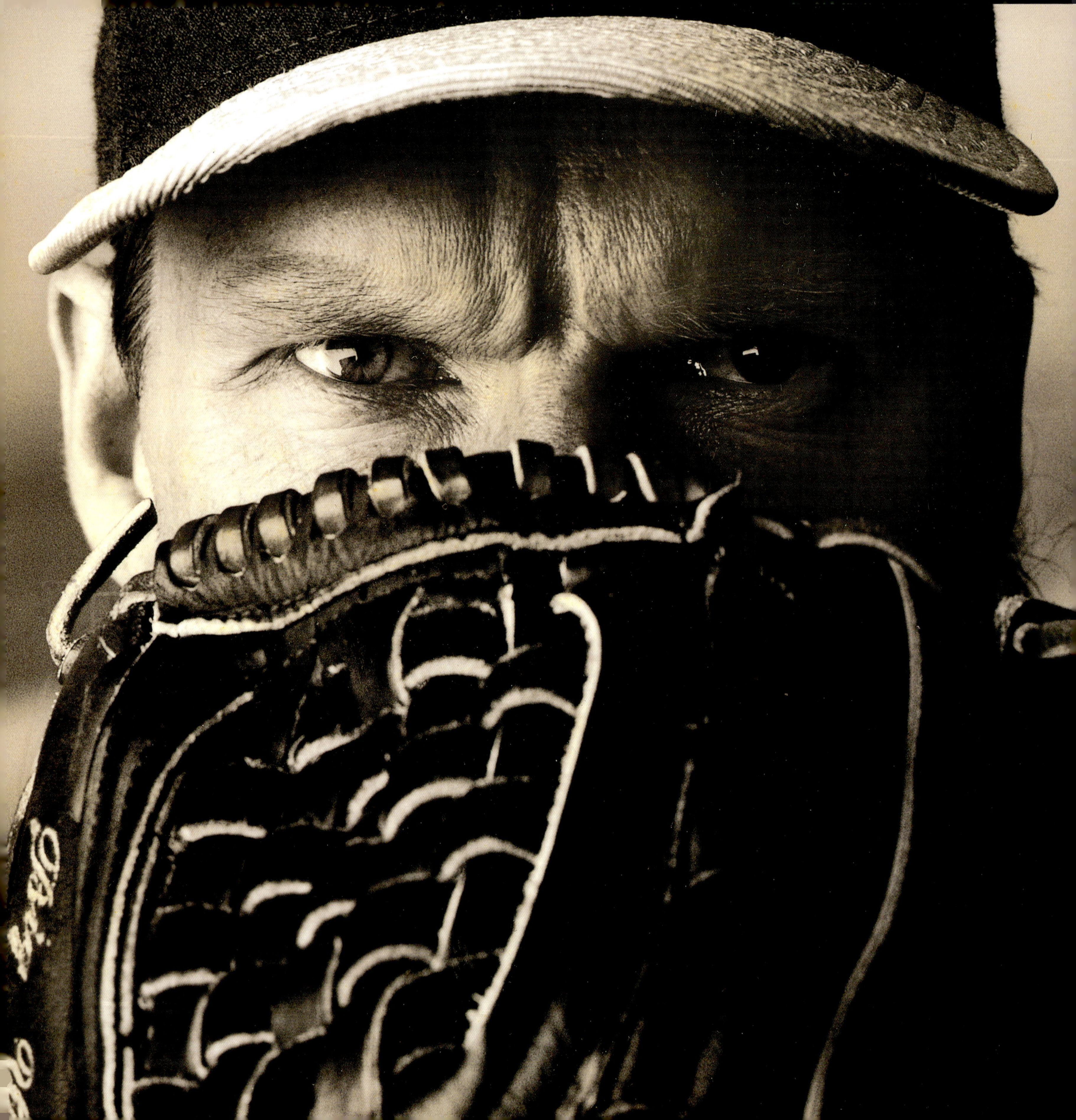

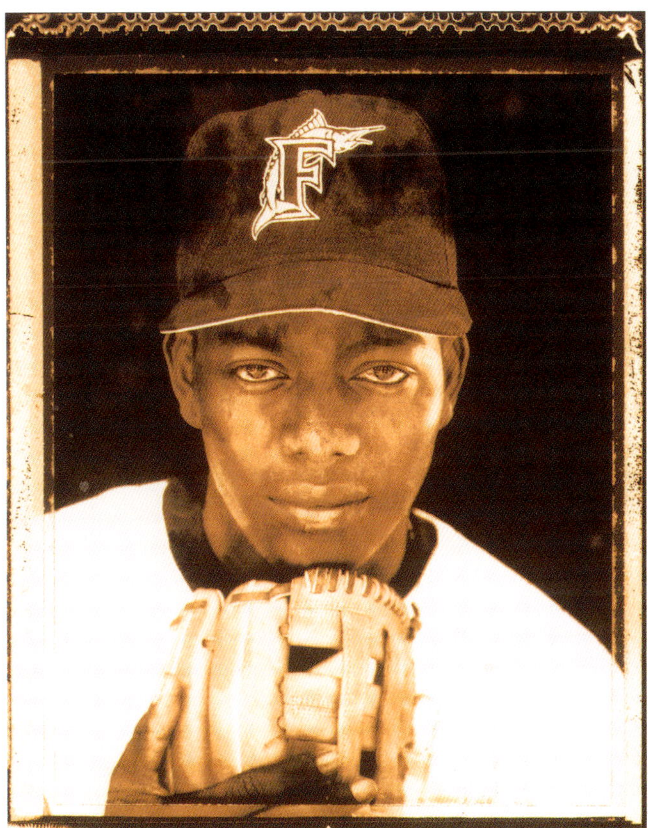

RANDY JOHNSON, Peoria, Arizona, 1997 **EDGAR RENTERIA,** Miami Beach, Florida, 1997

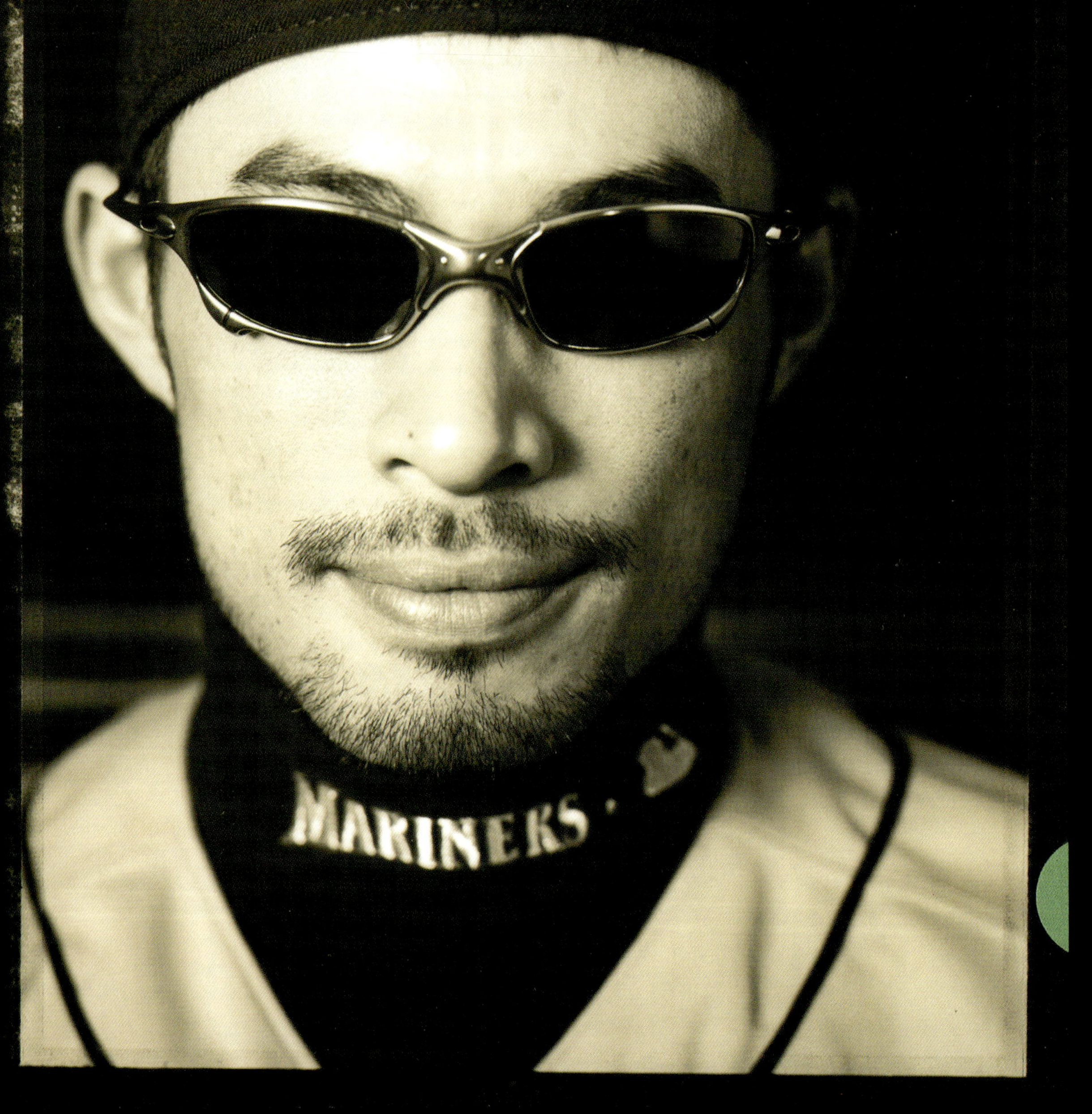

ICHIRO SUZUKI, Anaheim, California, 2001 **DEREK JETER,** Tampa, Florida, 2000

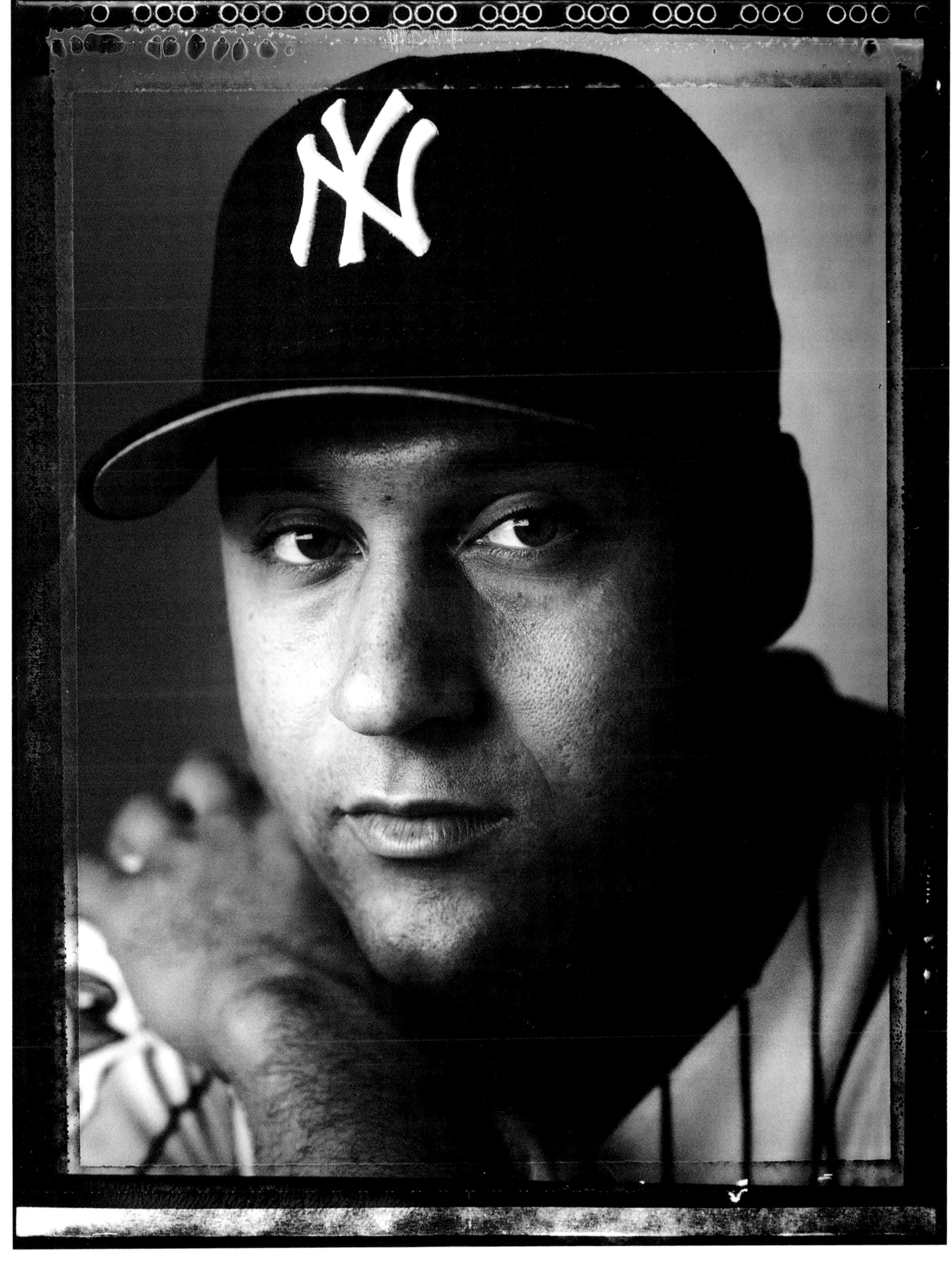
NY

PARKS

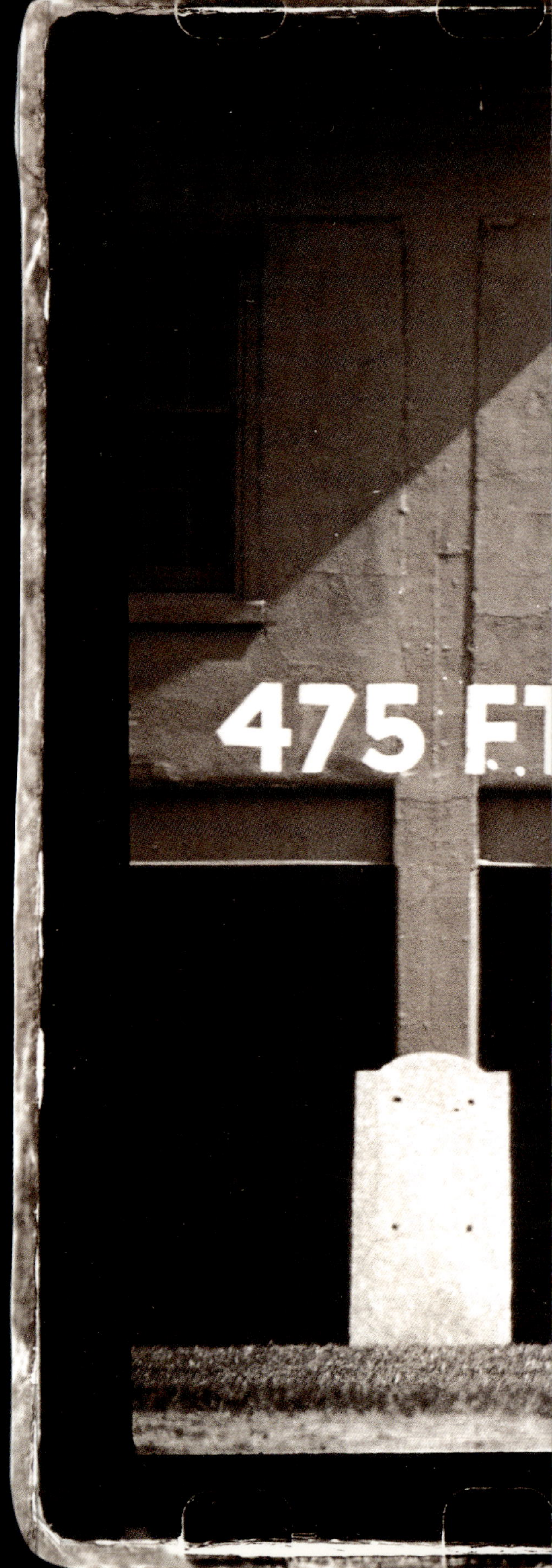

POLO GROUNDS, New York—R. L. Miller—1962

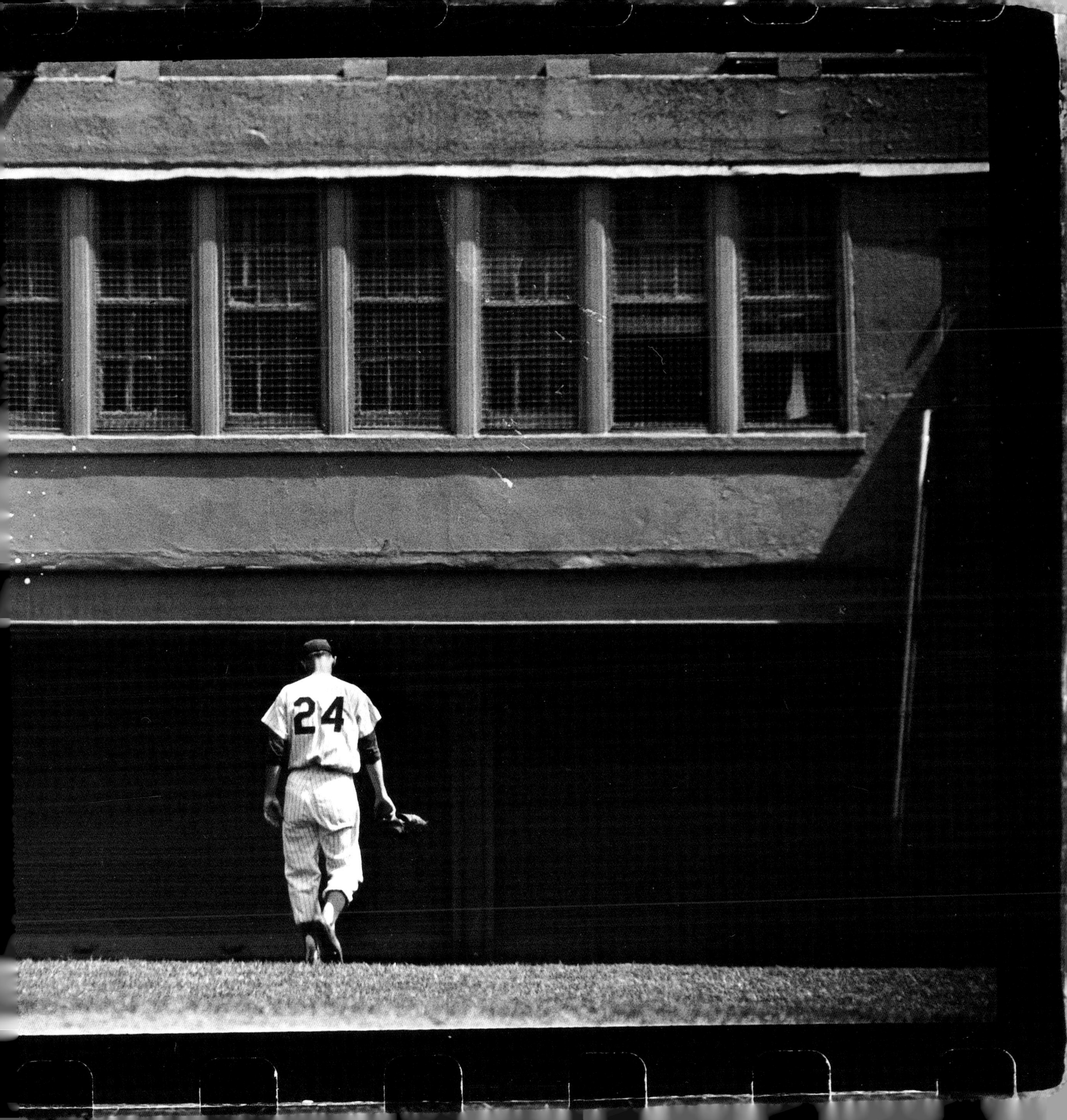
24

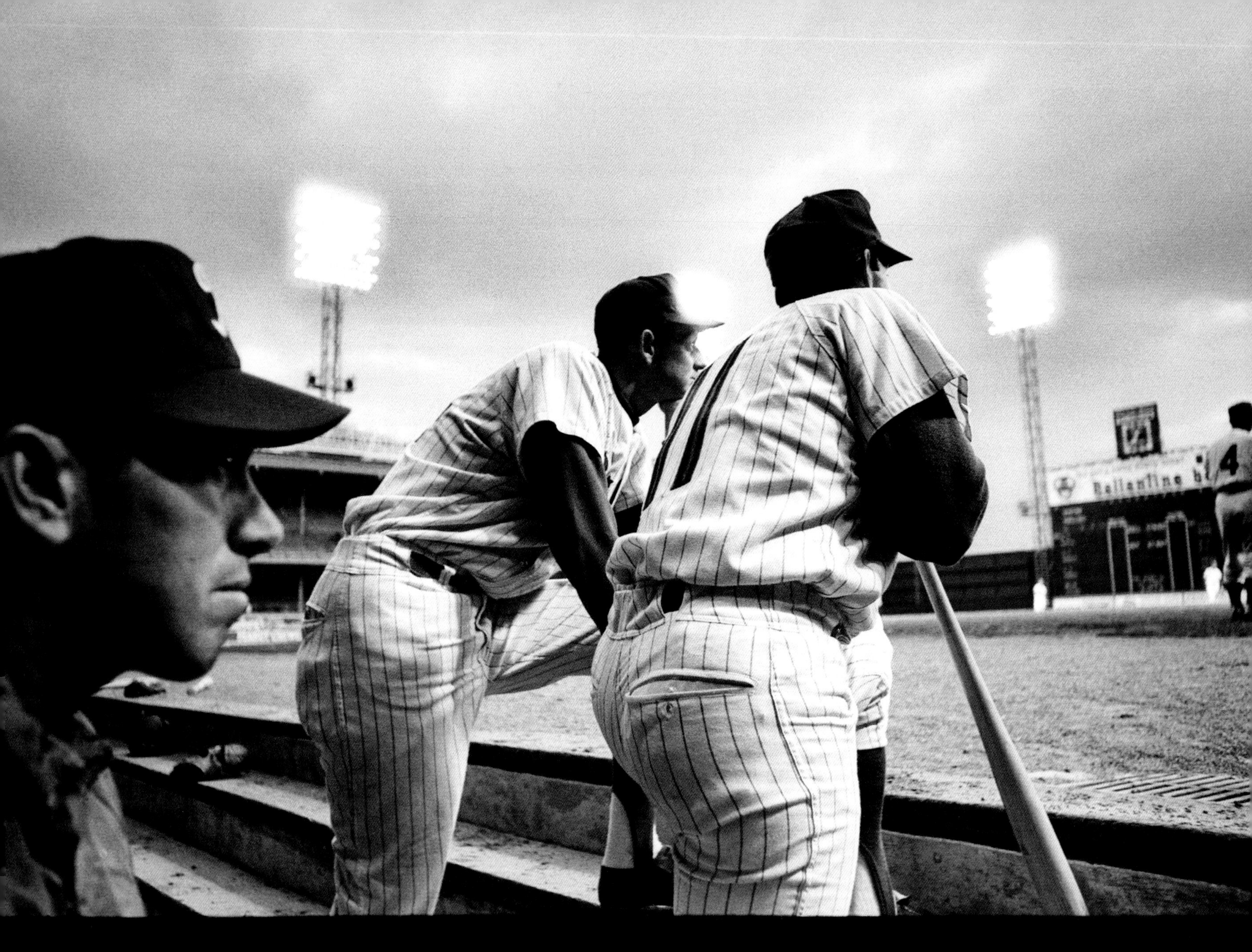

CONNIE MACK STADIUM Philadelphia: Phillies dugout—Cal McLish, Don Demeter, Clay Dalrymple 1963

BALLPARKS. NOT STADIUMS, BALLPARKS. Stadiums are mostly those monstrosities that emerged in the mid-1960s and early 1970s that often resembled one another. Wake up at midnight and look around Busch Stadium in St. Louis, Three Rivers Stadium in Pittsburgh, Riverfront Stadium in Cincinnati, or Atlanta–Fulton County Stadium and you wouldn't know which one you were in. Each was basically the same as any of the other three. And when any of those stadiums eventually imploded, not many people cared. Ballparks are different. You could fall in love with a ballpark, as many have. As Walter Iooss Jr. did with Connie Mack Stadium in Philadelphia. While visiting his father in Brooklyn as a boy, young Walter enjoyed going to Dodgers games at Ebbets Field, the ultimate ballpark. But by the time he was a freelance sports photographer in high school in New Jersey, the Dodgers had deserted Ebbets Field for Los Angeles and the Giants had departed the Polo Grounds for San Francisco. With its rooftop facade, New York City's remaining baseball field, Yankee Stadium, was, and is, a ballpark in spirit, but the nearest real ballpark for Walter was, despite its formal name, Connie Mack Stadium, a train ride away. Take the Pennsylvania Railroad to the North Philly station and walk a few blocks.

"I loved Connie Mack," Iooss says.

With steel girders supporting the roof over its double-decker grandstand, Connie Mack Stadium opened in 1908 and was known as Shibe Park until 1953, when it was renamed in honor of baseball's winningest manager. It resembled Ebbets Field. So did Tiger (formerly Briggs) Stadium in Detroit, now gone too. Only two classic ballparks have endured as baseball monuments for nearly a century: Fenway Park in Boston and Wrigley Field in Chicago.

"The Wall in Fenway is great," Iooss says, "but the best light in baseball is the sun coming through the portals at Wrigley Field around seven o'clock before a night game during the two weeks before and after June 21, the longest day of the year."

Iooss considers Camden Yards in Baltimore by far the best of the new ballparks. "It's cozy," he says. "The brick warehouse beyond right field makes it." But he talks so lovingly about Connie Mack Stadium, it's as if it were still there, as if he could shoot the scene tomorrow. With the Dodgers and the Giants no longer in New York, and before the Mets arrived, if he wanted to go to a National League game, he had to take the train down to Connie Mack and shoot the Phillies.

"That was my ballpark," he says. "My team."

But when the Mets restored National League baseball to New York in 1962, he couldn't resist going to the Polo Grounds. Perched in upper Manhattan across the Harlem River from Yankee Stadium, the Polo Grounds had been the home of the New York Giants until that franchise moved to San Francisco, following the Brooklyn Dodgers' move to Los Angeles, for the 1958 season.

The only major-league ballpark shaped like a rectangle, the Polo Grounds had been without baseball for four seasons before the Mets arrived as an expansion team and lost a record 120 games in 1962. But those Mets of manager Casey Stengel were so bad, they were good—at least as subjects for a photographer.

In his travels for *Sports Illustrated*, Walter also discovered the nuances of other ballparks in other cities, notably the unique overhang that shaded the Pittsburgh Pirates bullpen in old Forbes Field, as well as the palm-tree backdrop in spring-training ballparks that have always resembled the coziness of small minor-league ballparks, unlike the vast expanses of major-league stadiums.

It was in one of those parks that Walter made a classic portrait of Yogi Berra and Whitey Ford, often a World Series battery and now revered Hall of Famers. The men were in spring training with the Yankees as instructors at Legends Field in Tampa.

More than three decades earlier, Iooss had photographed several young Yankees just having fun in the same Florida sun—Tony Kubek, Joe Pepitone, Phil Linz, Tom Tresh, and Jake Gibbs playing a game called "flip" among themselves. On another day, he found Stan Musial, nicknamed "Stan the Man" by an Ebbets Field fan out of respect for how often he demolished the Dodgers, about to fall backward into a circle of St. Louis Cardinal teammates—that era's version of weight lifting.

"The best light in spring training," Iooss says, "is just before a night game. All the other photographers would get their pictures early and leave. I'd have it all to myself."

That's all any sports photographer ever asks: to have it all to himself. Not just the subject, but the light. Walter Iooss is more sensitive to light than most photographers. Remember how he talked about the light at Wrigley Field just before a night game in June. The light often makes the difference between somebody who just takes pictures and somebody who understands the art of photography.

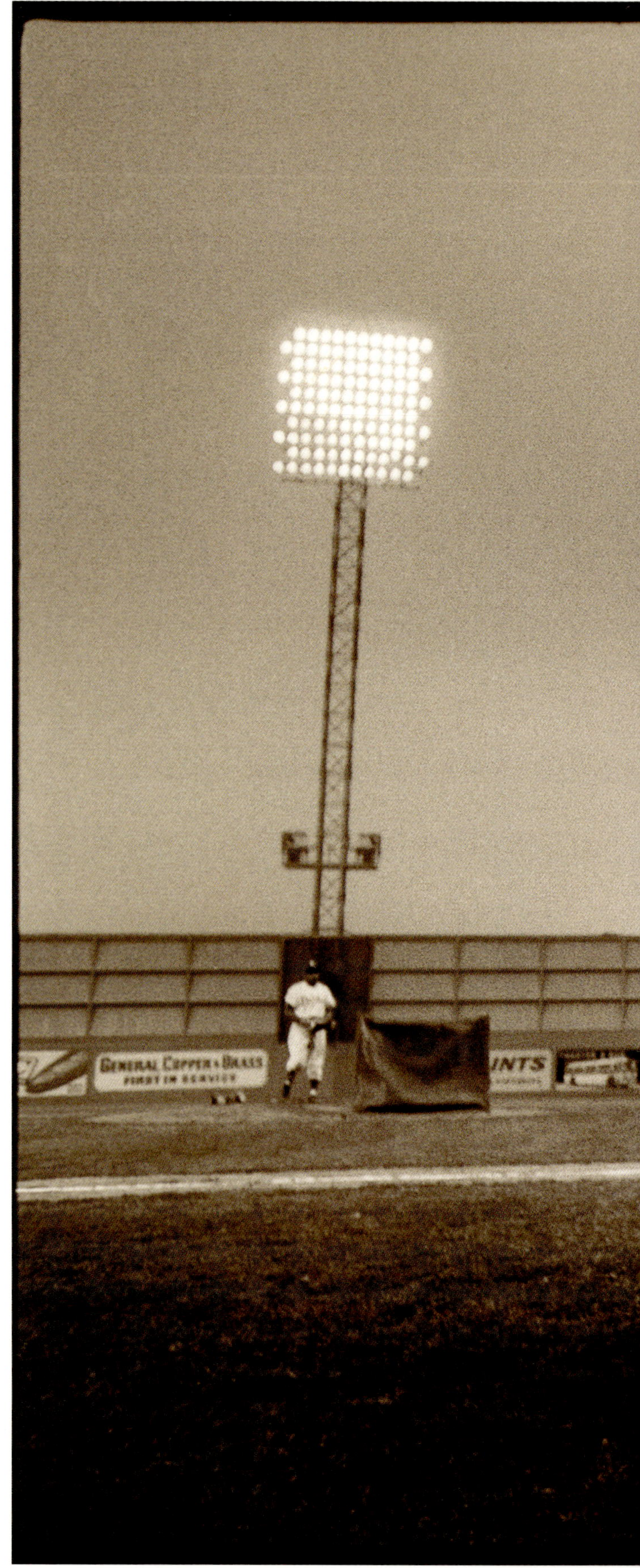

CONNIE MACK STADIUM, Philadelphia, 1963

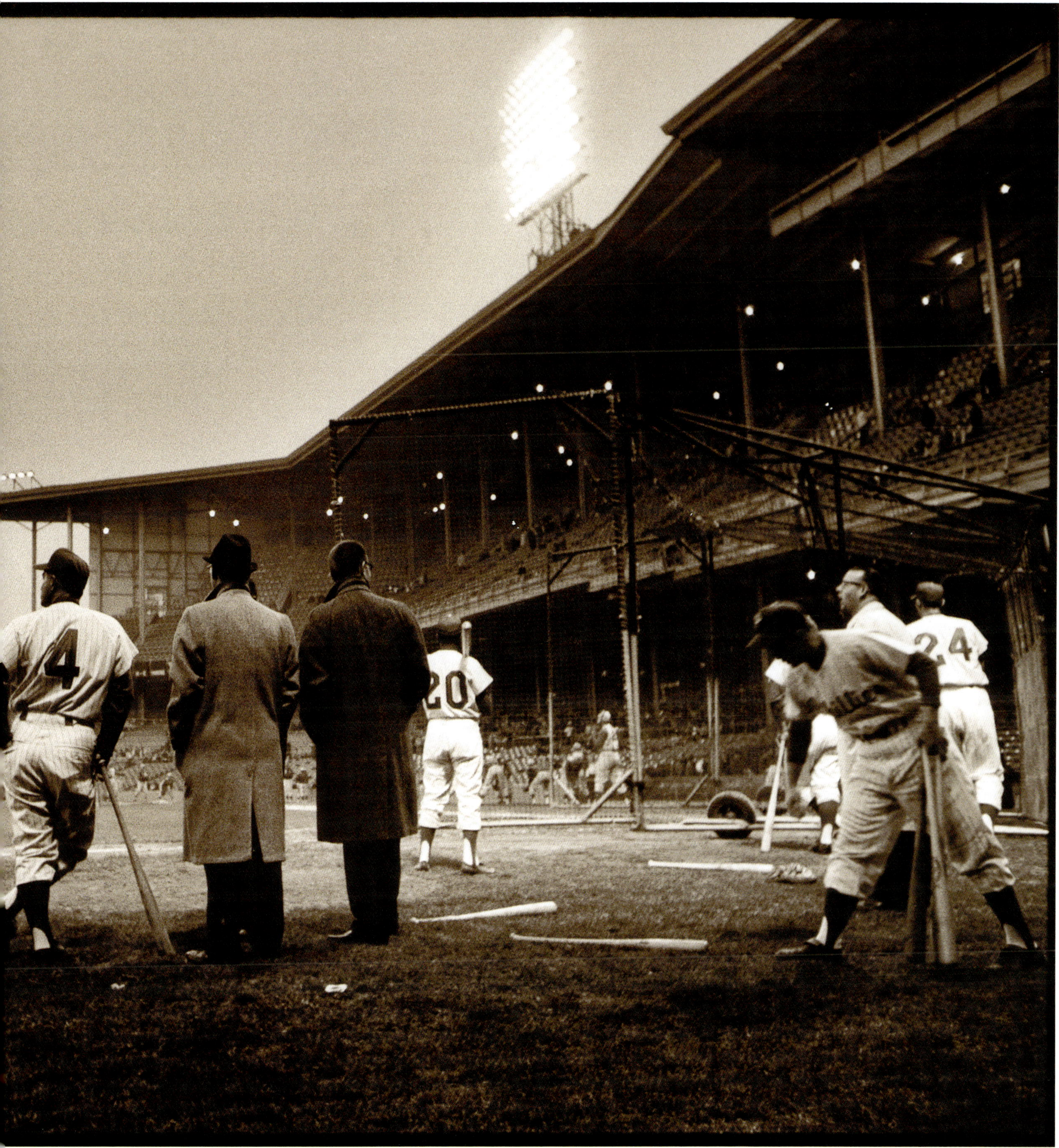

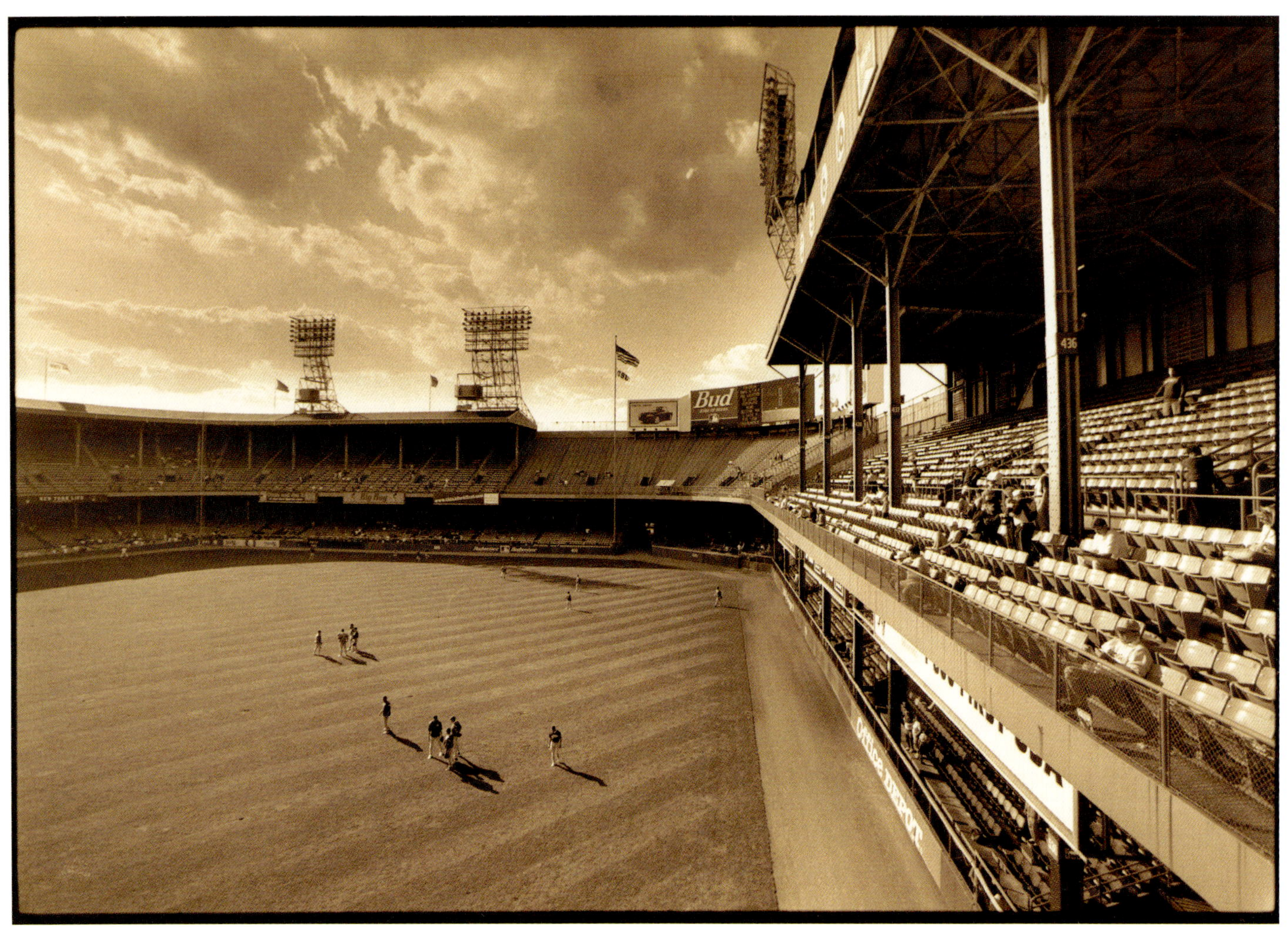

TIGER STADIUM, Detroit, 1999

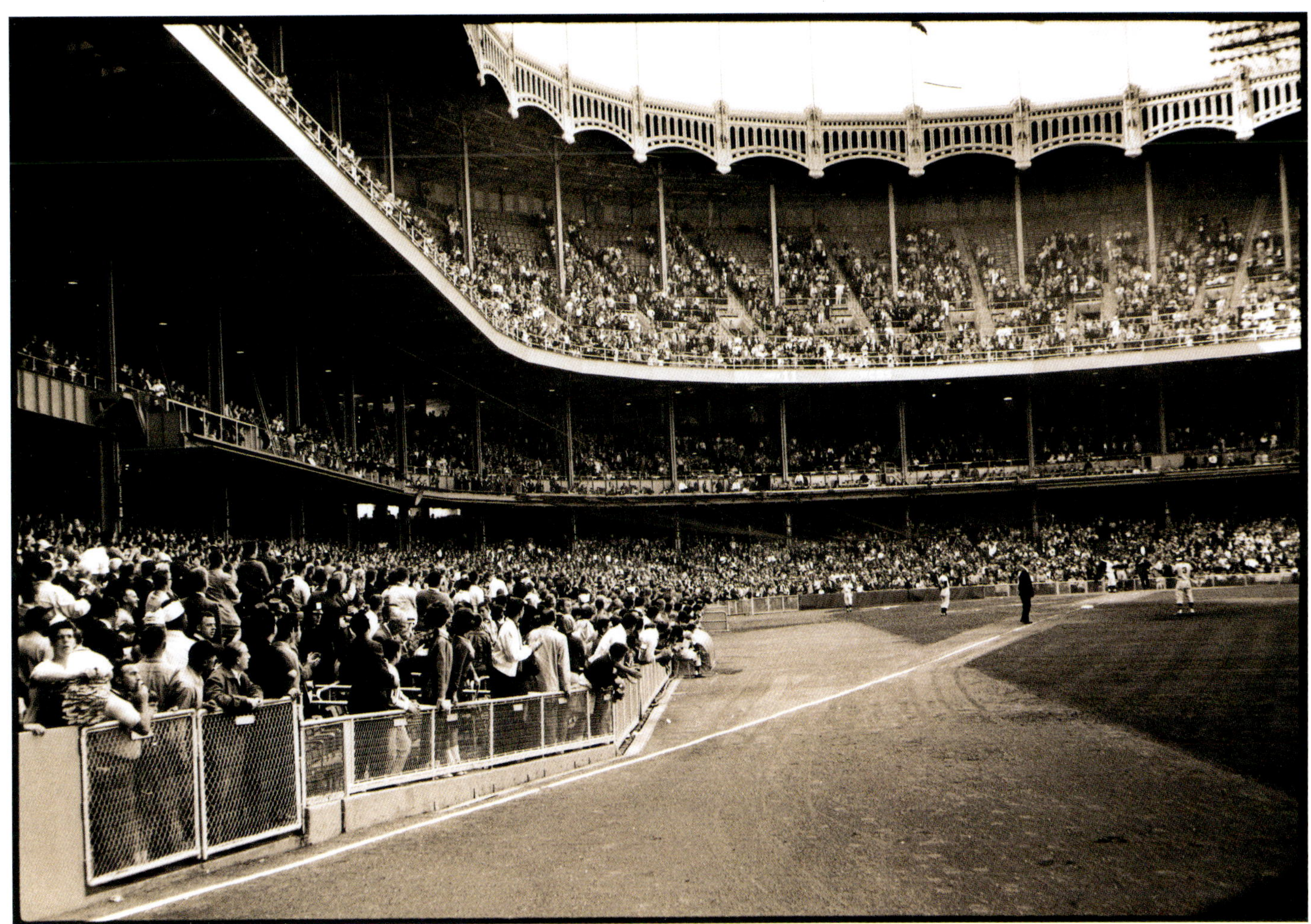

YANKEE STADIUM, New York, 1961

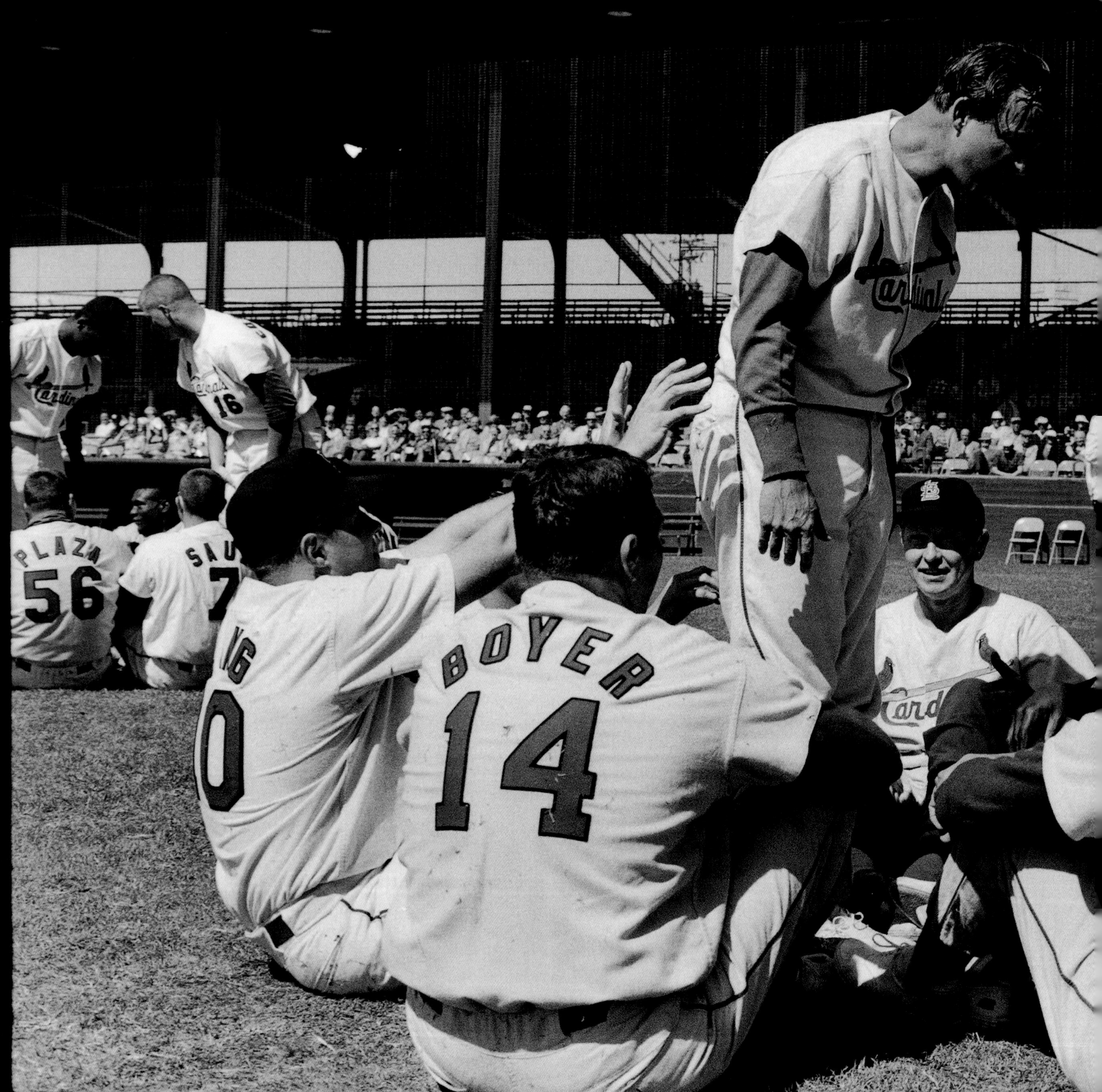
PLAZA
56
16
BOYER
14

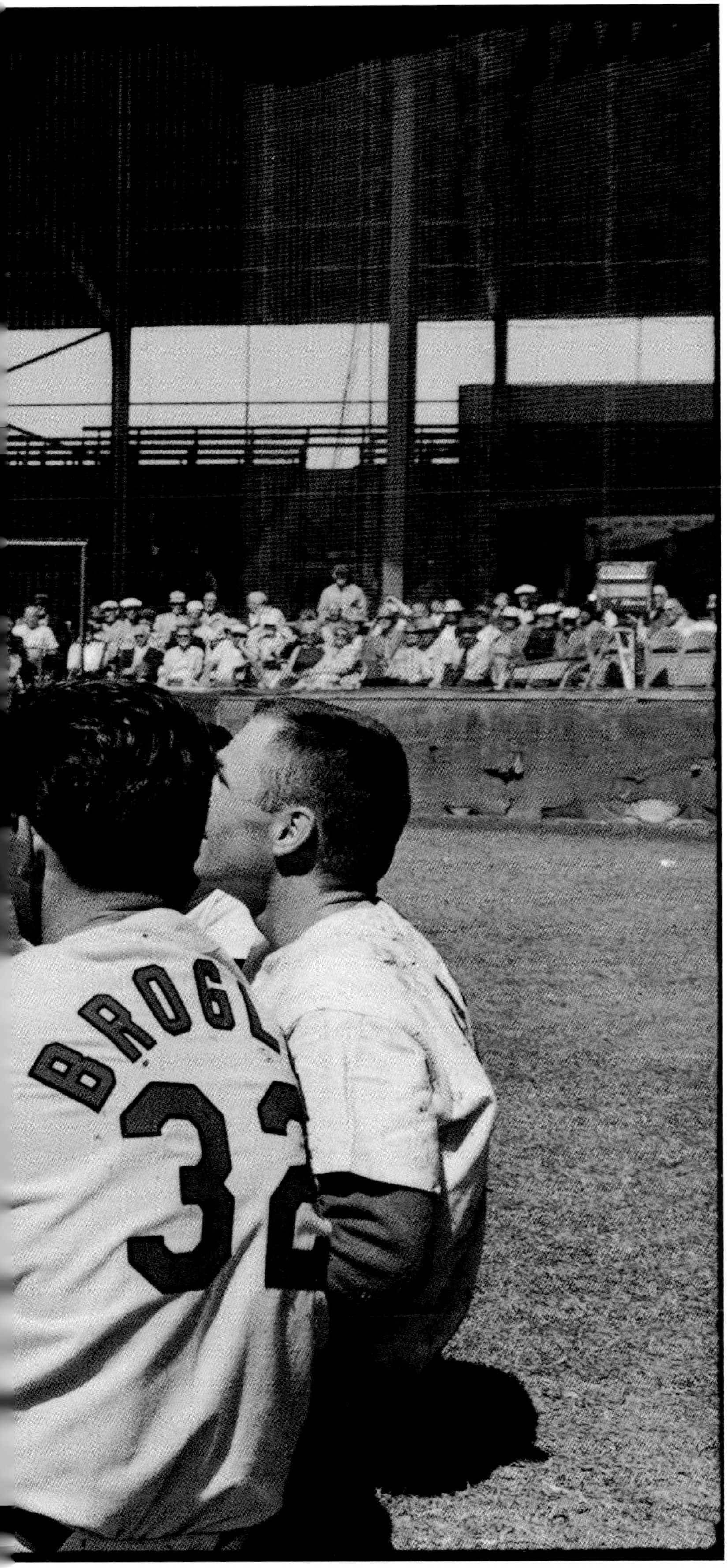

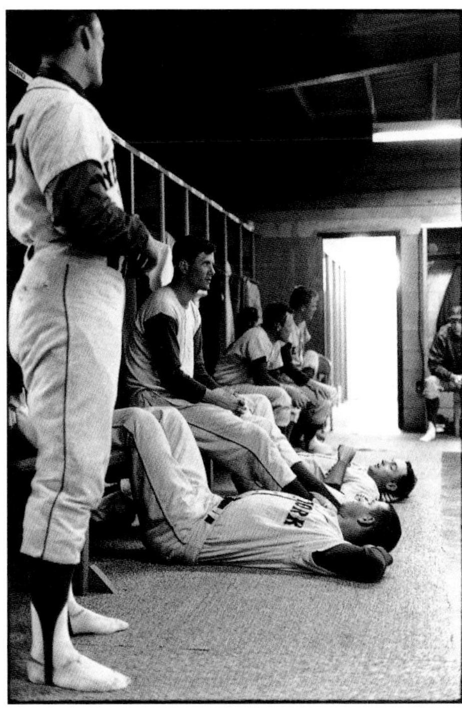

STAN MUSIAL, St. Petersburg, Florida, 1963 (LEFT)

N.Y. METS LOCKER ROOM, St. Petersburg, Florida, 1963 (ABOVE)

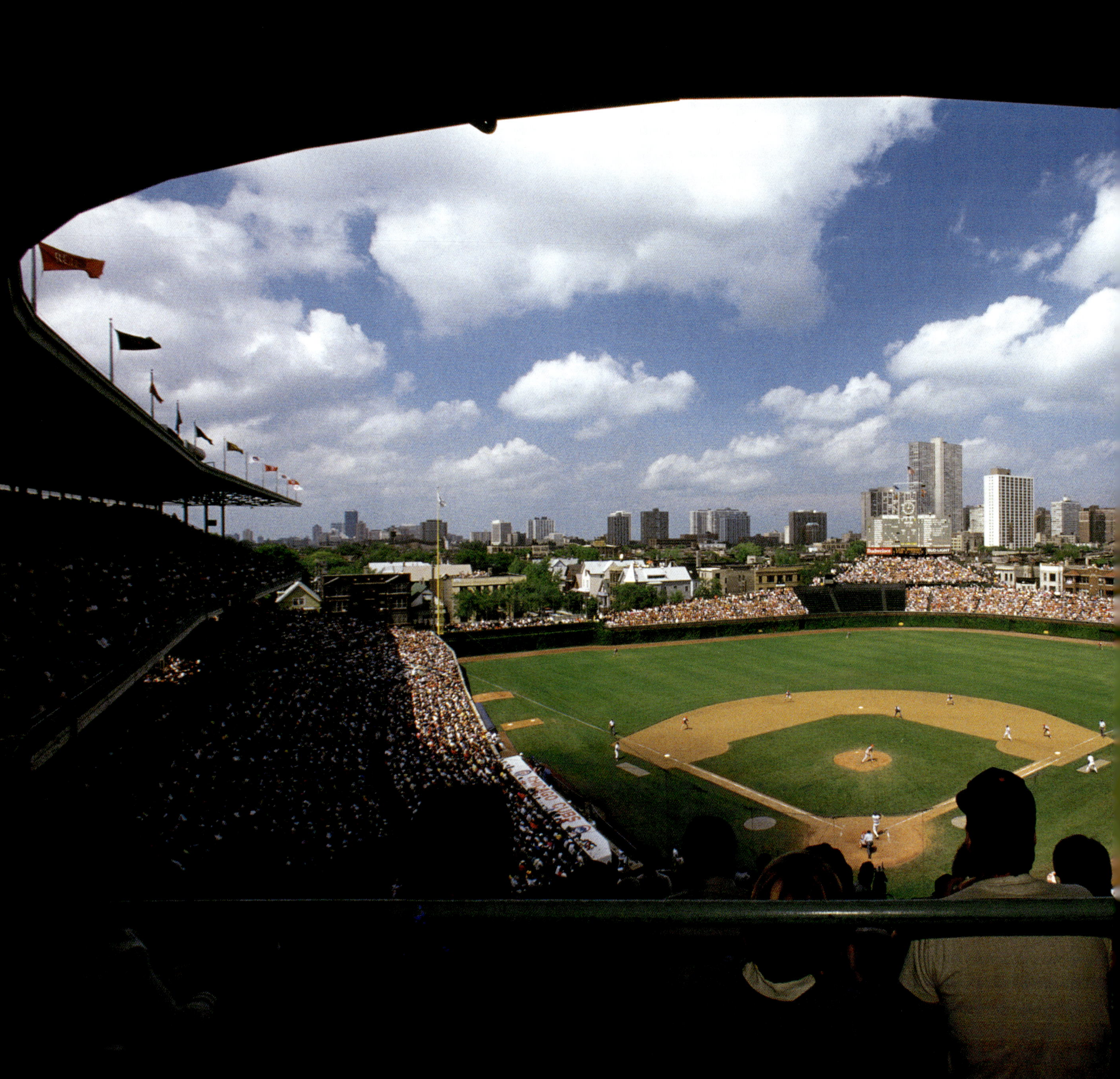
CHICAGO CUBS

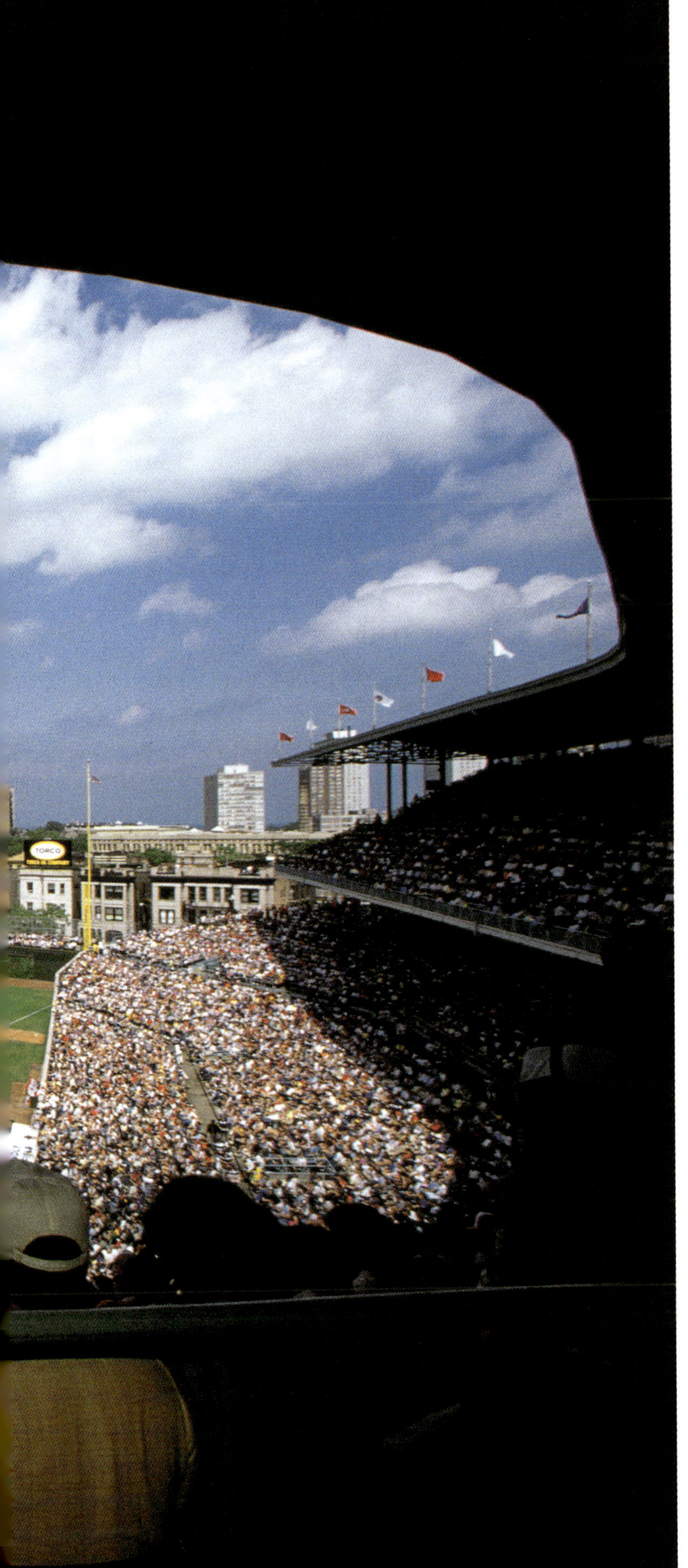

WRIGLEY FIELD, Chicago, 1985

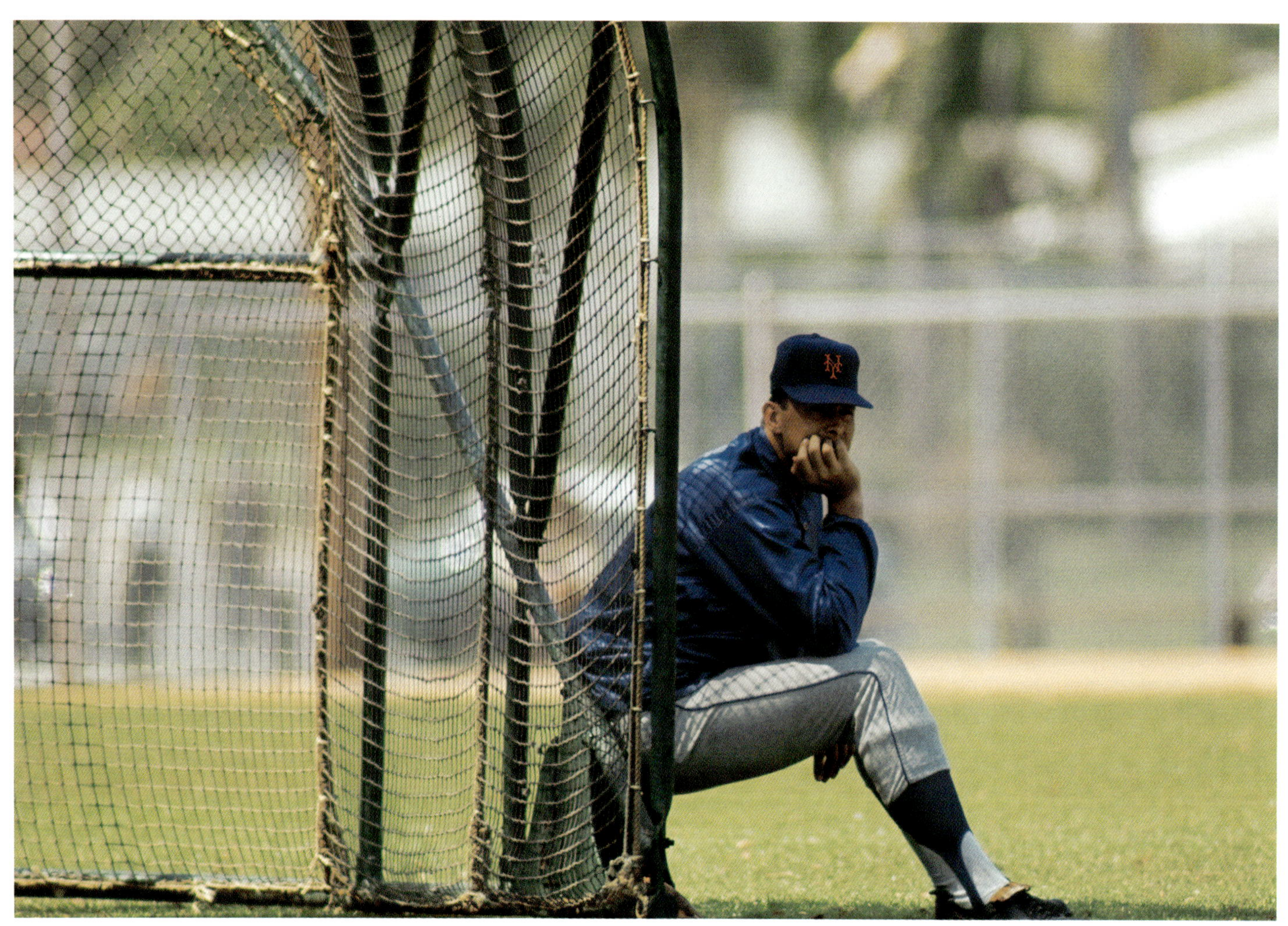

JERRY KOOSMAN, St. Petersburg, Florida, 1967

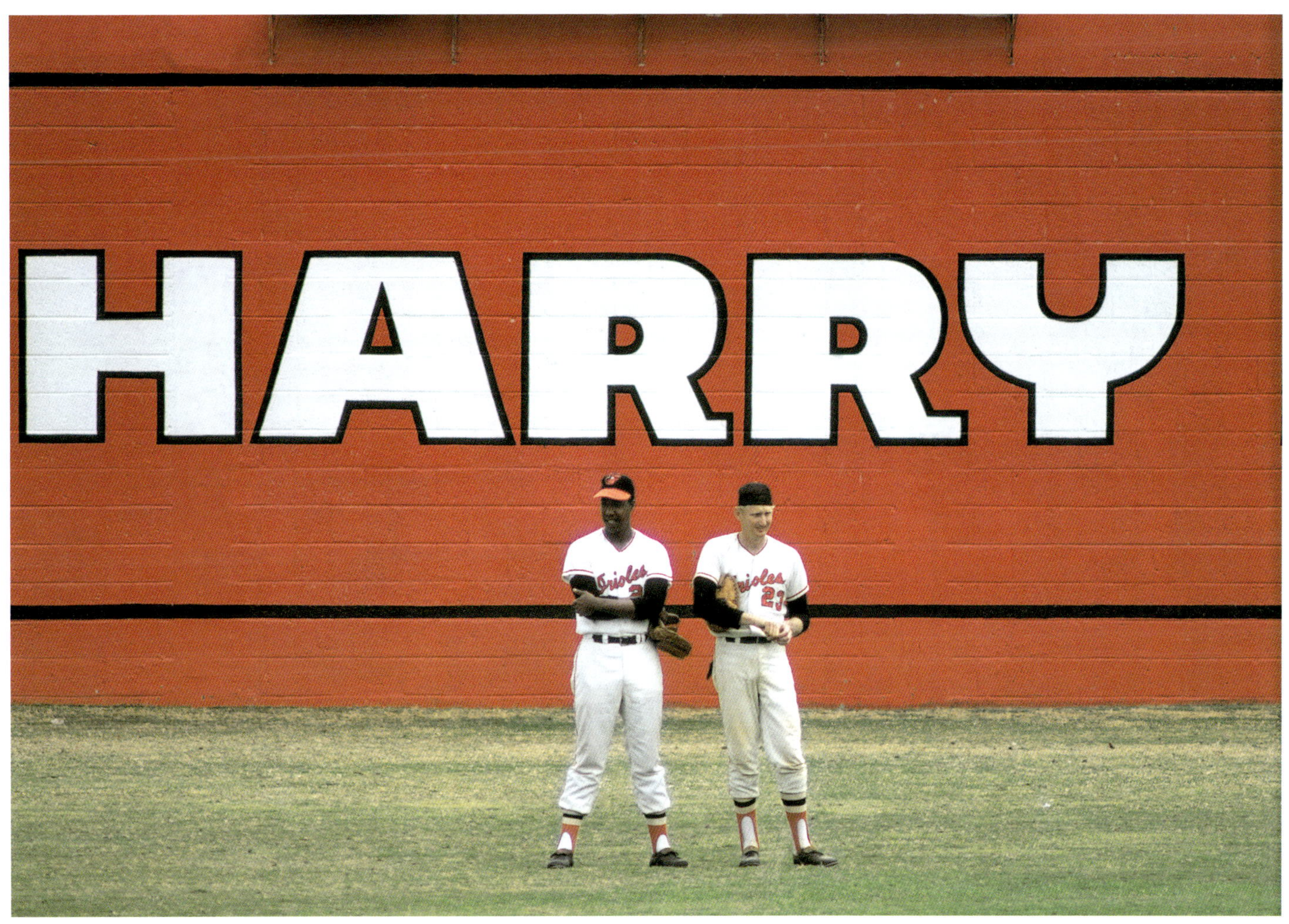

BALTIMORE ORIOLES, Miami, Florida, 1969

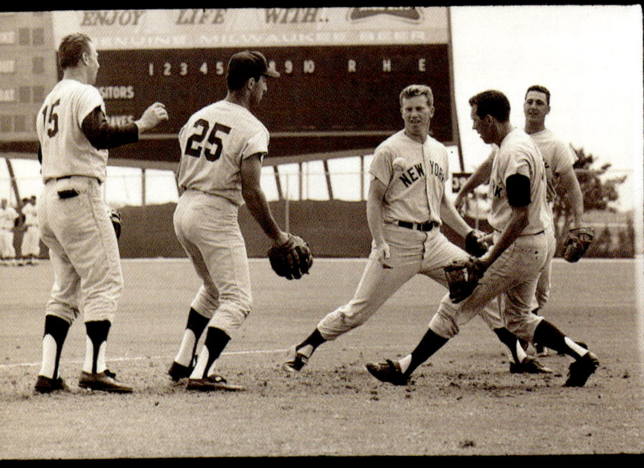

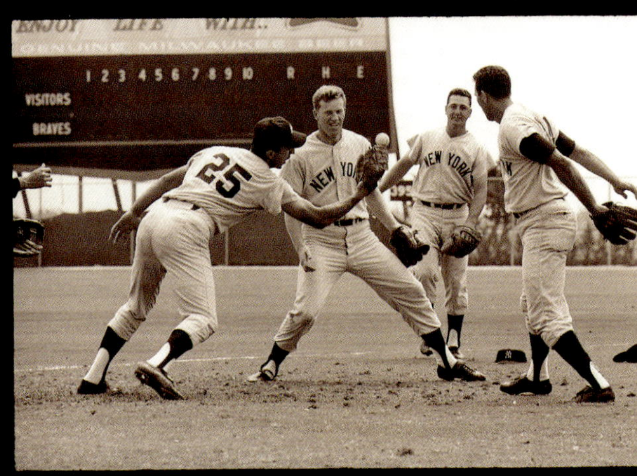

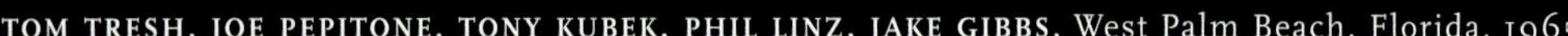

TOM TRESH, JOE PEPITONE, TONY KUBEK, PHIL LINZ, JAKE GIBBS, West Palm Beach, Florida, 1965

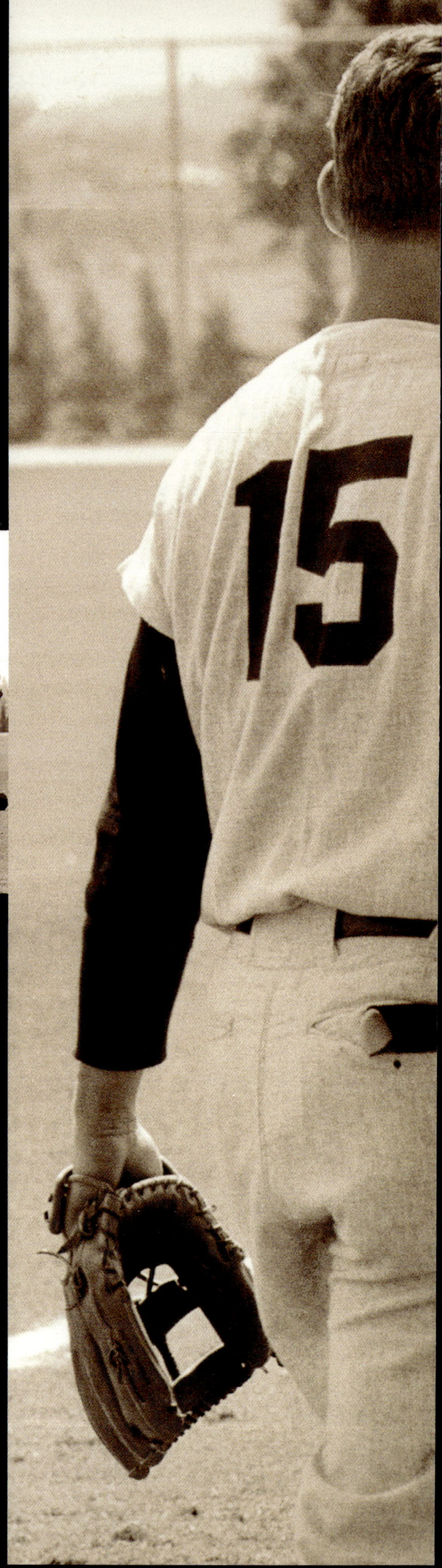

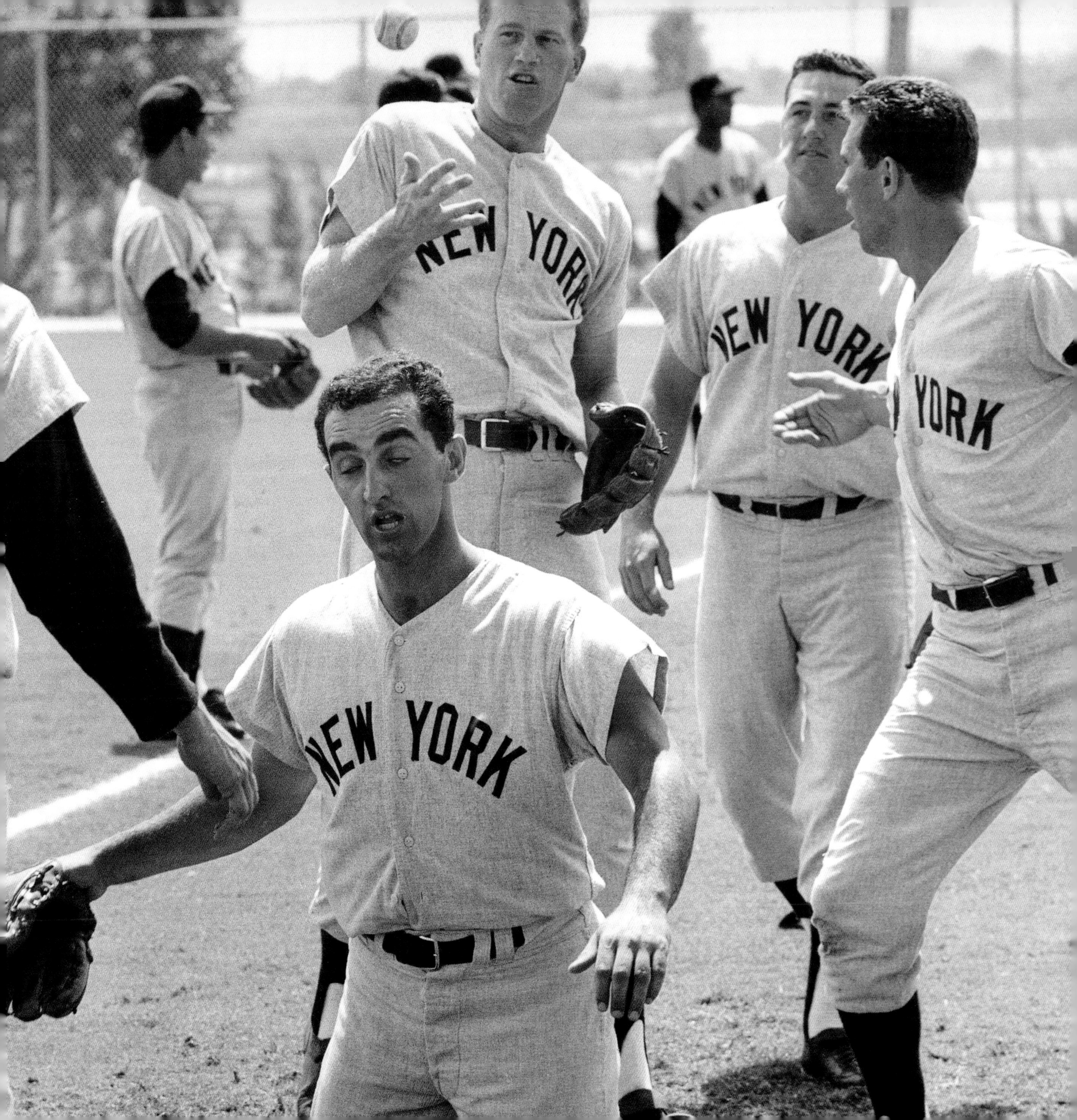
NEW YORK
NEW YORK
NEW YORK
YORK

BOSTON RED SOX SPRING TRAINING, Winter Park, Florida, 1988

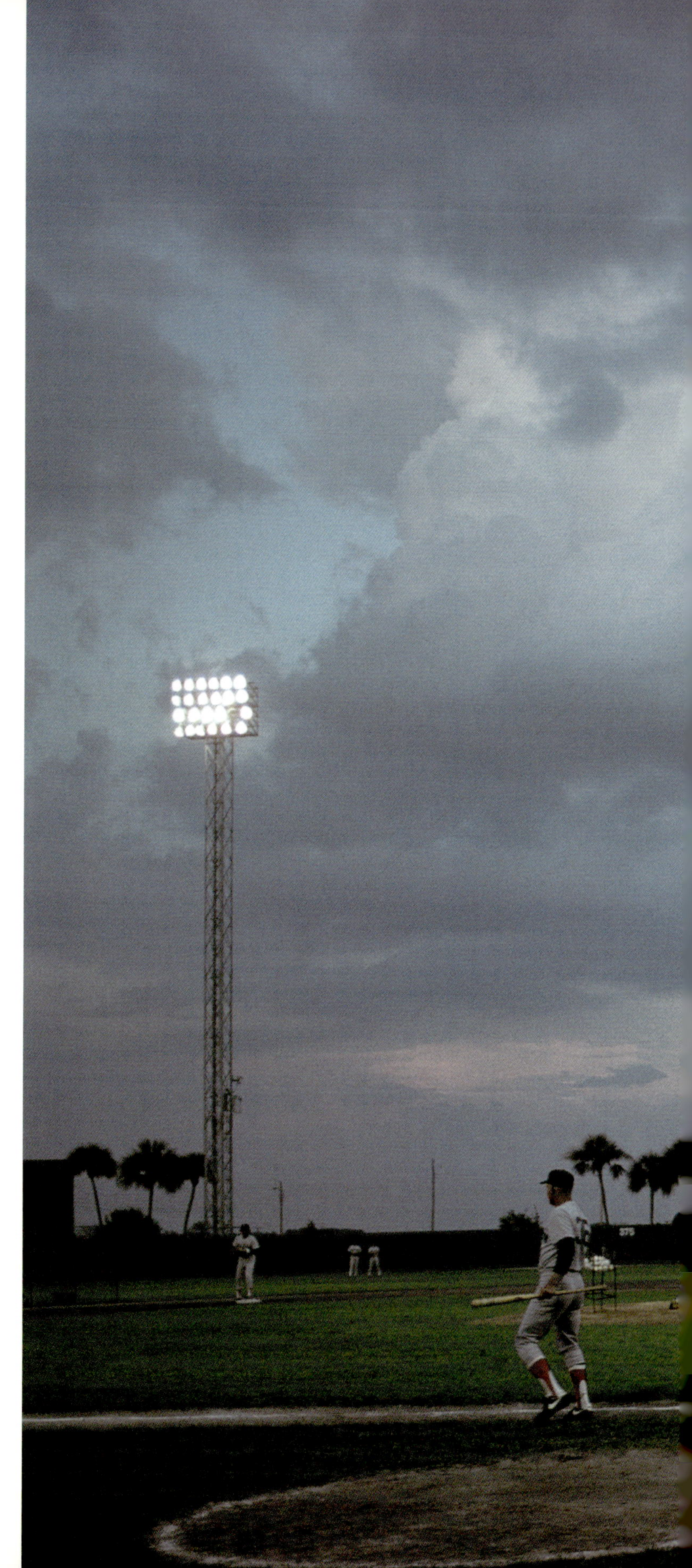

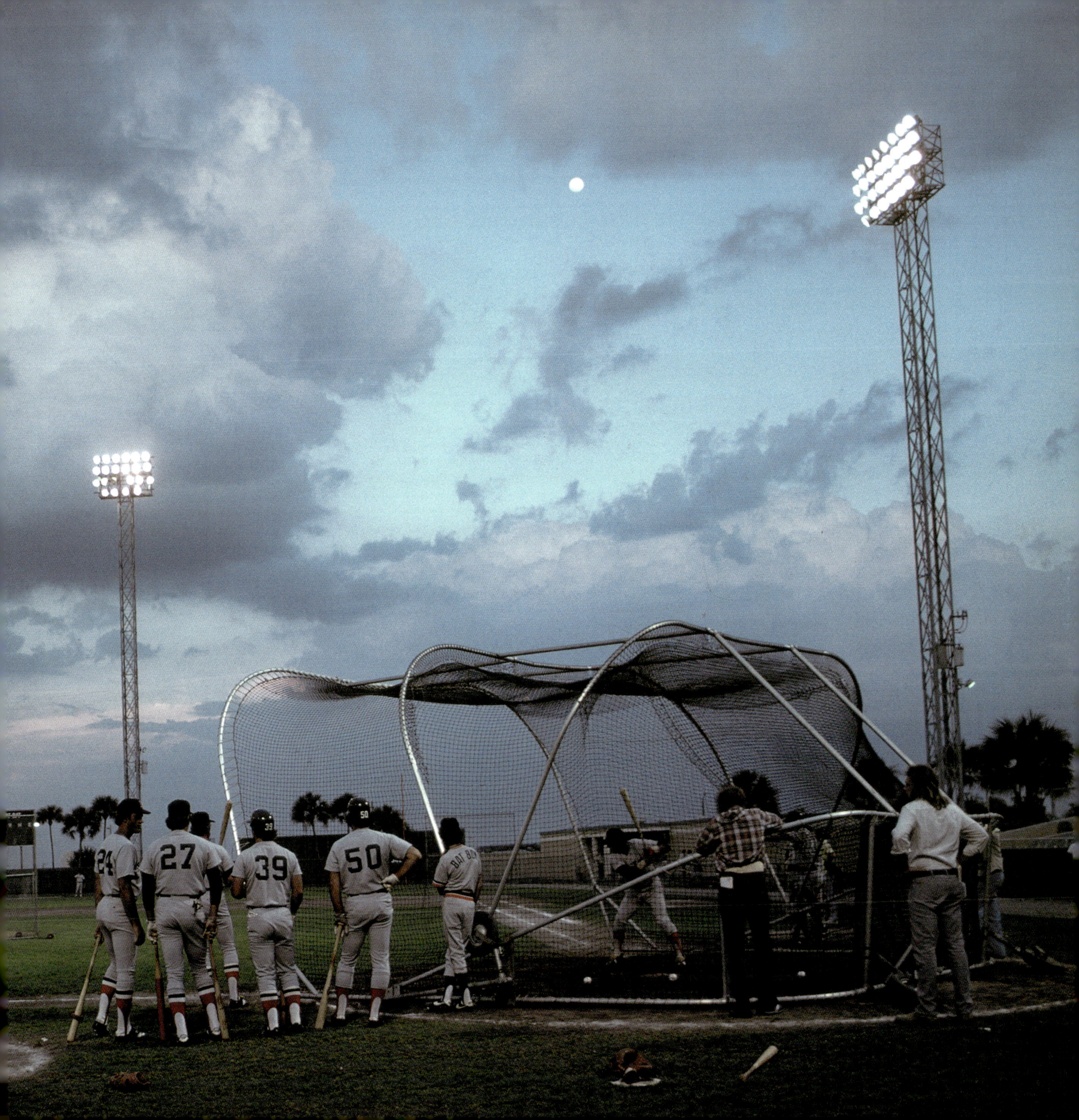
24
27
39
50
BAT BOY

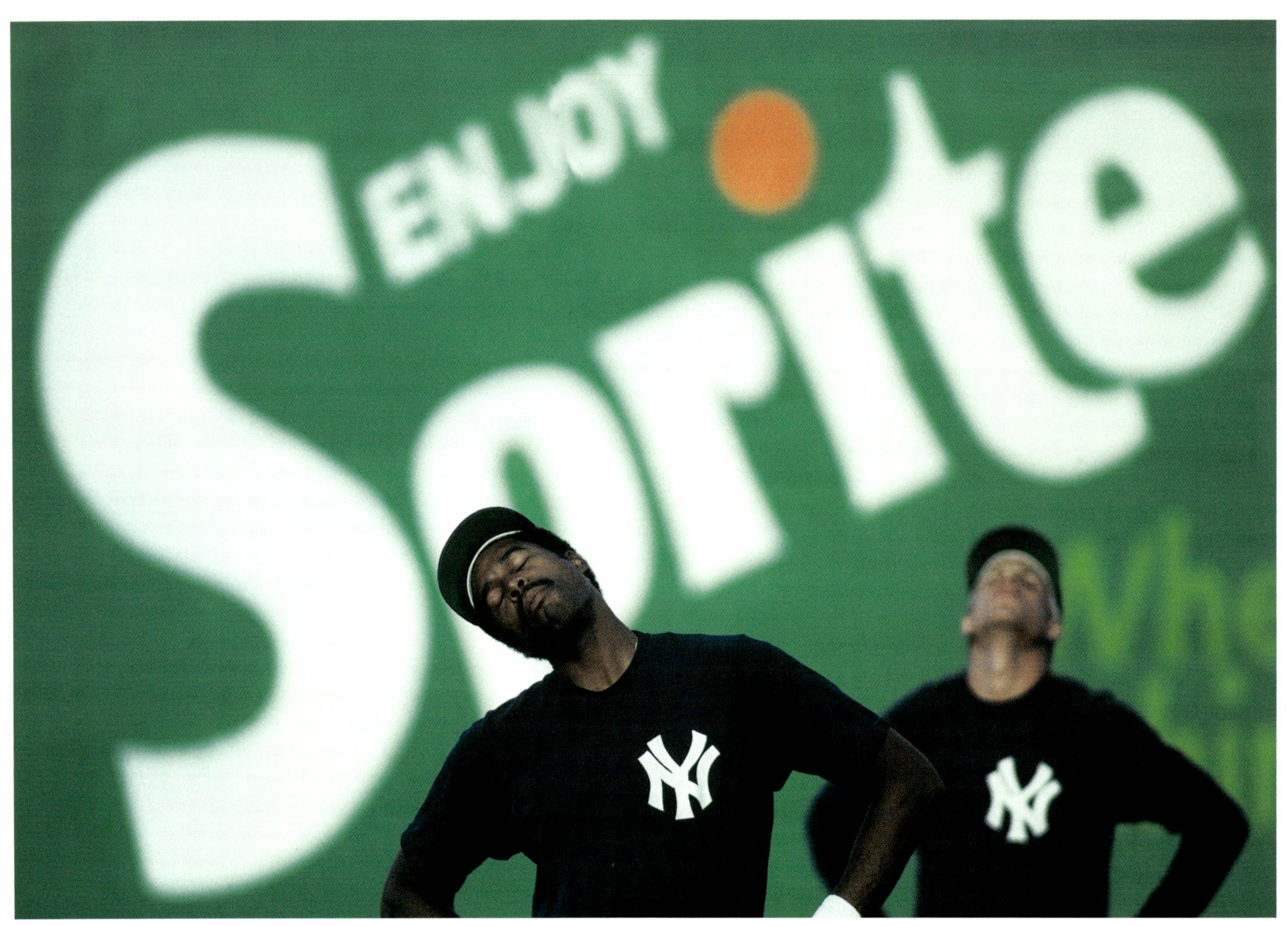

DAVE WINFIELD, Tampa, Florida, 1981

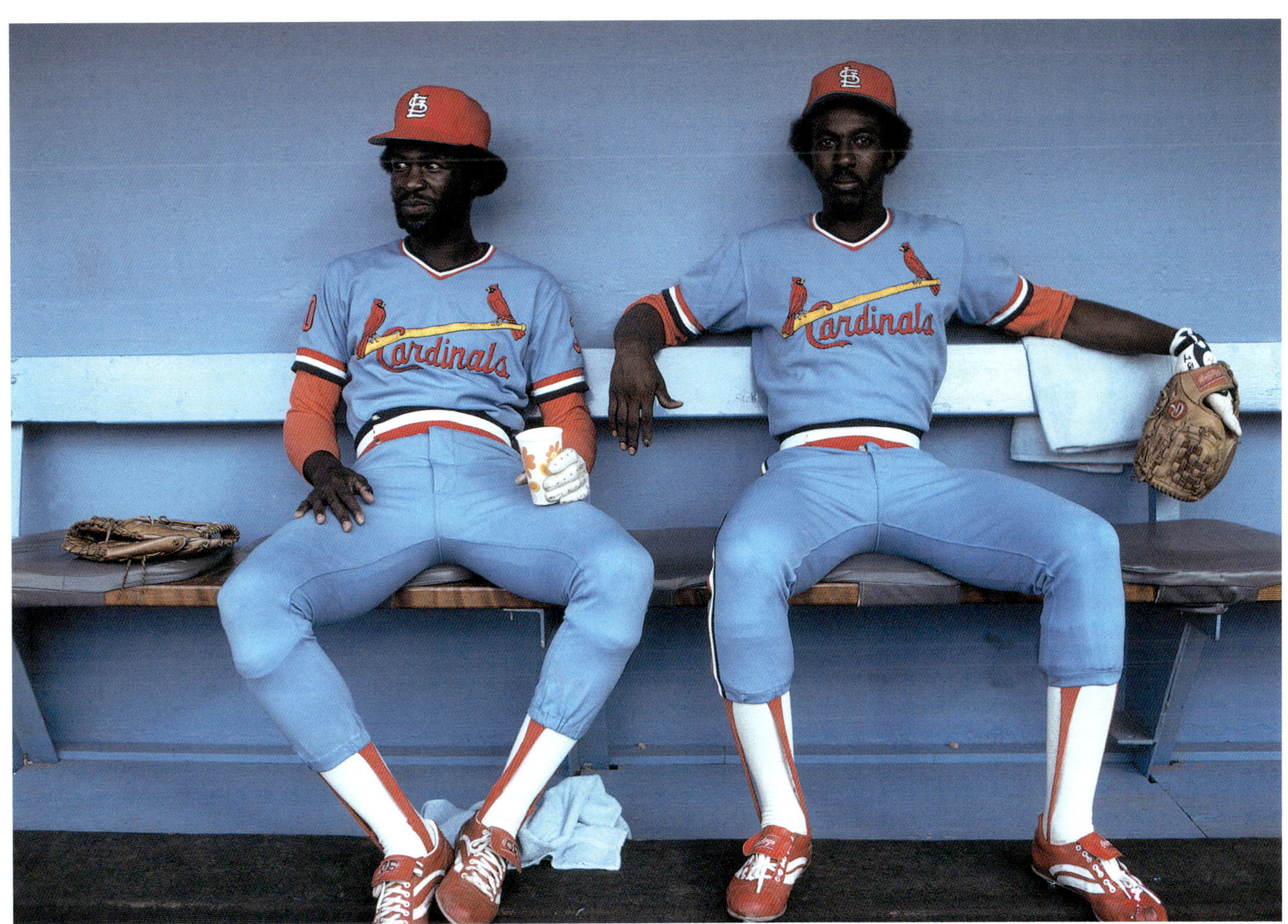

TONY SCOTT, GARRY TEMPLETON, Los Angeles, 1979

TONY GONZALEZ, Philadelphia, 1964

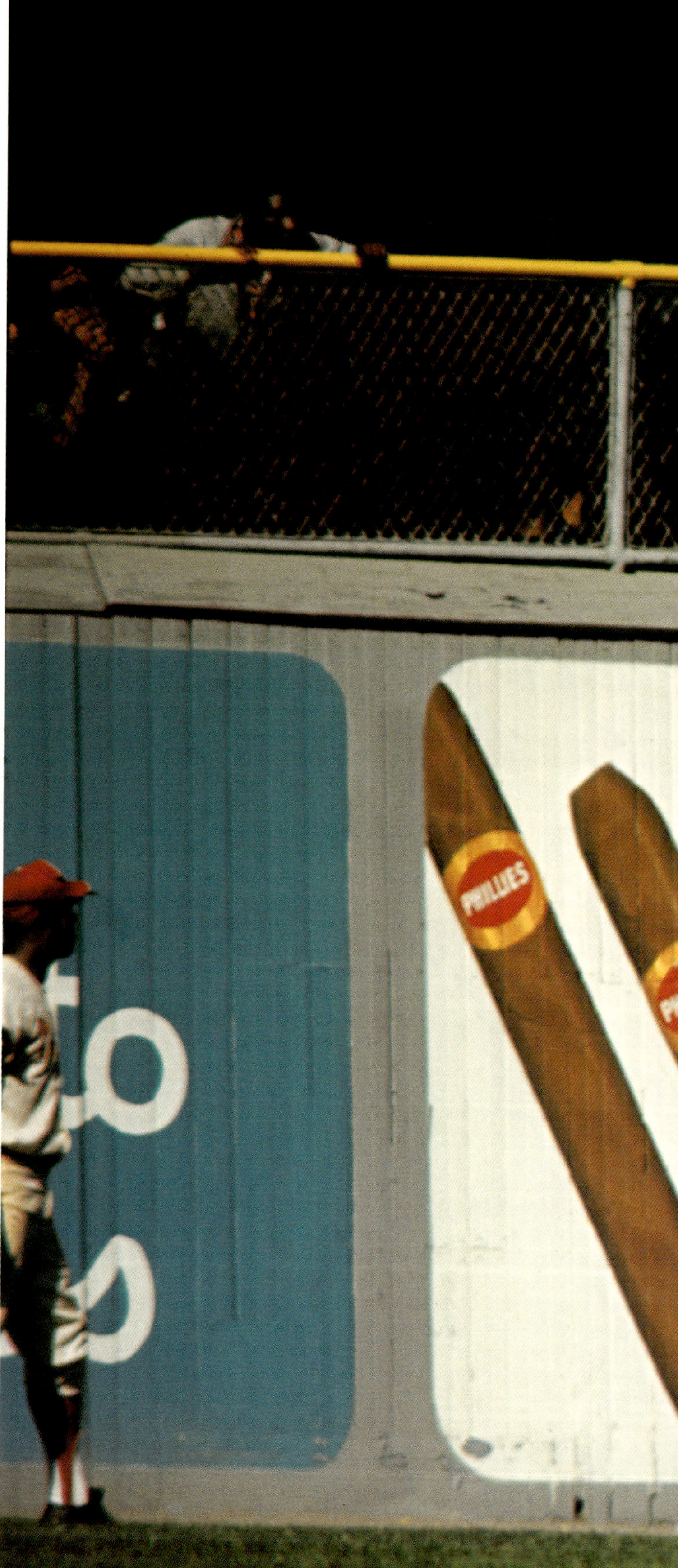

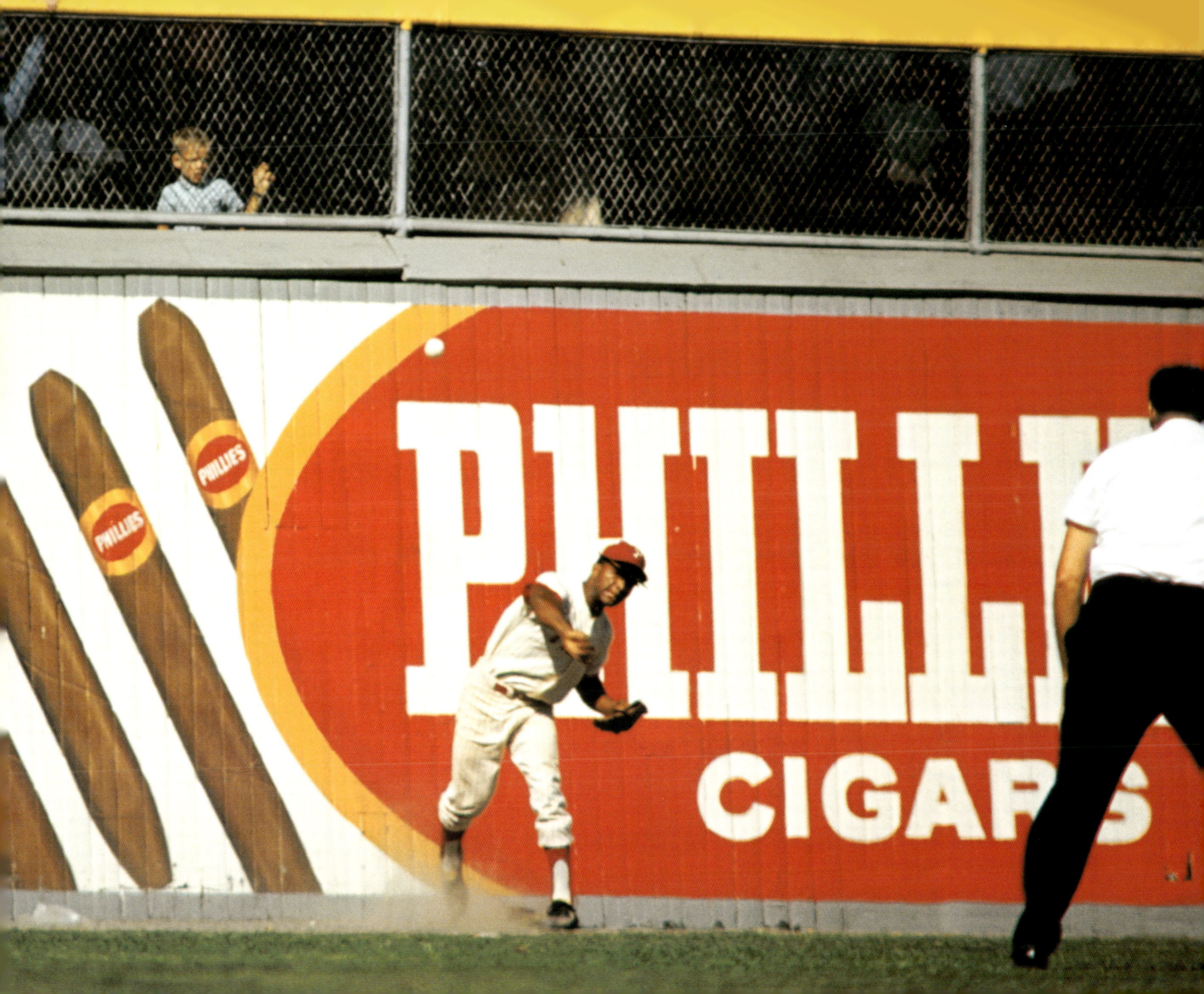
PHILLIES
PHILLIES
PHILLI
CIGARS

WADE BOGGS, Boston, 1992

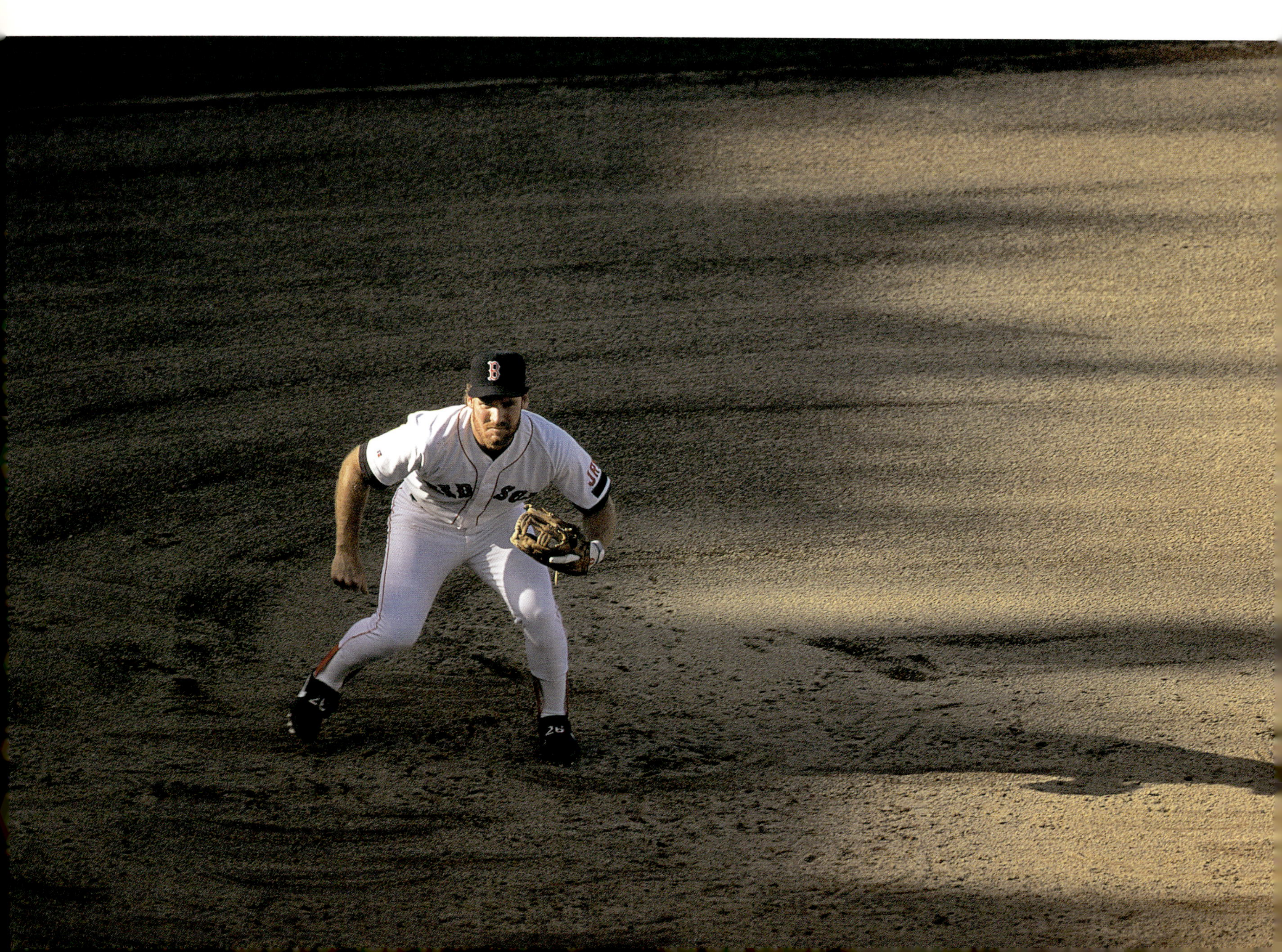

JIM RICE, Fenway Park, Boston, 1979

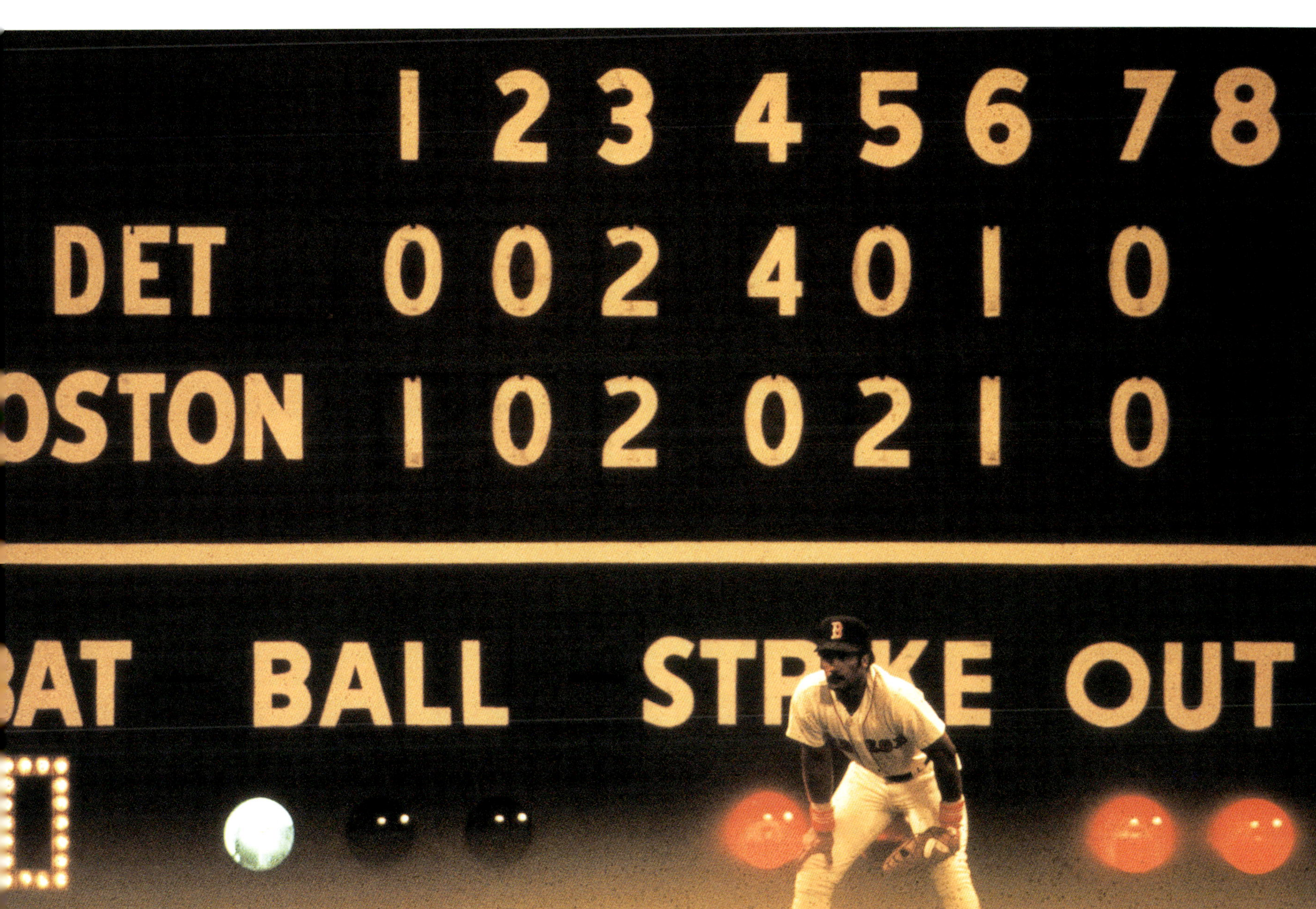

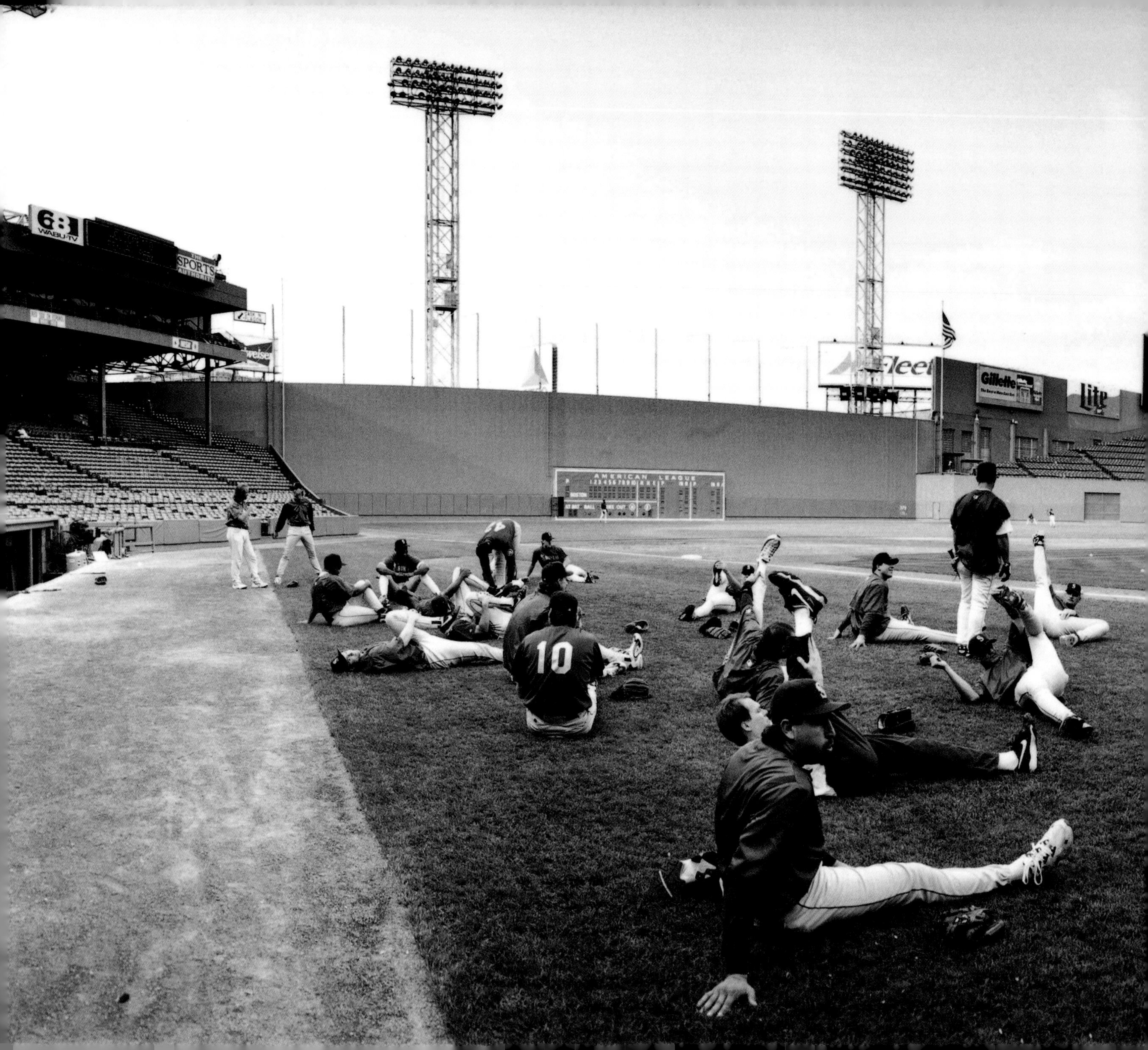
WABU-TV
SPORTS
Fleet
Gillette
Lite
AMERICAN LEAGUE
10

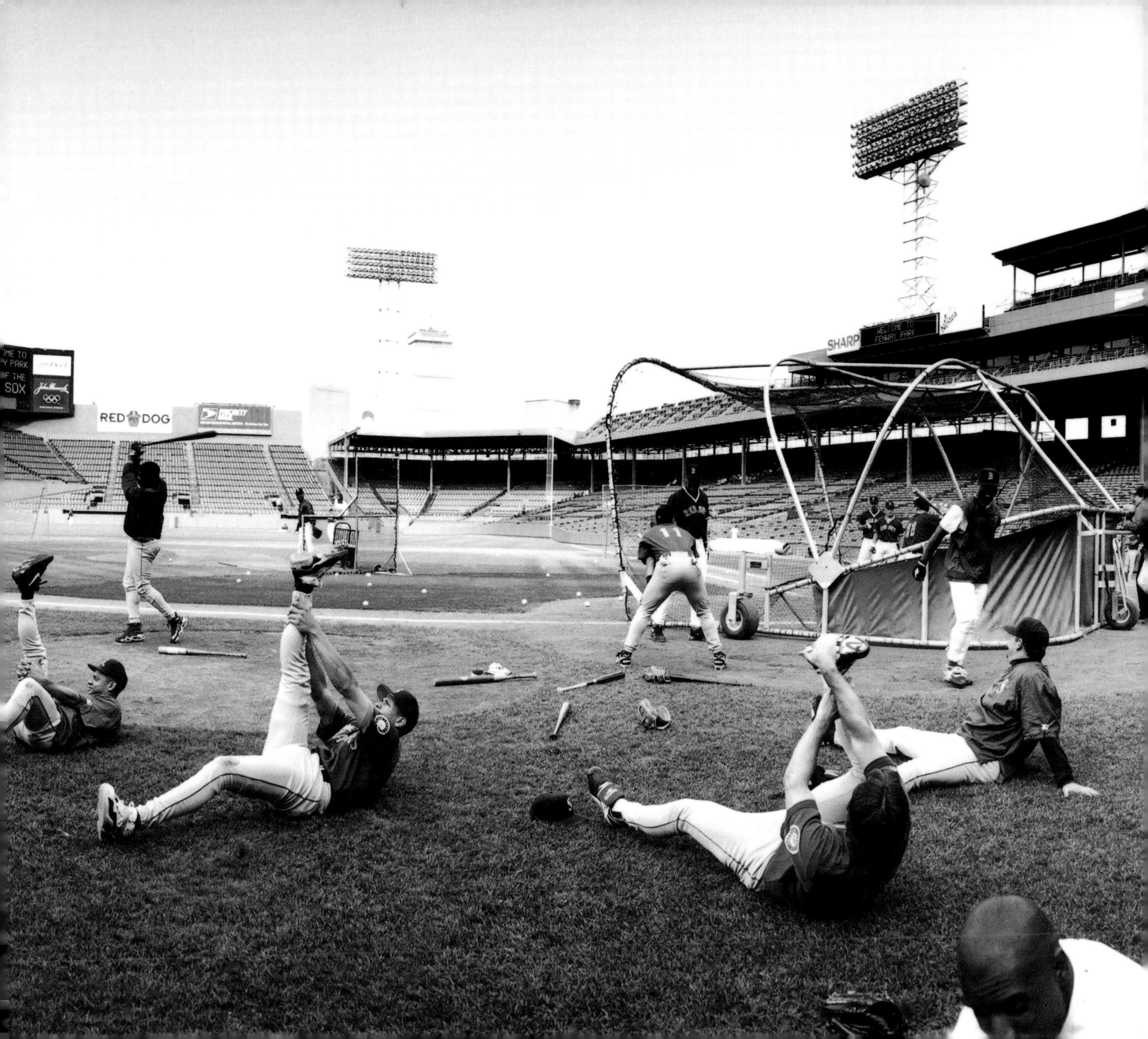
RED DOG
SHARP
WELCOME TO
FENWAY PARK

REGGIE SANDERS, Los Angeles, 1993

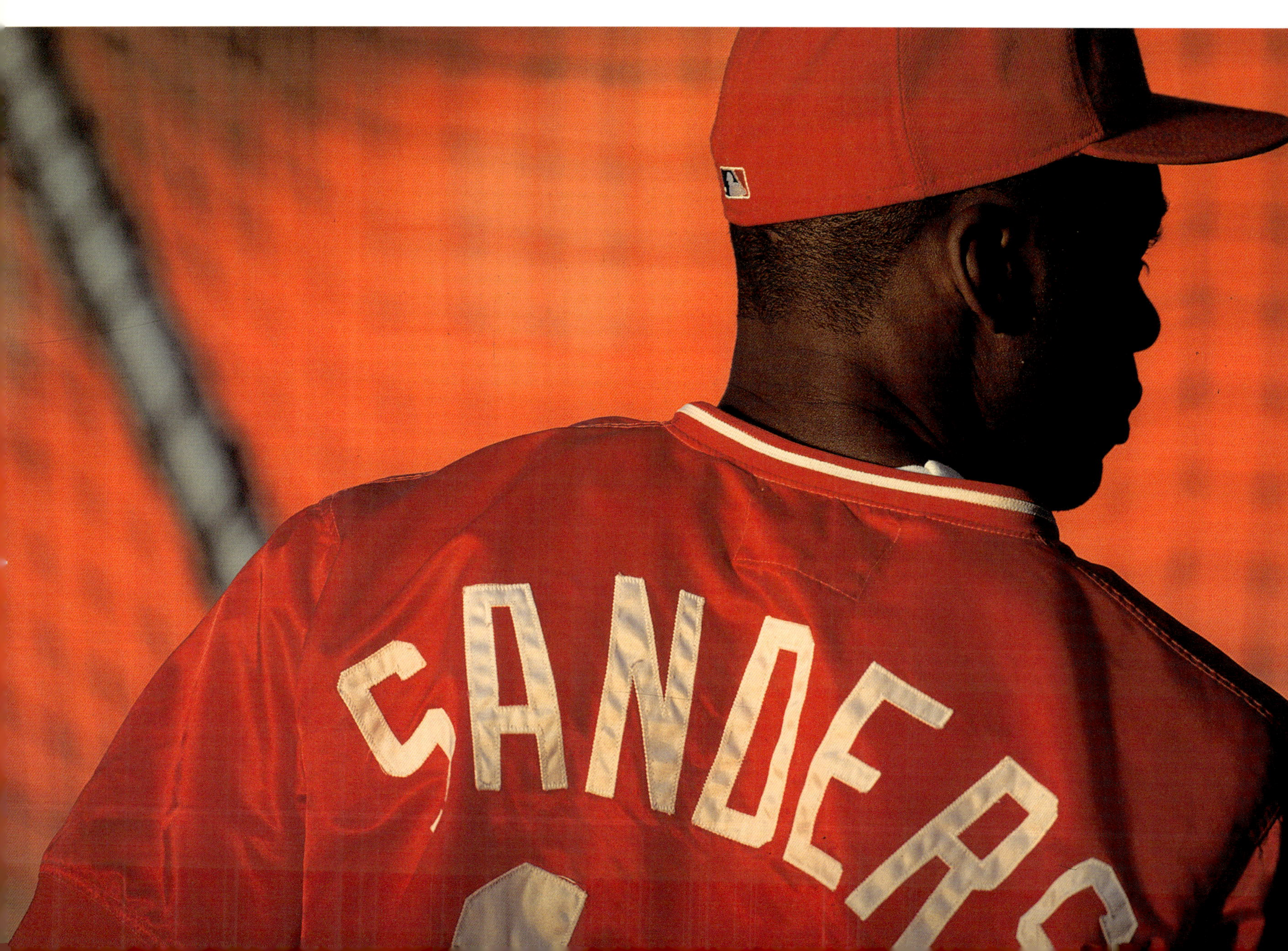

KEVIN MITCHELL, San Francisco, 1993

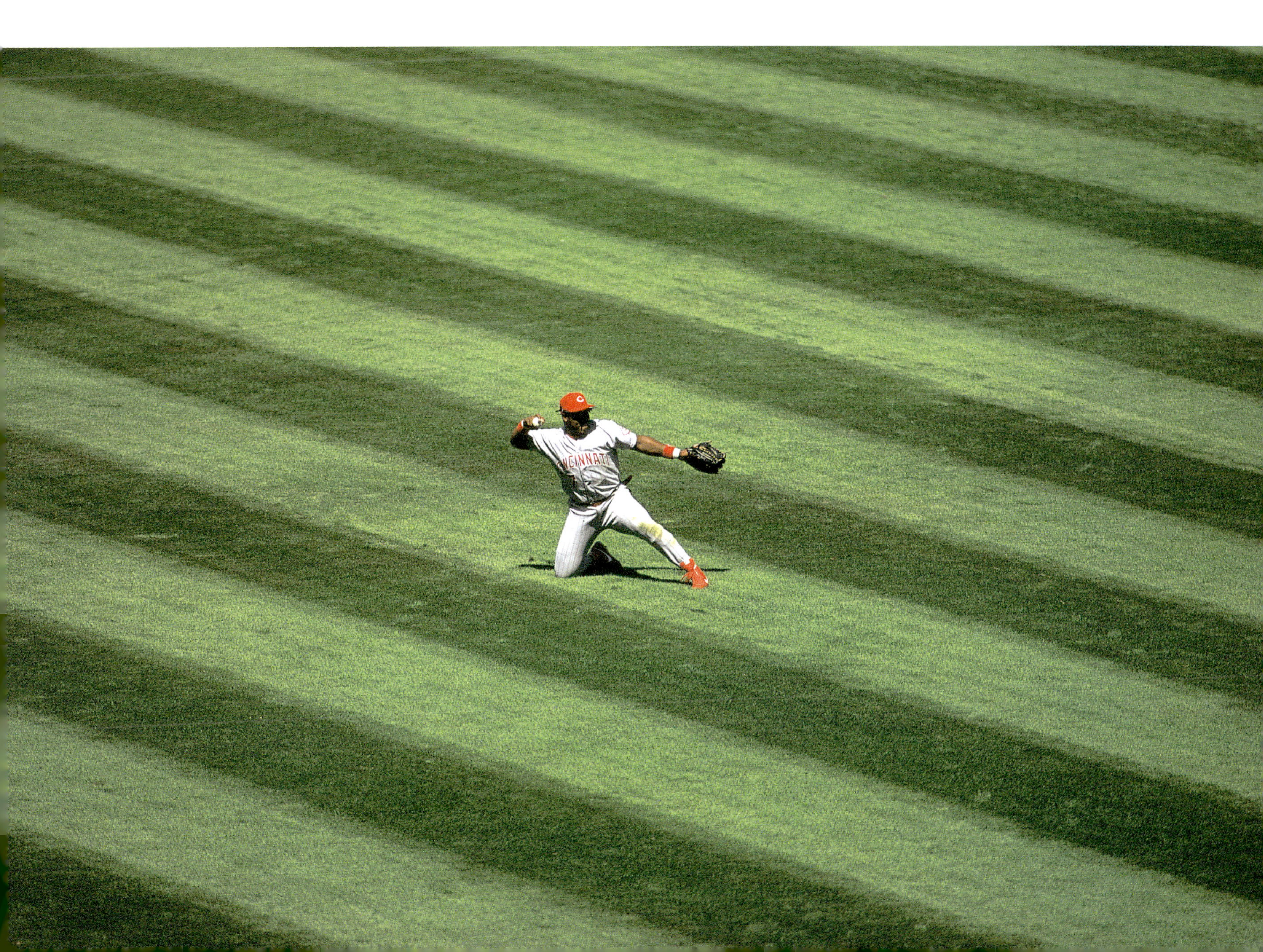

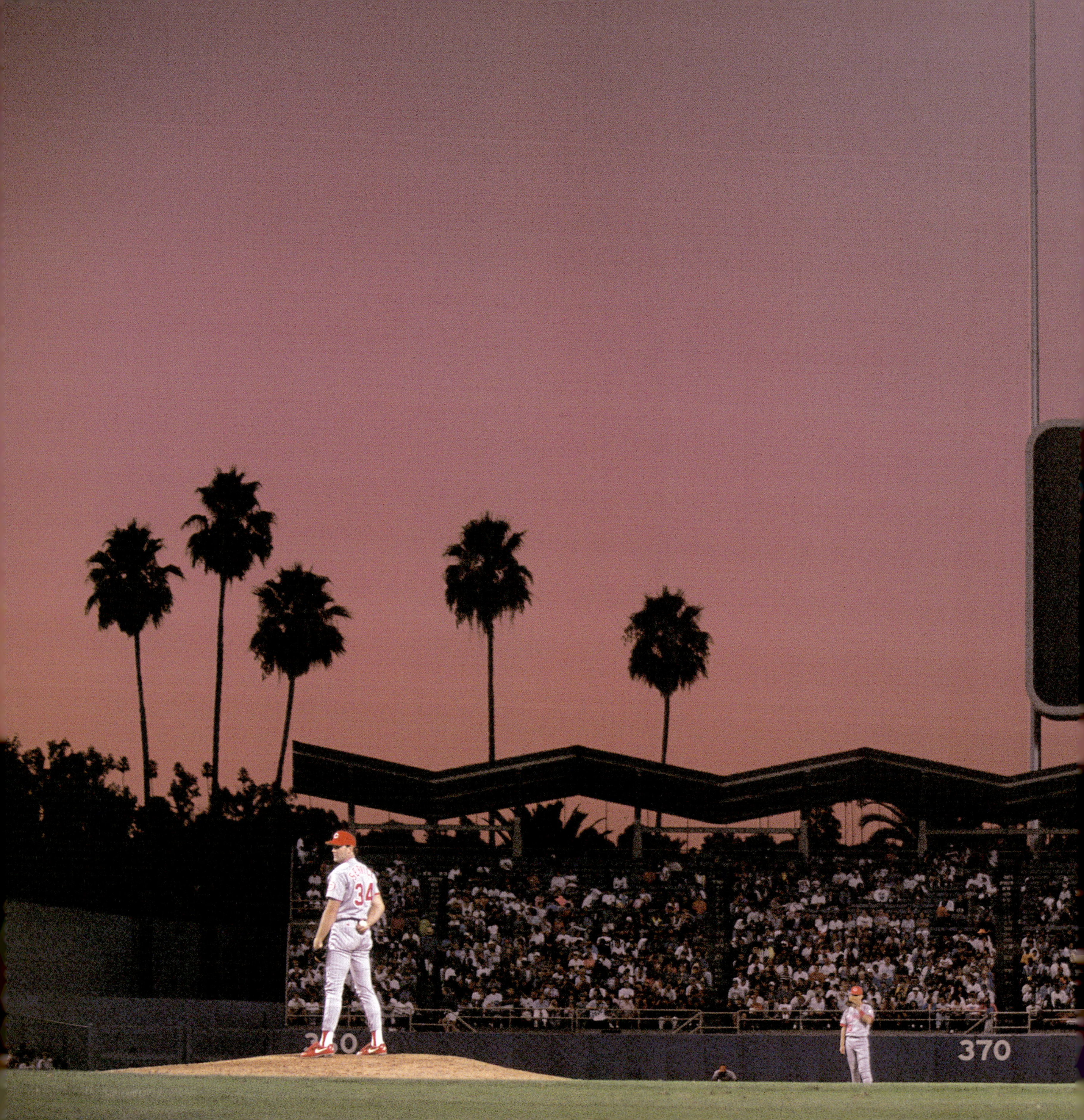
34
370

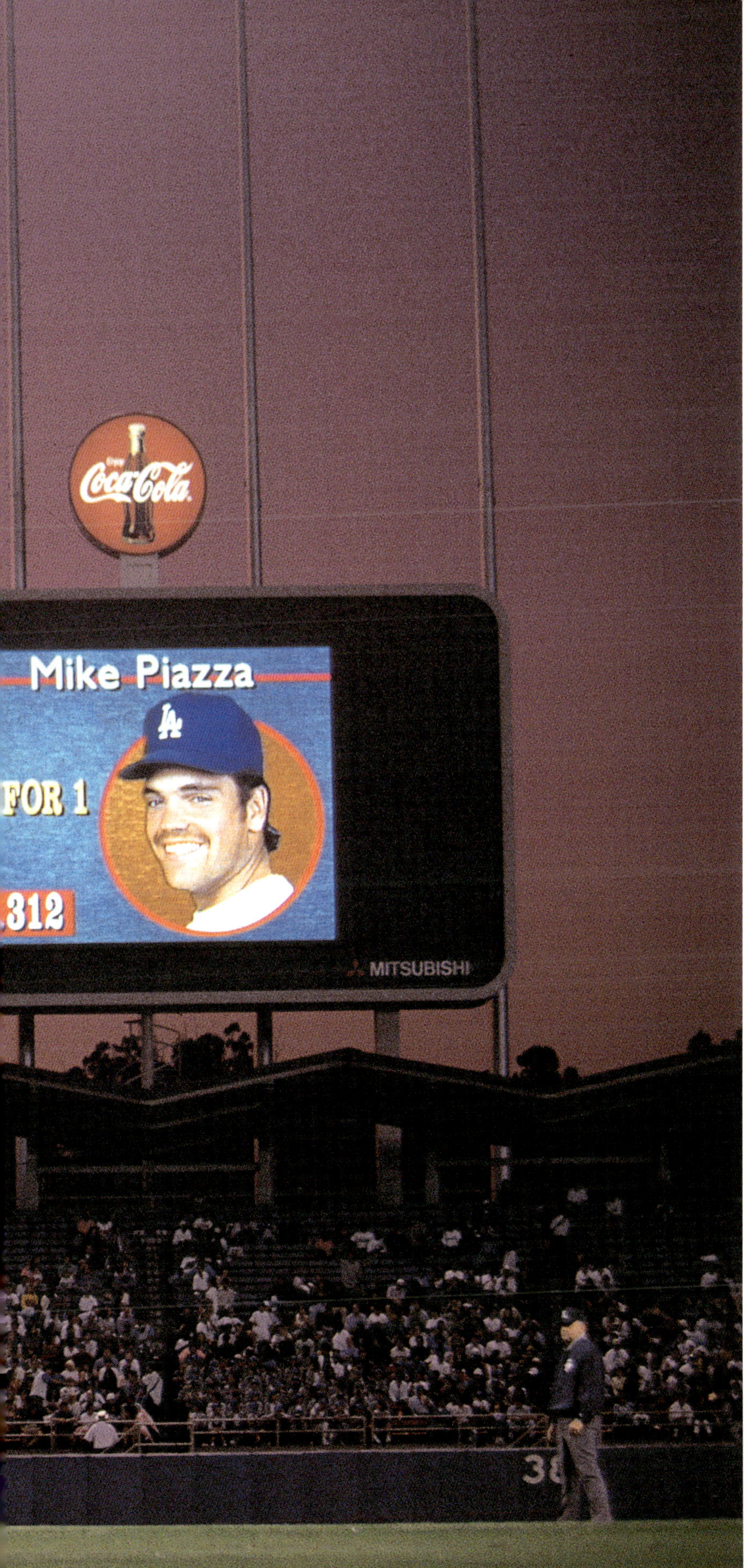

DODGER STADIUM, Los Angeles, 1993

WRIGLEY FIELD SCOREBOARD, National Anthem, Chicago, 1985

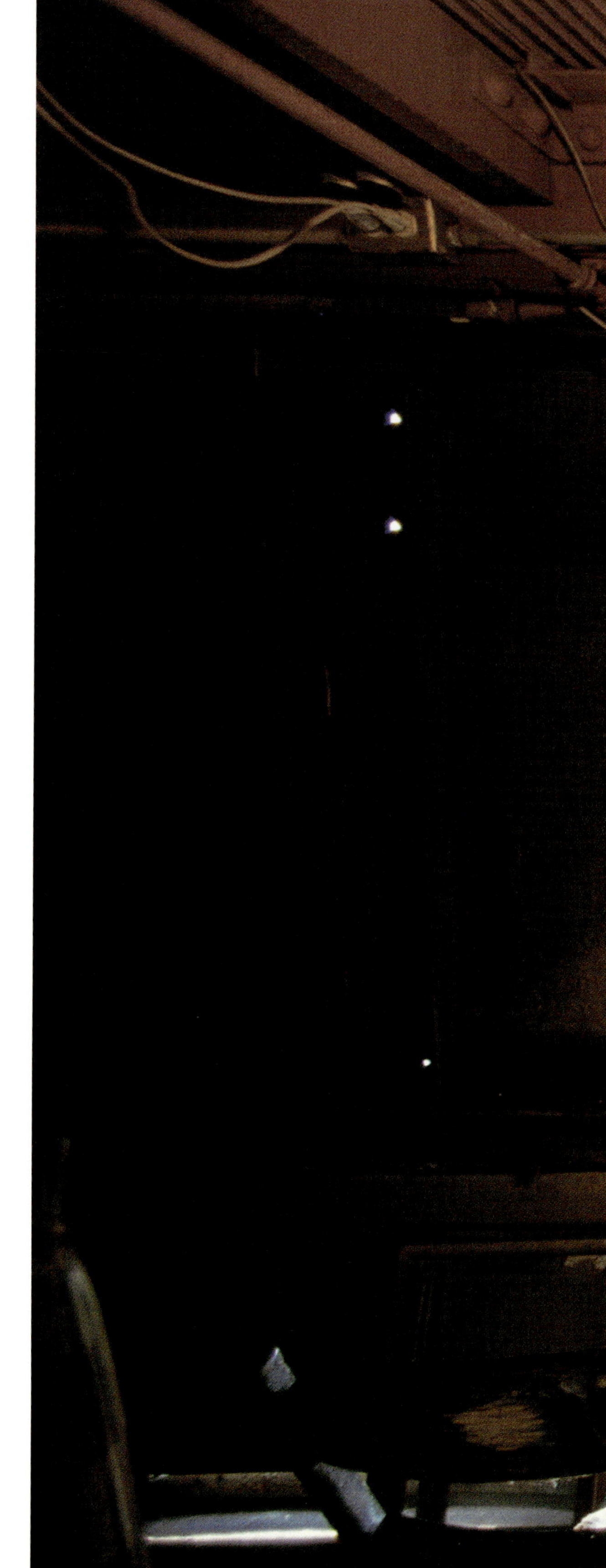

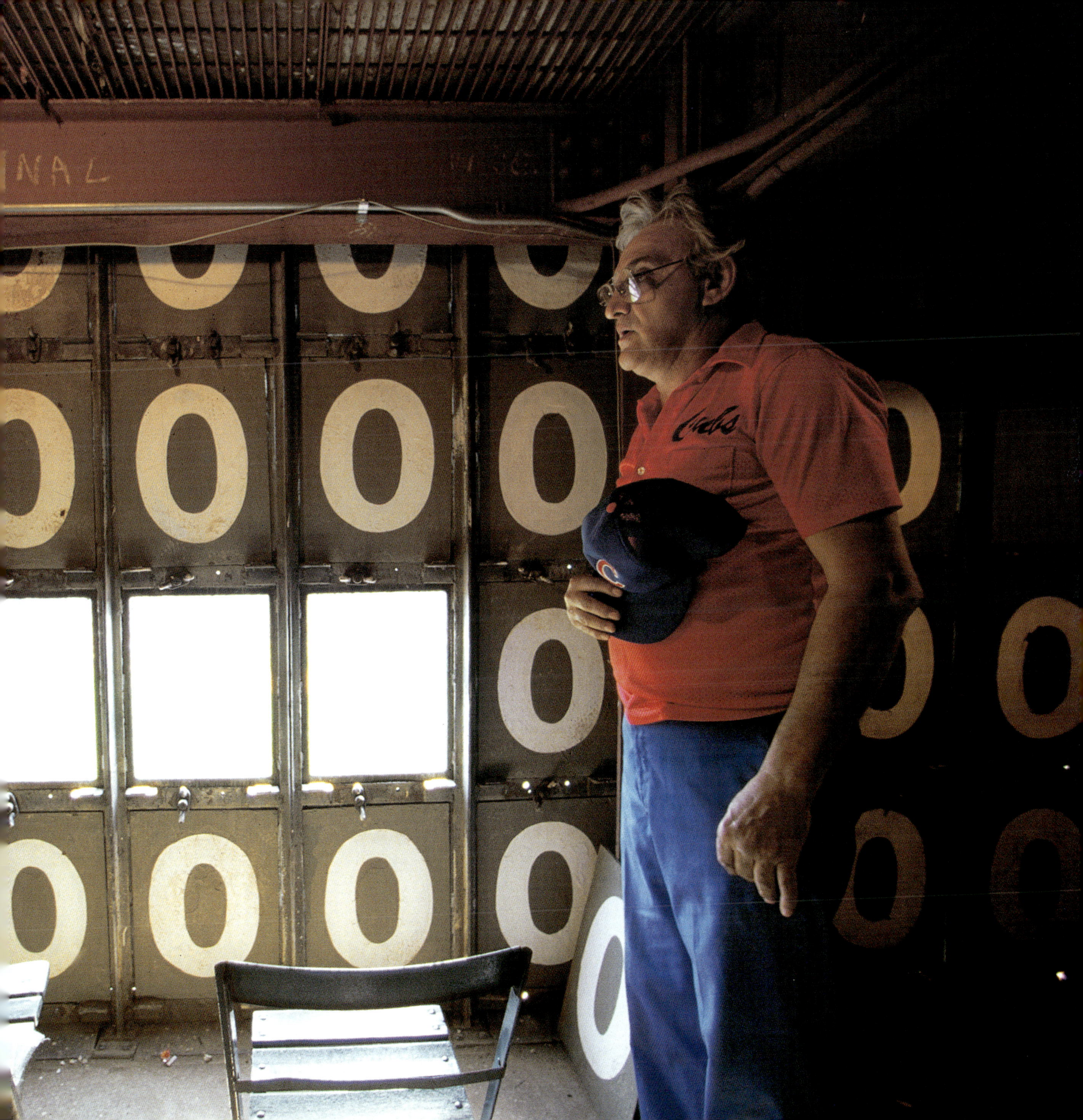
NAL
Cubs

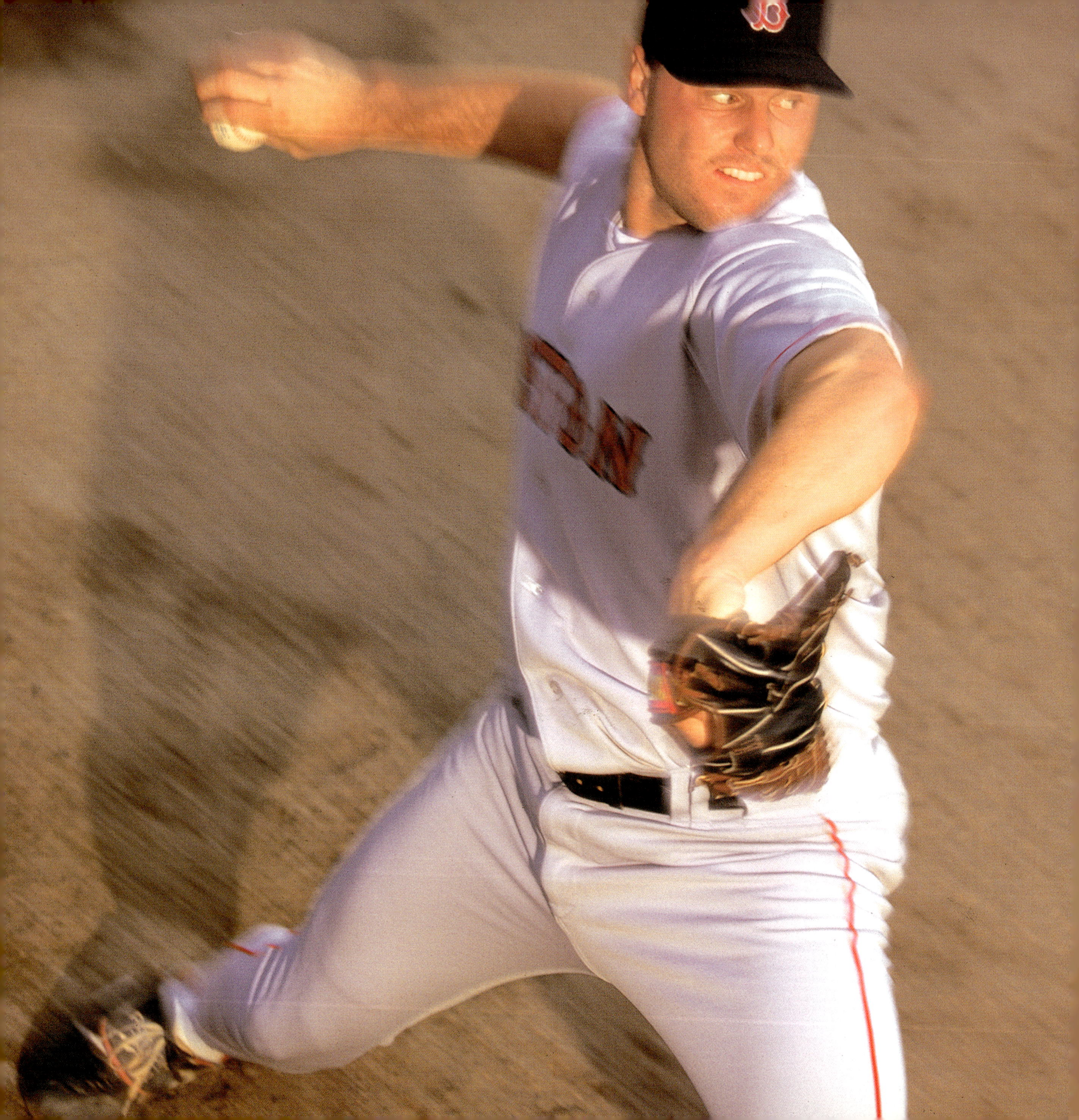

PITCHERS

ROGER CLEMENS, Baltimore, 1993

PITCHERS ARE A PHOTOGRAPHER'S DREAM. Their windup. Their throwing motion. Their follow-through. Their reaction of joy or sadness. On every pitch, their mound is a stage. And of all the pitchers, if not all the ballplayers, that Walter Iooss Jr. has photographed, Sandy Koufax was the most compelling subject. "In his first season with the Dodgers in 1955, Sandy didn't get into many games," Iooss remembers. "He was a twenty-year-old bonus baby who couldn't be sent to the minors under the rules then, and he seldom was trusted to pitch because he was so wild. I guess I was lucky to see him pitch in Ebbets Field that season." For all his future Hall of Fame grandeur, Koufax had a 2–2 record as a Brooklyn Dodgers rookie in 1955, appearing in only 12 games with only 5 starts. But both of his victories were complete-game shutouts. Although he struck out 30 with that famous fastball, he walked 28—wildness that he didn't tame until years later, after the Dodgers had moved to Los Angeles.

On June 4, 1964, Iooss was lucky again. He was in Connie Mack Stadium in Philadelphia the night Koufax pitched his third of four no-hitters, a 3–0 victory over the Phillies. He struck out twelve, walked one.

With the scoreboard identifying the bottom of the eighth inning, here is Koufax taking the sign against the backdrop of the Dodgers batting order: center fielder Willie Davis, shortstop Maury Wills, third baseman Jim Gilliam, left fielder Tommy Davis, first baseman Ron Fairly, right fielder Wes Parker, catcher Doug Camilli, second baseman Dick Tracewski, and Koufax.

And after the final out in the ninth inning, here is Koufax bursting from the mound.

In 1965, Iooss was in Minnesota for the decisive seventh game of the World Series between the Dodgers and the Twins. His left arm resembling a slingshot, here is Koufax firing his second shutout, 2–0, with ten strikeouts, three walks. In 24 innings in that World Series, he struck out 29. During the regular season, he struck out 382 in a 26–8 record with eight shutouts. But after a 27–9 season with a 1.73 earned-run average in 1966, Koufax's arthritic elbow convinced him to stop pitching.

"He was the best," Iooss says. "The best pitcher I ever saw, maybe the best pitcher anyone ever saw or will see."

The same year, 1964, that Iooss was in Connie Mack Stadium for Koufax's no-hitter, he suffered as a Phillies fan. With a six-and-one-half game lead and only twelve games remaining, the Phillies appeared sure to clinch the National League pennant. But they then lost ten straight. On the final day of the season, Iooss watched right-hander Jim Bunning, who had pitched a perfect game that year against the Mets at Shea Stadium on Father's Day, shut out the Reds in Cincinnati, 10–0, but when the Cardinals beat the Mets in St. Louis that Sunday, the Cardinals won the pennant.

"Bunning had the best follow-through of any pitcher," Iooss says. "After that final game in Cincinnati, I sat with him in the dugout. Just the two of us. I think I was sadder than he was."

Warren Spahn, whose 363 victories are the most of any left-hander, was remarkably durable. With managers now so dependent on relief pitchers, complete games are a rarity. In Spahn's era, they were expected. While winning twenty or more games in thirteen seasons, he also had twenty or more complete games in twelve seasons. He led the league in victories eight times, in complete games nine times.

"What a pitcher," Iooss says.

And here is Spahn, in one of his final years with the Milwaukee Braves, pitching against the backdrop of shirt-sleeved fans in the Polo Grounds centerfield bleachers on a hot, sunny afternoon. But when Iooss wanted to do a portrait of Spahn years later in his Braves cap and uniform shirt, Spahn's reaction was typical of his grumpy reputation.

"He told me, 'I just had eye surgery. I can't do this now. Call me another time.'" Iooss recalls.

When Iooss called again, Spahn agreed. Sitting in a dugout, Spahn took a drag on a cigarette whenever Iooss looked up from his camera. "Keep smoking," Iooss said, "you look good with a cigarette in your hand." Then, trying to get some emotion in Spahn's grumpy face, Iooss got grumpy, barking, "Sit up straight." With a sneer, Spahn straightened up.

"How's your arm now?" Iooss wondered.

"I just have arthritis in one finger."

"Which opposing pitchers did you admire in the late '50s and early '60s?" Iooss asked, but when Spahn didn't answer, Iooss said, "How about Marichal?"

"The hell with him," Spahn snapped.

"Not personally, but as a pitcher."

"He beat me, 1–0, in 16 innings."

On July 2, 1963, on Spahn's way to a 23–7 record that season at age forty-two, his duel with Juan Marichal in Candlestick Park ended when Willie Mays hit a home run with one out in the sixteenth inning. Over his fifteen and one-third innings, Spahn allowed only eight other hits, struck out two, and walked one. After Iooss's photo shoot that day years later, a friend of Spahn's told Iooss that in the duel with Marichal, it was estimated that Spahn threw at least 250 pitches.

"These days," Iooss says, "after 120 pitches, the starting pitcher is out of the game."

Not every pitcher will be inducted into the Hall of Fame in Cooperstown, New York, as Koufax, Bunning, and Spahn were, but every pitcher is a subject. Ernie Broglio is best remembered as the Cardinals right-hander who was traded to the Cubs for Lou Brock, but to Iooss, he had a classic windup.

Then there was Mets right-hander Bob Miller, usually identified as Robert L. Miller to separate him from another Mets pitcher, Lefty Bob Miller.

After having been selected in the expansion draft from the Cardinals, right-hander R. L. Miller had a 1–12 record in 1962 when the Mets lost 120 games. Have you ever seen a pitcher so bewildered after having been battered for a grand-slam home run that he squatted on the mound? Walter did.

In twenty-one starts that season, R. L. Miller had only one complete game. Whenever he was removed, other photographers focused on the new pitcher, but Walter preferred to follow R. L. Miller plodding toward his shower in the Mets clubhouse beyond center field. Walter's angle was the best angle.

SANDY KOUFAX, No-hitter, Philadelphia, 1964 (OVERLEAF) **SANDY KOUFAX,** World Series, Minneapolis, 1965 (GATEFOLD) **DON DRYSDALE** (GATEFOLD OVERLEAF) **SANDY KOUFAX AND DON DRYSDALE,** World Series victory celebration, Minneapolis, 1965 (FOLLOWING PAGE)

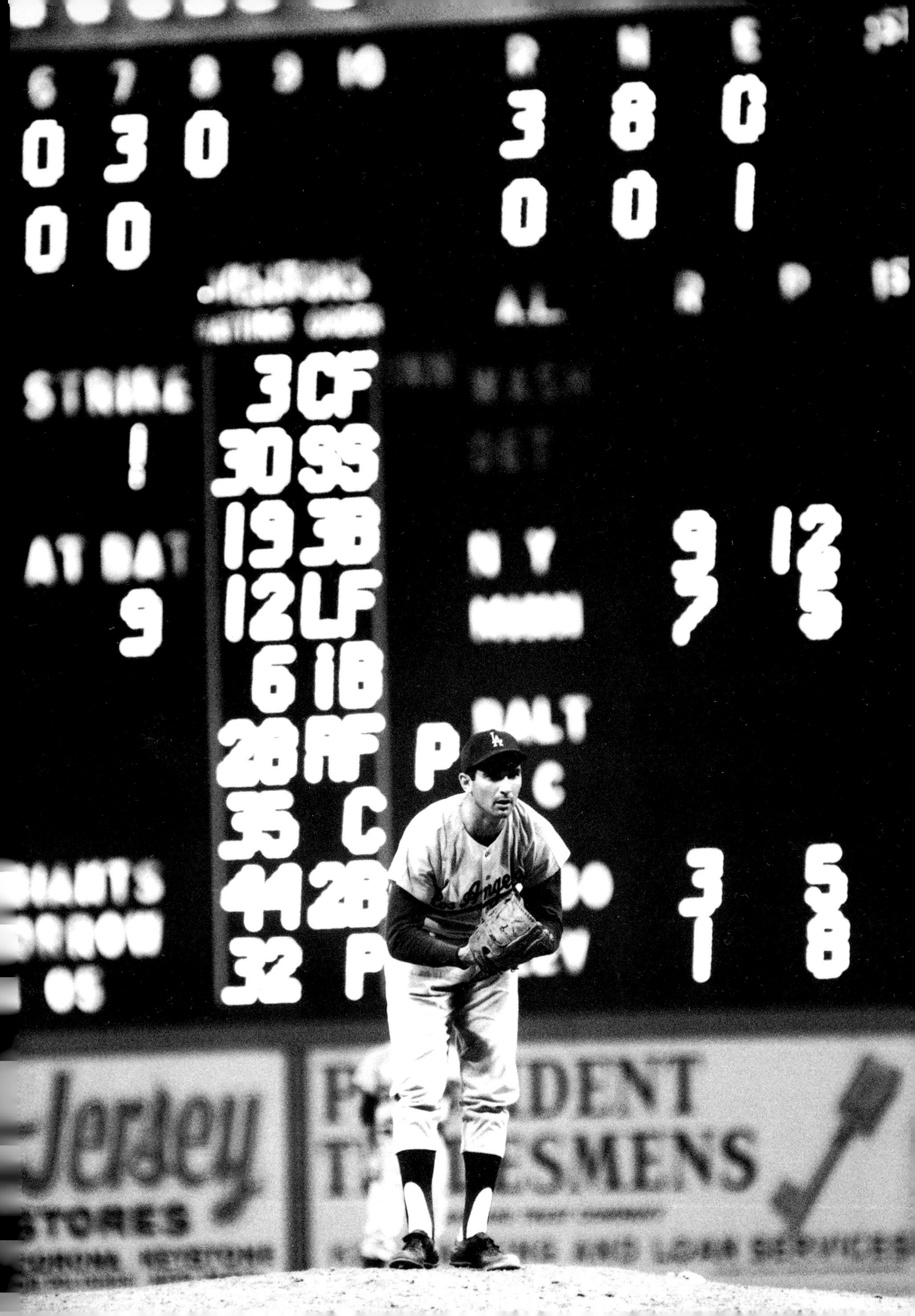

STRIKE
AT BAT
A.L.
N.Y.
BALT
Jersey
STORES
TRADESMENS

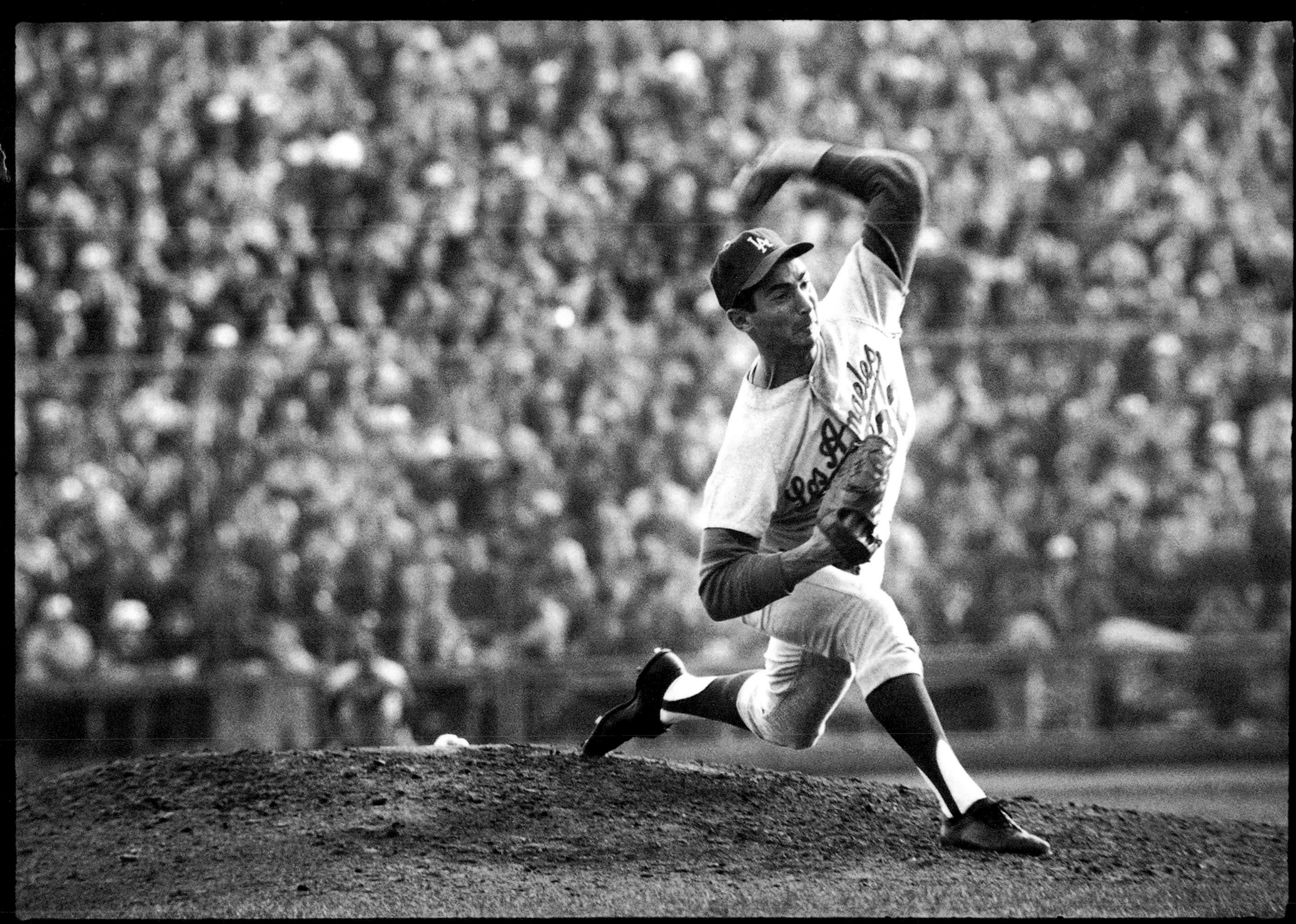
KODAK SAFETY F
Los Angeles
6
6A

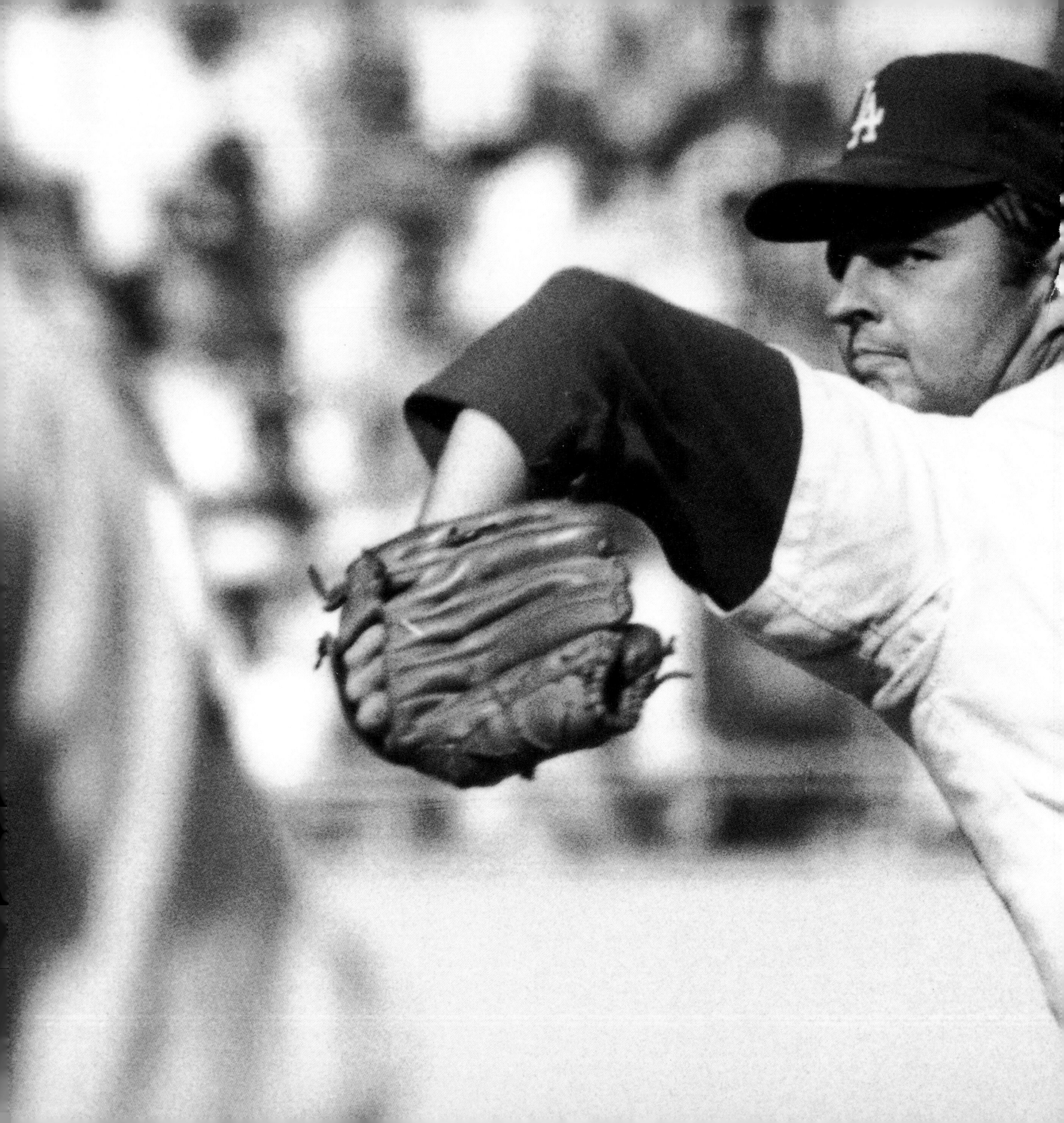

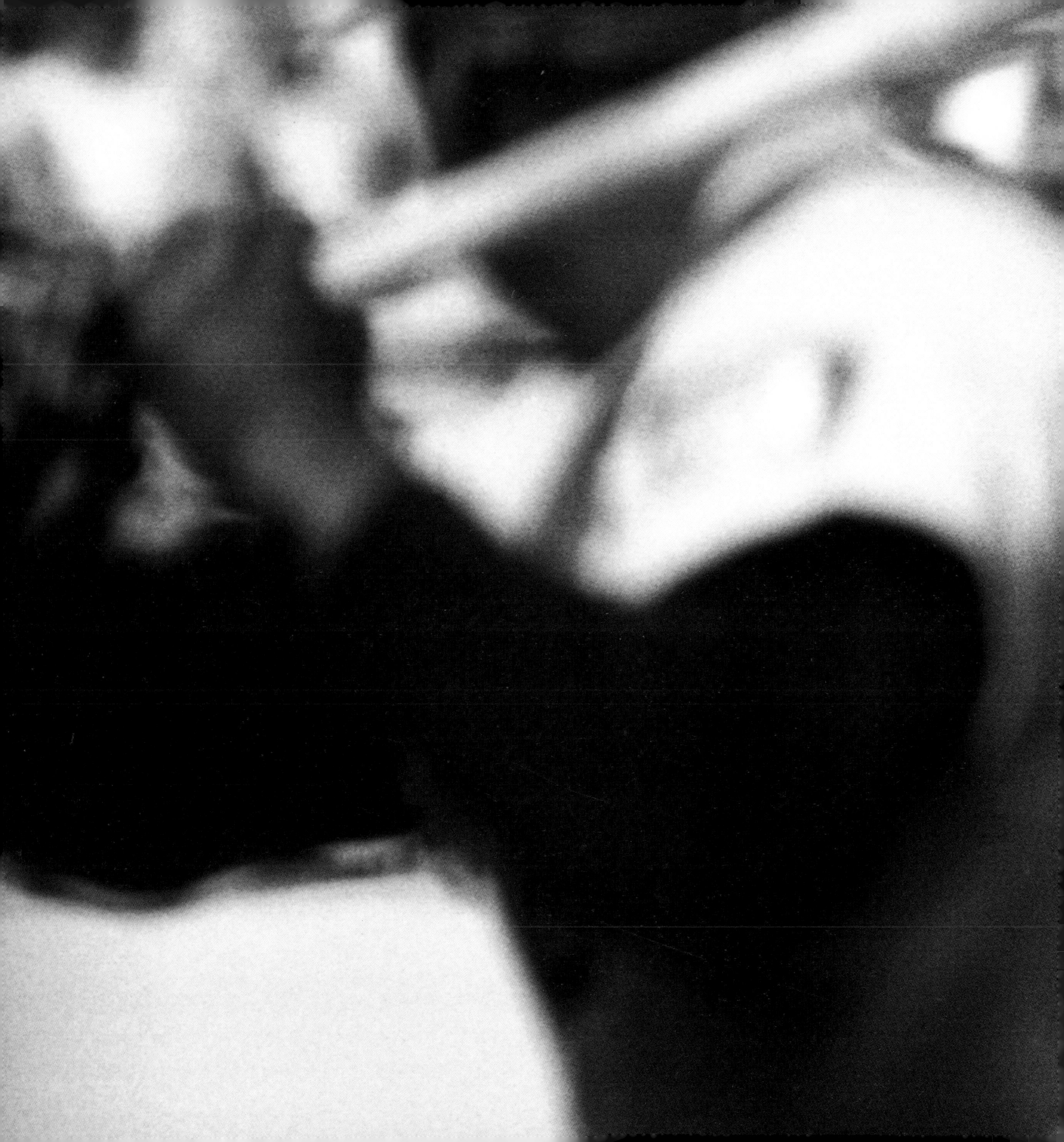

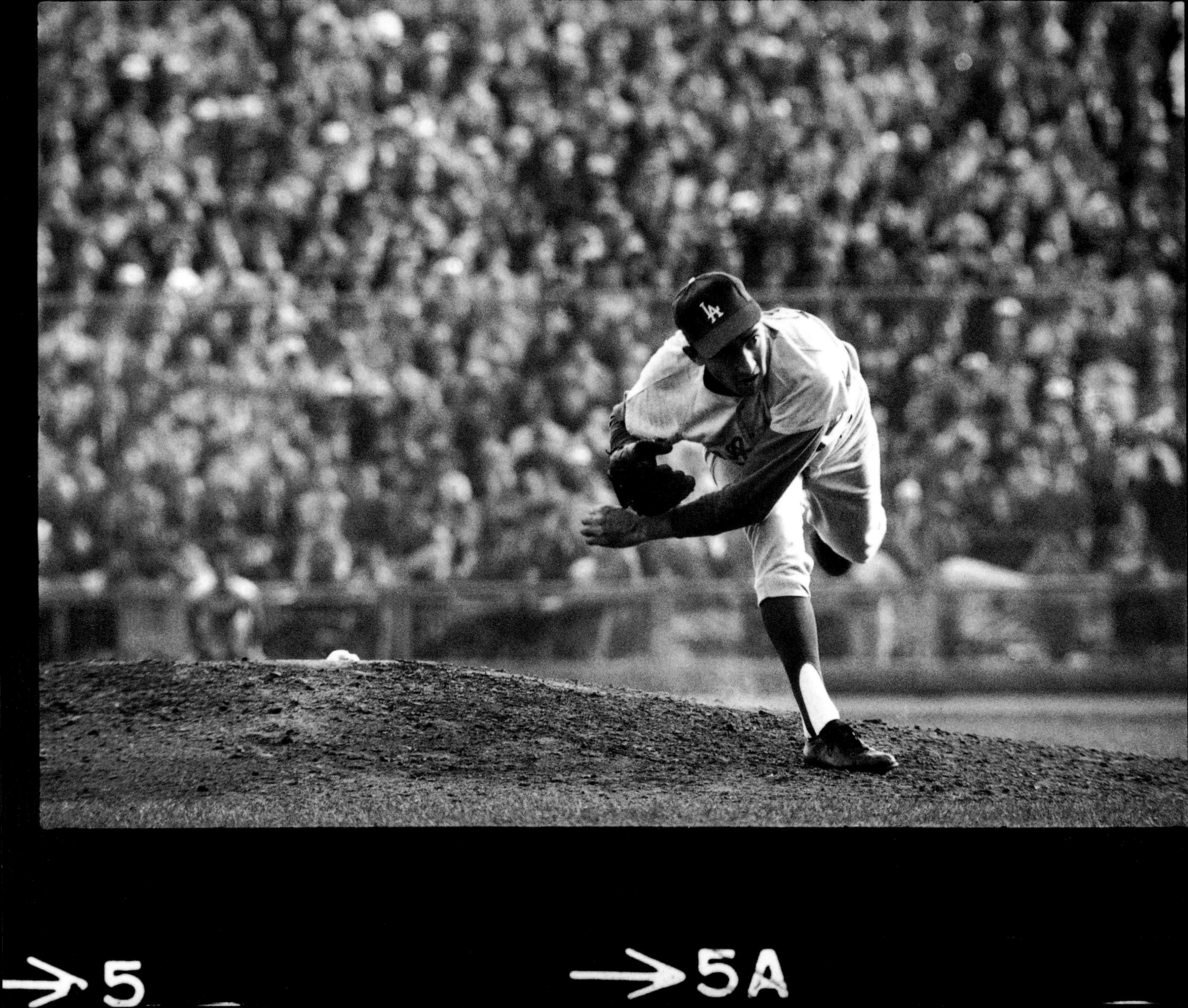

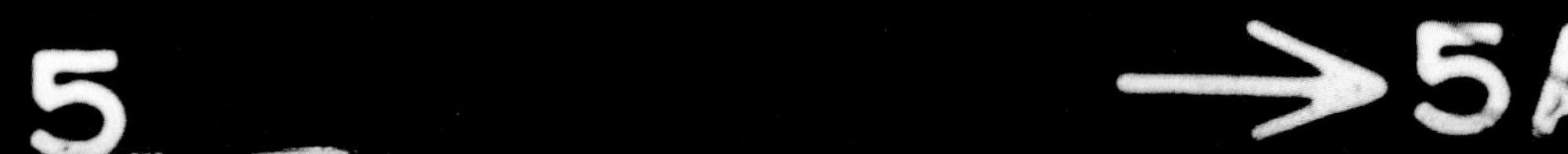
→5
→5A

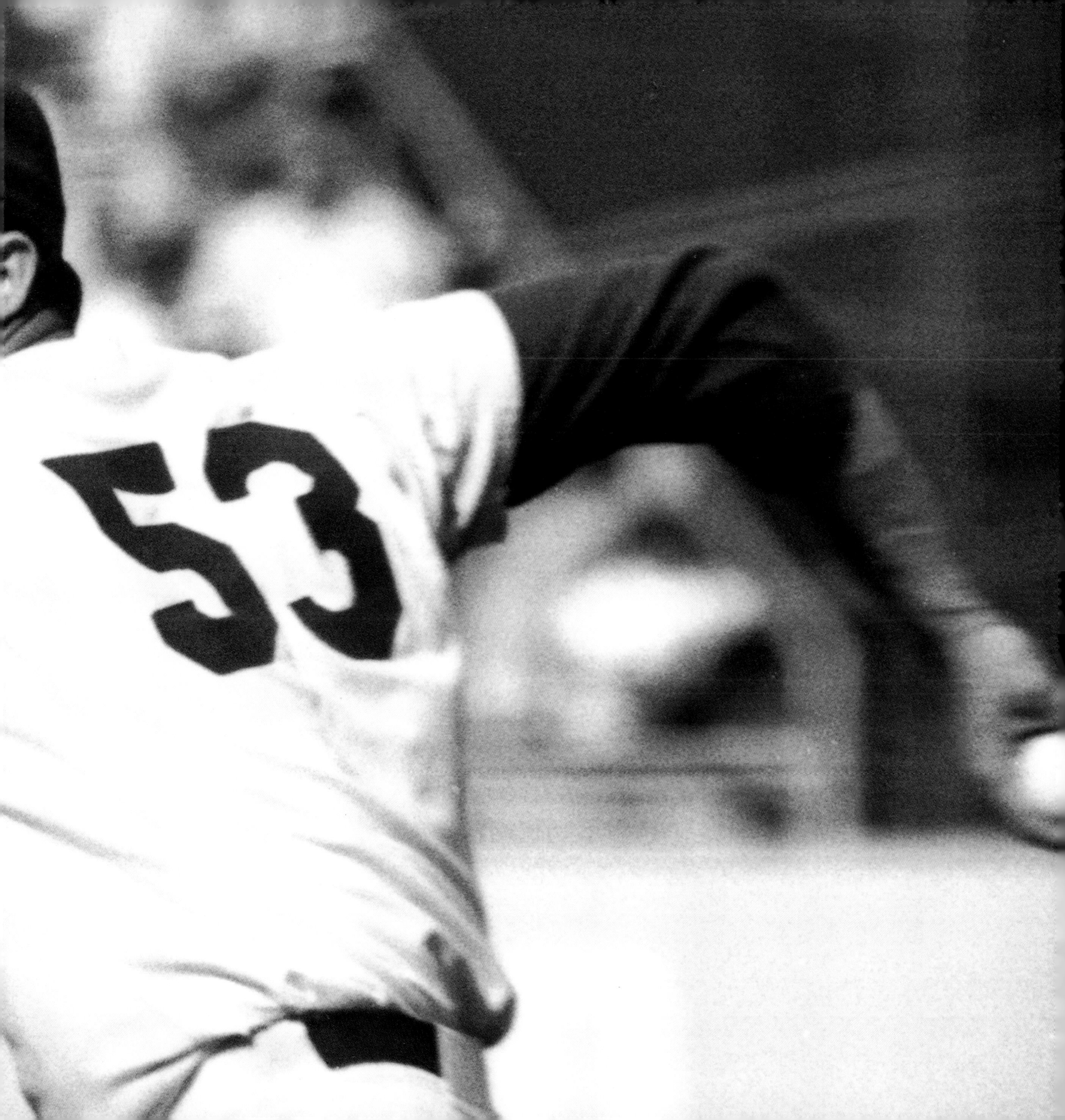
53

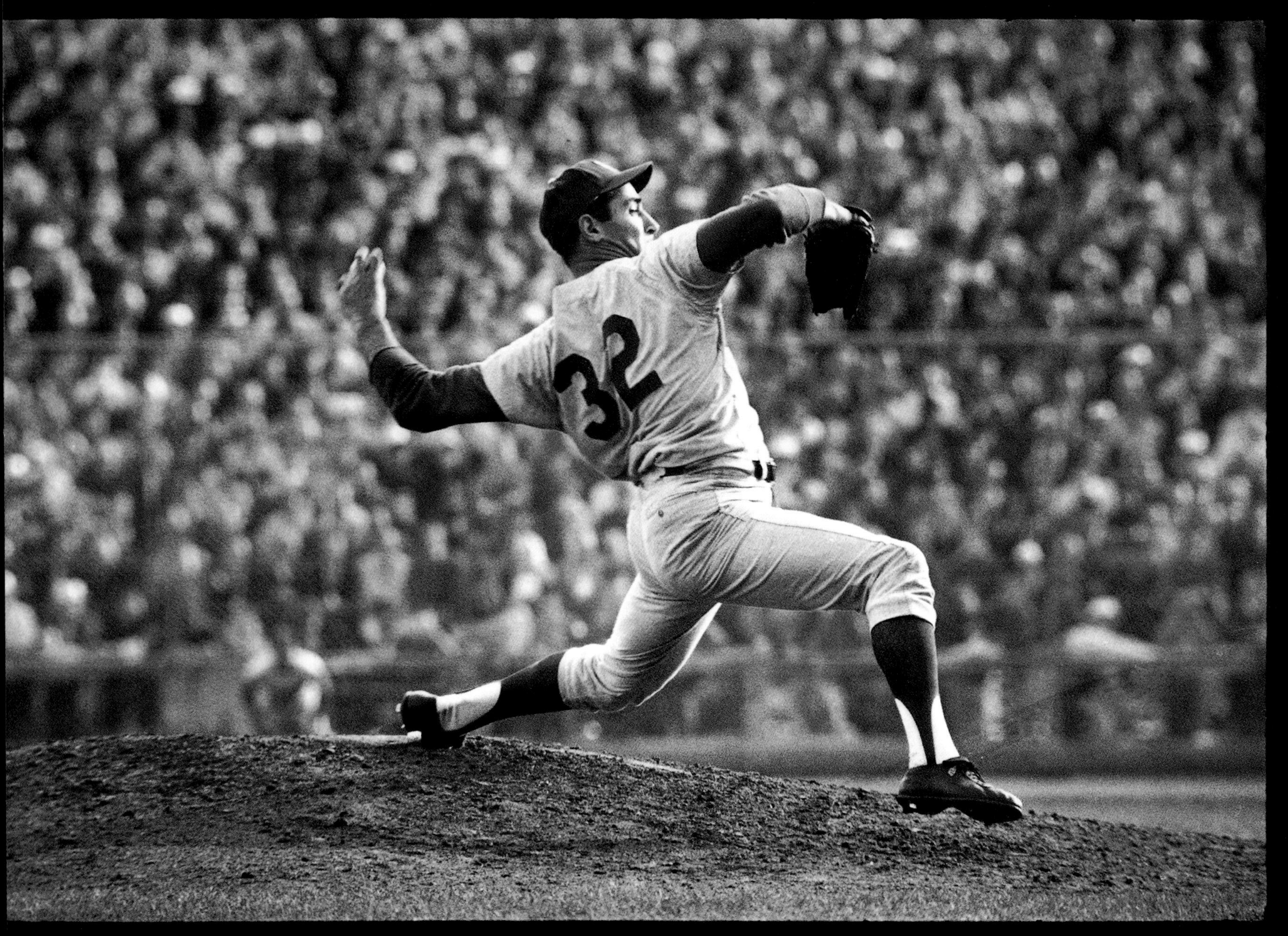
KODA
32
8
→8A

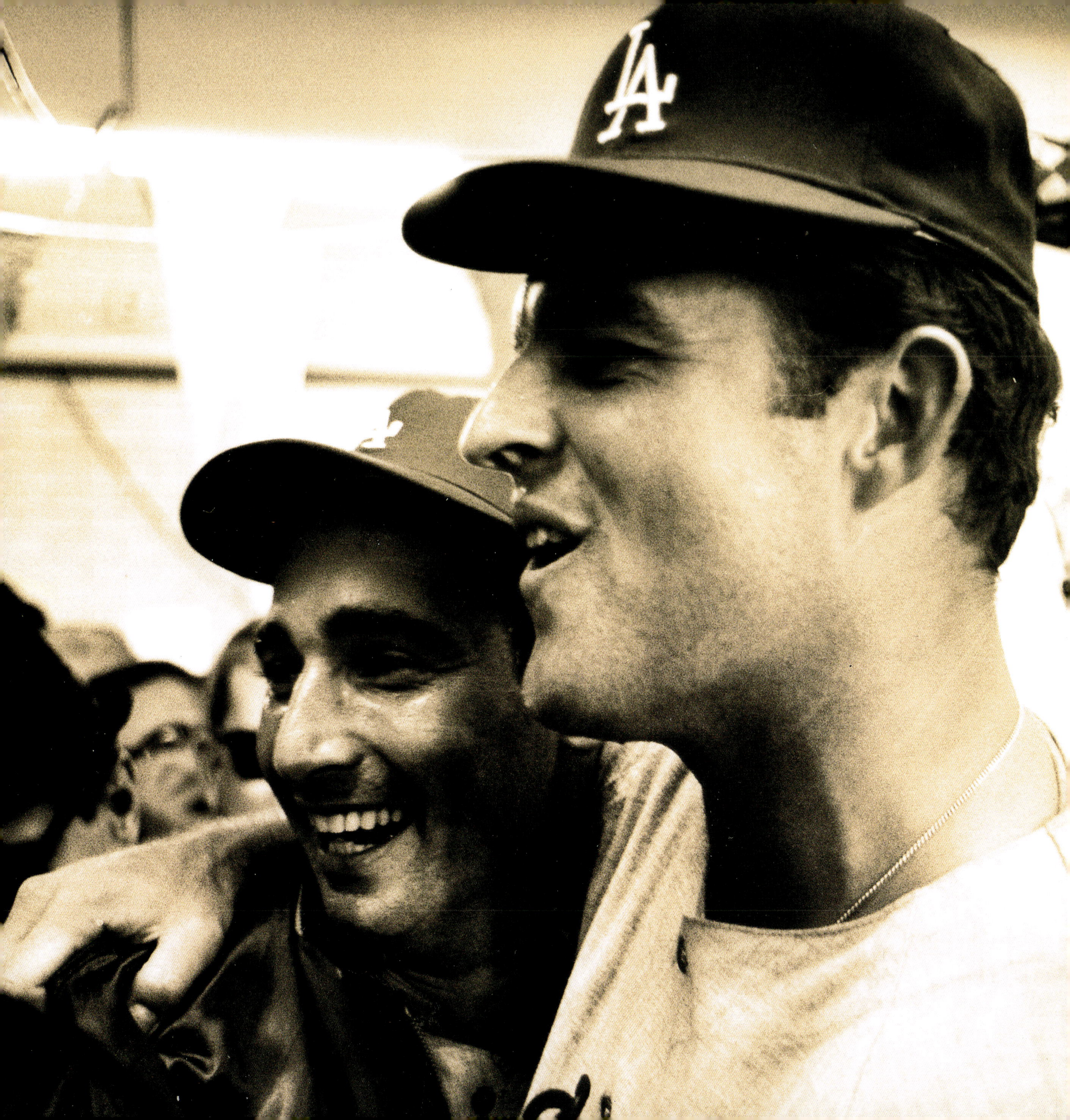
LA

JUAN MARICHAL, Philadelphia, 1961

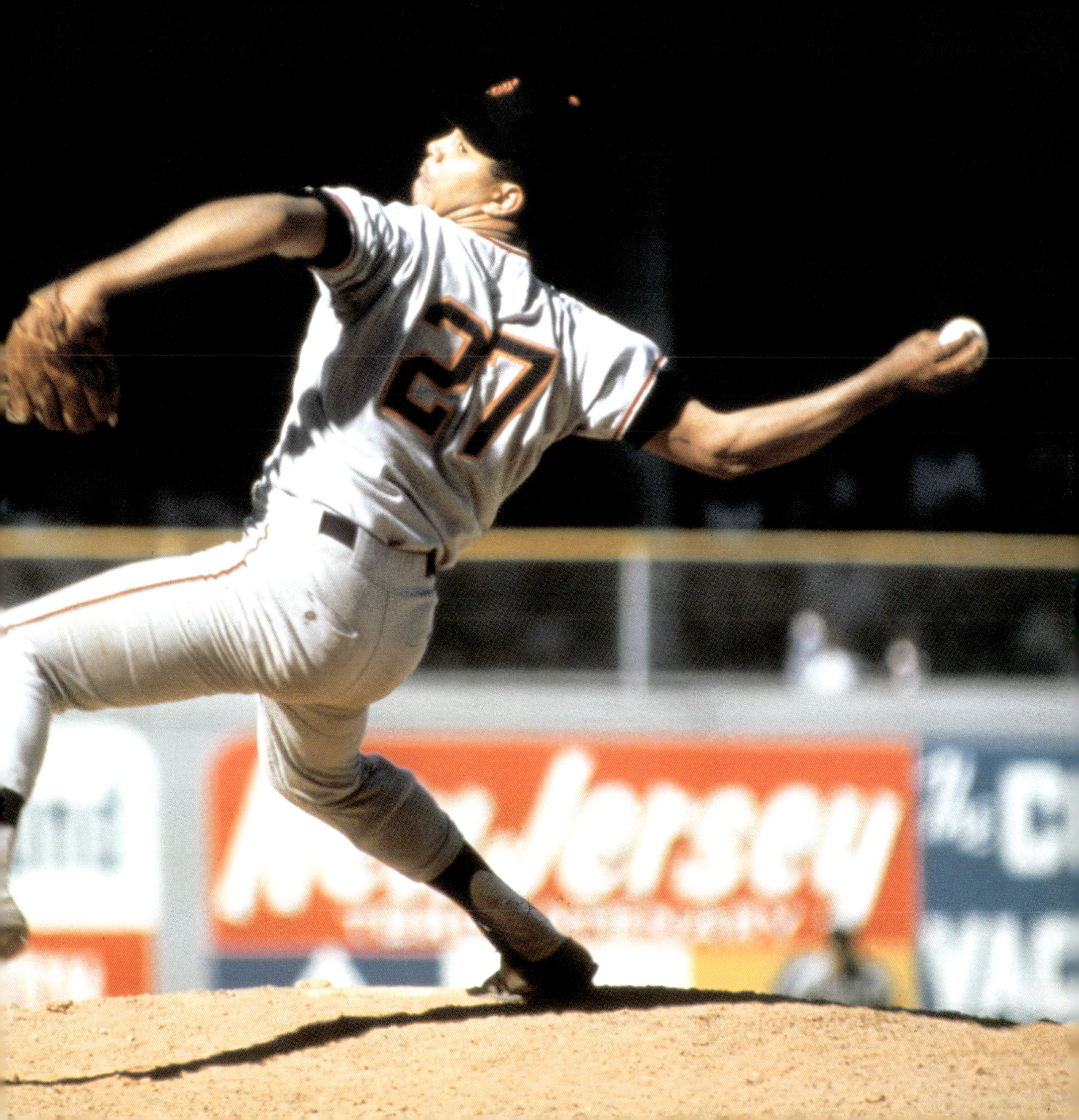
27
Jersey

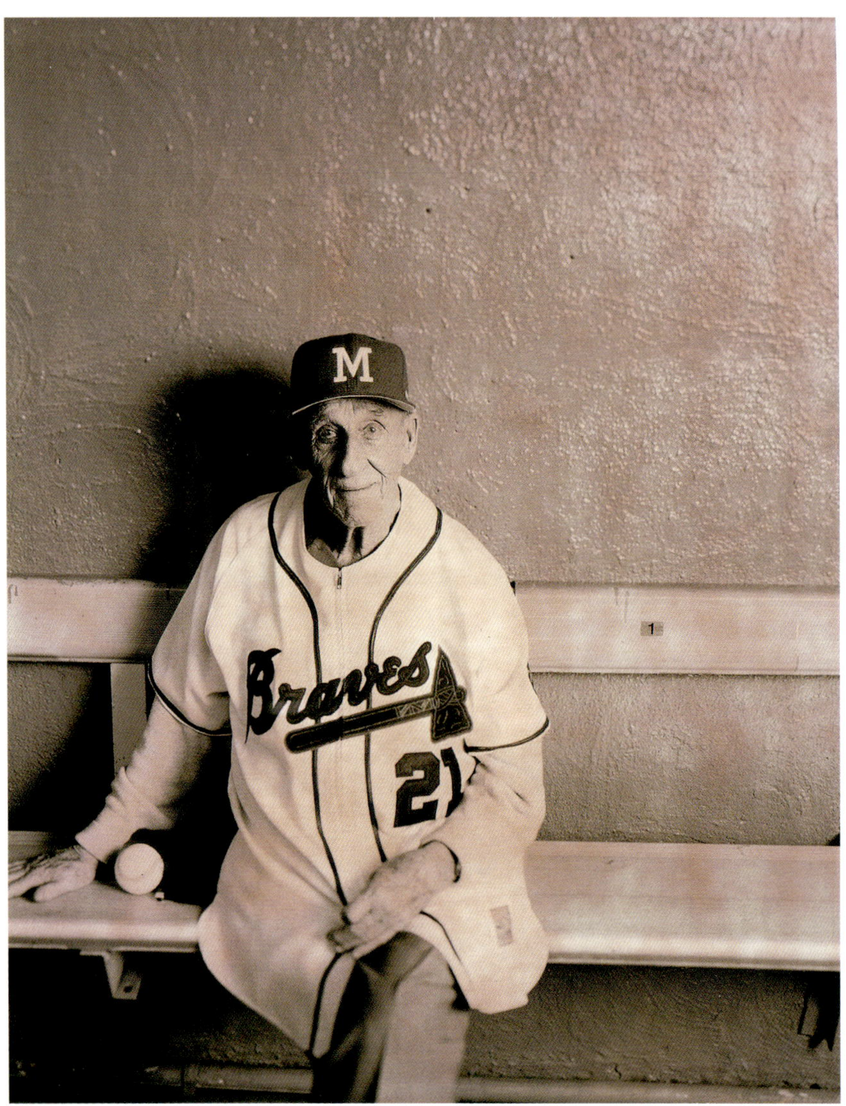

WARREN SPAHN, Tulsa, Oklahoma, 2001

WARREN SPAHN, Polo Grounds, New York, 1962

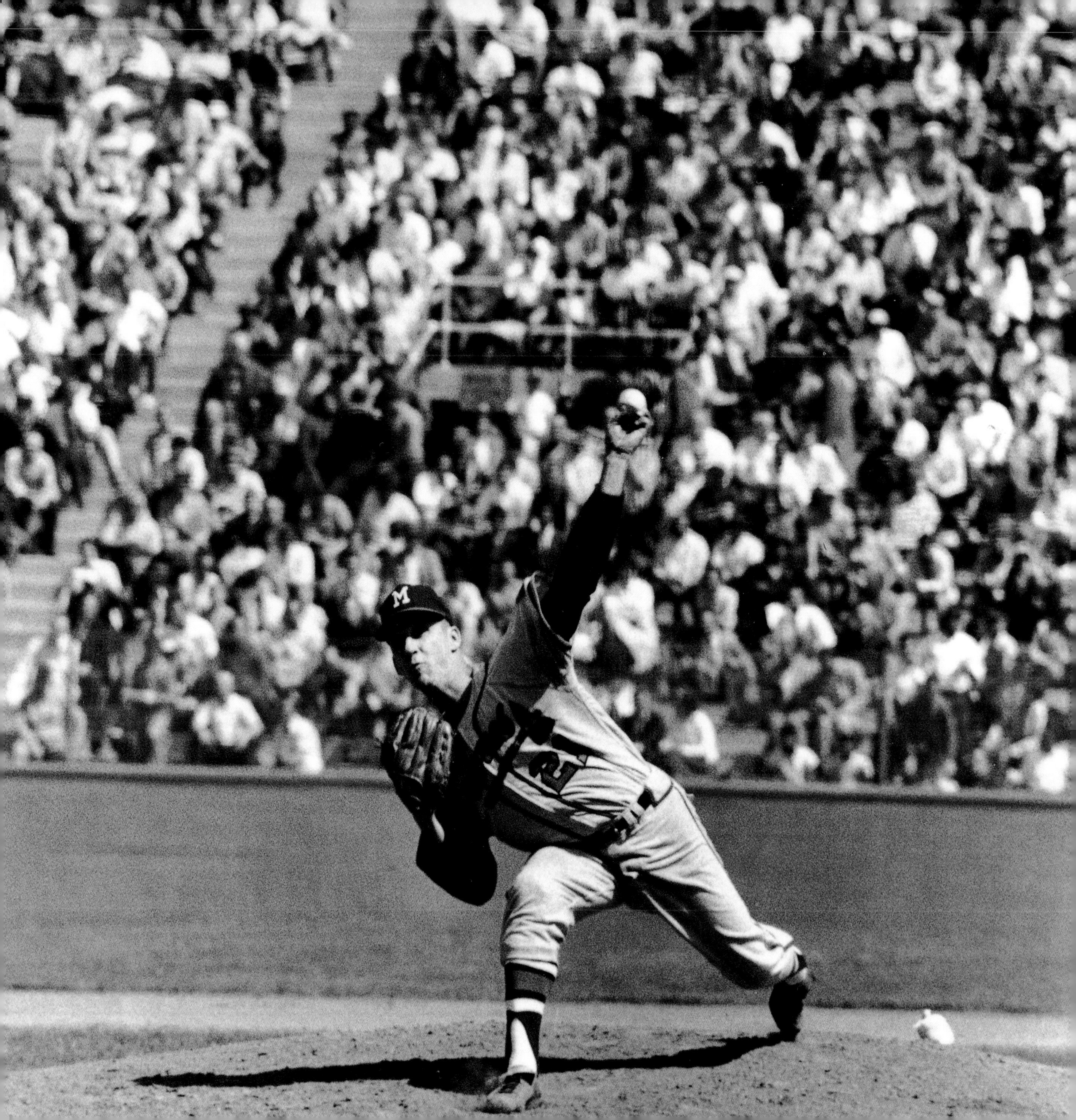

R. L. MILLER AND GIL HODGES, New York Mets, Polo Grounds, New York, 1962

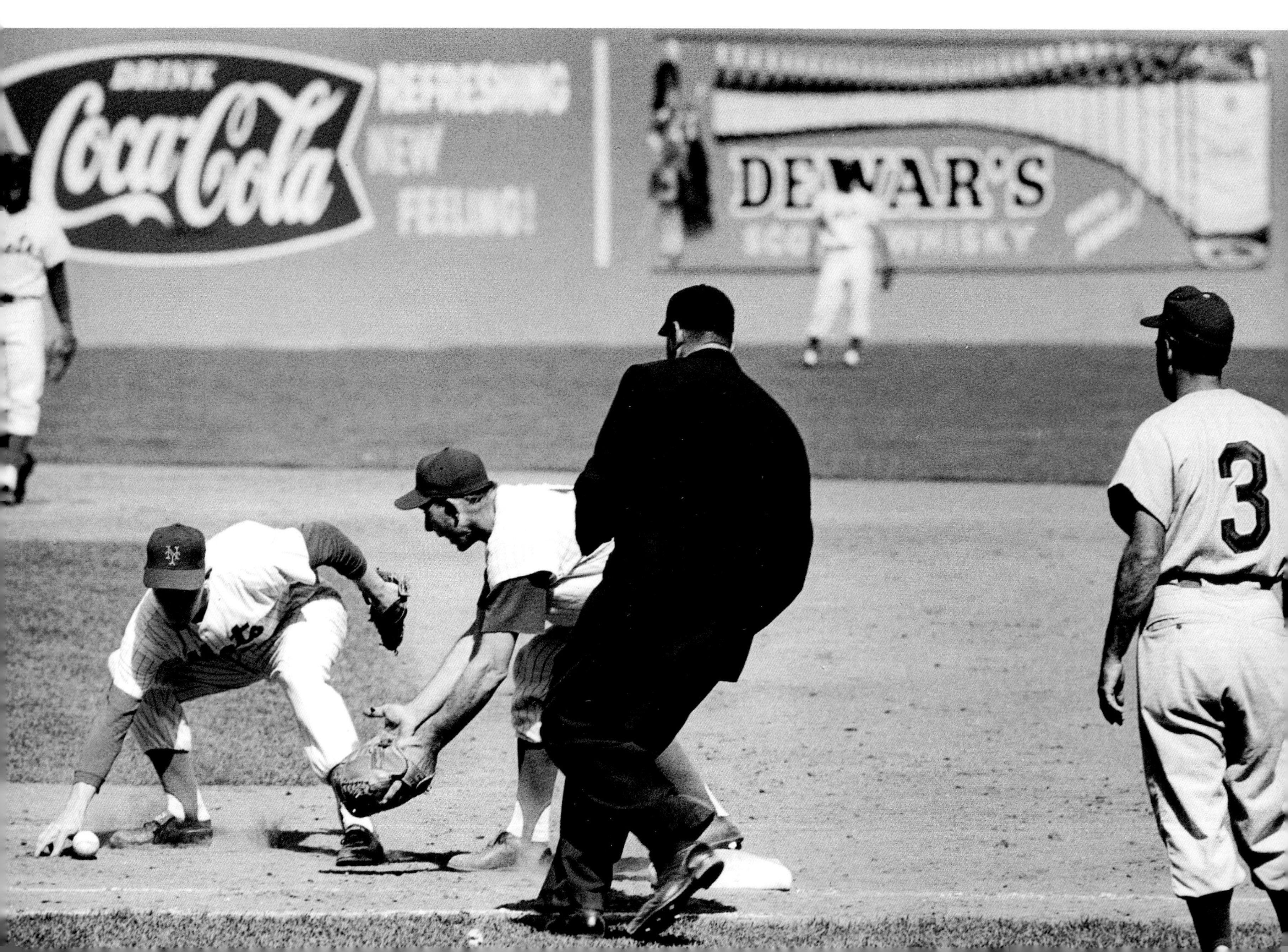

R. L. MILLER, Polo Grounds, New York, 1962

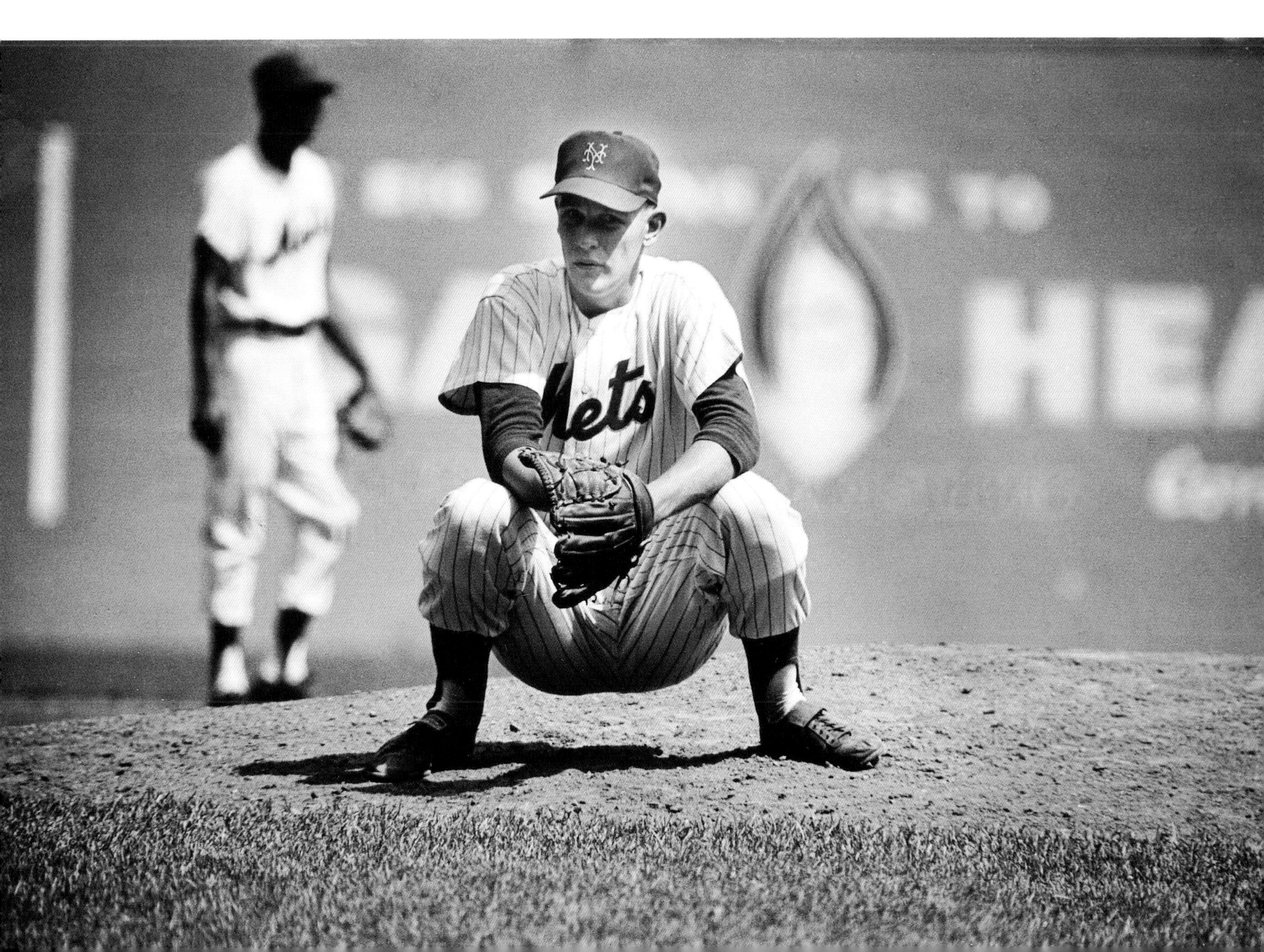

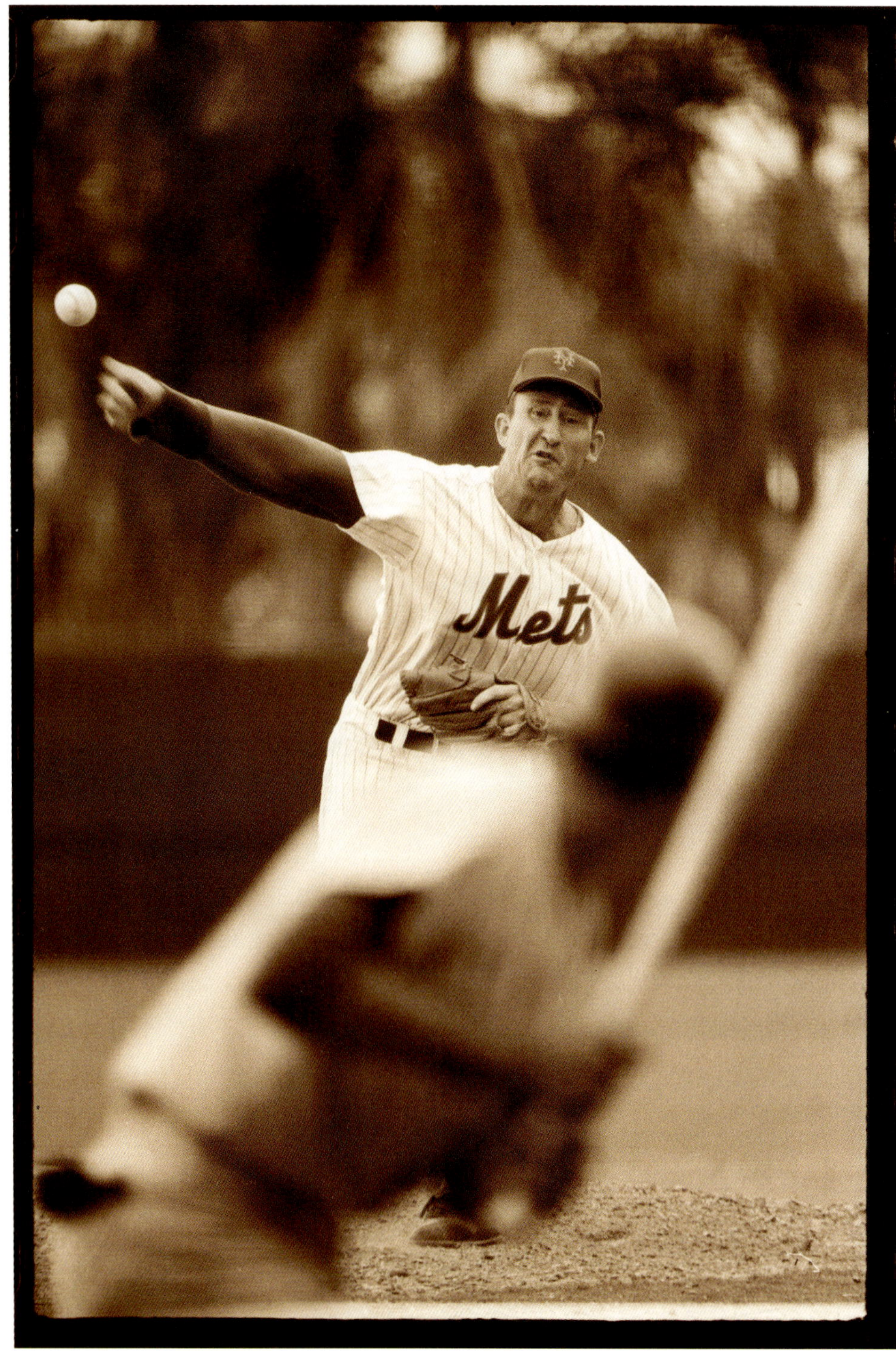

ROGER CRAIG, Polo Grounds, New York, 1962

FORBES FIELD, Pittsburgh Pirates Bullpen (Smoky Burgess and Elroy Face, standing; coach Sam Narron, left; coach Don Osborn, right), 1964

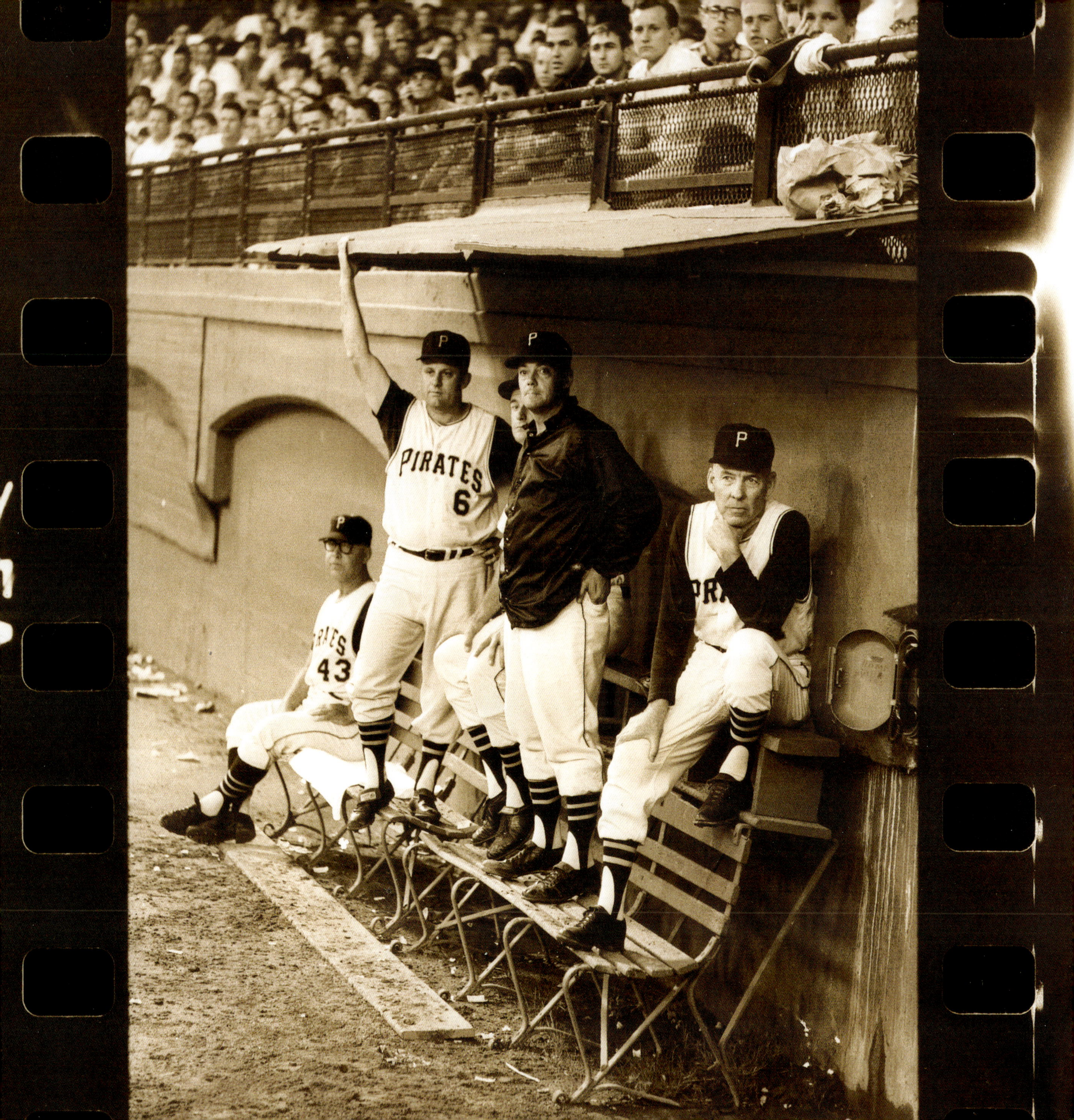
PIRATES
6
43

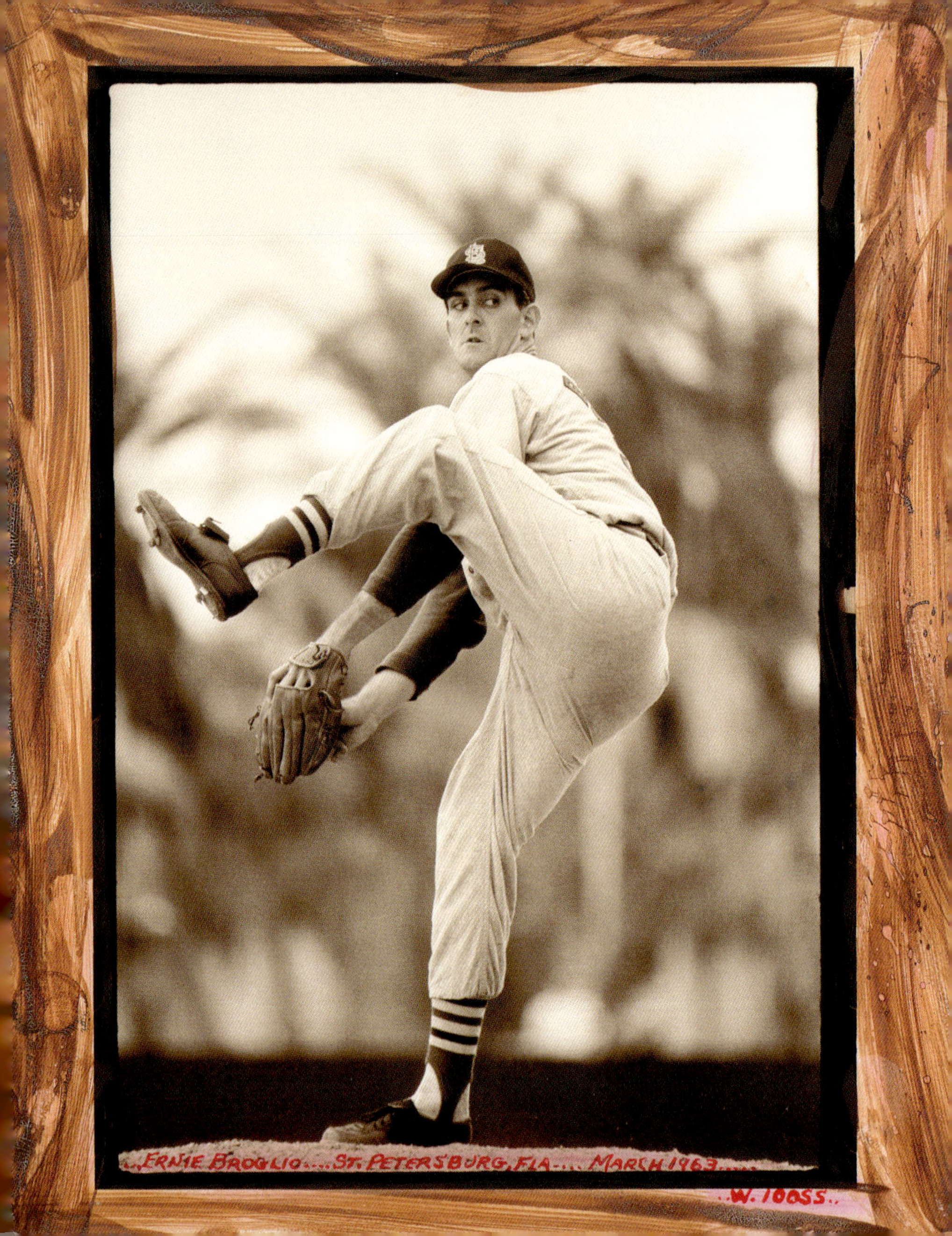
..ERNIE BROGLIO....ST. PETERSBURG, FLA.... MARCH 1963.....
..W. IOOSS..

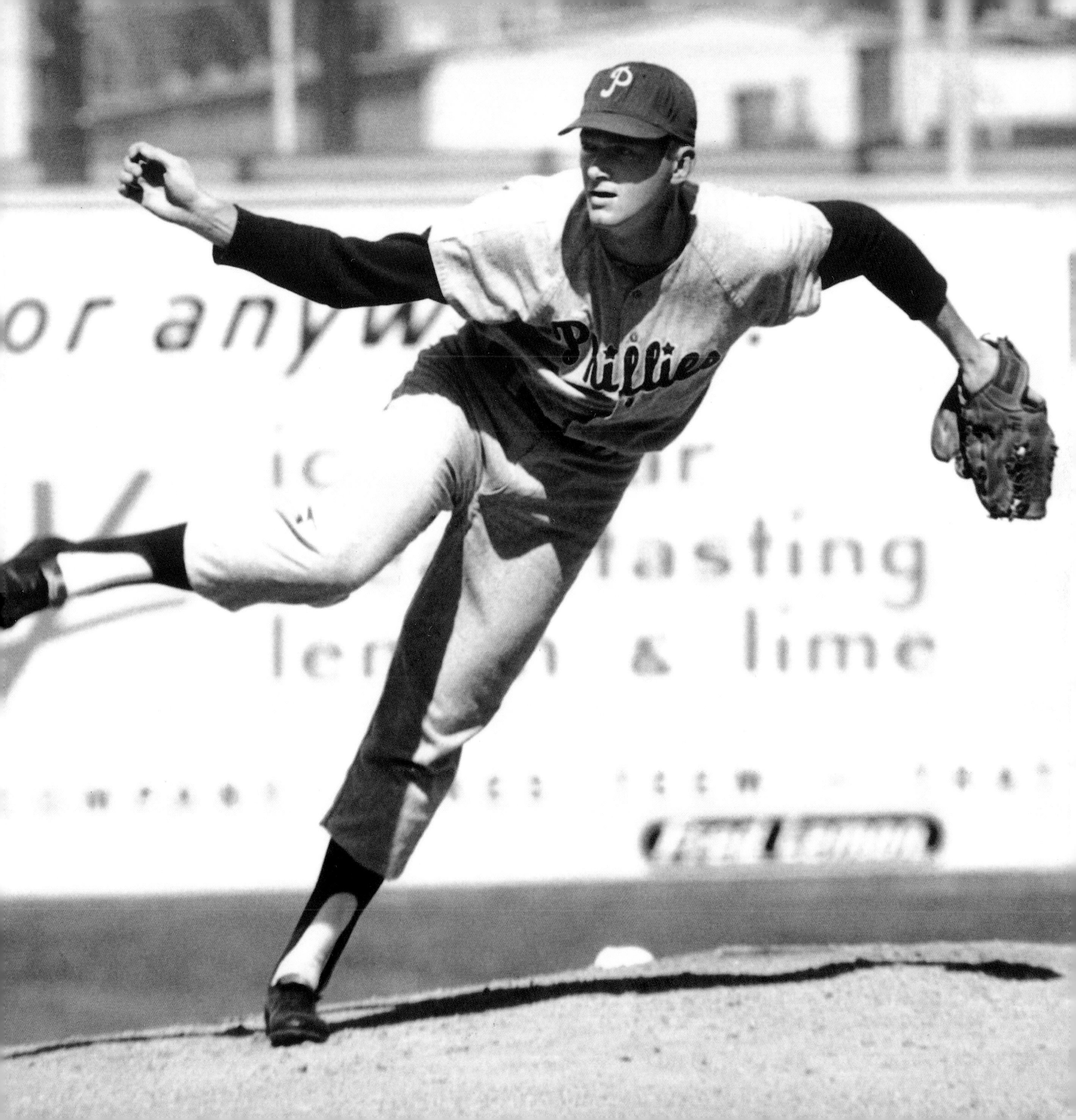
Phillies
& lime

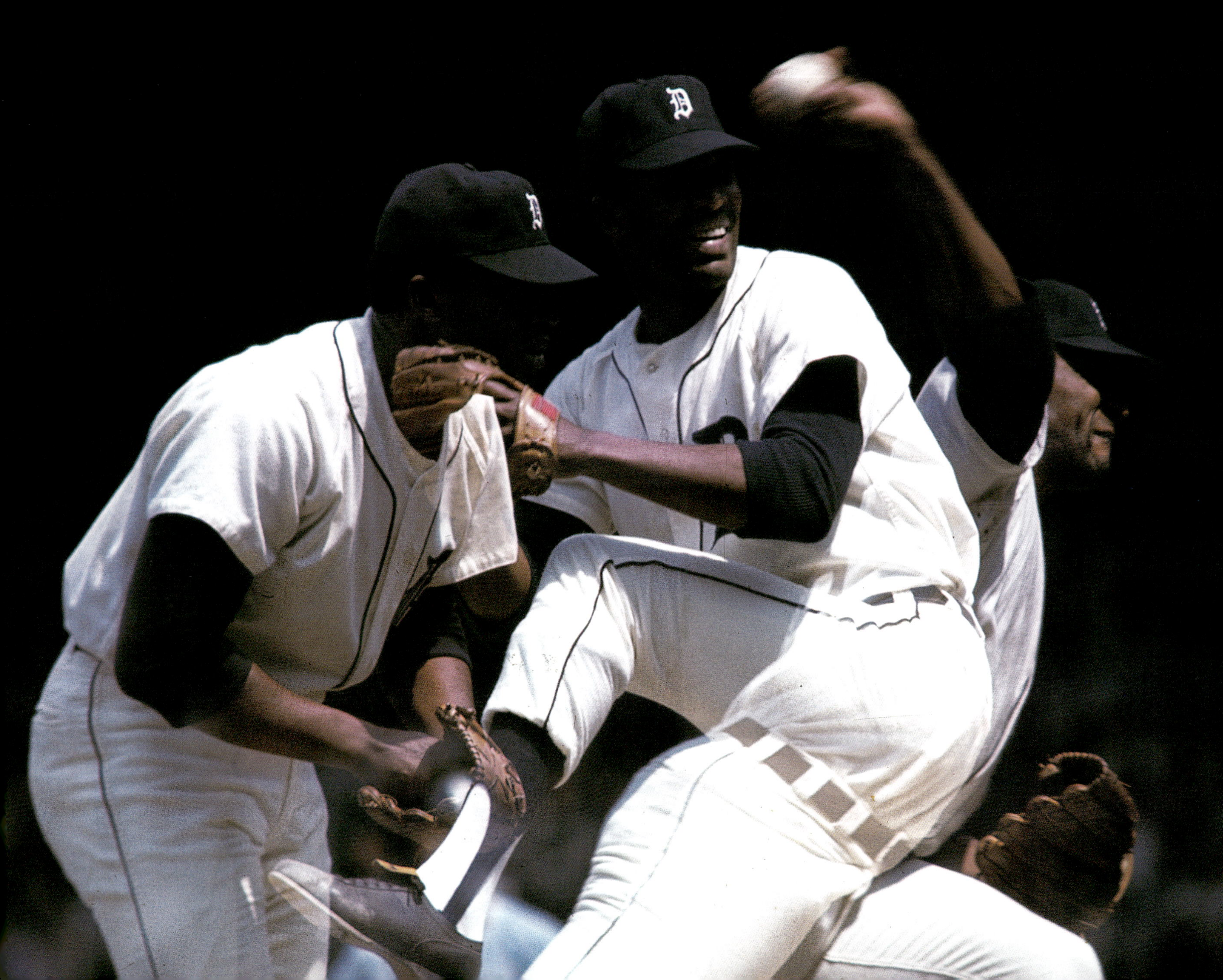

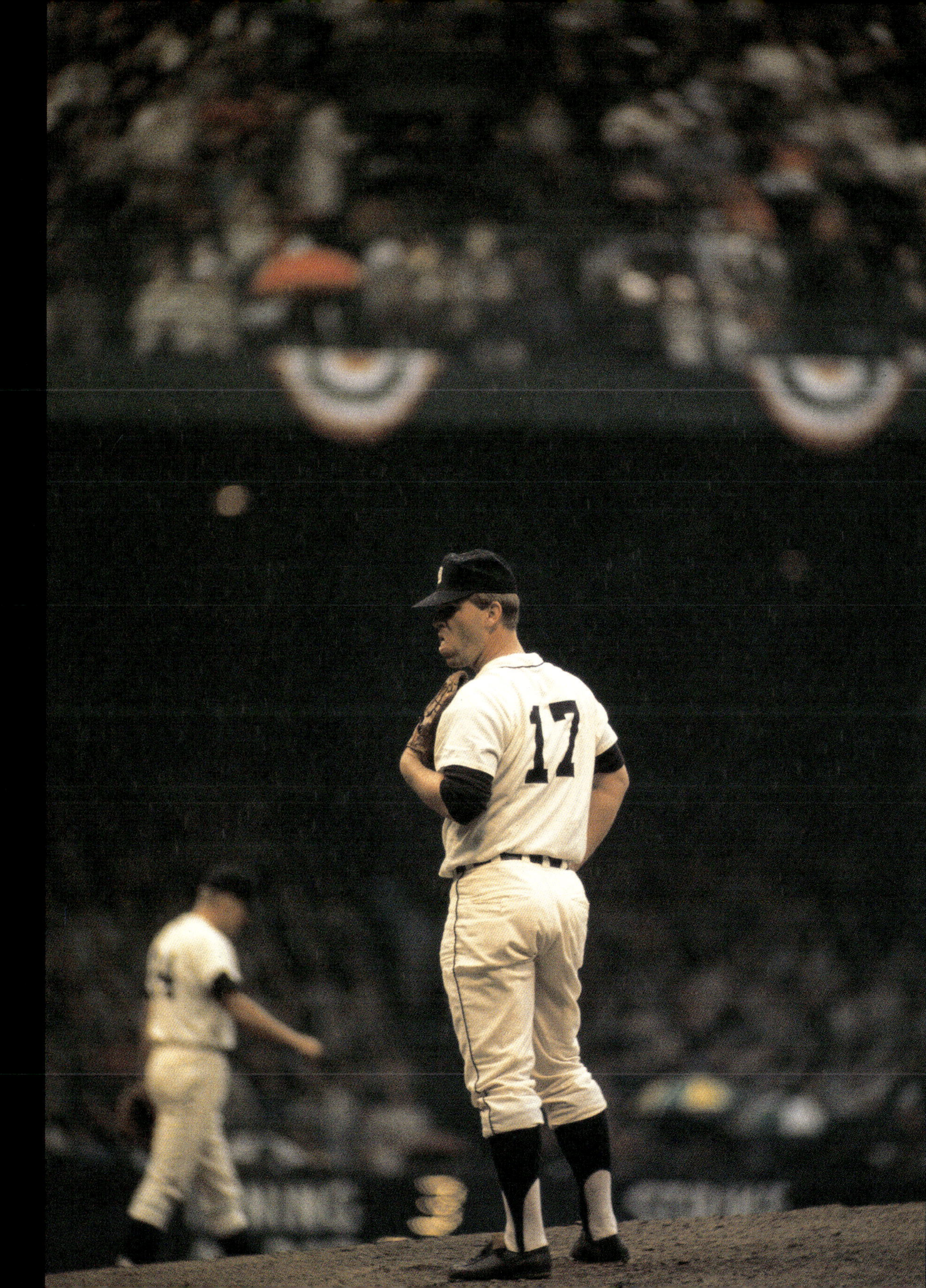
17

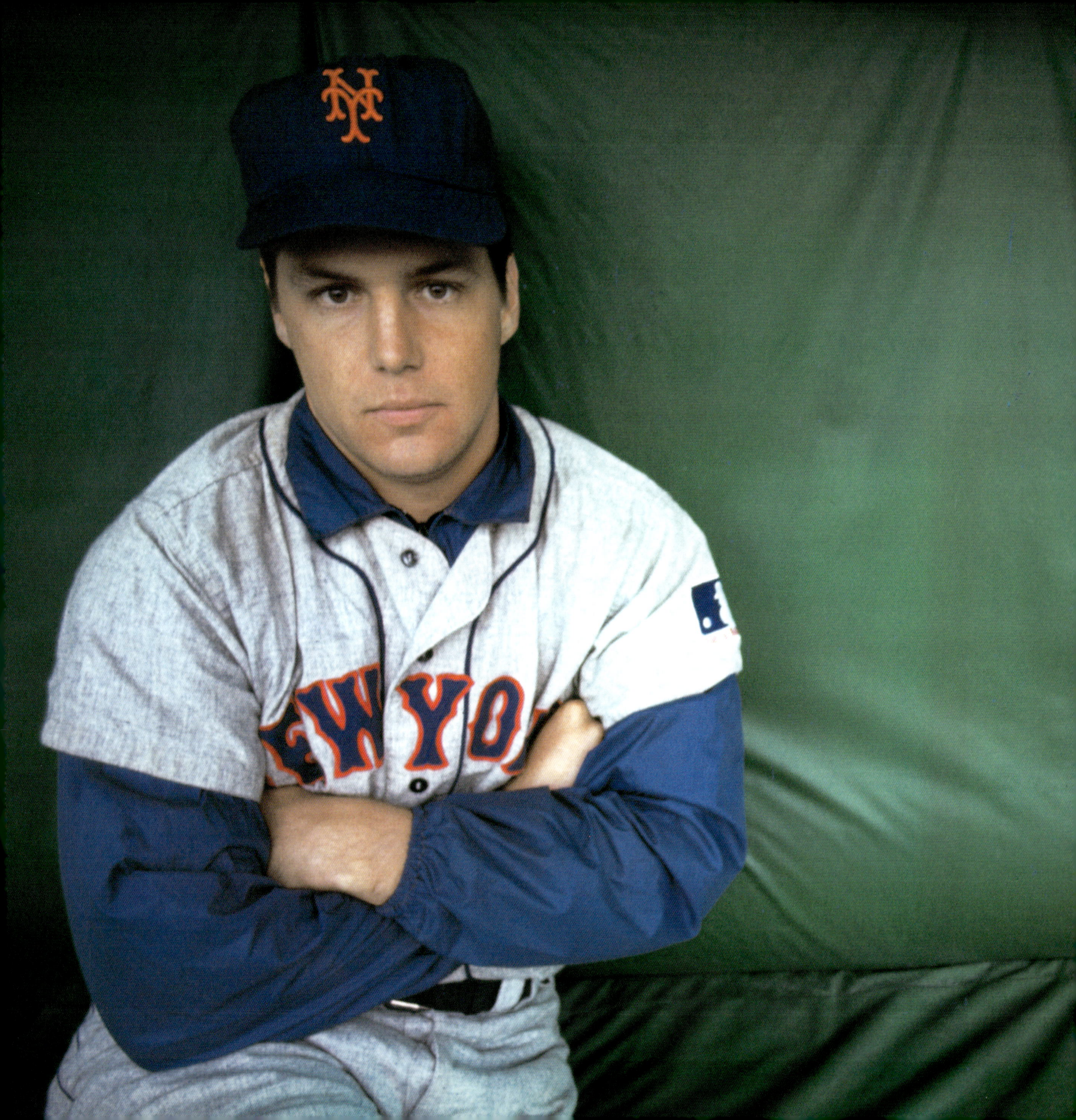

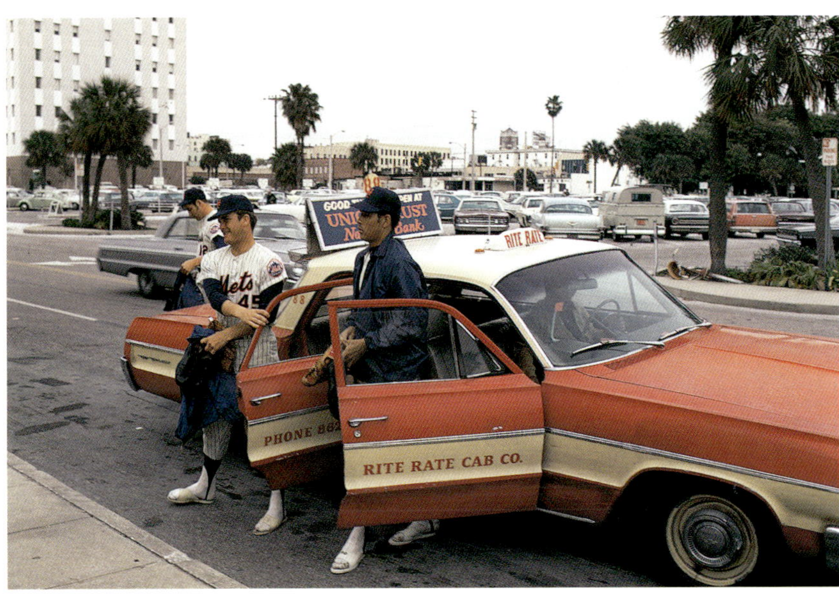

TOM SEAVER, Montreal, 1969 (LEFT)

TUG MCGRAW AND TEAMMATES, St. Petersburg, Florida, 1969 (ABOVE)

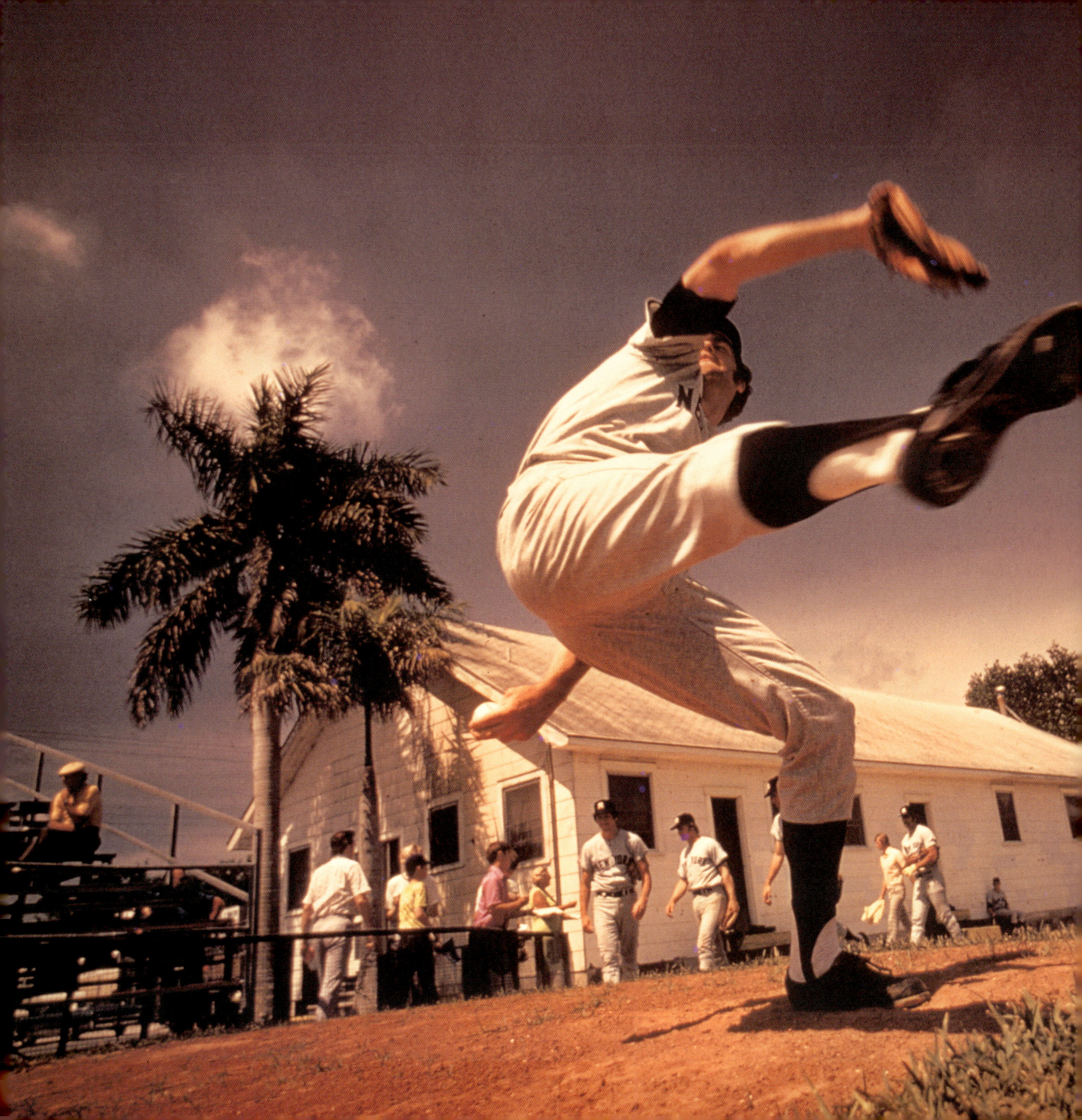

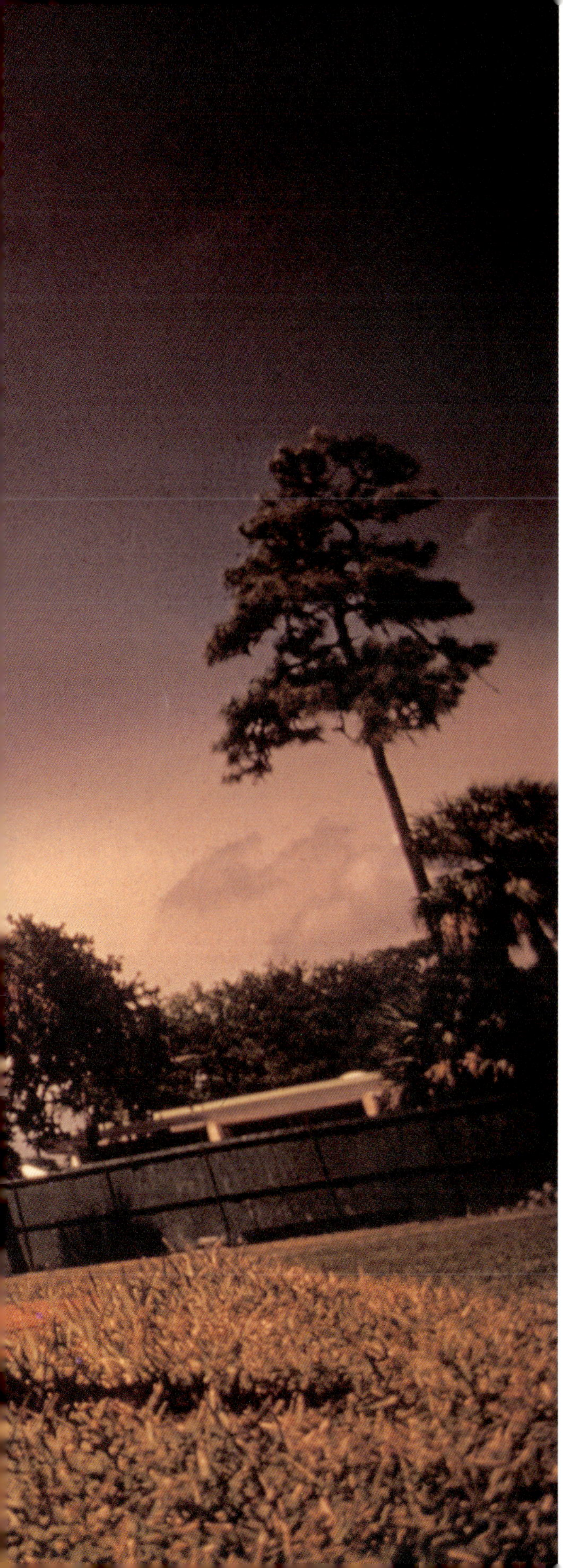

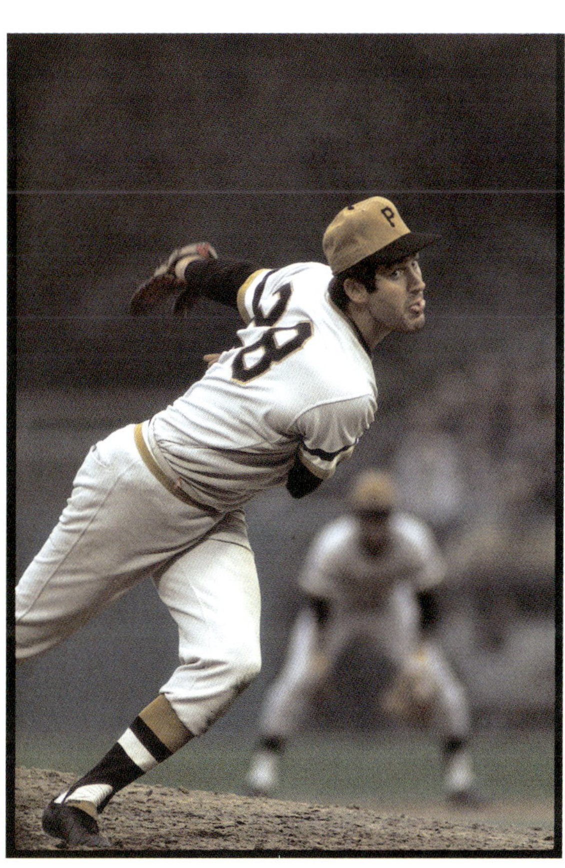

STEVE BLASS, World Series, Pittsburgh, 1971 (ABOVE)

SAM MCDOWELL, Bradenton, Florida, 1974 (LEFT)

BOOG POWELL, Detroit, 1966

BOB GIBSON, St. Louis, 1973 (OVERLEAF)

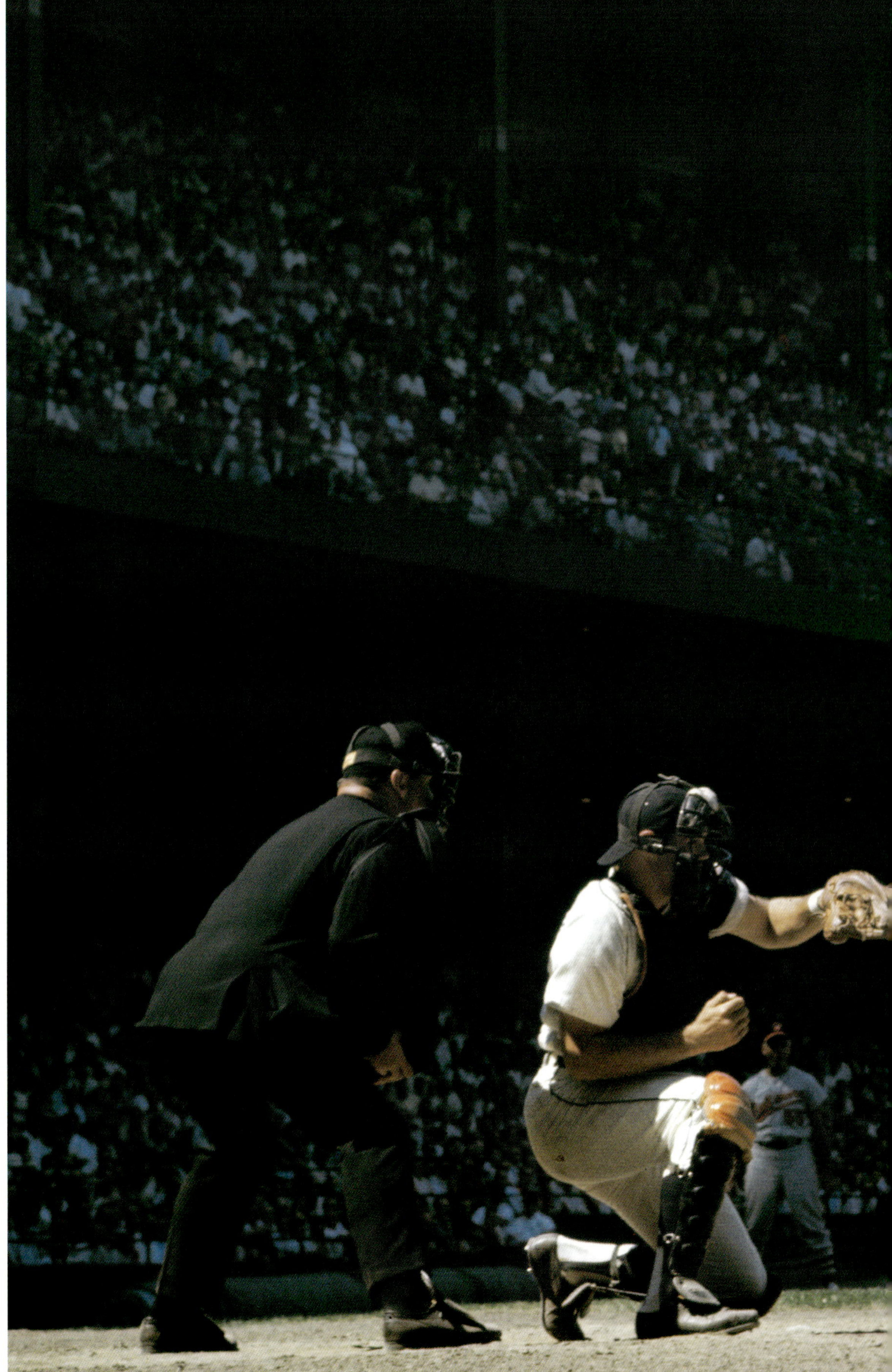

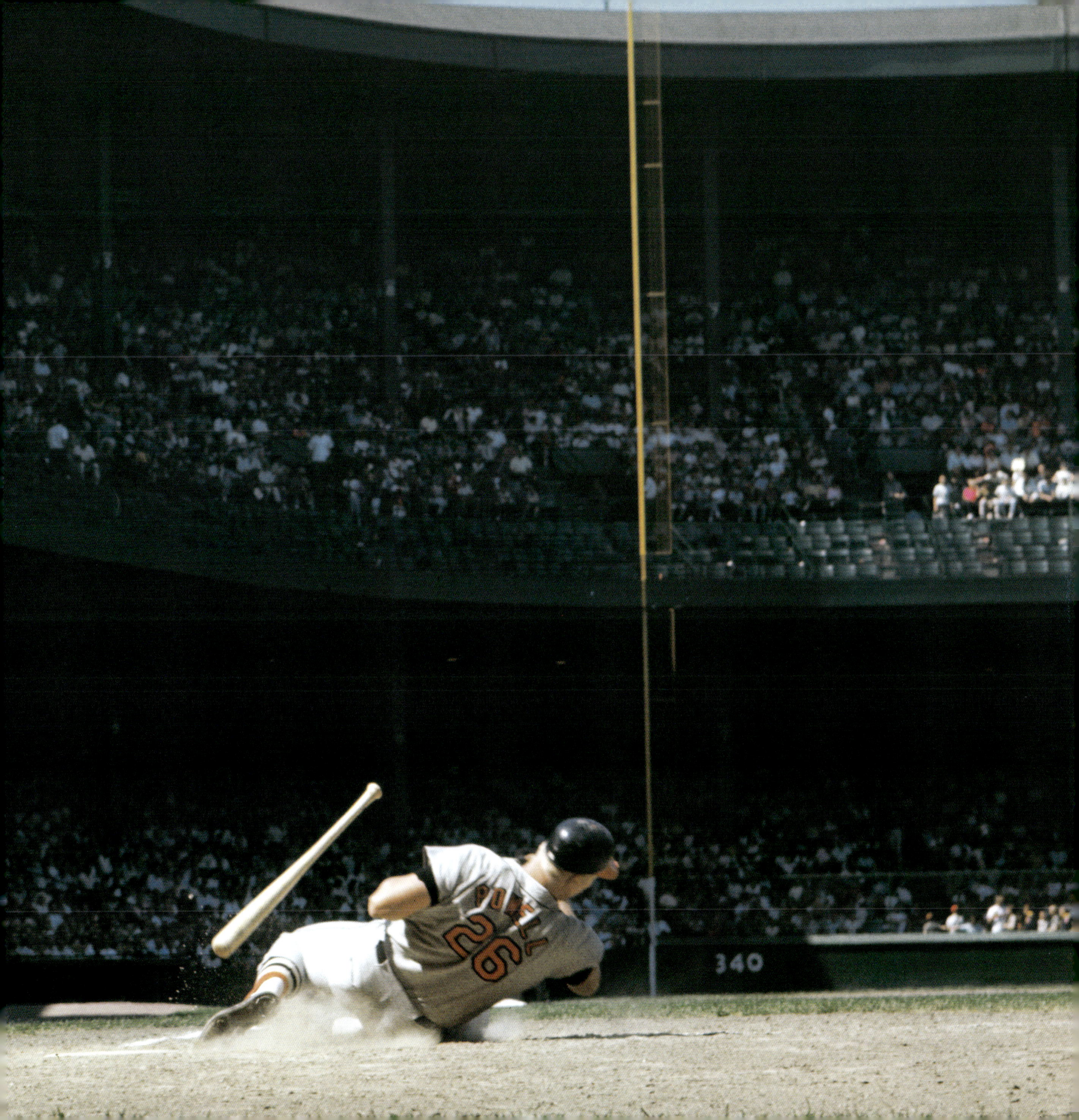
26
340

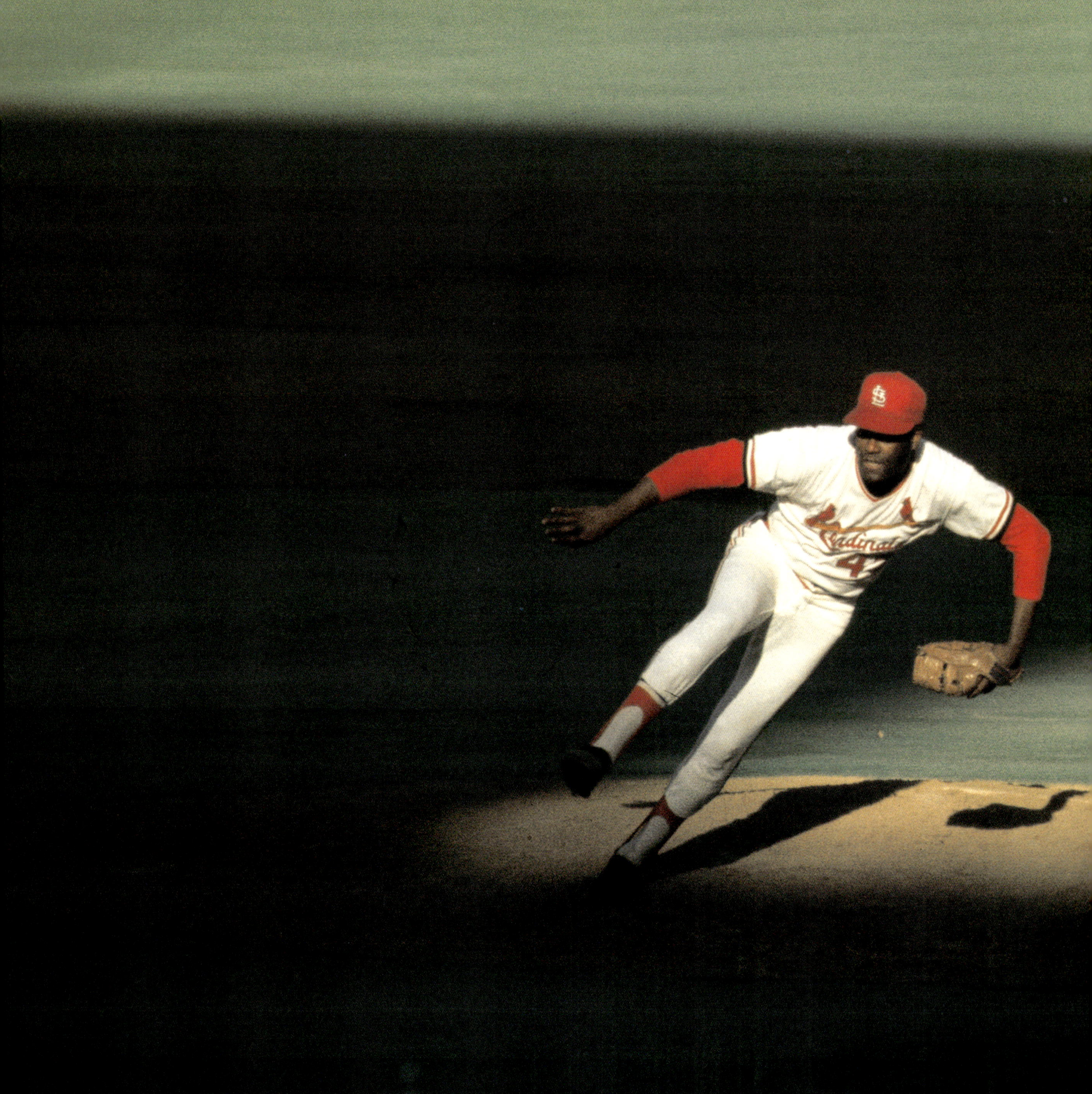

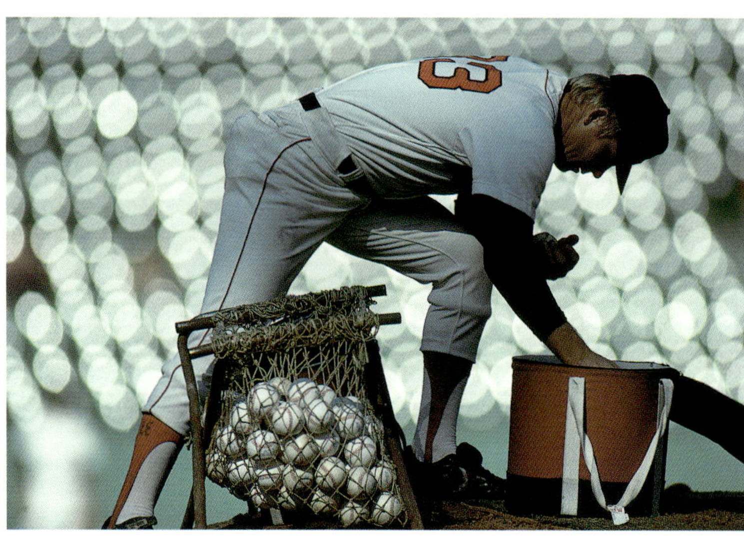

WALT HRINIAK pitching batting practice, Boston, 1979 (ABOVE)

GREG MADDUX, Chicago, 1993

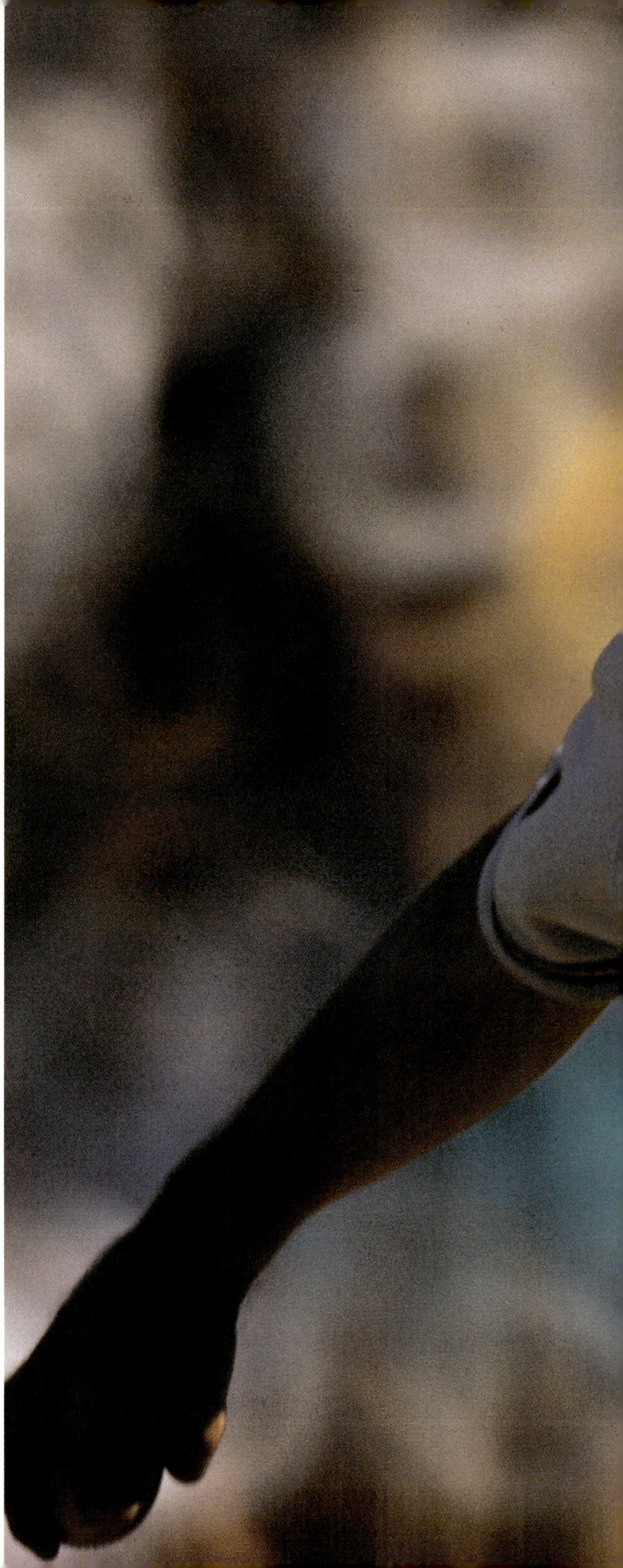

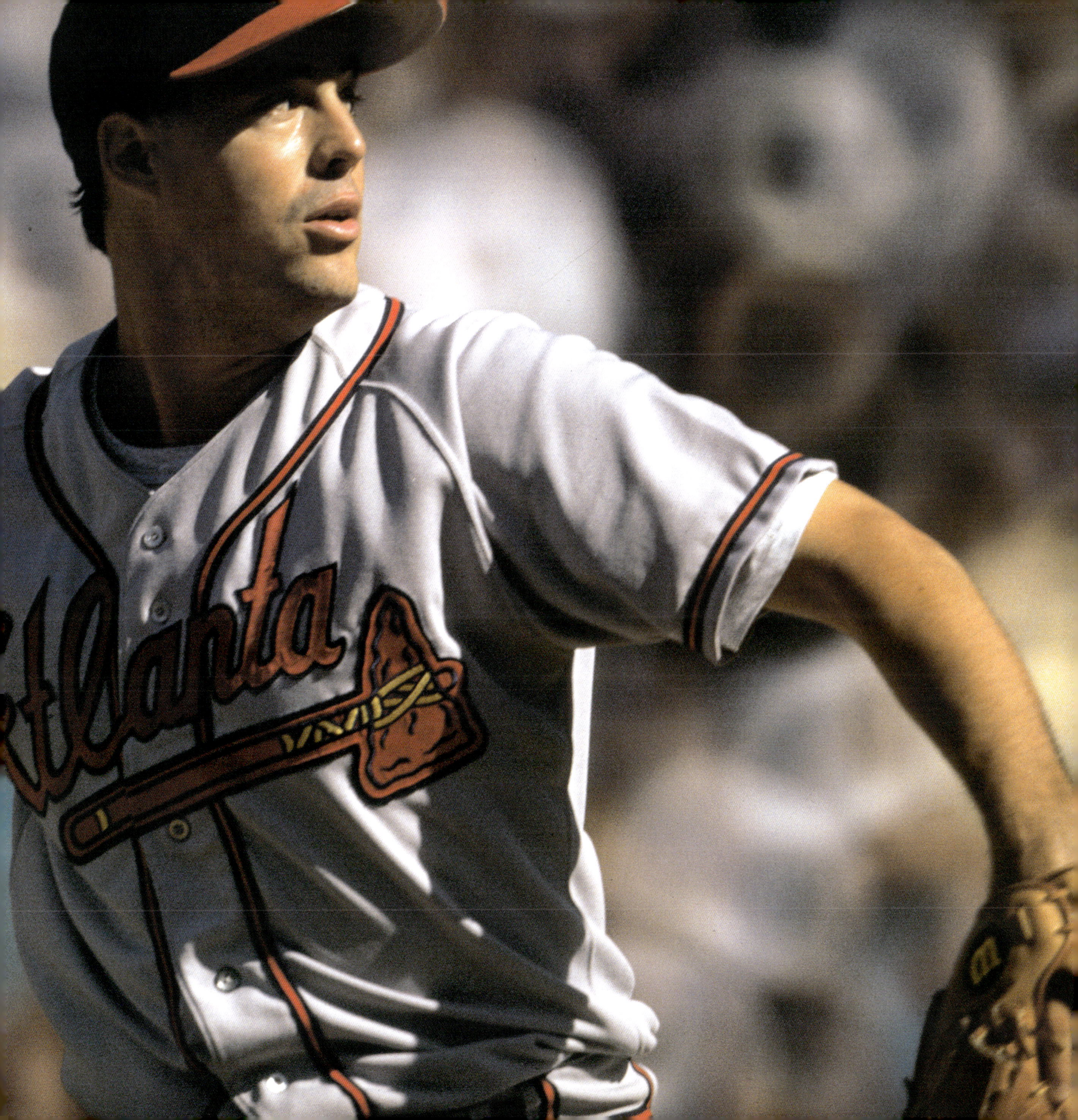

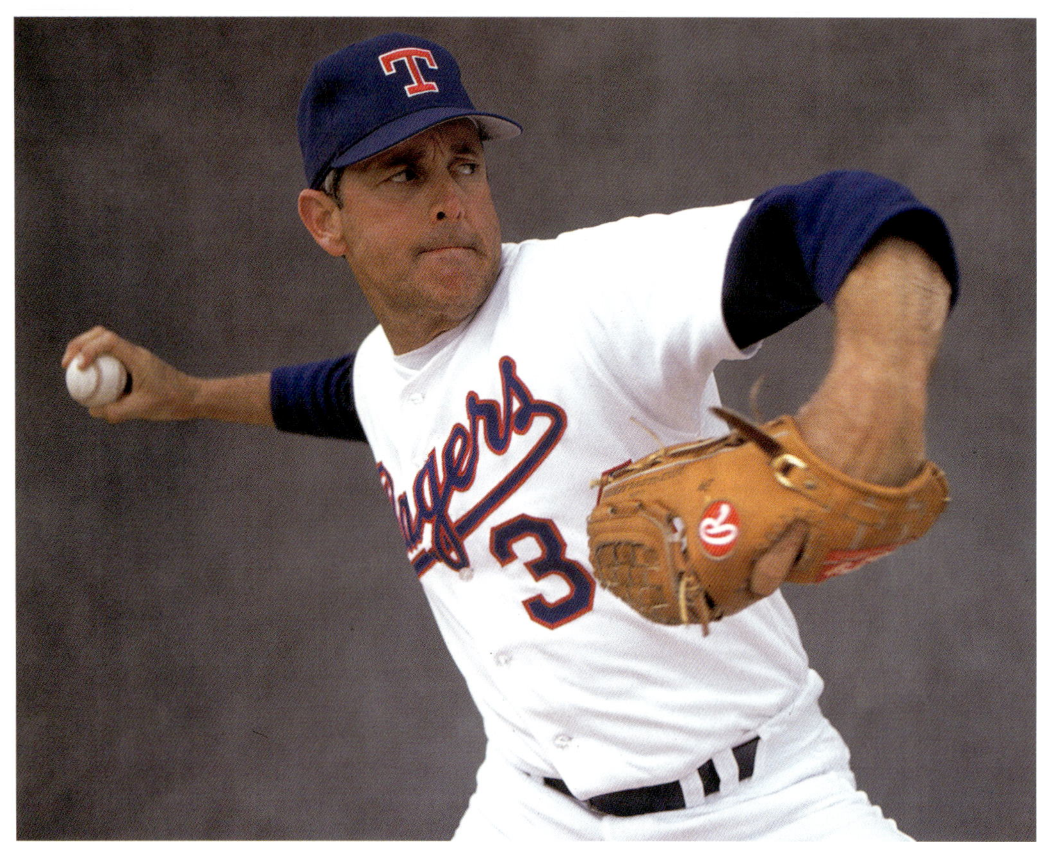

NOLAN RYAN, Port Charlotte, Florida, 1991

TOM SEAVER, Tampa, Florida, 1981

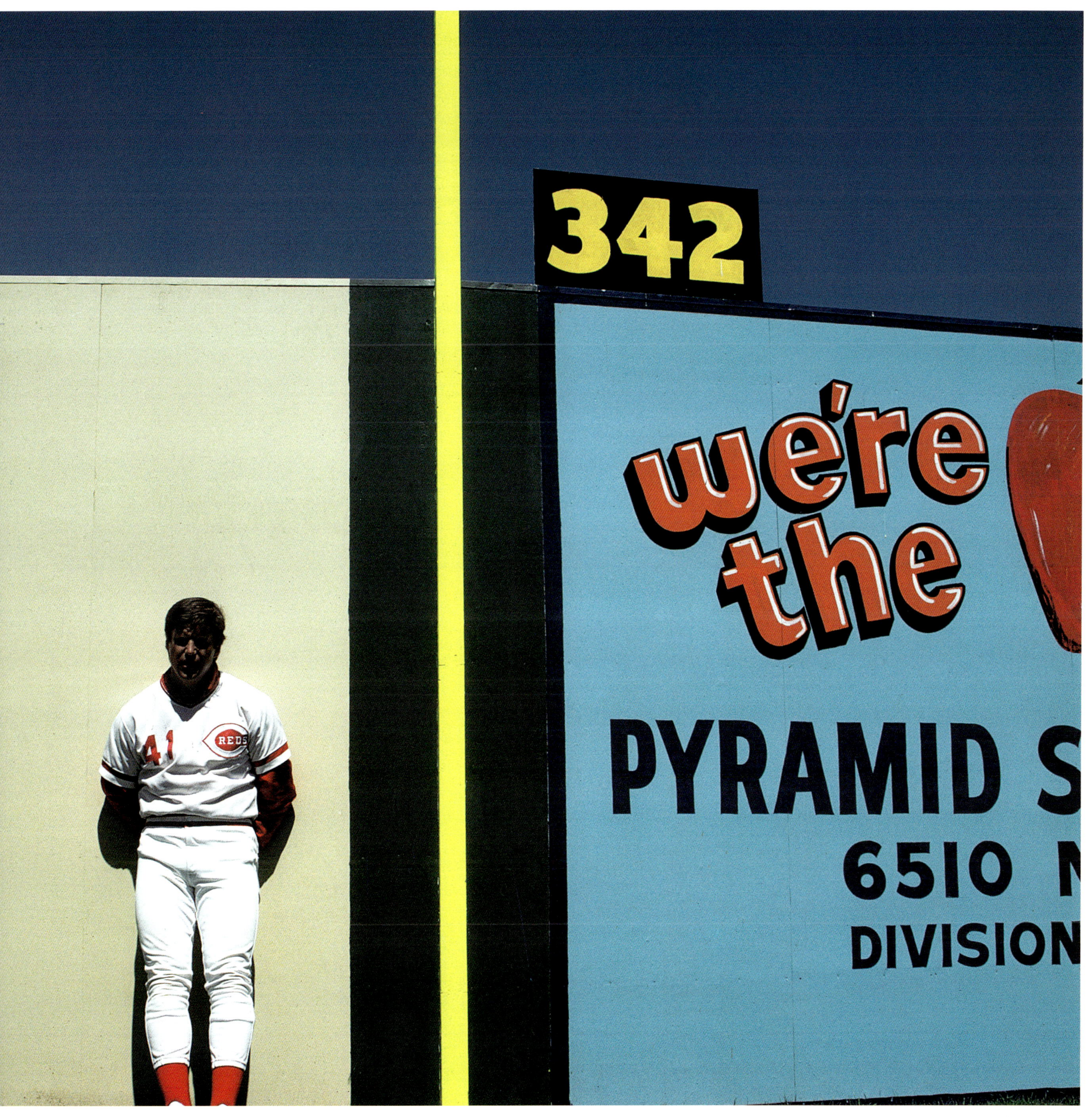
342
41
REDS
we're the
PYRAMID S
6510 N
DIVISION

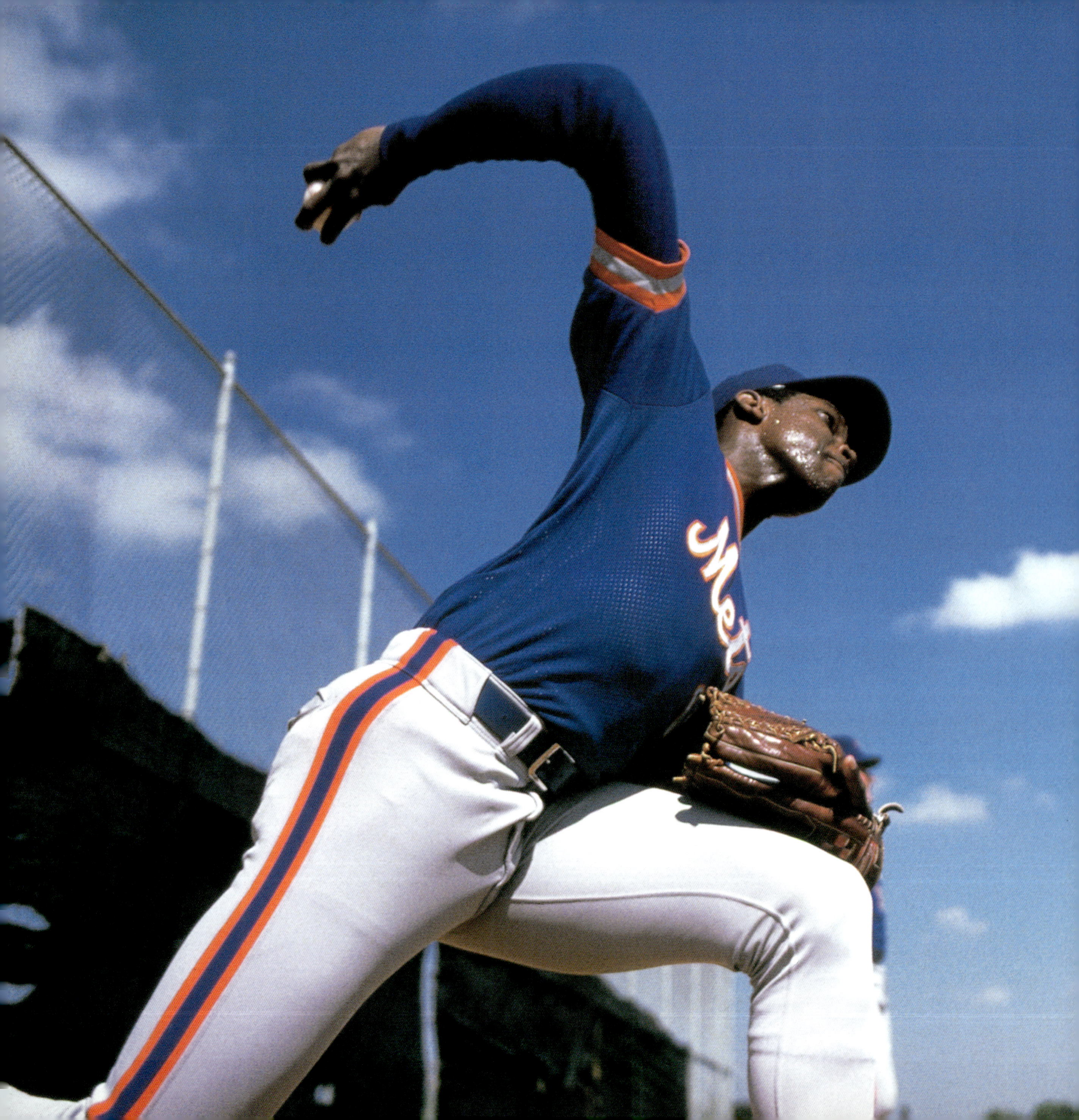

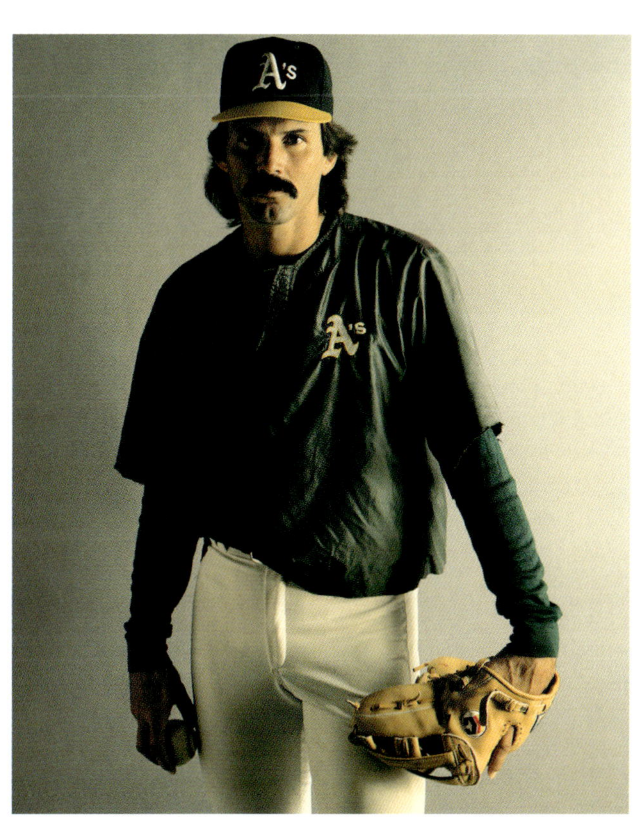

DWIGHT GOODEN, St. Petersburg, Florida, 1985 (LEFT)

DENNIS ECKERSLEY, Oakland, California, 1990 (ABOVE)

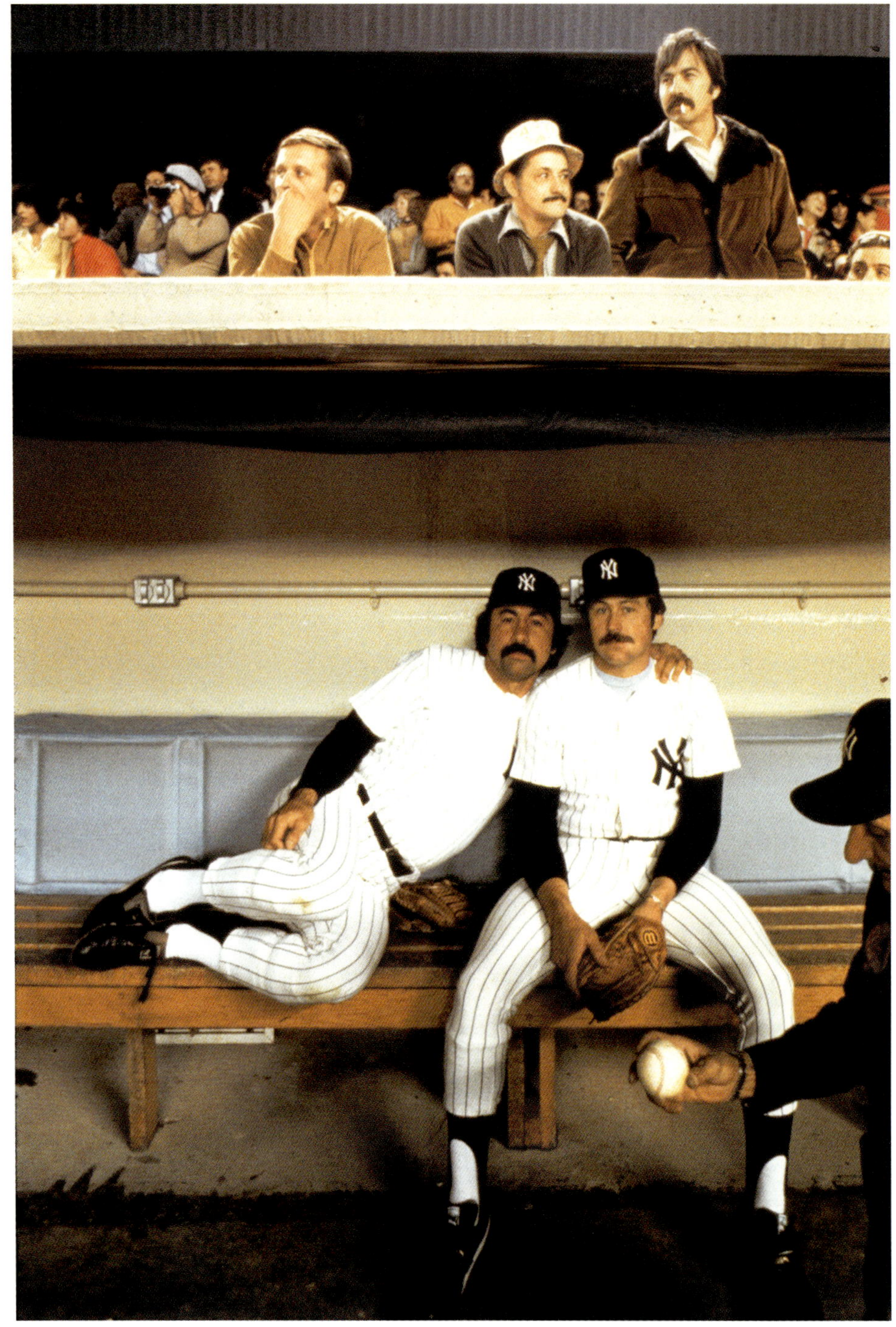

ED FIGUEROA AND CATFISH HUNTER, Yankee Stadium, 1975

PEDRO MARTINEZ, Fort Myers, Florida, 2001

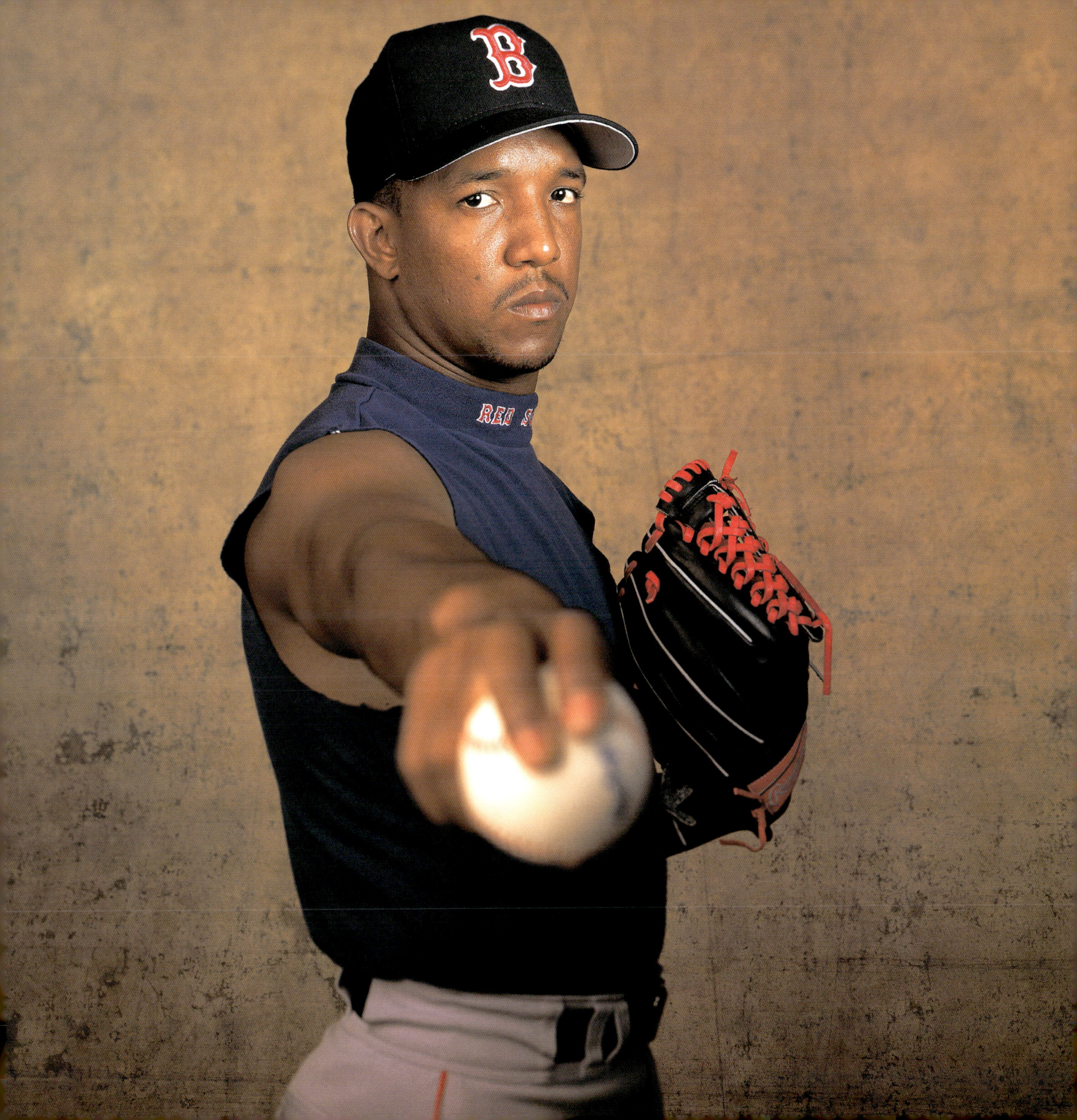

HITTERS

FRANK THOMAS, Chicago, 1994

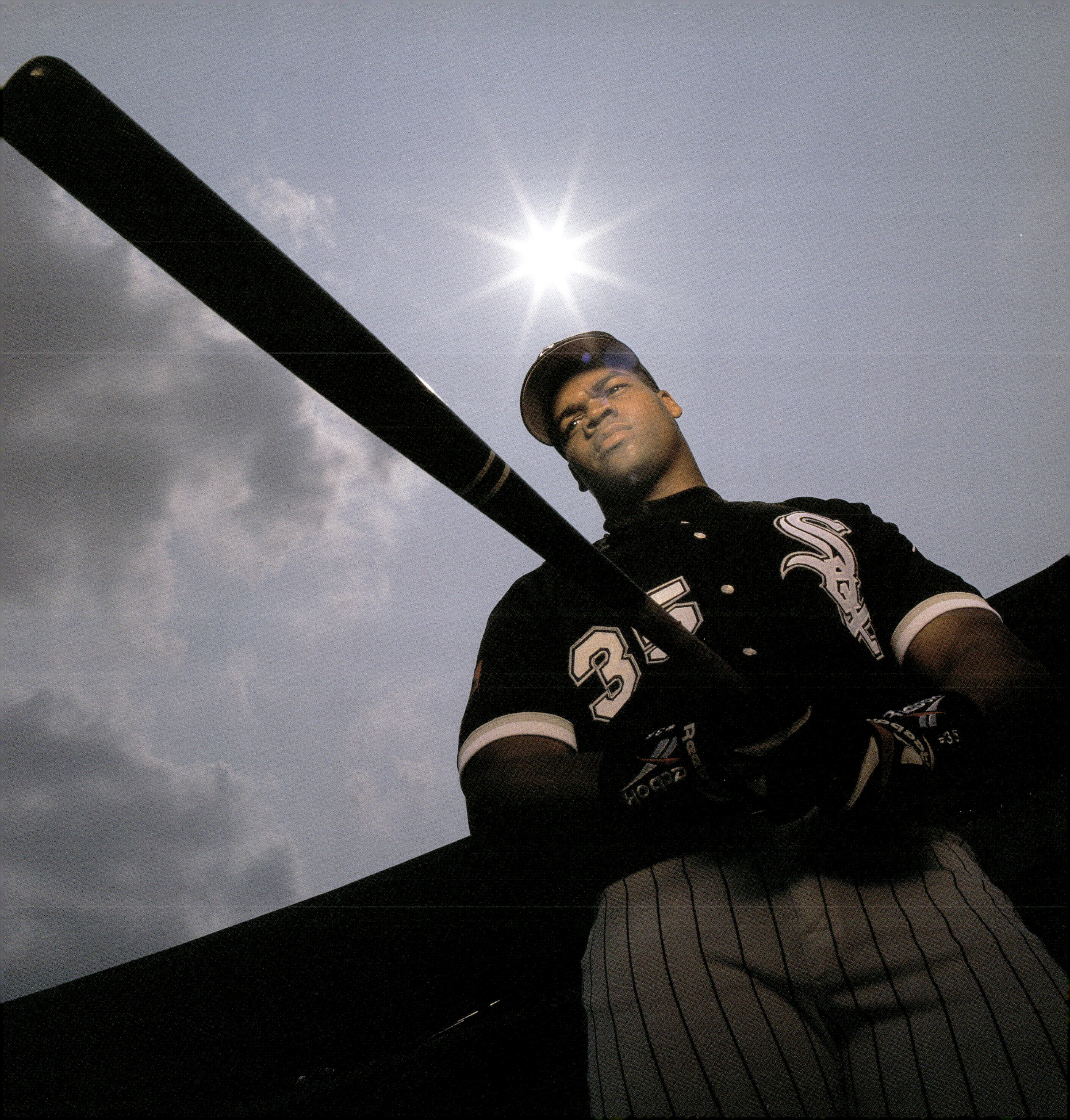

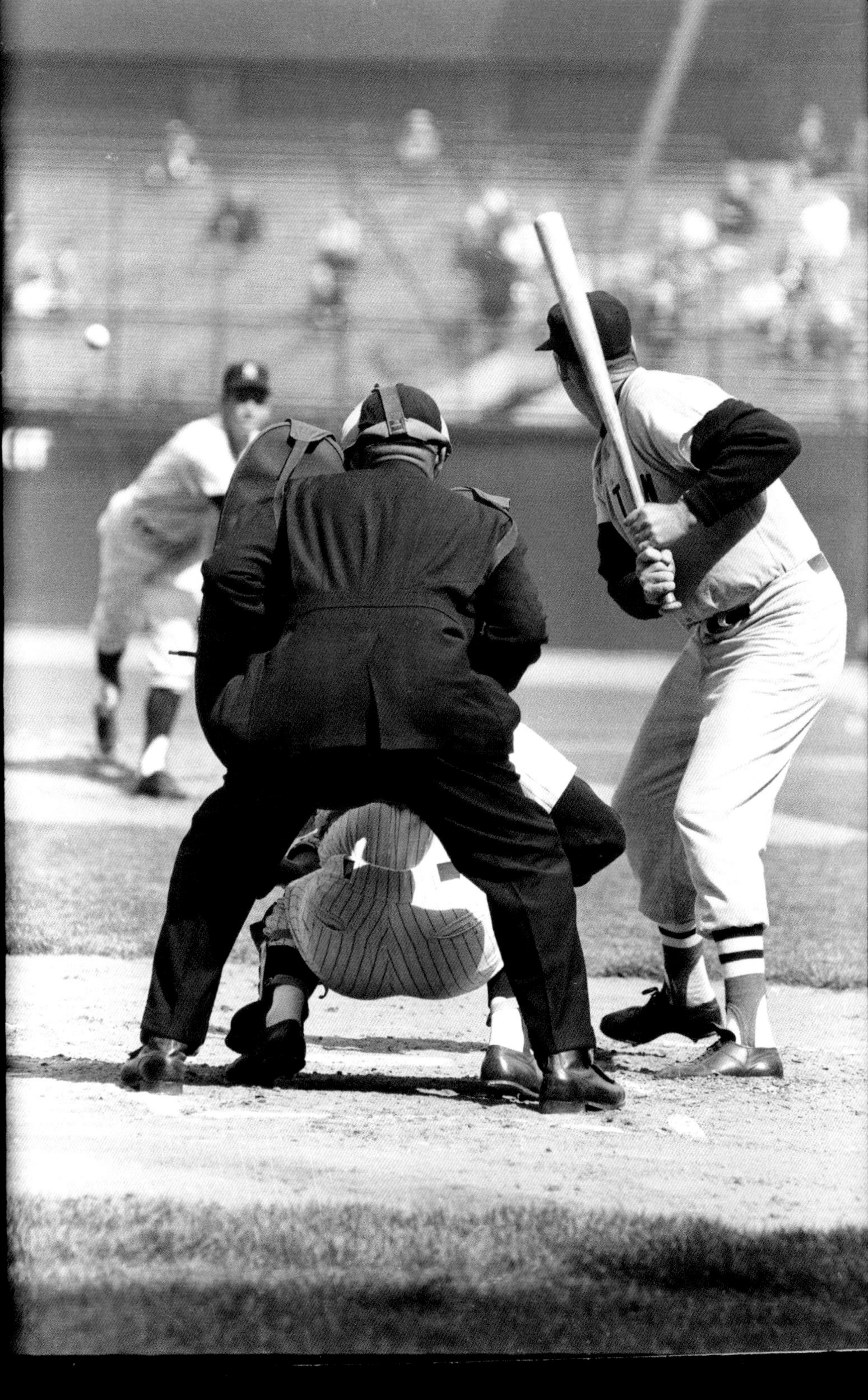

TED WILLIAMS, Yankee Stadium, 1960

OF ALL THE HITTERS he has photographed, Walter Iooss Jr. never got to talk to the one he most wanted to talk to. "Mickey Mantle," he says. "Mickey was my hero as a kid, but I could never get any access to him. I could never get close enough to talk to him. I wish I'd talked to him." Even so, from various angles at the old Yankee Stadium, Iooss was close enough to project the power in his hero's swing. Two decades later, he did talk to a Yankee slugger, Reggie Jackson, the one and only Mr. October, and asked him a favor. "I needed a shot of Reggie standing at the plate watching one of his home runs soaring into the stands," Iooss says. "I told him where I'd be, out in the first row of the right-field stands, near where I was when Roger Maris hit his 61st homer. I had the same lens I used for Maris and I told Reggie, 'If you hit one deep, drop the bat, stand there, and watch it.' I knew he'd do it. He loves the camera."

His first time up, Jackson went deep, but not deep enough. The ball was caught on the warning track.

"He had stood there like I wanted," Iooss says. "When he came out to play right field, he came over to me and said, 'How's that?' I said, 'That was good, but you've got to take him deep.'"

His next time up, Jackson hit a soaring home run into the right-field stands.

"When he came out to right field after the homer," Iooss says, "he looked at me and said, 'How's that?' I told him, 'Pretty good, but you didn't stand there long enough.' And all around me, fans are yelling at me, 'What are you talking to Reggie about?'"

On that hot, humid New York afternoon, Jackson was wearing a navy blue long-sleeved sweatshirt under his uniform.

"When I asked him why," Iooss says, "he told me, 'I want the other team to know that Reggie can take the heat.'"

With two other hitters, Iooss's angle from behind is enough to tell you who they were. Even if Ted Williams and Stan Musial had traded their Red Sox and Cardinals uniforms, anyone who ever saw them in a batter's box would know instantly who was who. Musial about to uncoil from his stance that resembles a question mark, the muscles in his left forearm tense, his feet planted. Williams, already striding with his raised front foot, his hands low, his bat poised, his eyes still deciding if the pitch is good enough to hit. Maybe he'll swing. Maybe he won't.

Here is Hank Aaron, in his straight-up stiff-legged trot, doing what he did 755 times, more than any other big-league hitter: turning toward the batboy and the dugout after a home run.

Here is Willie Mays, returning to Connie Mack with the San Francisco Giants, his eyes following the ball as he follows through with his sweeping swing, and here he is in the on-deck circle with that boyish smile.

"Willie exuded joy," Iooss says.

Here is Ken Griffey Jr., as seen by Iooss from the

catwalk high above home plate in the Kingdome, at the moment of impact between his bat and the pitch.

Here is Wes Covington, one of Iooss's favorites with the Phillies, about to unwind himself after a swing and a miss.

Here is Vic Power, a Cleveland Indians first baseman, objecting in open-mouthed annoyance to the umpire's forefinger above Yankee catcher Elston Howard on a dreary day when almost all the seats beyond the left-field foul pole were empty.

Here is Matt Stairs, an Oakland Athletics slugger, lifting his front leg as he awaits a pitch in Tiger Stadium's last hours.

"I took that with an old Speed Graphic camera," Iooss says. "I wanted to take a picture that looked like 1956, the way the film looked back then. Everything in it is so sharp."

And here is Tony Oliva, who won three American League batting titles with the Minnesota Twins, finishing his follow-through in old Metropolitan Stadium in the 1965 World Series.

"What a swing," Iooss says. "It's a left-handed version of that famous photo of Joe DiMaggio's follow-through in Griffith Stadium in Washington."

DiMaggio stopped playing after the 1951 World Series, so Iooss never had an opportunity to photograph the Yankee Clipper, except at an Old-Timers Day when his swing had lost some of its elegance. But if Iooss had been able to shoot "the great DiMaggio," as Santiago the fisherman called him in Ernest Hemingway's *The Old Man and the Sea,* he would have done it from the same angle as the photographer in Griffith Stadium.

"DiMaggio's body is big enough; his form is flawless," Iooss says. "You see the entire stadium. It's beautiful. It's one of the few photos that I would never change."

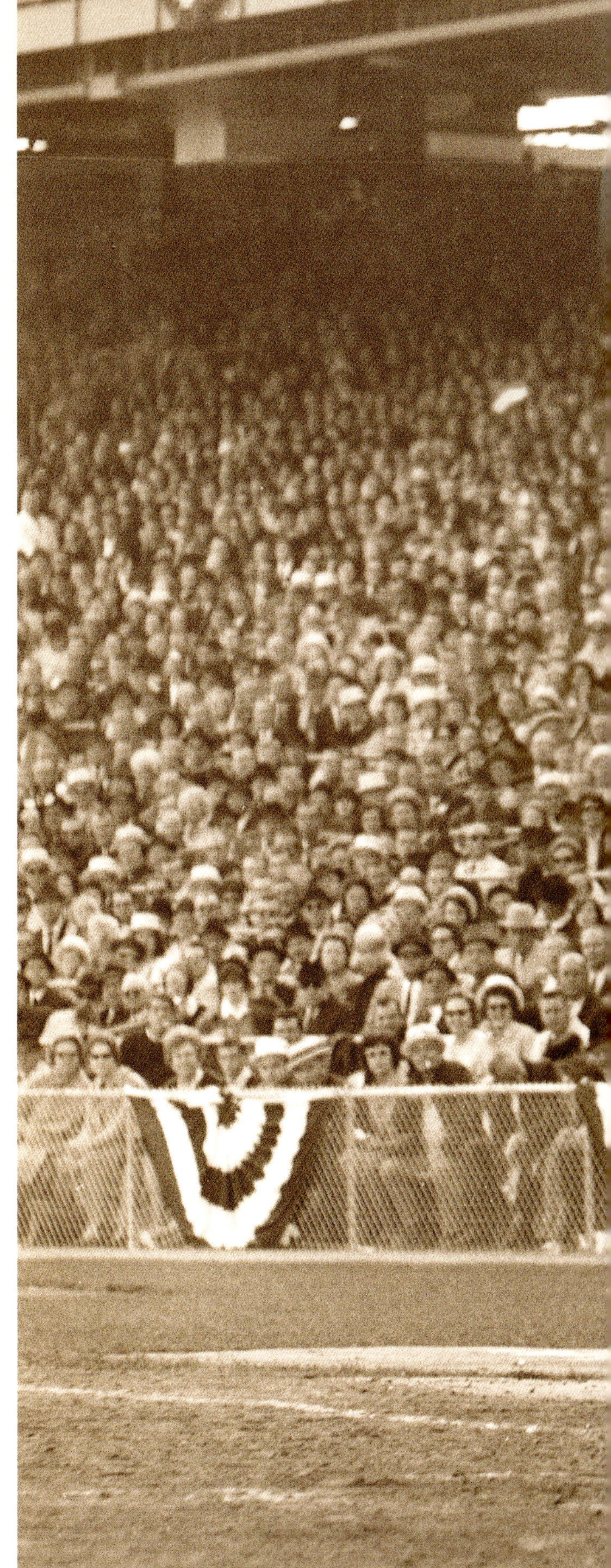

TONY OLIVA, World Series, Minneapolis, 1965

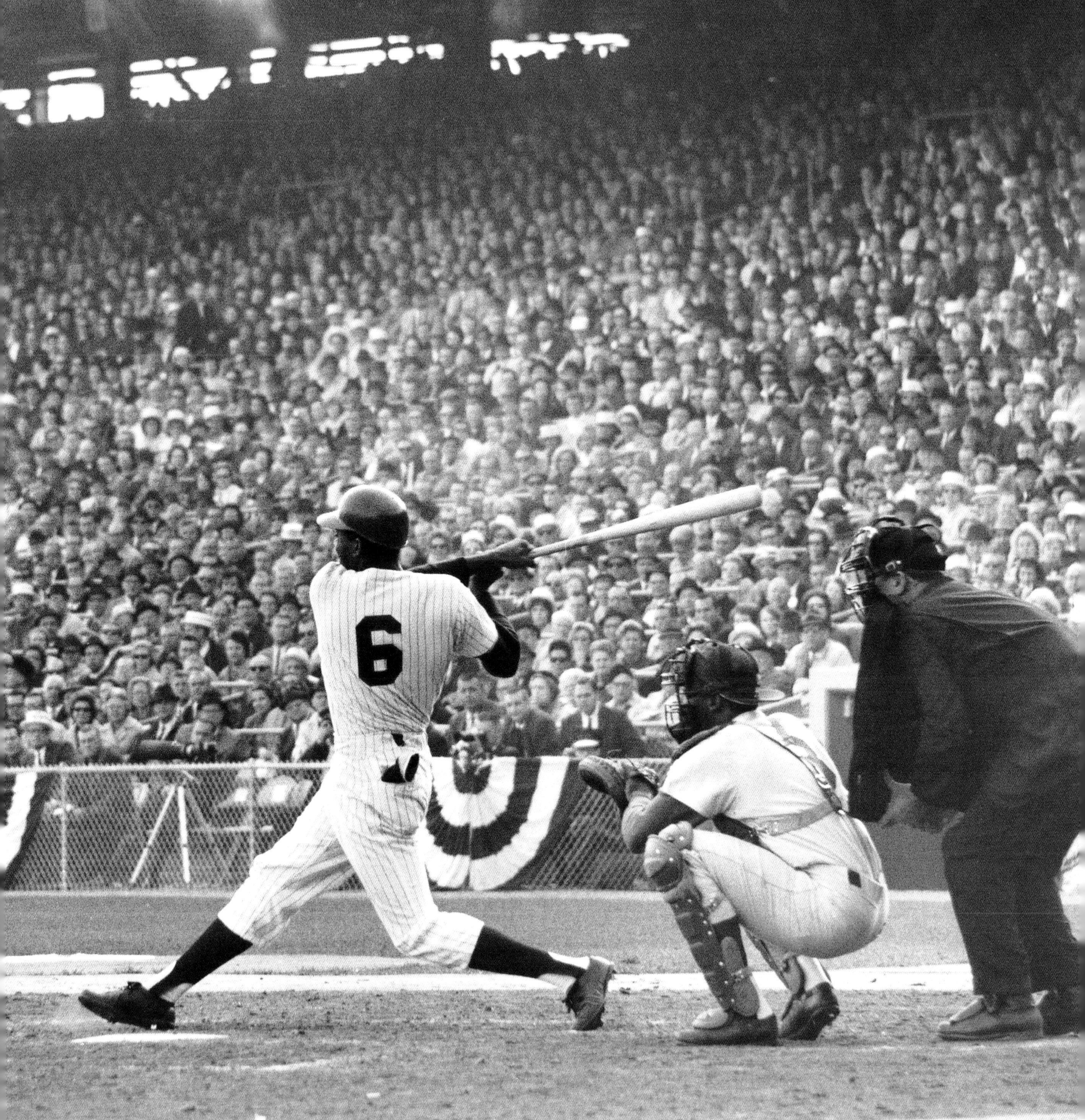

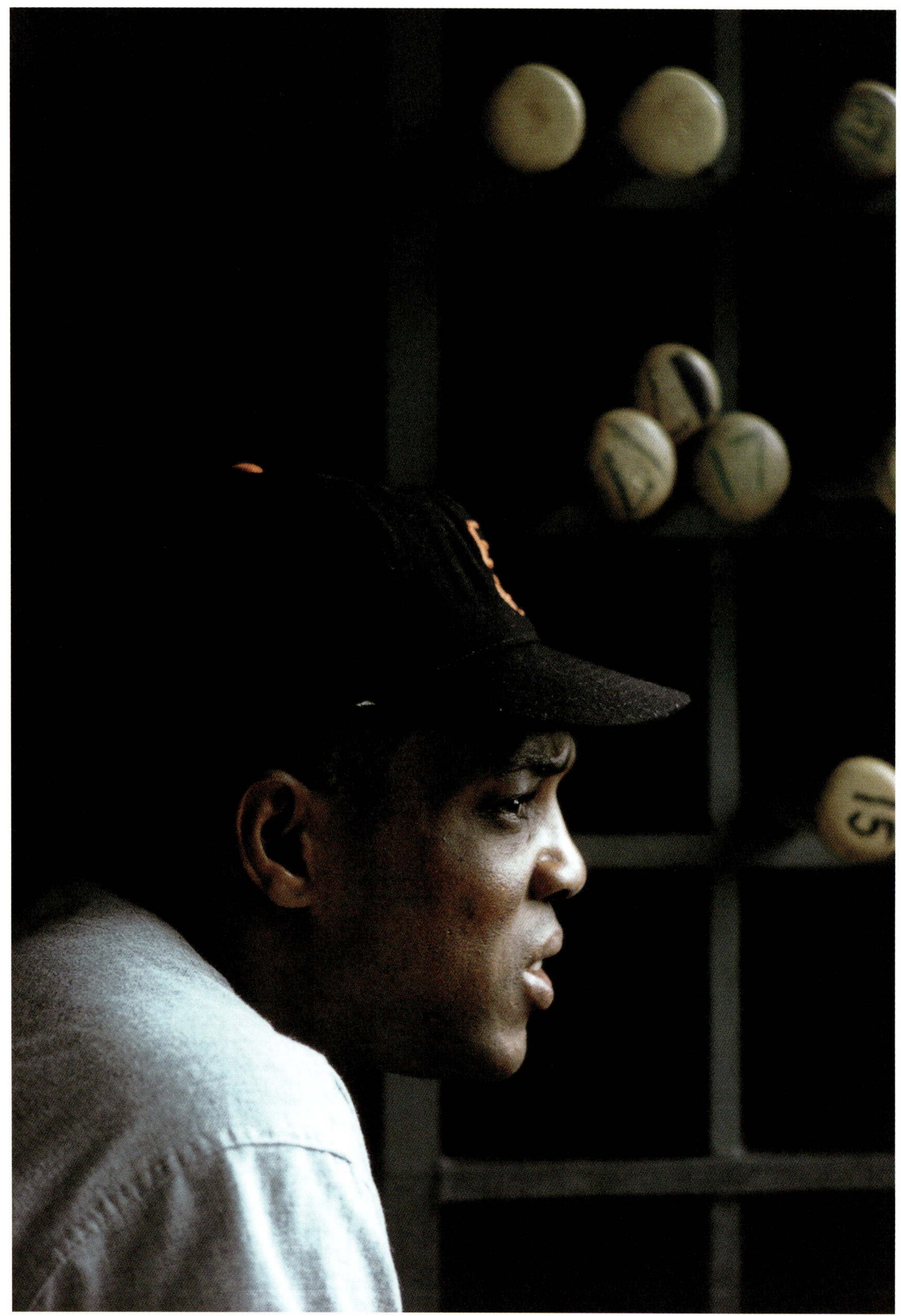

WILLIE MAYS, Milwaukee, 1966

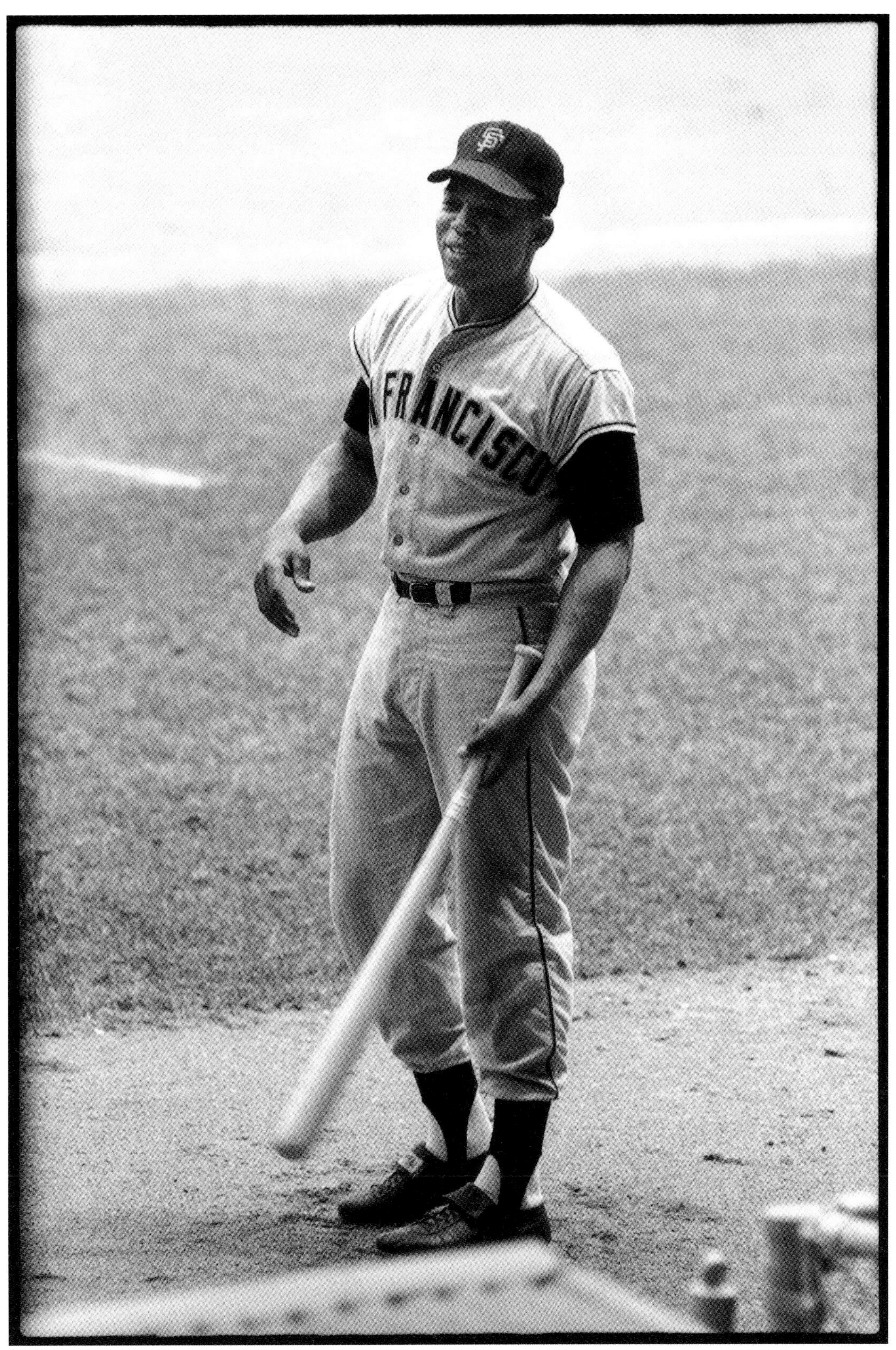

WILLIE MAYS, Philadelphia, 1963

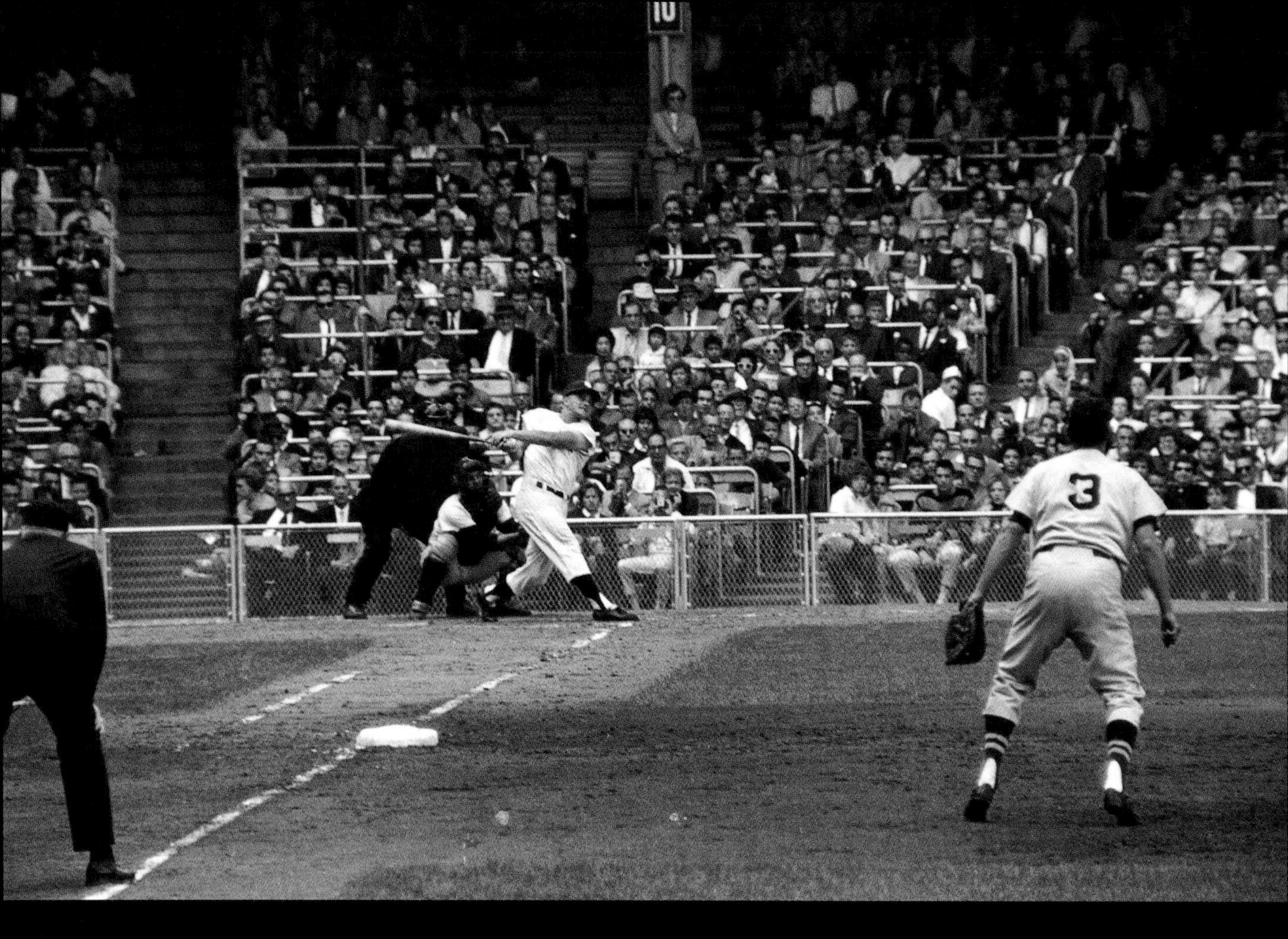

ROGER MARIS hits 61st home run, Yankee Stadium, 1961

MICKEY MANTLE, batting; **ROGER MARIS** on deck, Yankee Stadium, 1962

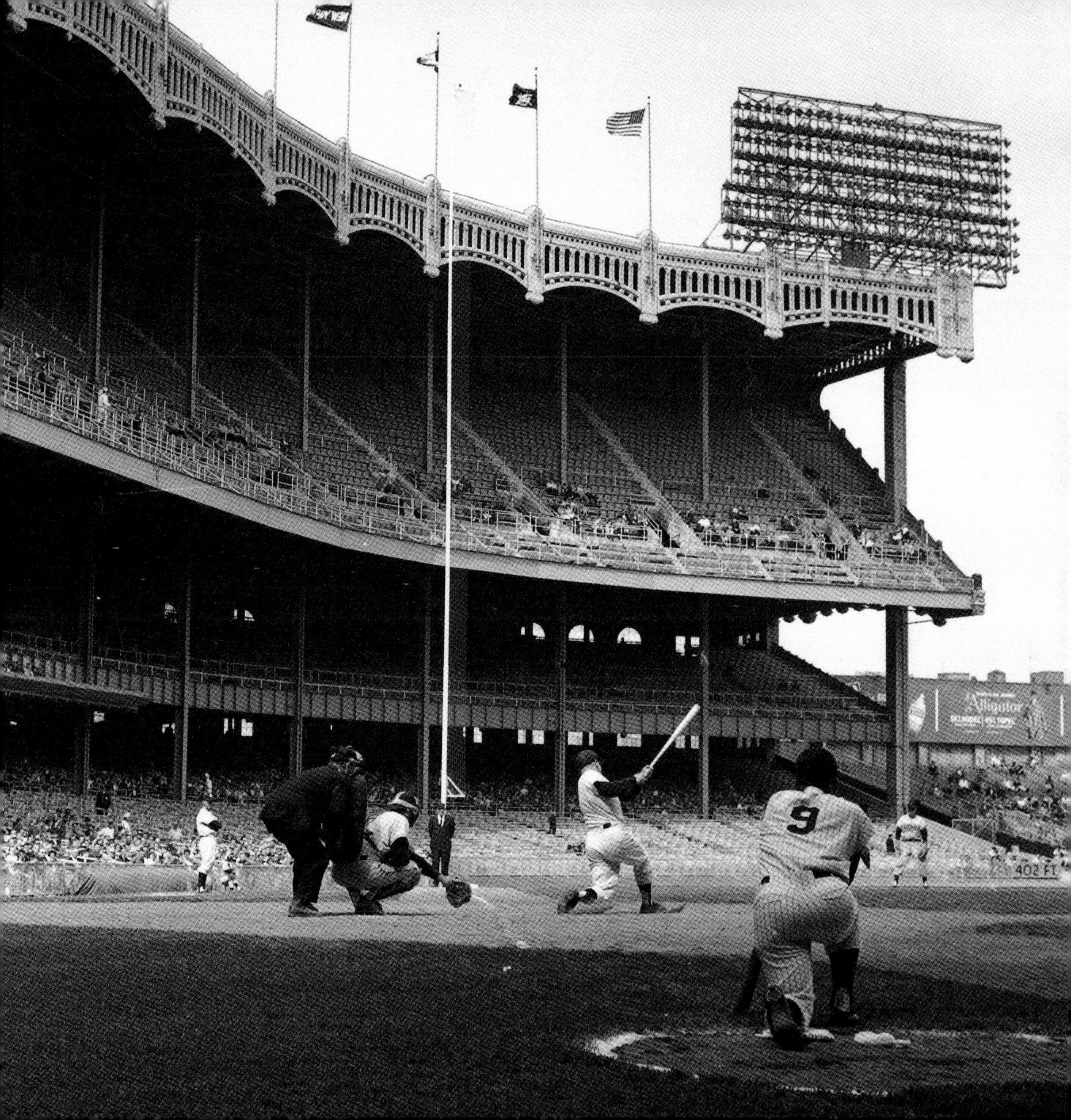

Alligator
9
402 FT

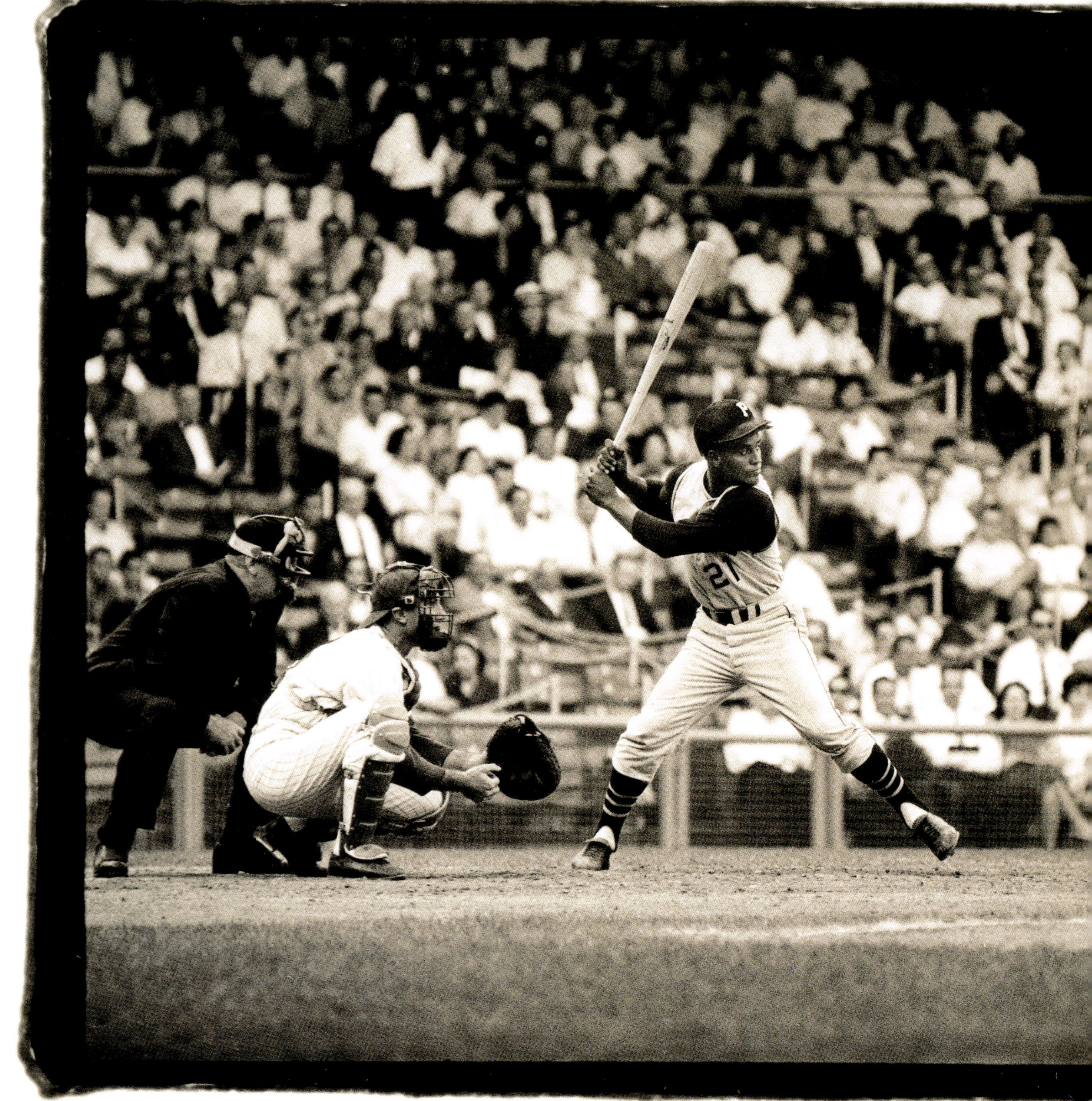
21

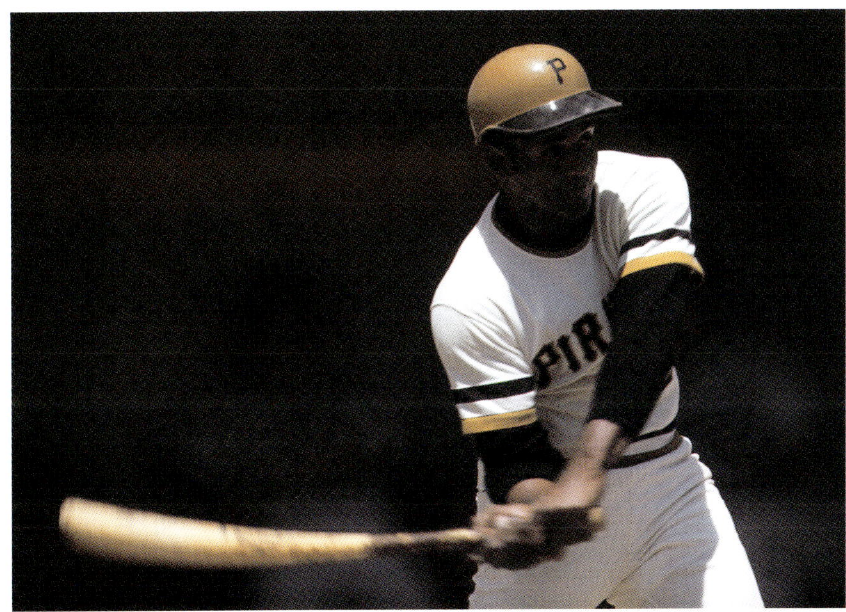

ROBERTO CLEMENTE, Polo Grounds, New York, 1962 (LEFT)
and at Pittsburgh, 1970 (ABOVE)

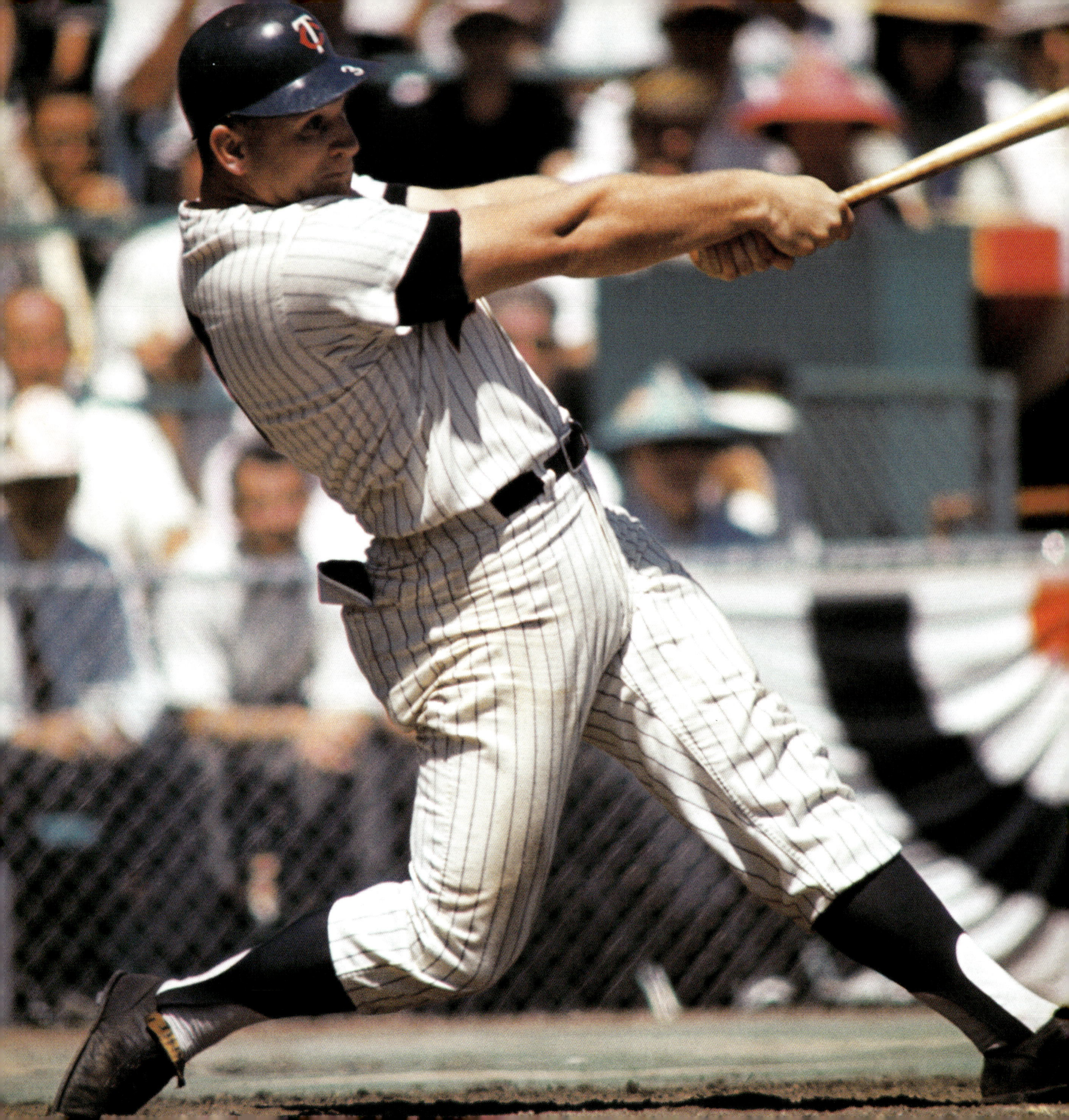

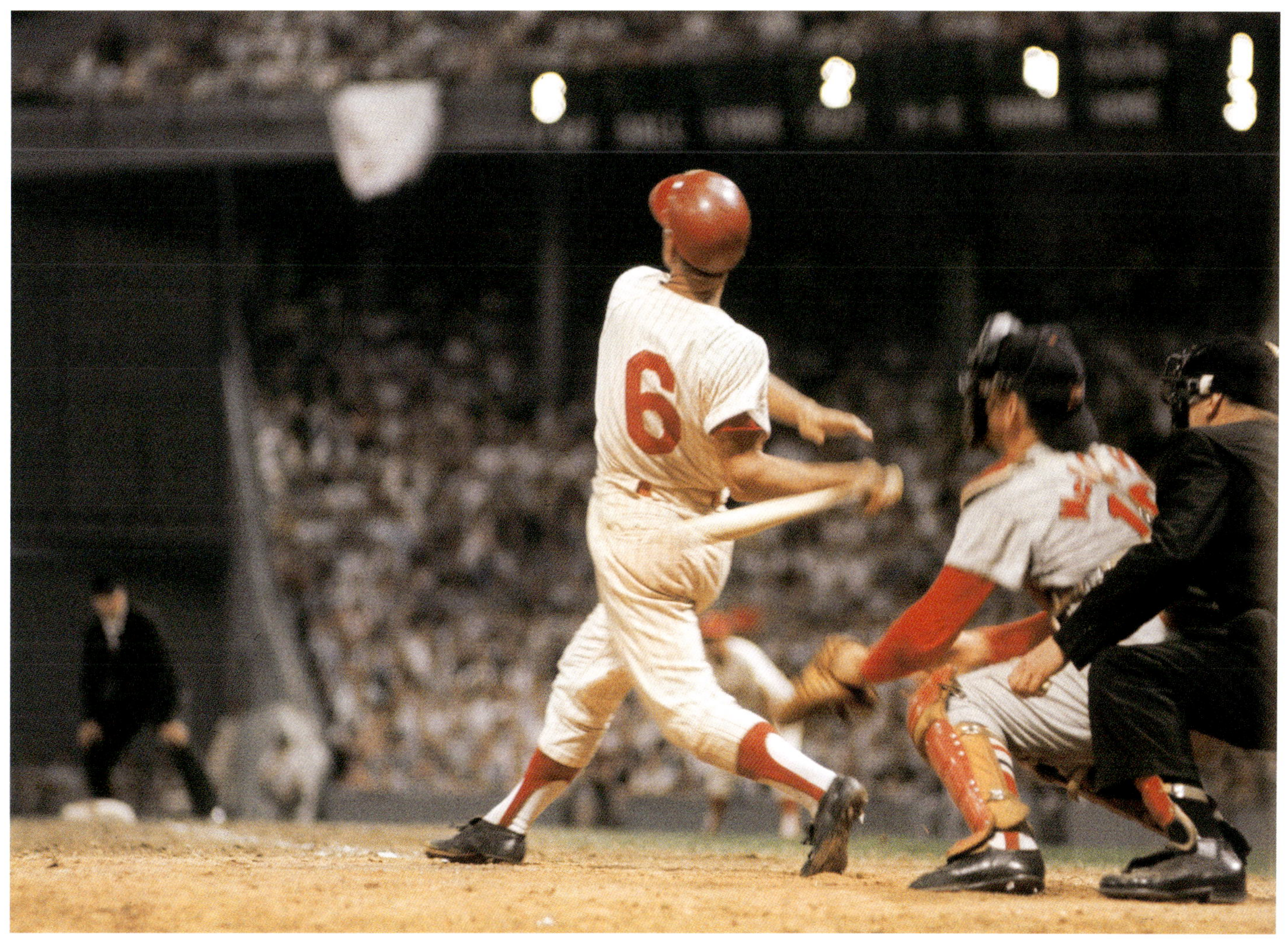

HARMON KILLEBREW, All-Star Game, Minneapolis, 1965 (LEFT)

JOHN CALLISON, Philadelphia, 1964 (ABOVE)

CARL YASTRZEMSKI, World Series, Fenway Park, Boston, 1967 (OVERLEAF)

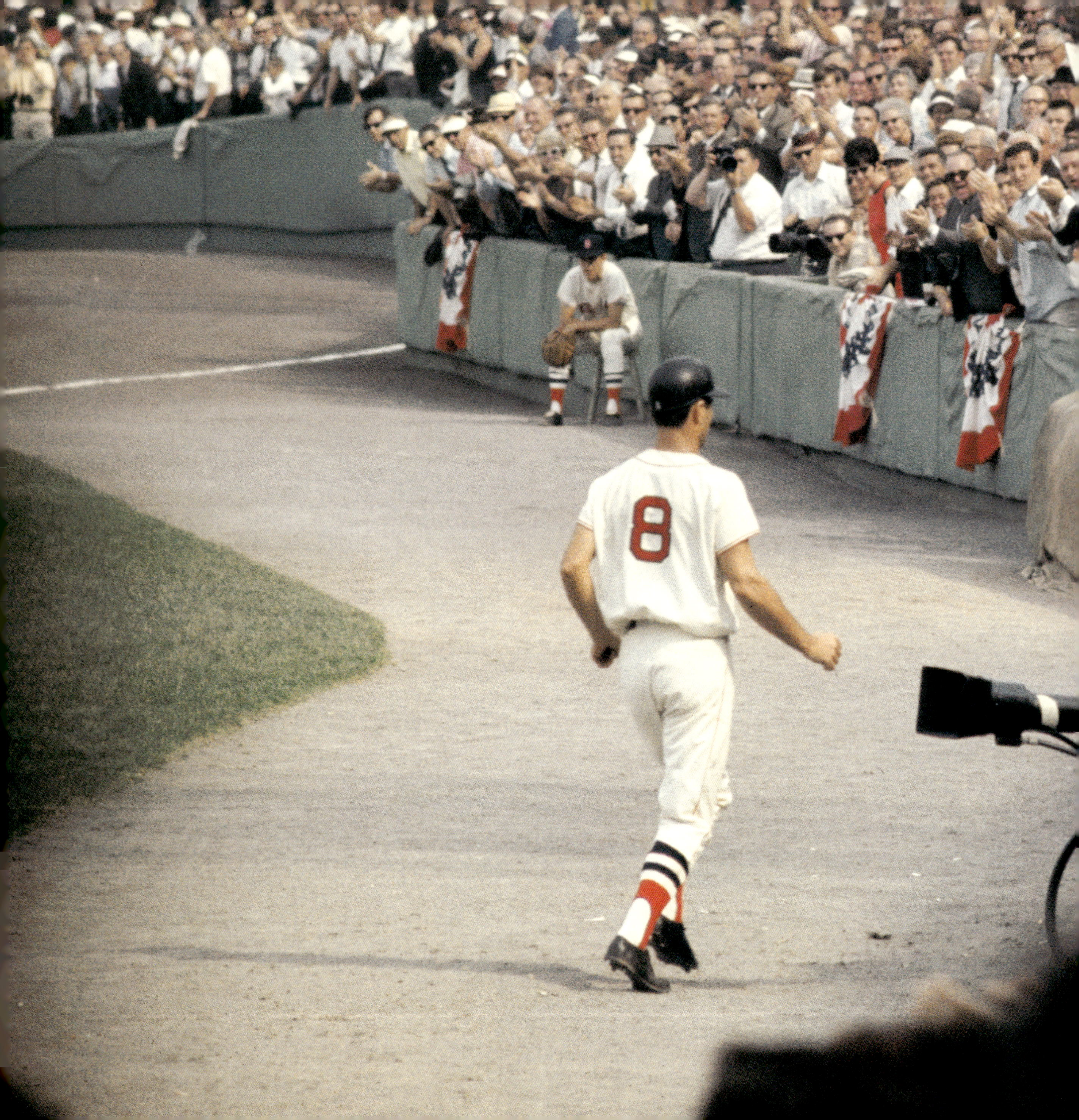

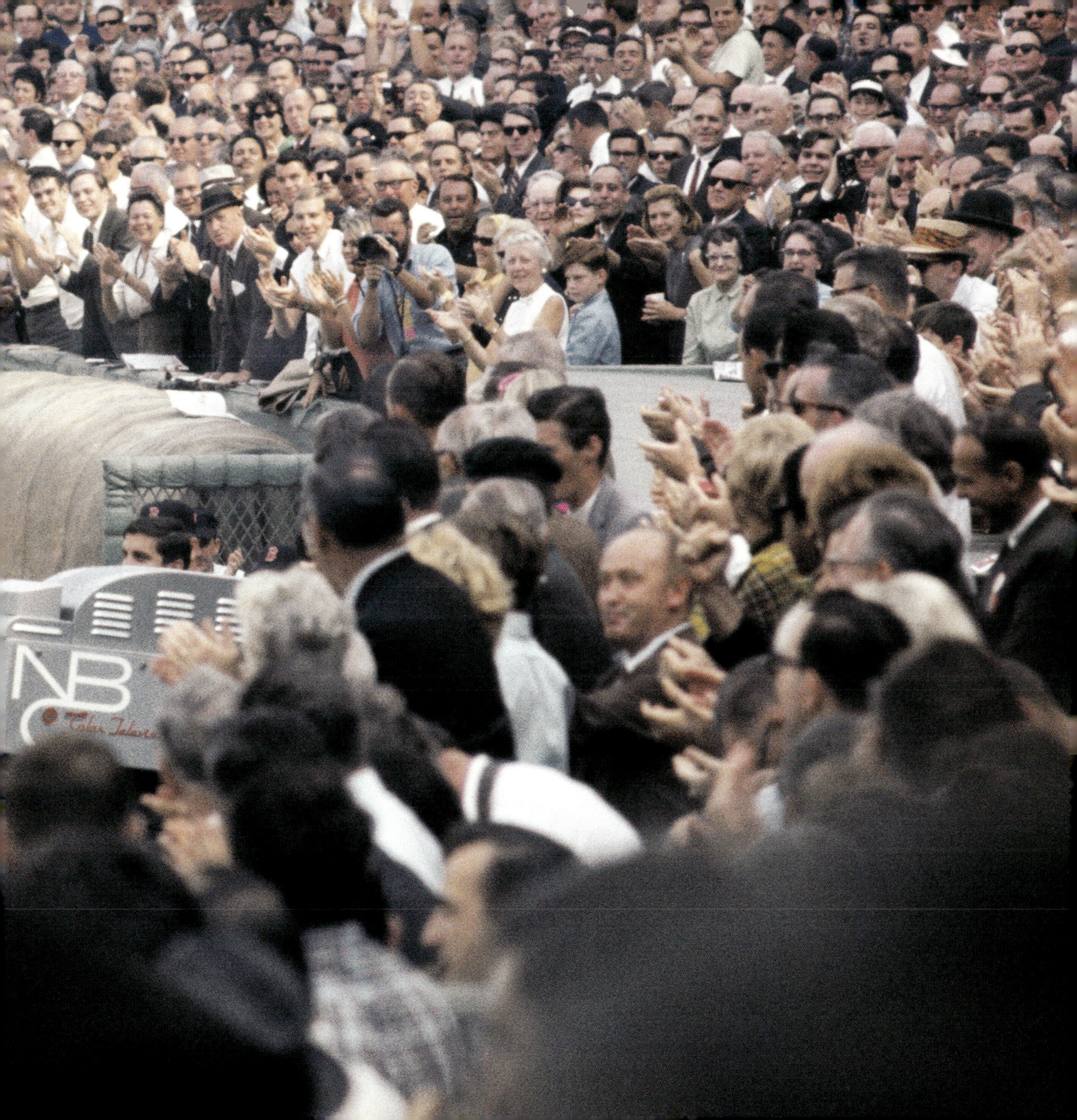
NBC

HANK AARON, Philadelphia, 1963

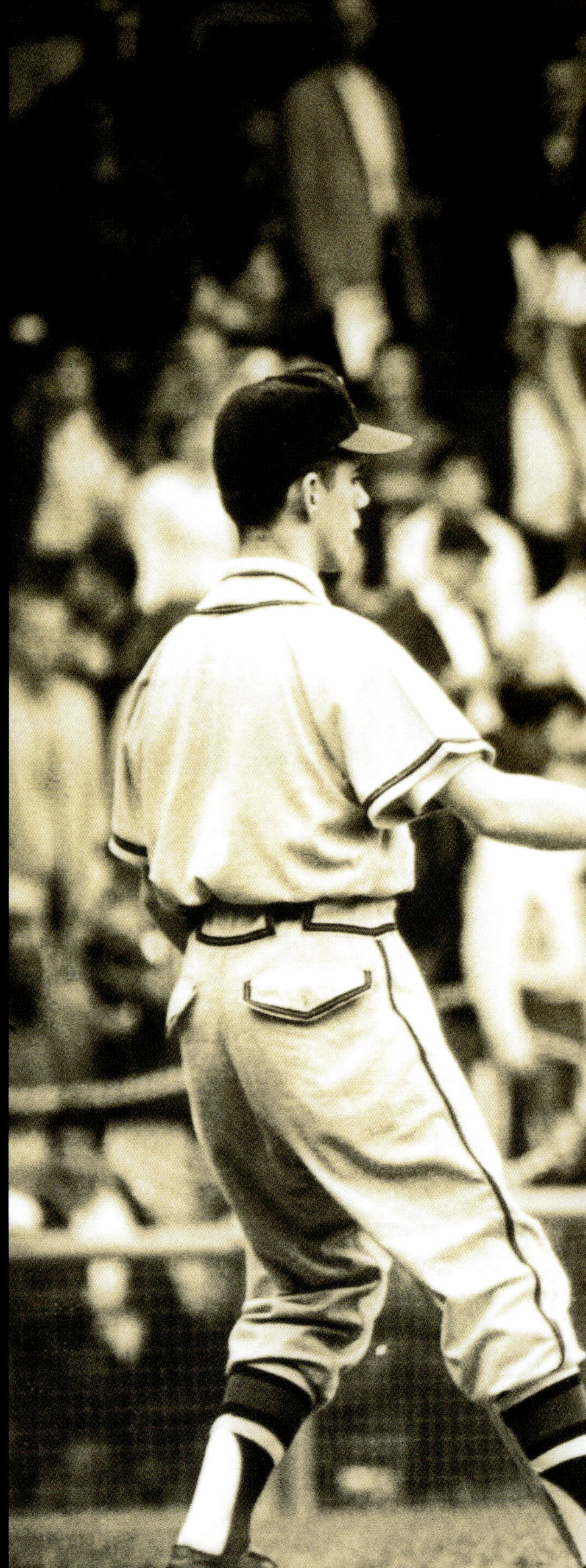

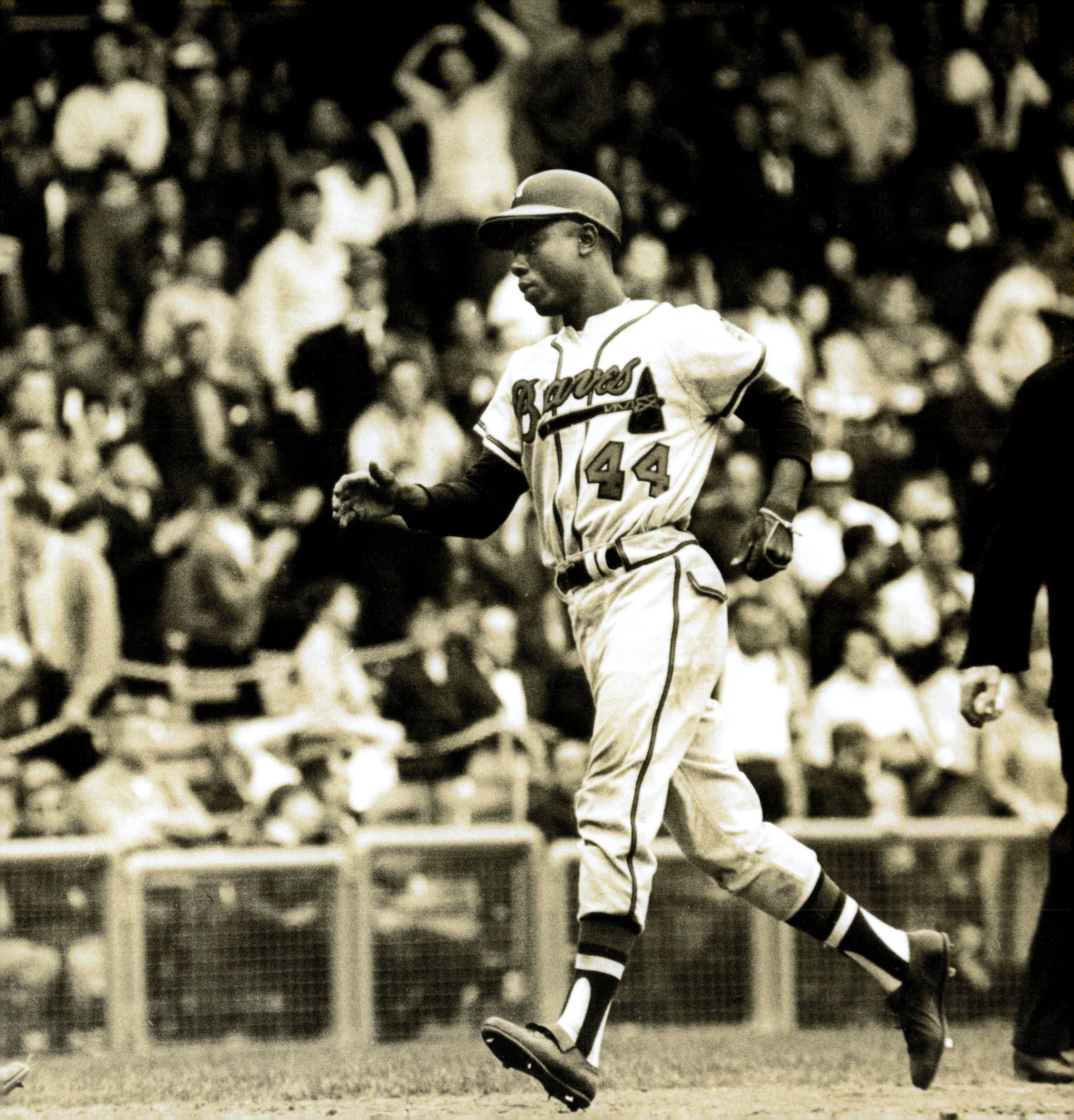
Braves
44

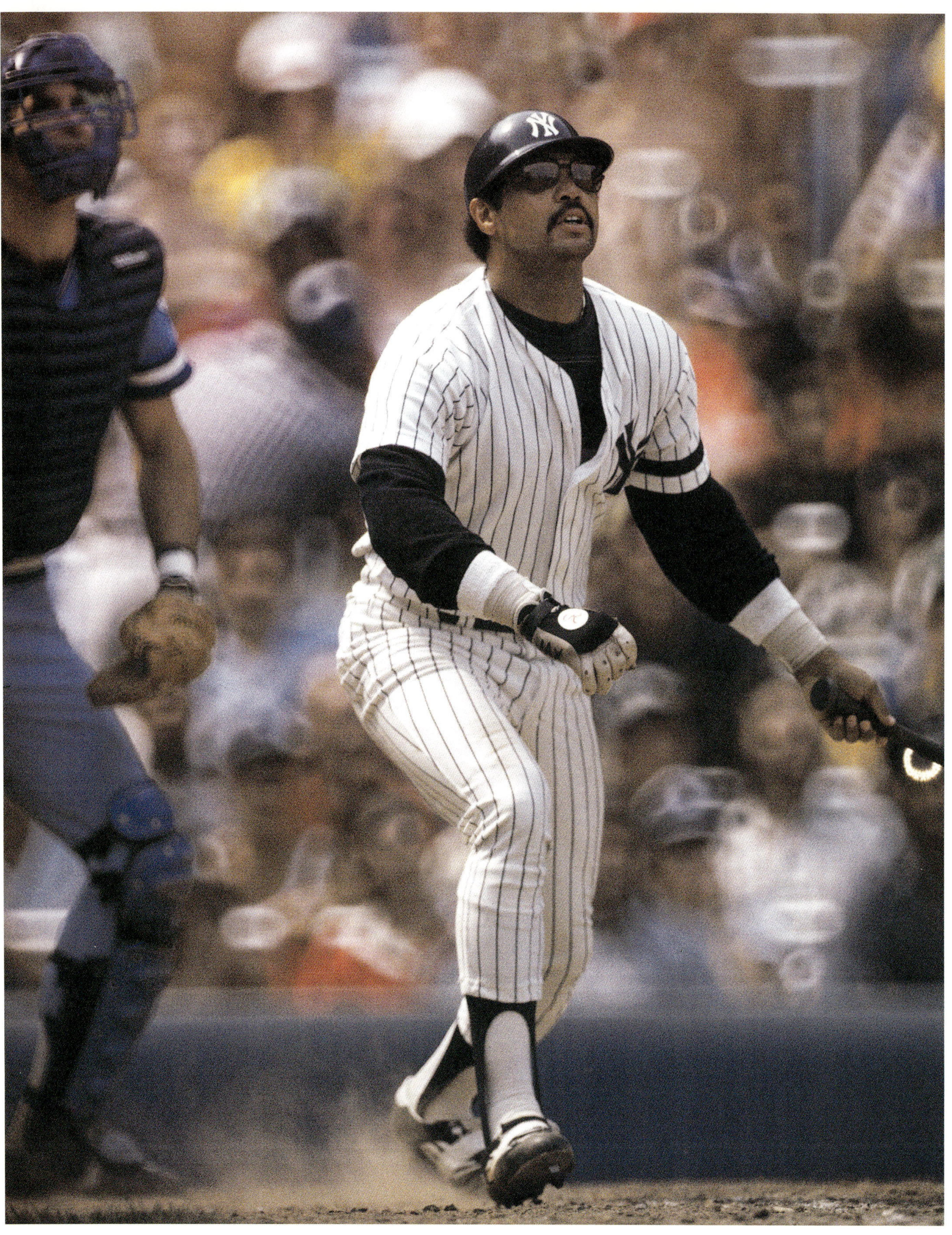

REGGIE JACKSON, Yankee Stadium, 1980

BROOKS ROBINSON, Detroit, 1967

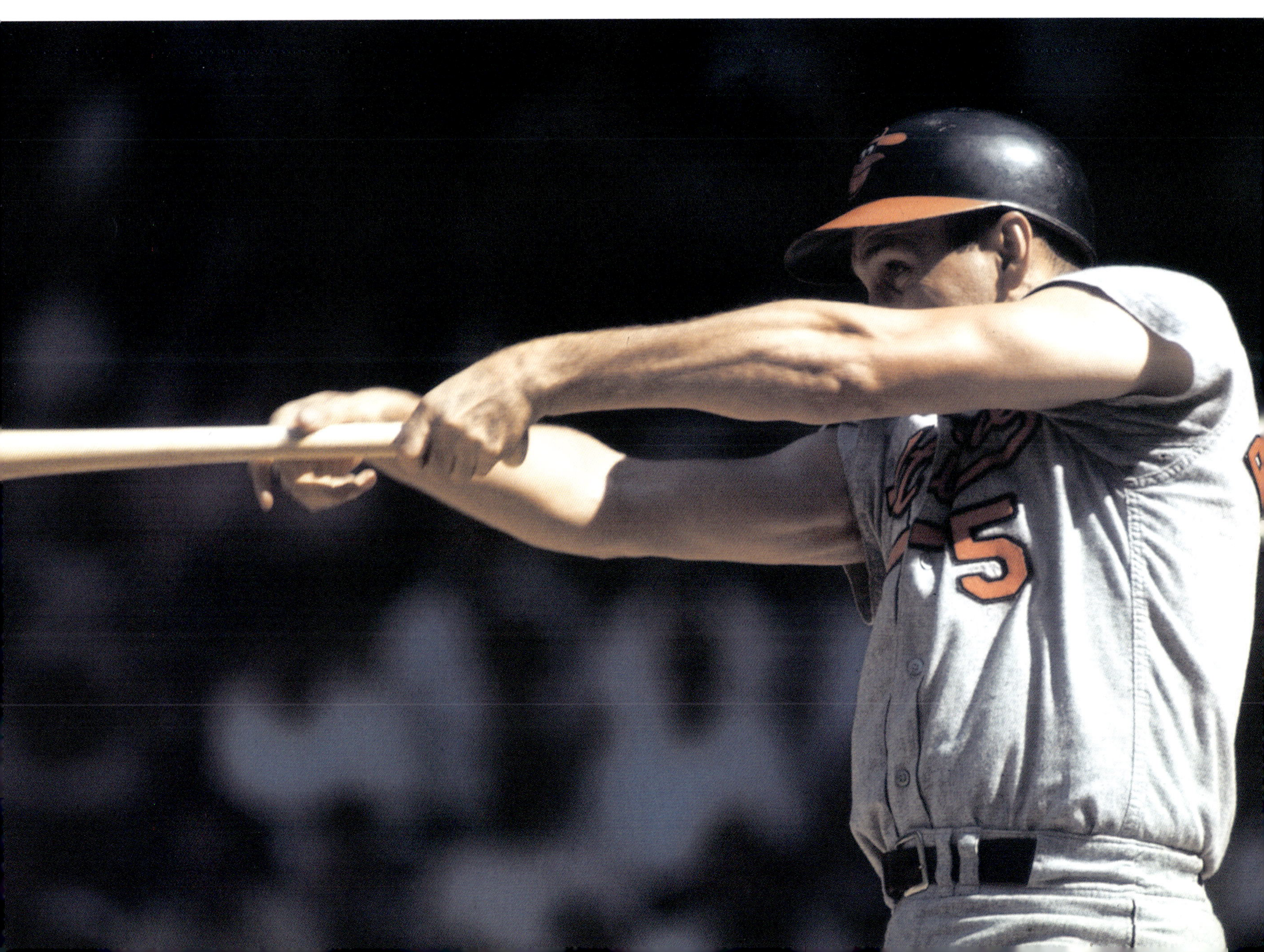

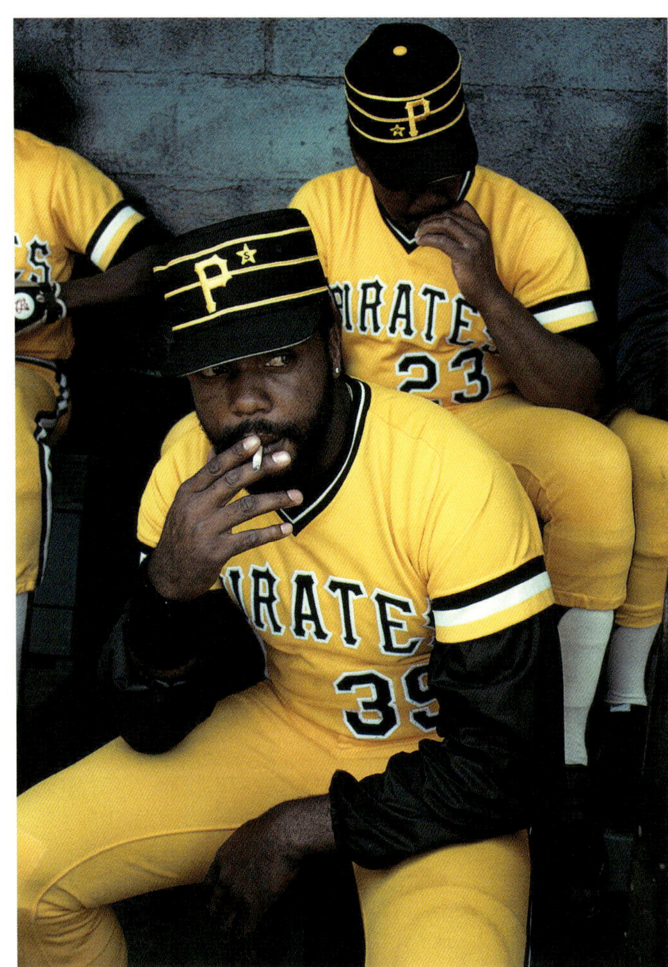

DAVE PARKER, Bradenton, Florida, 1980 (ABOVE)

WILLIE STARGELL, Montreal, 1977 (RIGHT)

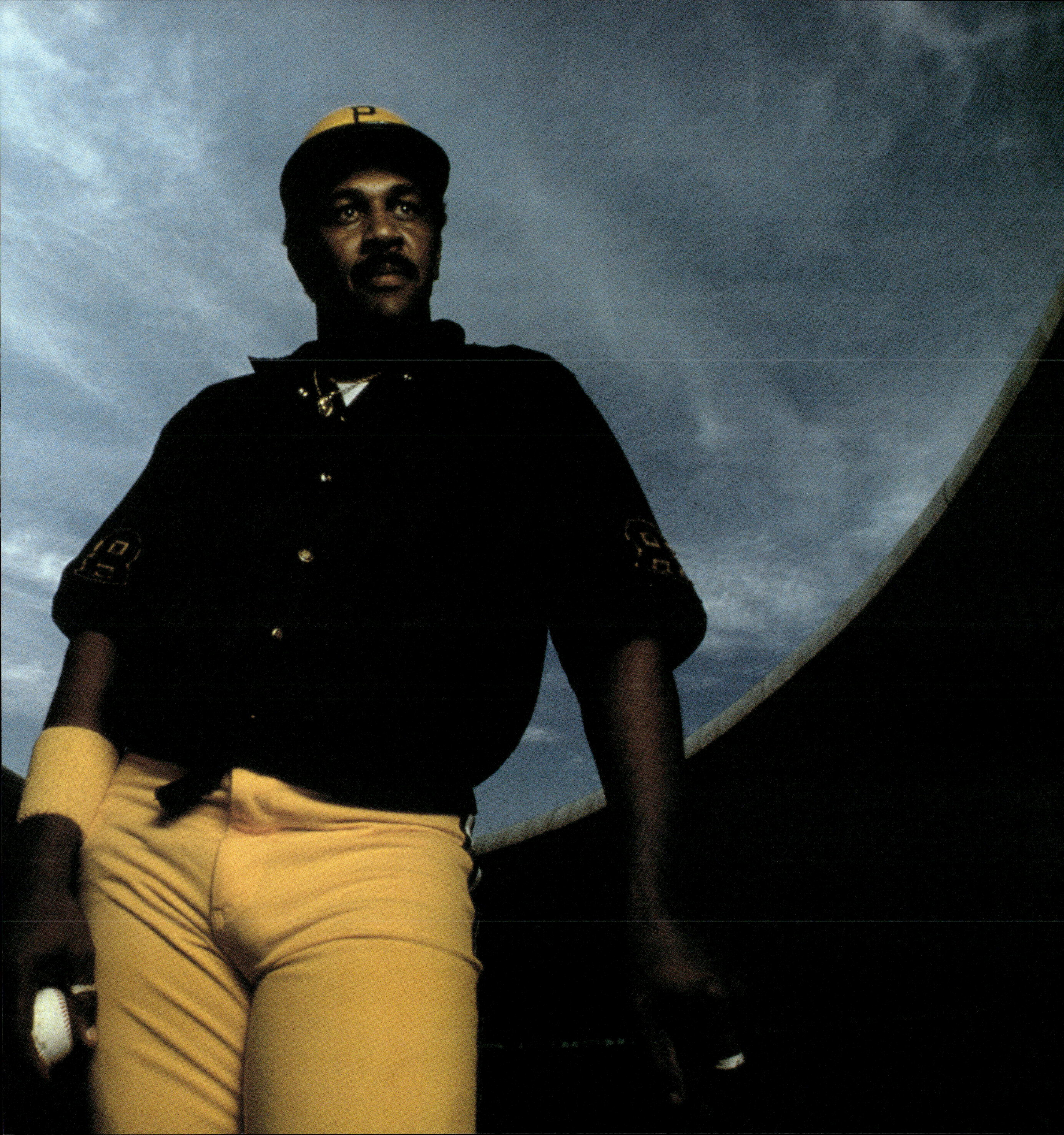

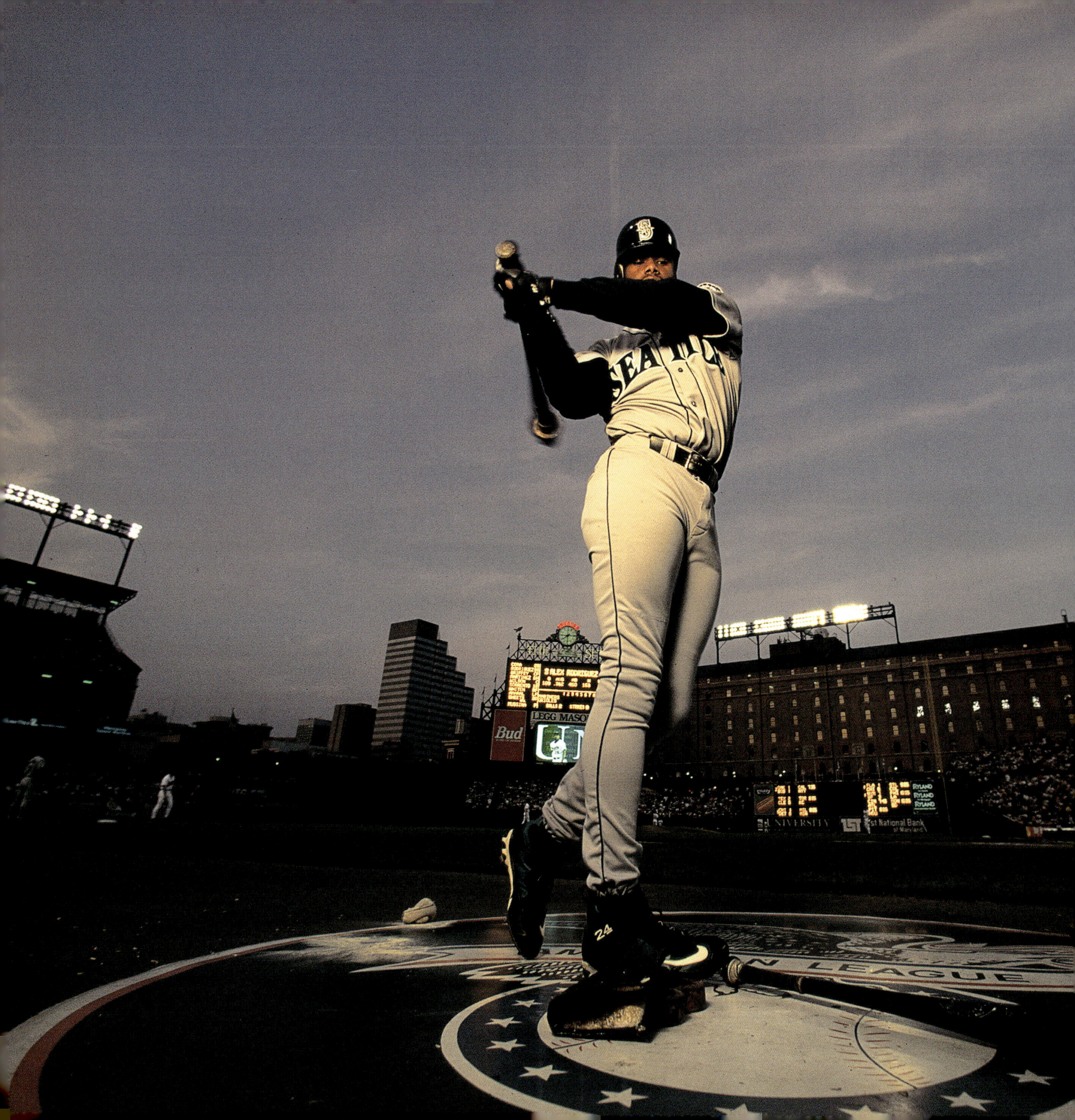
ALEX RODRIGUEZ
Bud
RYLAND
1st National Bank of Maryland

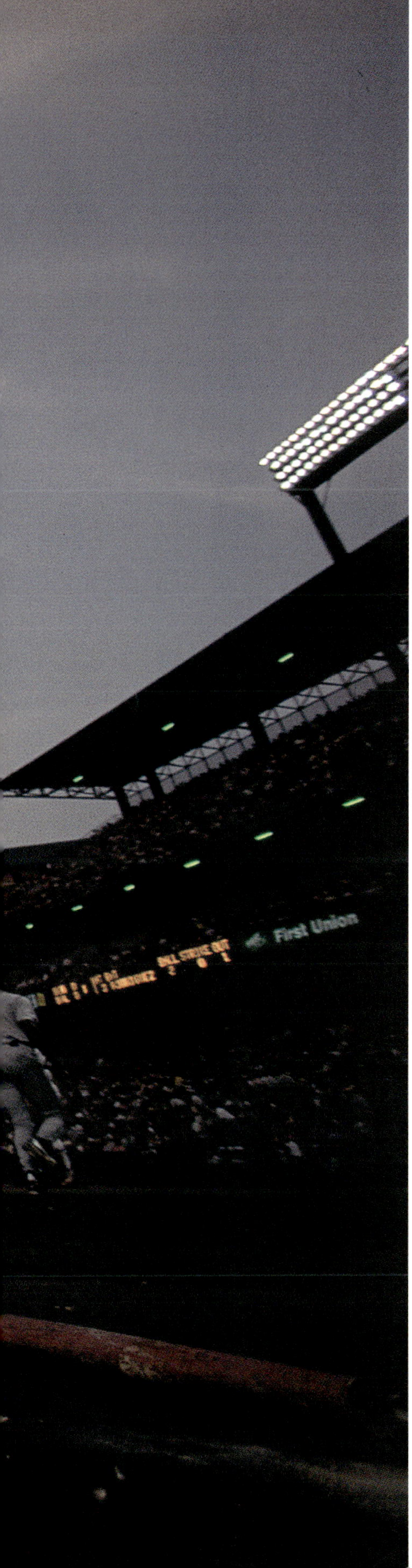

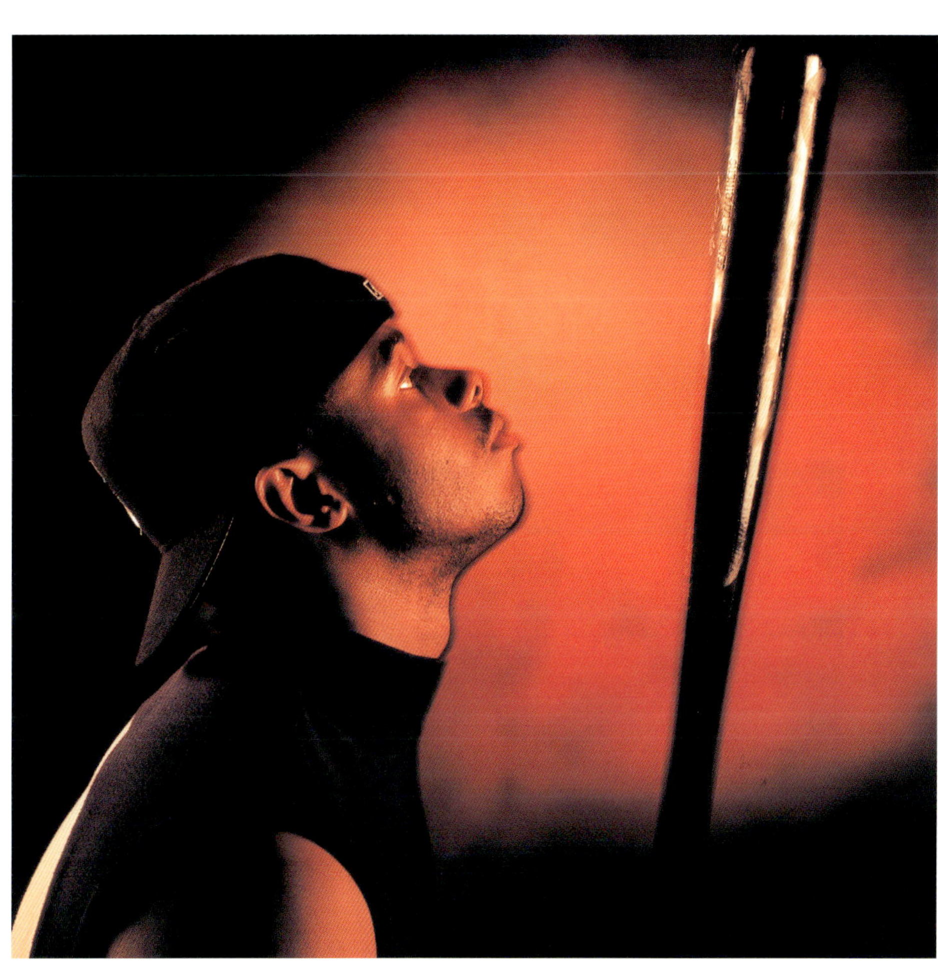

KEN GRIFFEY JR., Baltimore, 1995, and at Chicago, 1994 (ABOVE)

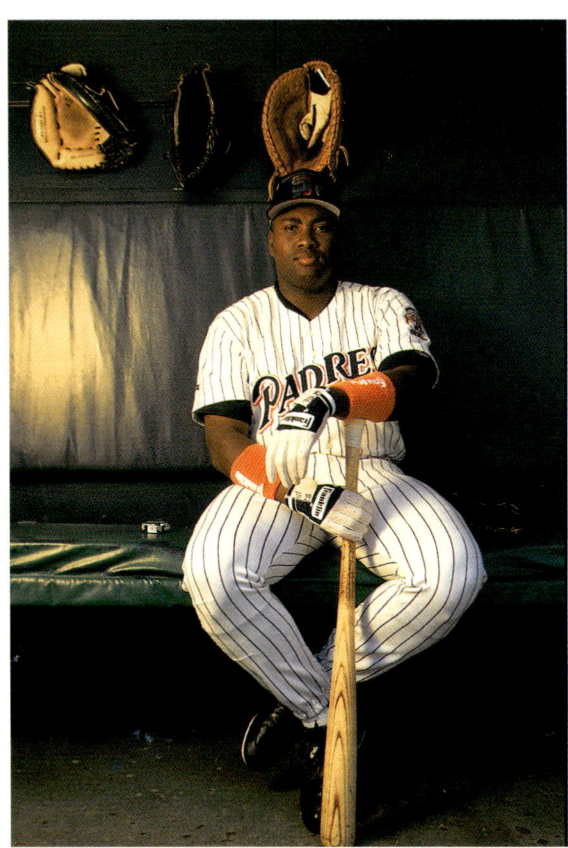

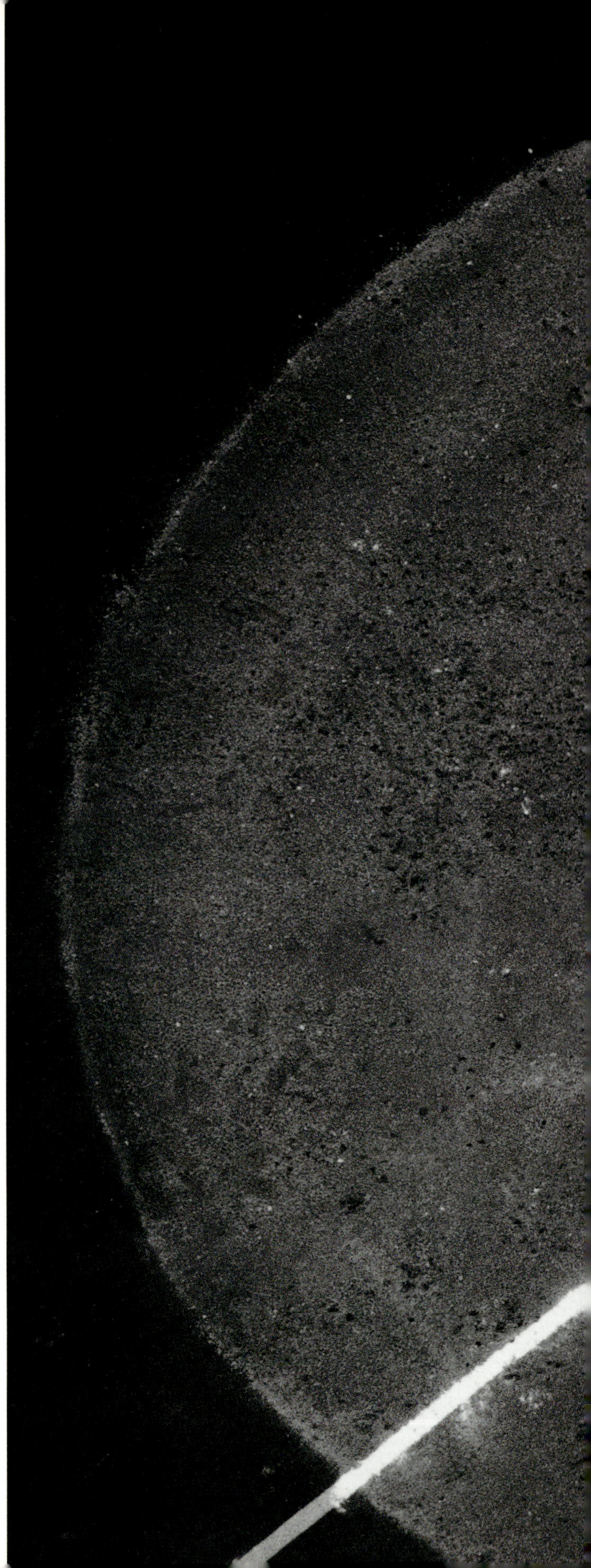

TONY GWYNN, San Diego, 1993 (ABOVE)

KEN GRIFFEY JR., Seattle, 1996 (RIGHT)

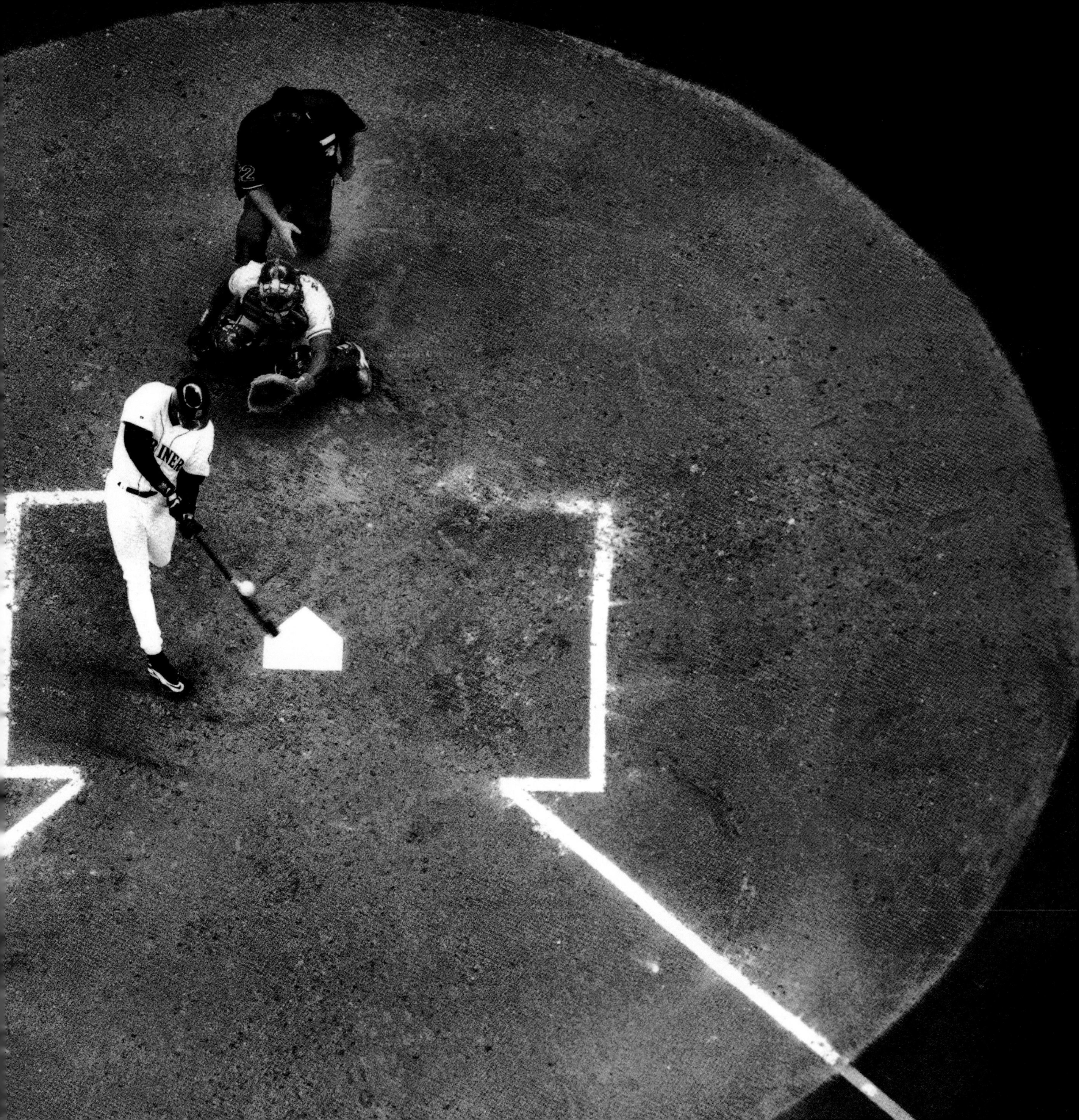

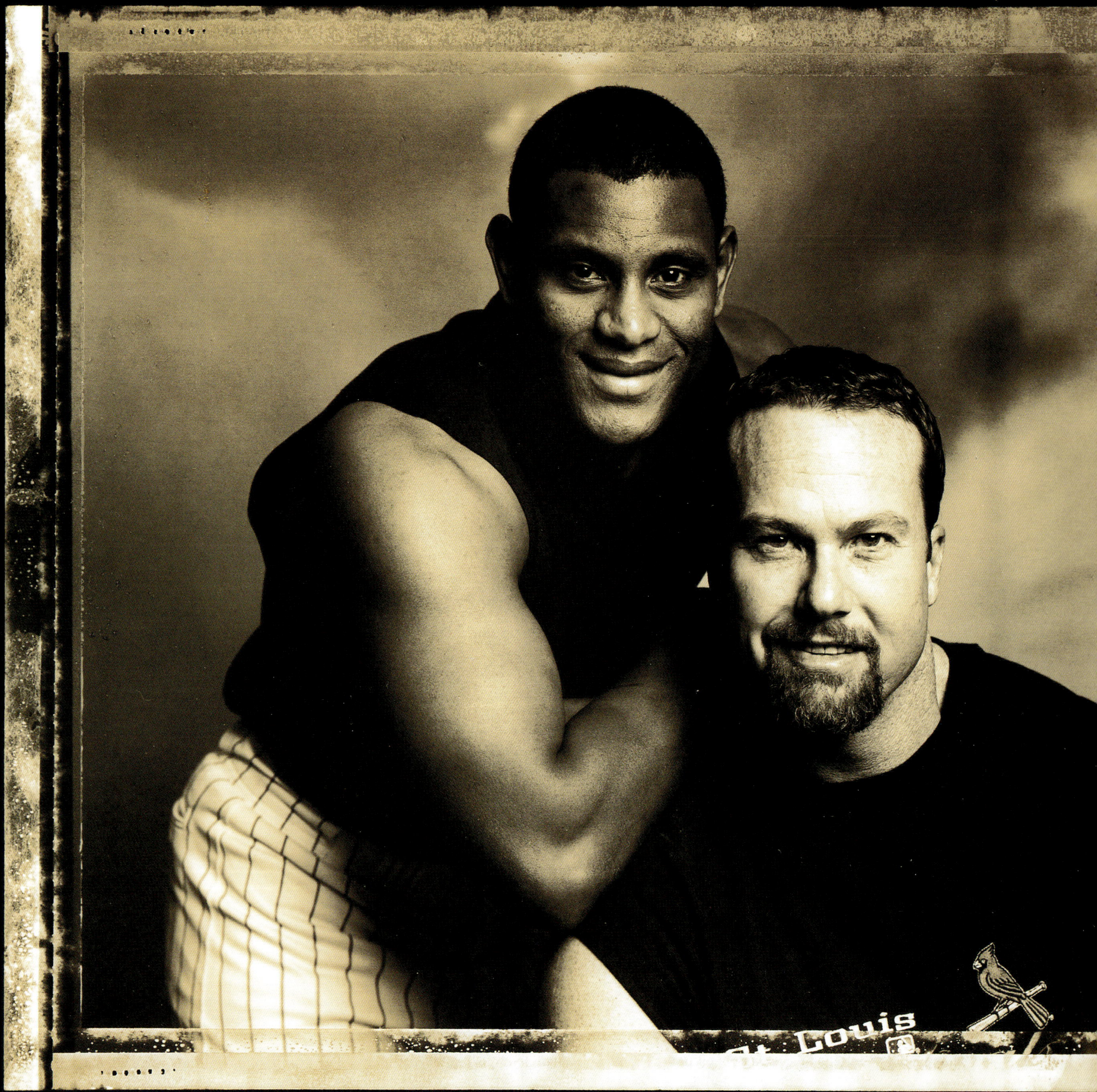
Louis

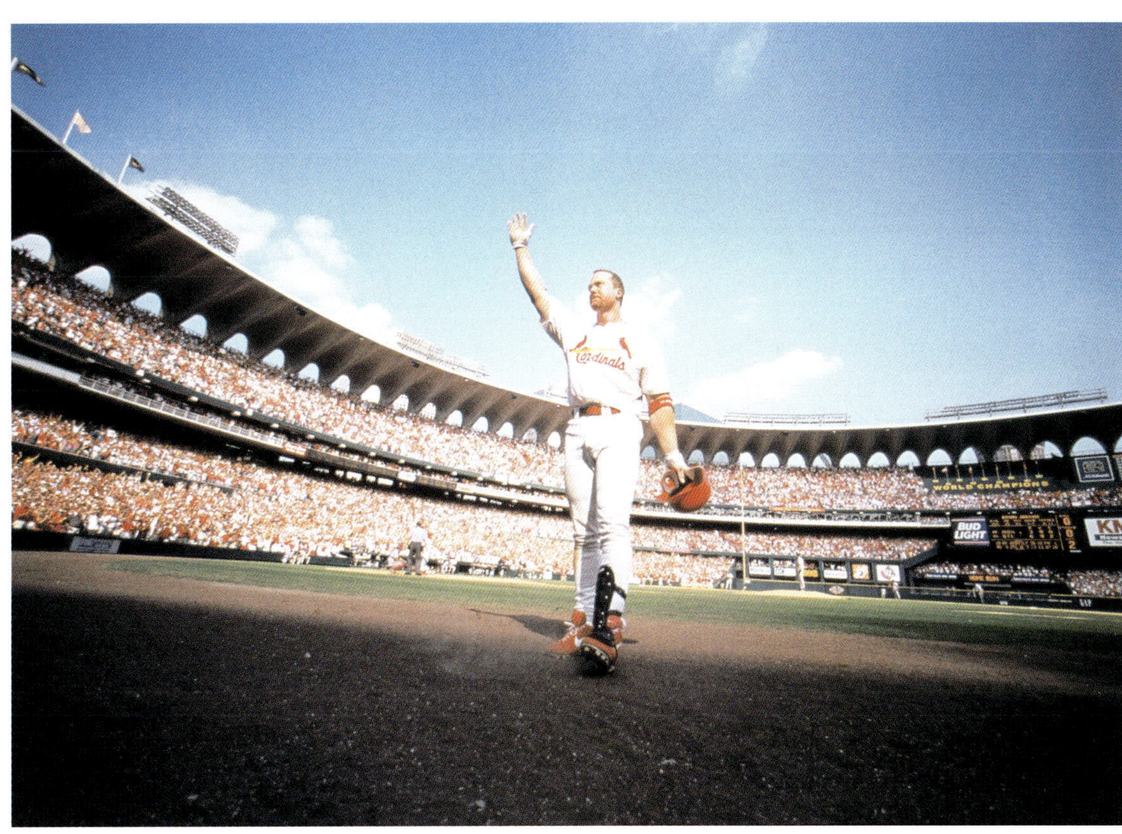

SAMMY SOSA AND MARK MCGWIRE, Los Angeles, 1999

MARK MCGWIRE after hitting his 70th home run, St. Louis, 1998

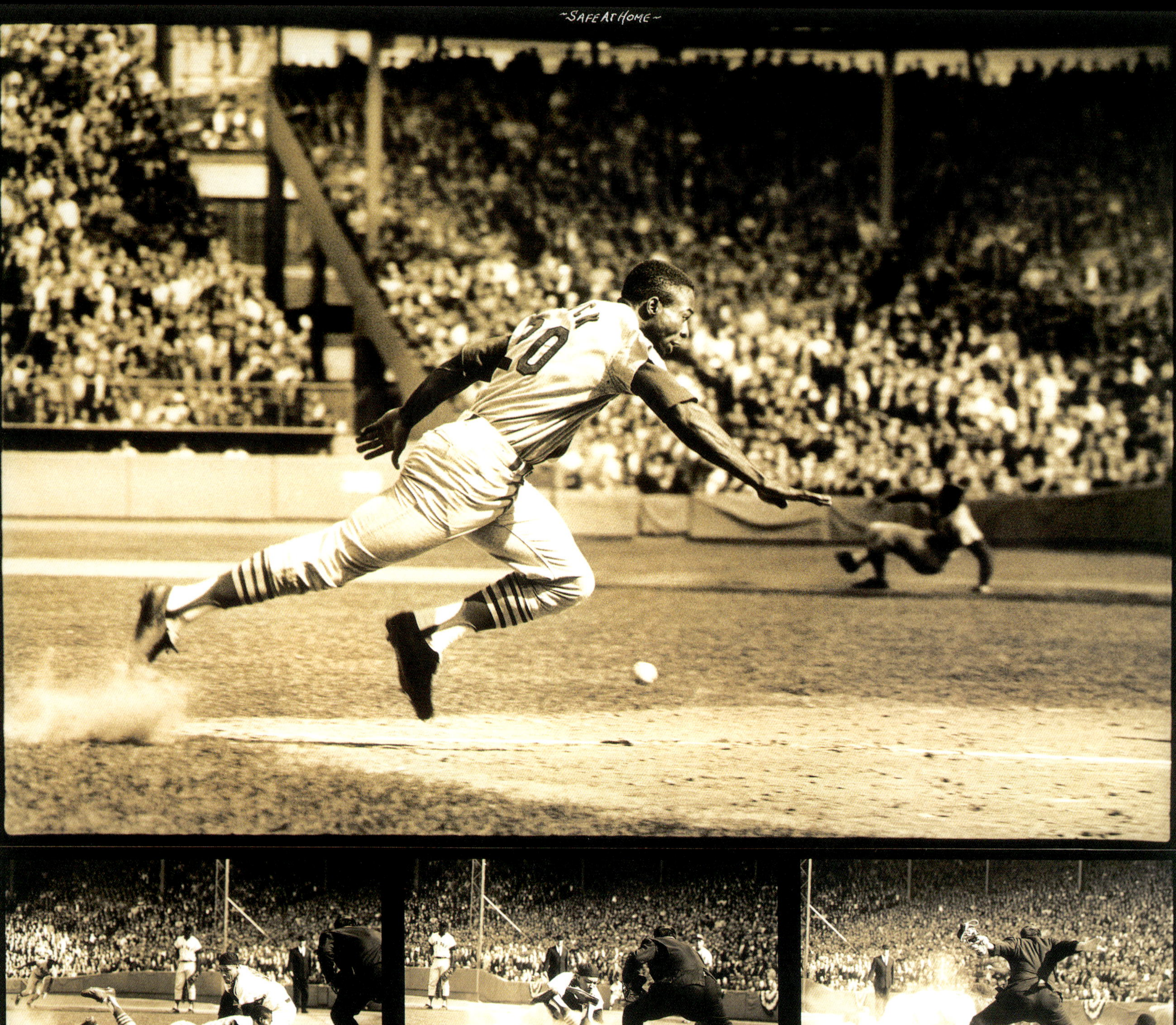

BASE RUNNERS

LOU BROCK, World Series, Boston, 1967

BASE RUNNING CAN BE BALLET or a cloud of dust. Sometimes both. Here is Phillies shortstop Bobby Wine aloft, Nureyev with a glove, while Reds outfielder Marty Keough kicks up a storm. "You can't pose these shots, you've got to anticipate them," Iooss says. "If you think there's going to be a play at second base, you prefocus on second base and wait for it to happen. Sometimes it does, sometimes it doesn't. If the base runner keeps going to third or to home, you try to refocus at third or at home to get the decisive moment." Base running is often a forgotten art. The ability to steal bases isn't always the difference between a good or bad base runner. With some players, it's instinct. Knowing when to steal, when to try to take the extra base, sometimes knowing when to slide. And how to slide.

Just as important is the instinct of the infielders or the catcher in trying to tag out a base runner. Knowing when to simply put down their glove (with the ball in it) and let the base runner slide into it. Knowing when to slap a quick tag on the base runner, if not a phantom tag to fool the umpire into calling out the base runner.

Two base-running teammates are seldom seen in the same frame, but Iooss once caught Giants teammates Willie Mays and Orlando Cepeda together.

Mays, who has slid home with a run, is on his knees while turning to check the whereabouts of Cepeda, about to slide for another San Francisco run. The throw, if there was one, is either much too late or already cut off because Phillies catcher Bob Oldis is standing in surrender, not crouched to brace himself for a collision.

"Other times," Iooss says, "you just focus on the base runner because you're hoping to portray his speed."

Here is Cardinals outfielder Lou Brock, resembling a leopard leaping out of a tree, about to slide headfirst into home at Fenway Park during Game 6 of the 1967 World Series. As Red Sox catcher Elston Howard takes the throw, Brock disappears in a cloud under umpire Ed Runge's safe sign.

"To get a sequence like that," Iooss says, "you need a motor drive."

Brock had a player's version of a motor drive. Over his career, he stole 50 or more bases in 12 seasons, a major-league record. With 938 steals, he is second to Rickey Henderson on the all-time list; his 118 in 1974 is the National League record; Henderson stole 130 with the Oakland Athletics in 1982.

"And sometimes," Iooss says, "you get a preview of history."

Here is Reds third baseman Chico Ruiz crashing into Phillies catcher Clay Dalrymple at home plate in 1964. Weeks later, in the opener of the ten-game losing streak that would cost the Phillies the pennant, Ruiz surprisingly tried to steal home in the sixth inning with two out and Hall of Fame slugger Frank Robinson at bat. When Dalrymple had to leap to the right to catch right-hander Art Mahaffey's wide pitch, Ruiz scored standing up, the difference in a 1–0 game.

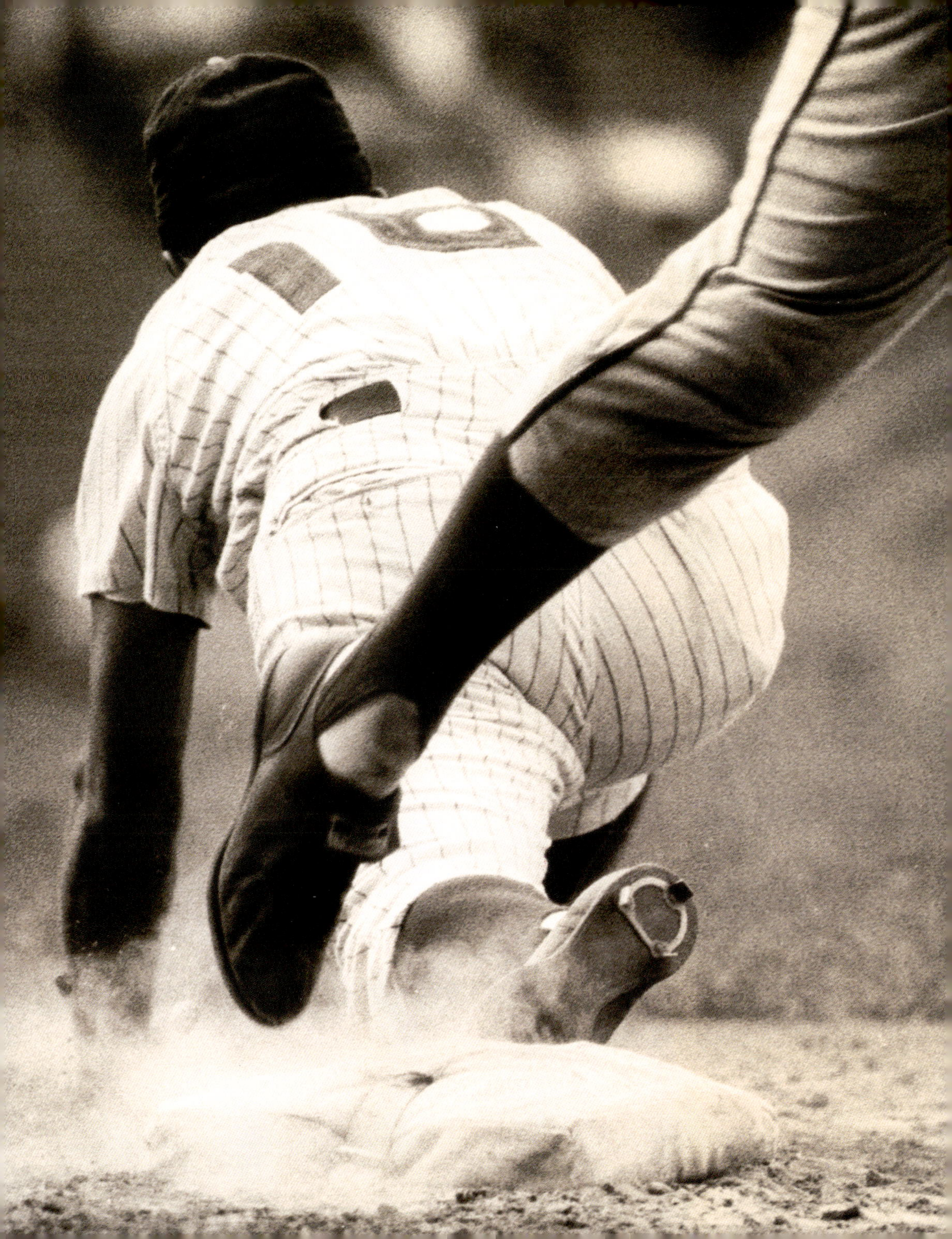

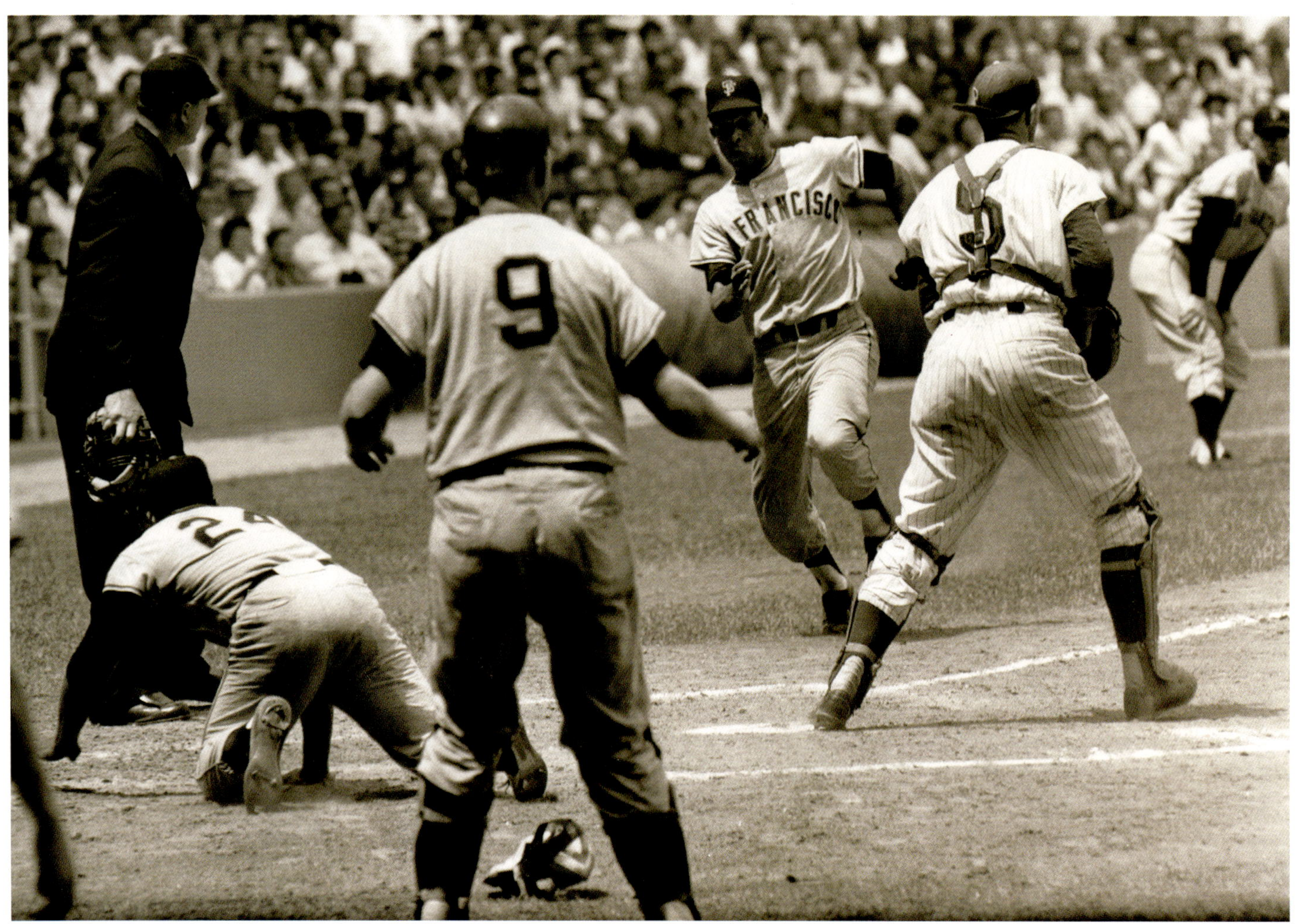

ORLANDO CEPEDA coming home, Philadelphia, 1962

RUBEN AMARO SR., Philadelphia, 1962

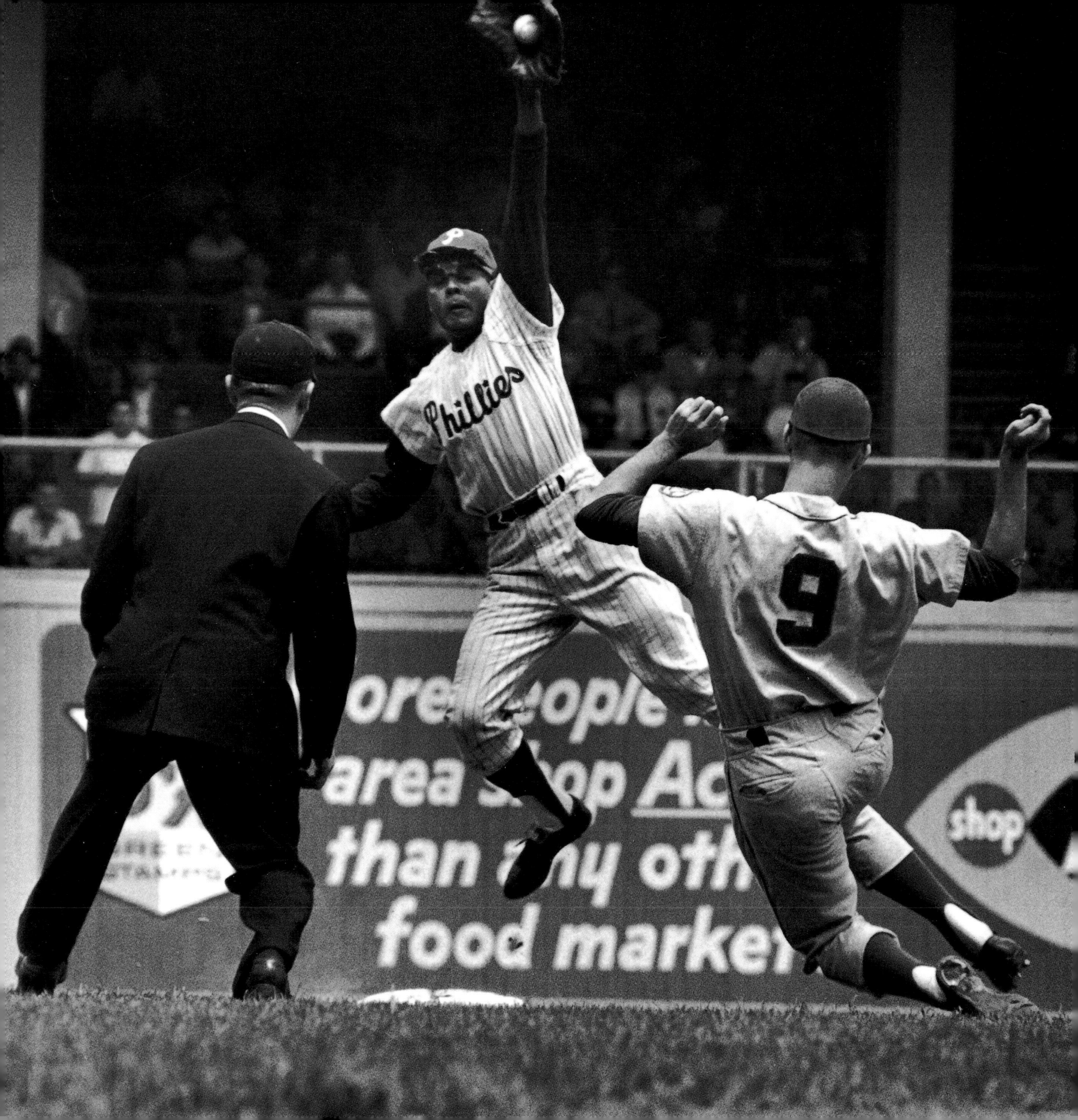

Phillies
9
area
than
food market

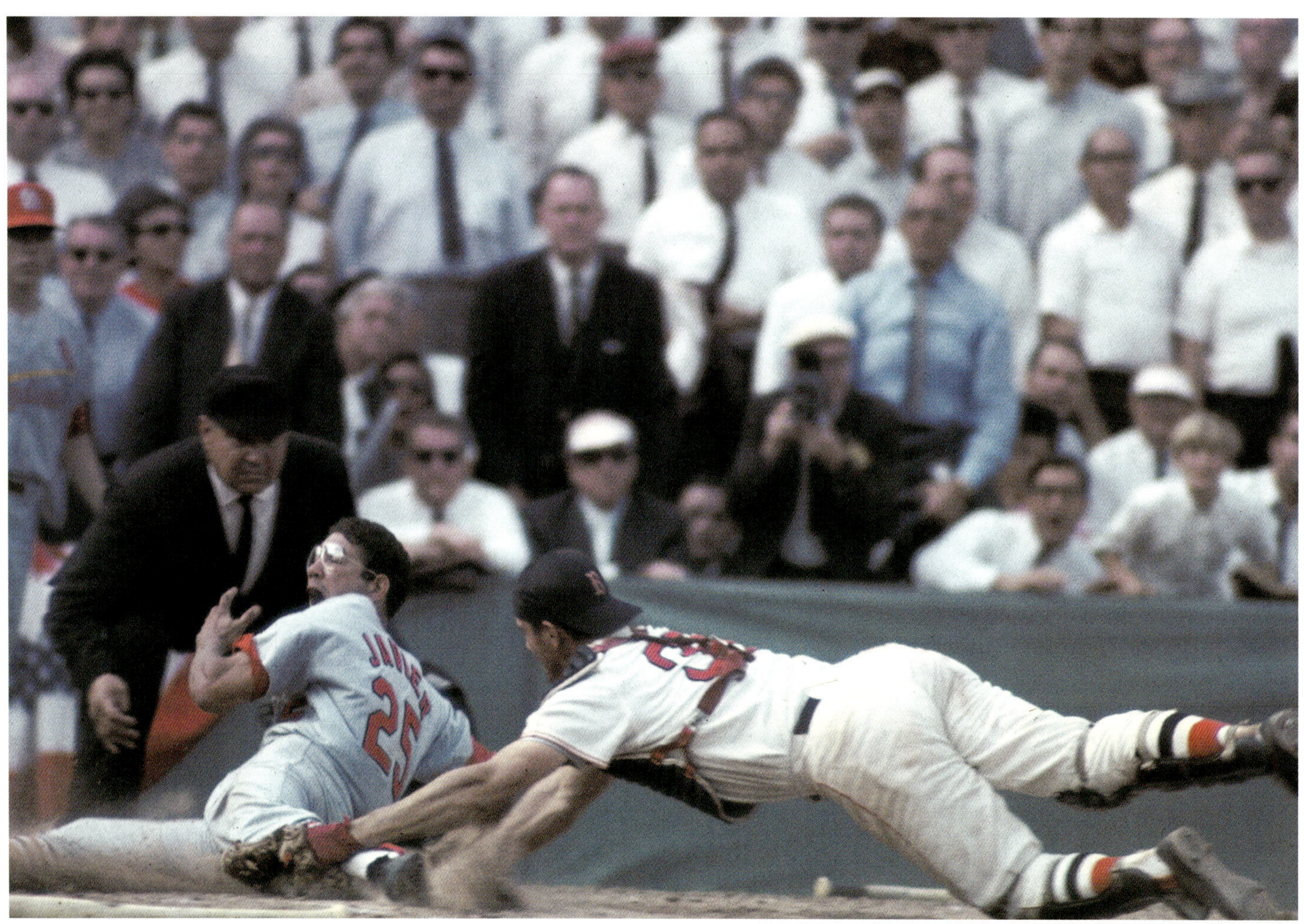

JULIAN JAVIER, World Series, Boston, 1967

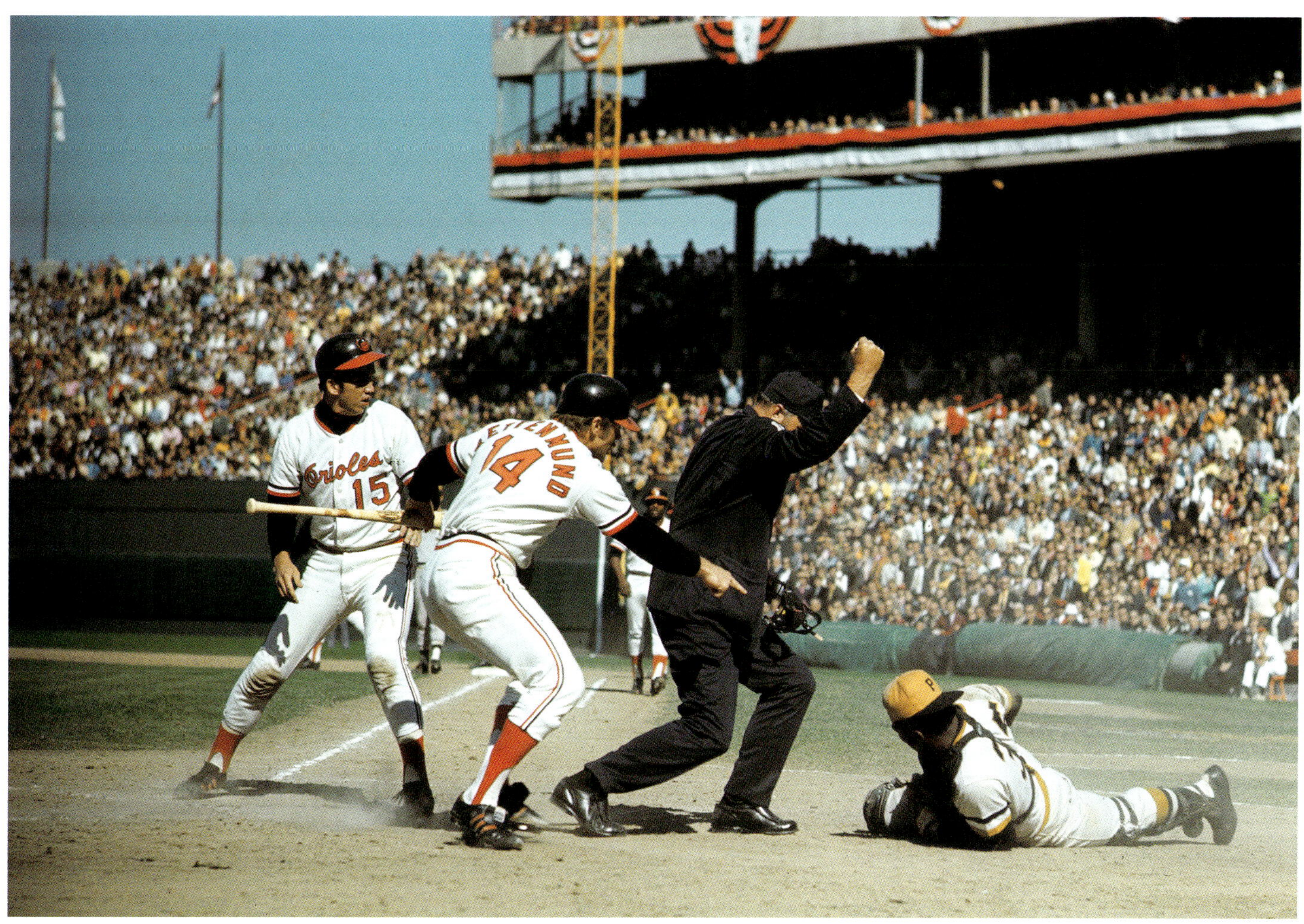

DAVEY JOHNSON, MERV RETTENMUND, MANNY SANGUILLEN, World Series, Baltimore, 1971

BROOKS ROBINSON, Detroit, 1966

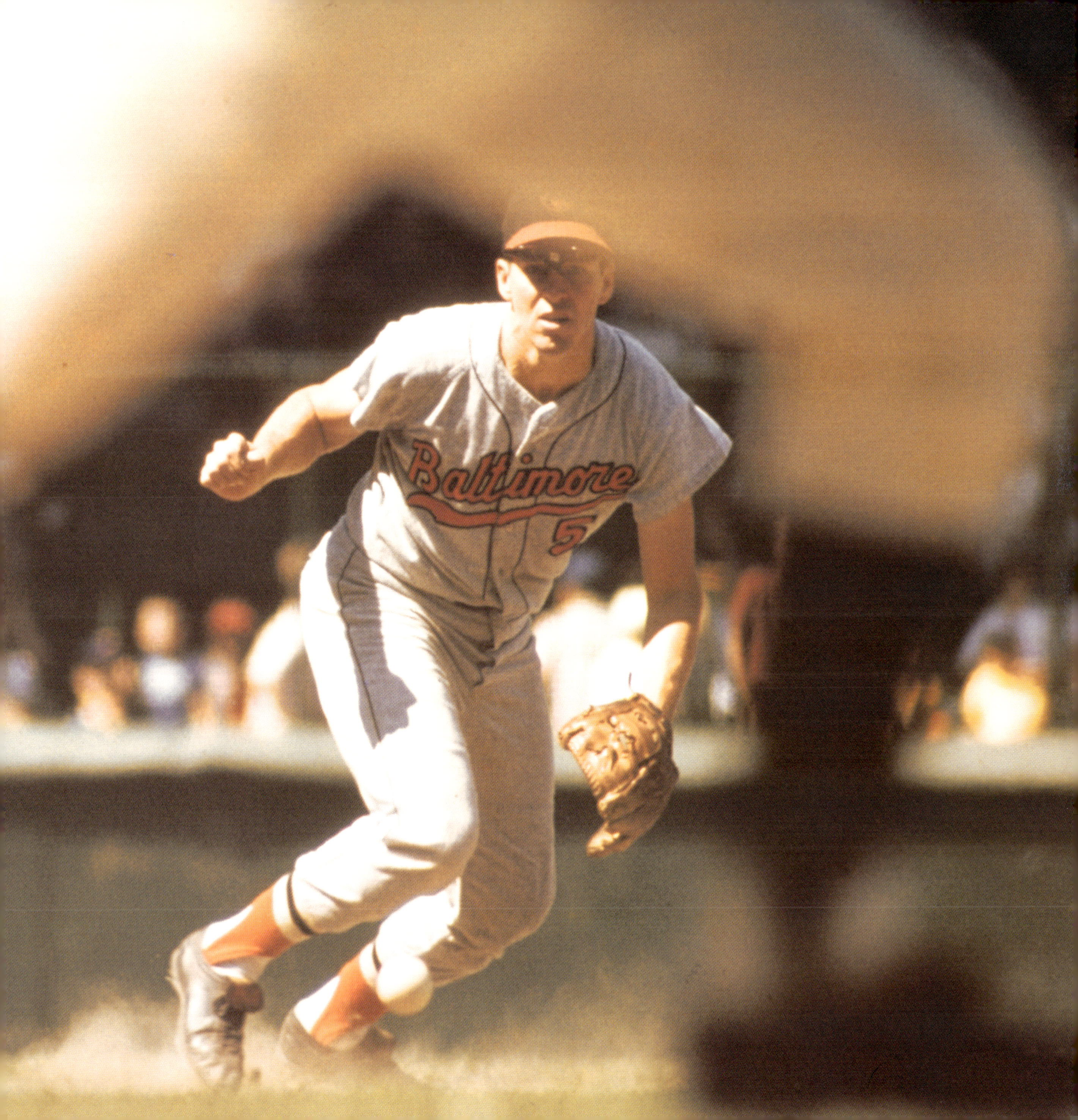
Baltimore
5

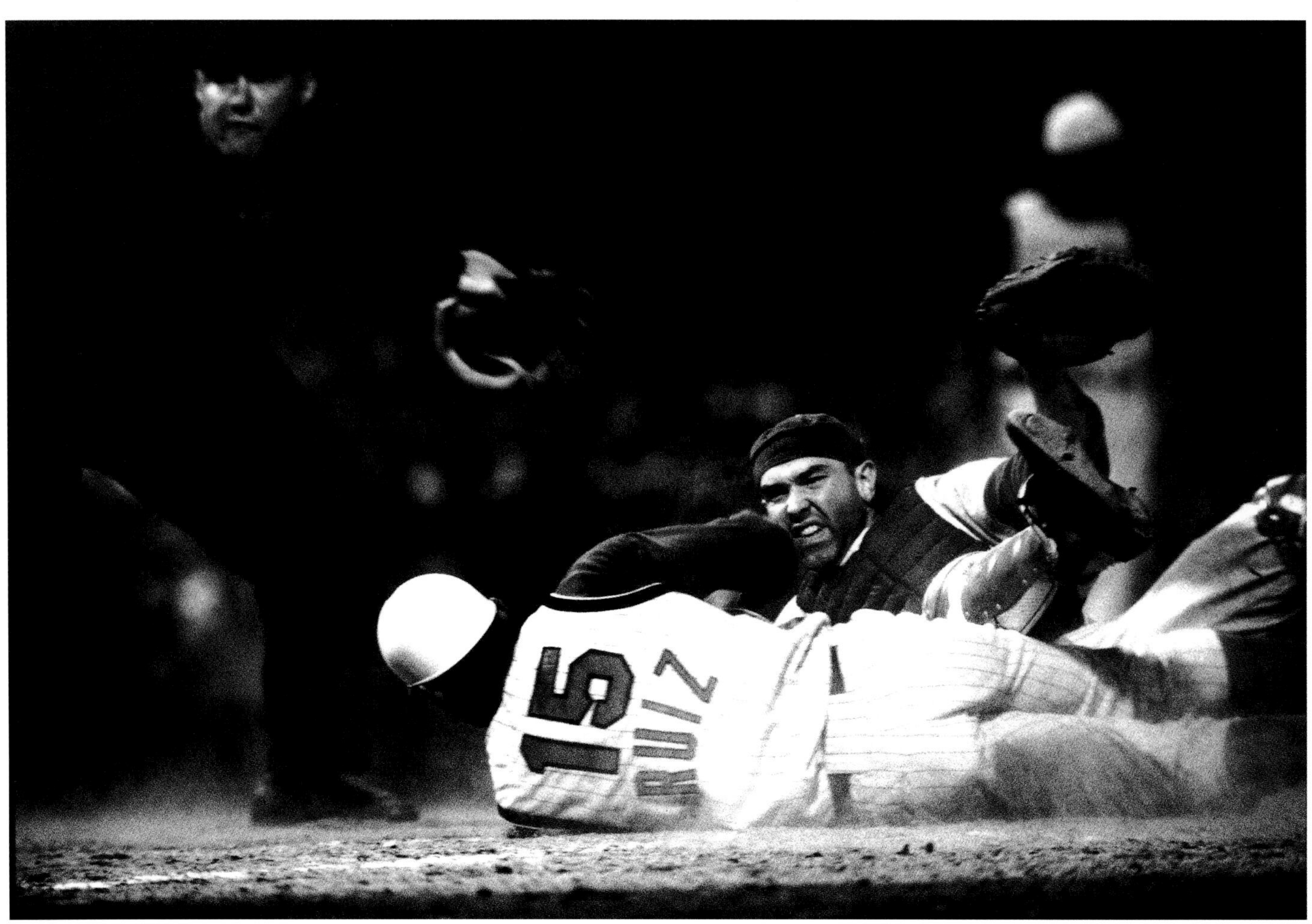

CLAY DALRYMPLE AND CHICO RUIZ, Philadelphia, 1964

BOBBY WINE, Philadelphia, 1962

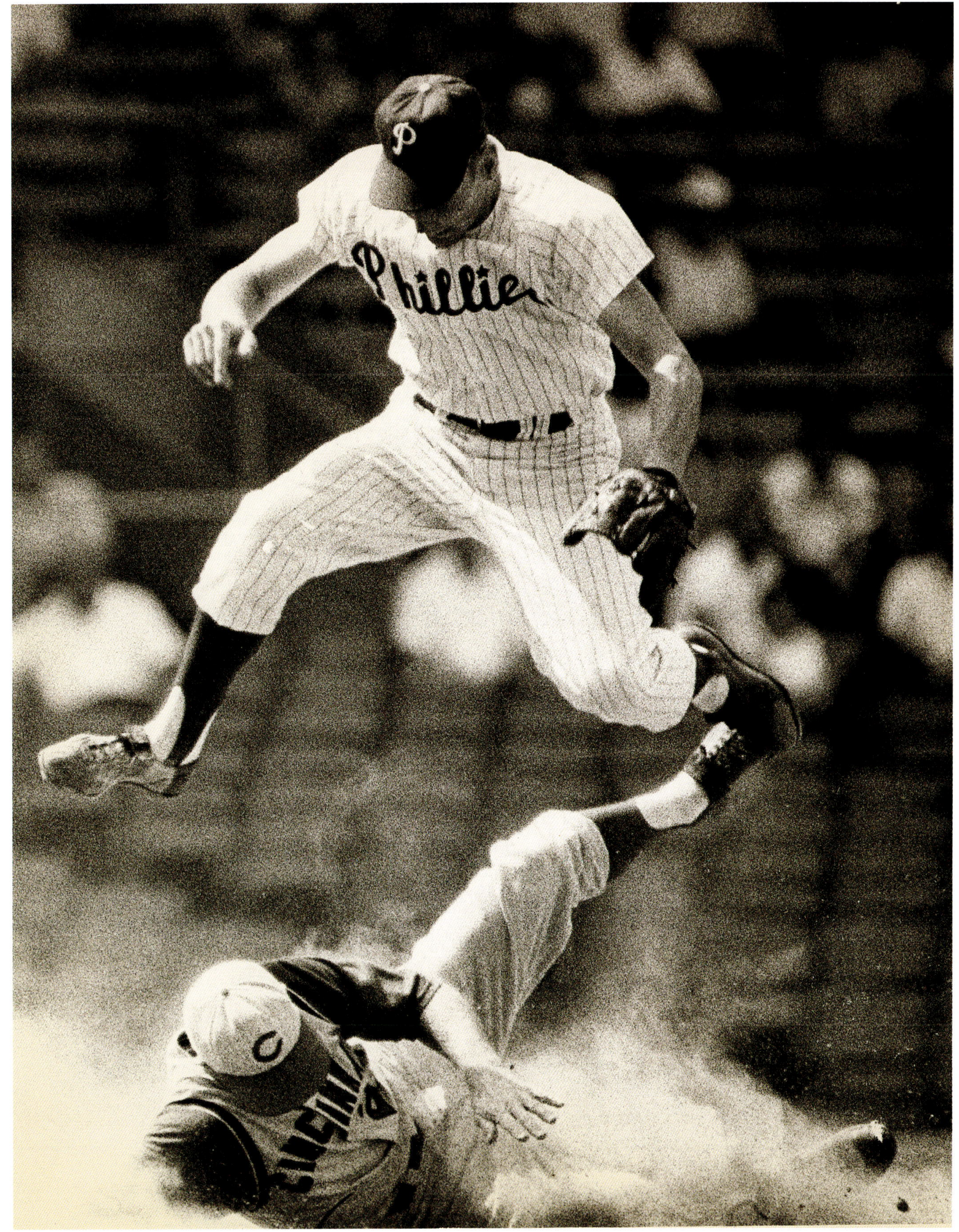

ALAN TRAMMELL, Detroit, 1993

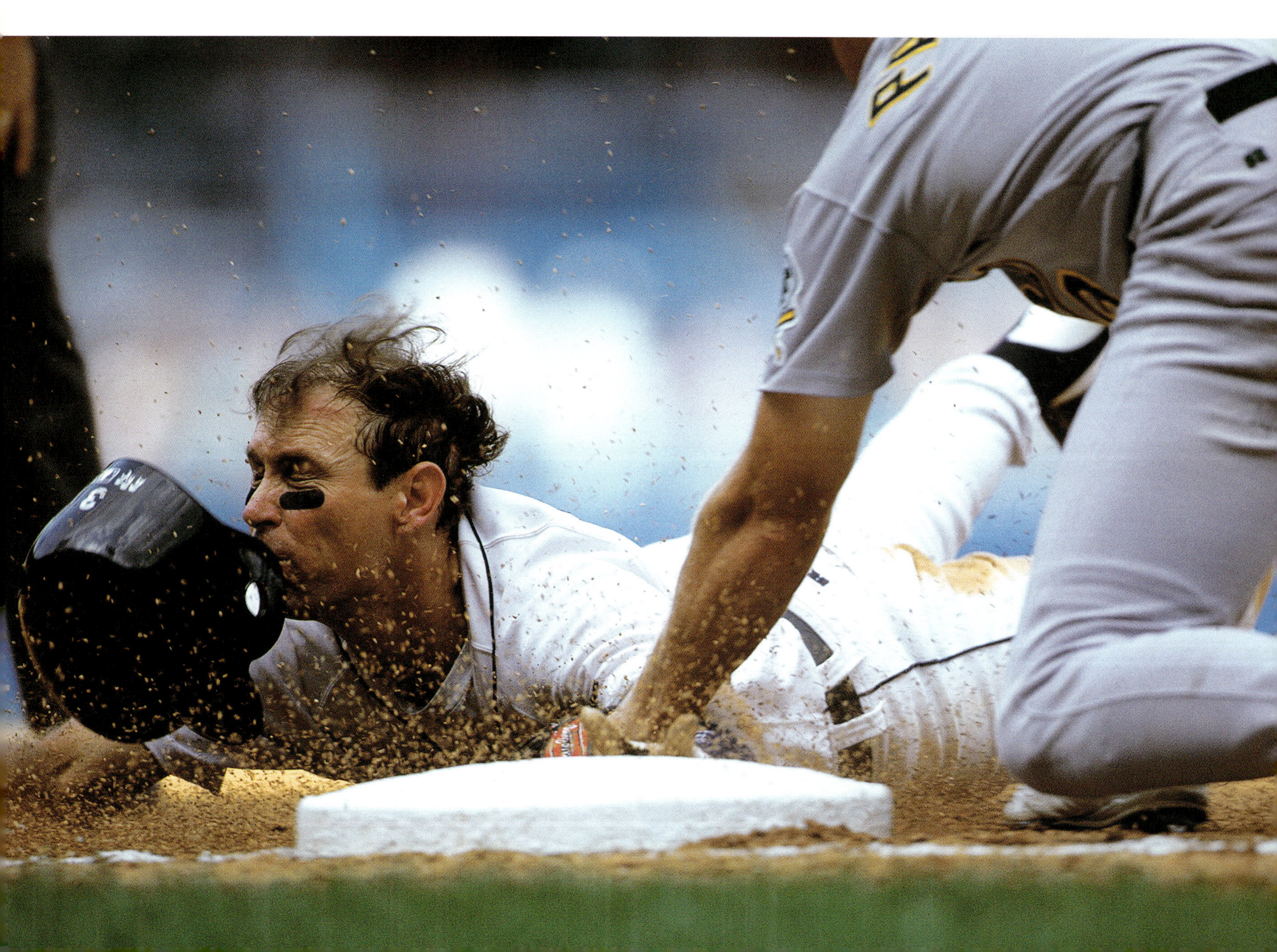

JOE MORGAN, World Series, Cincinnati, 1975

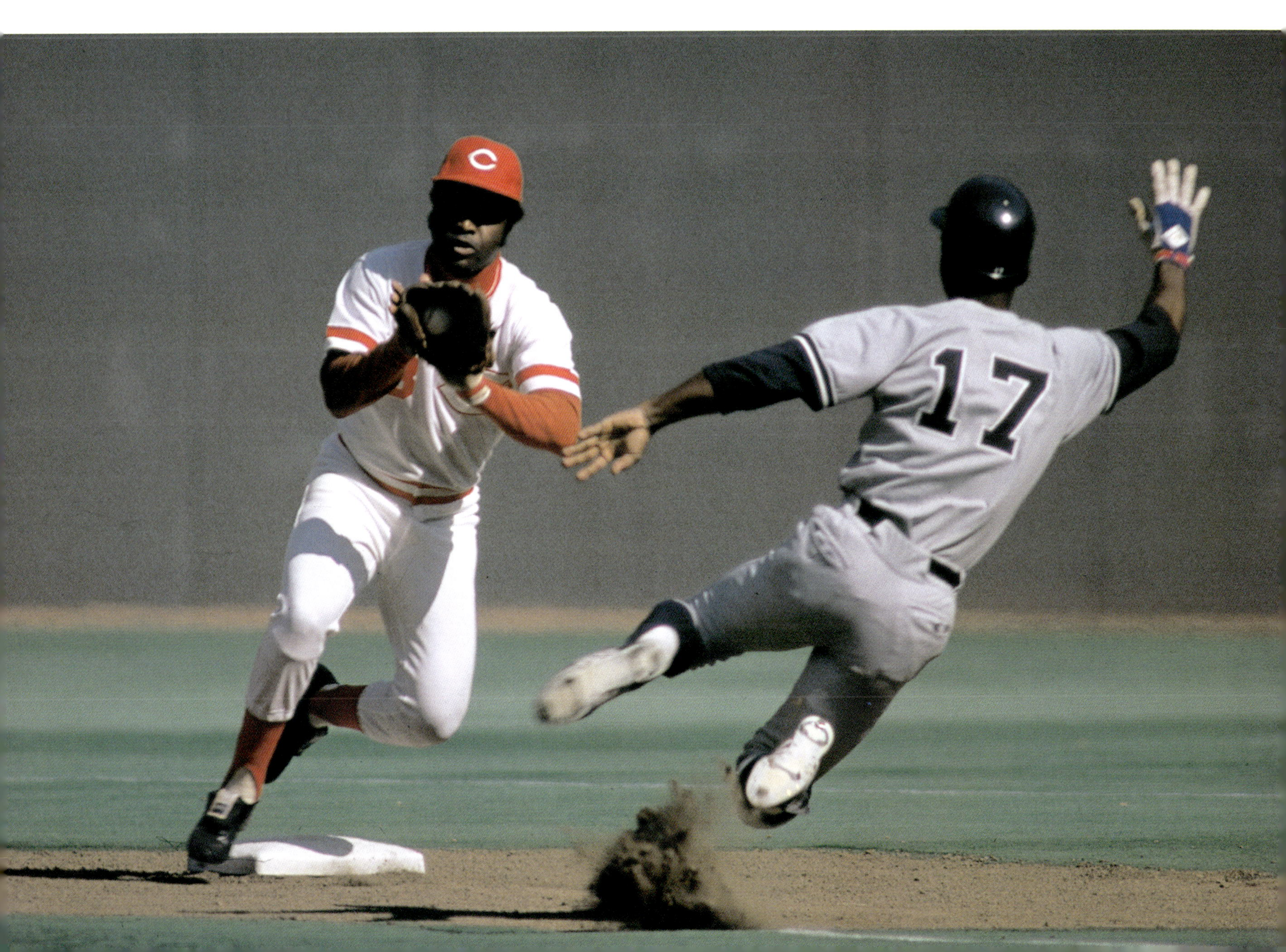

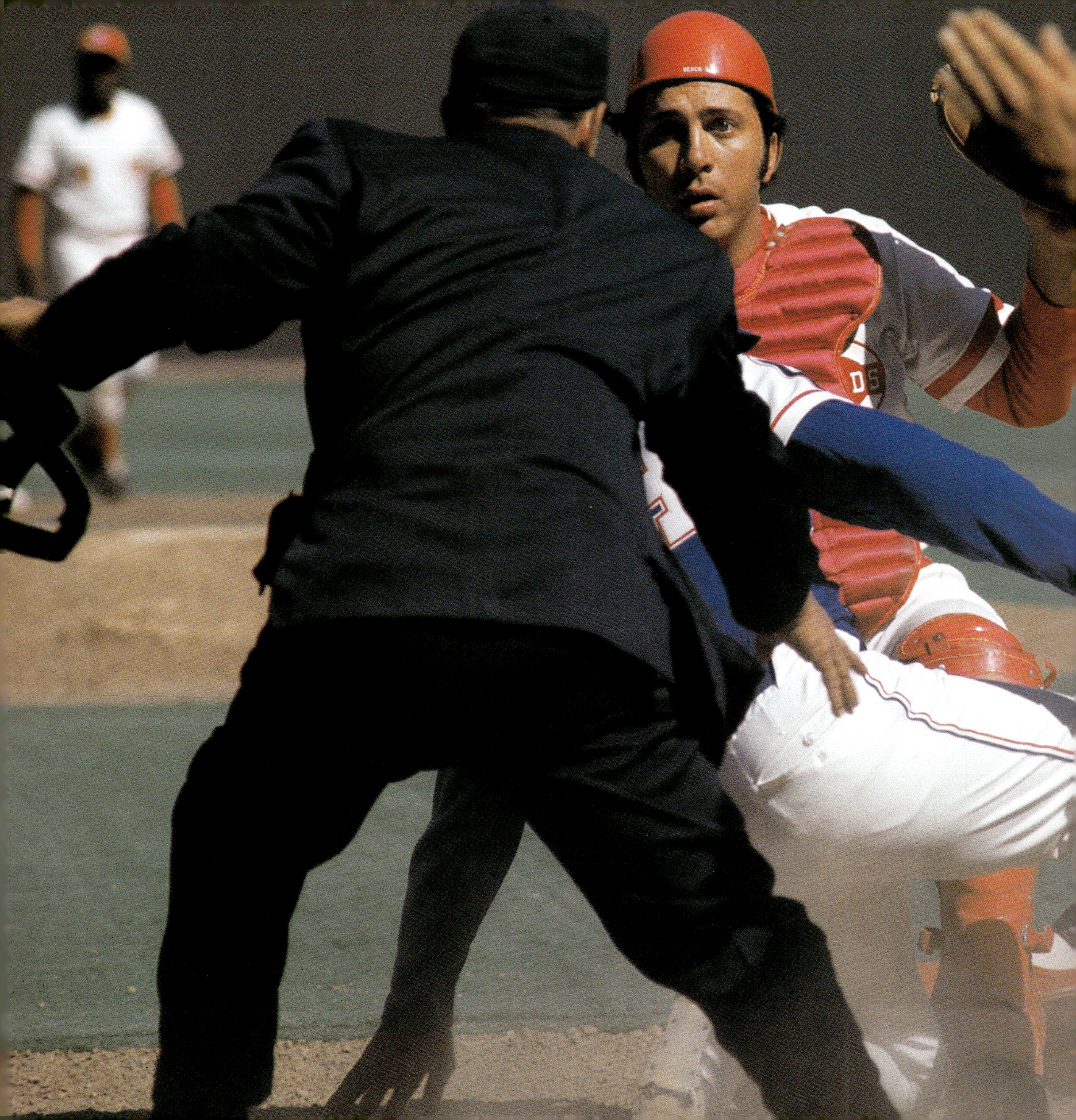

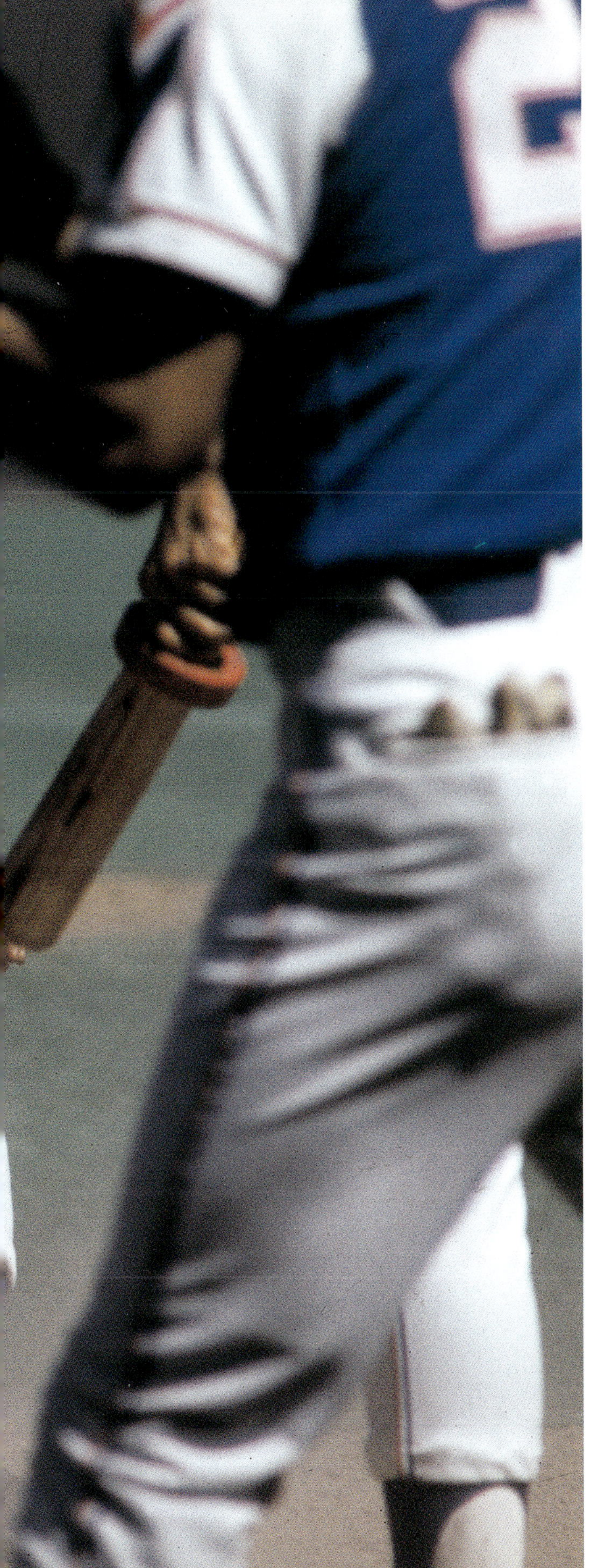

JOHNNY BENCH, Cincinnati, 1974

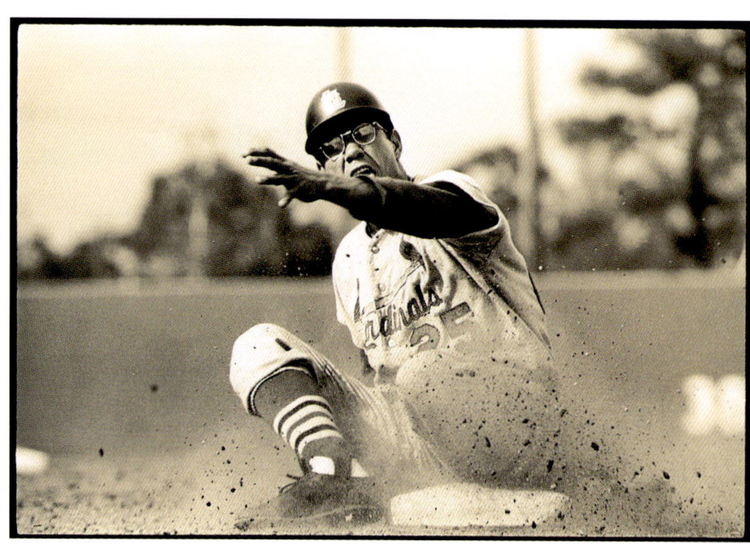

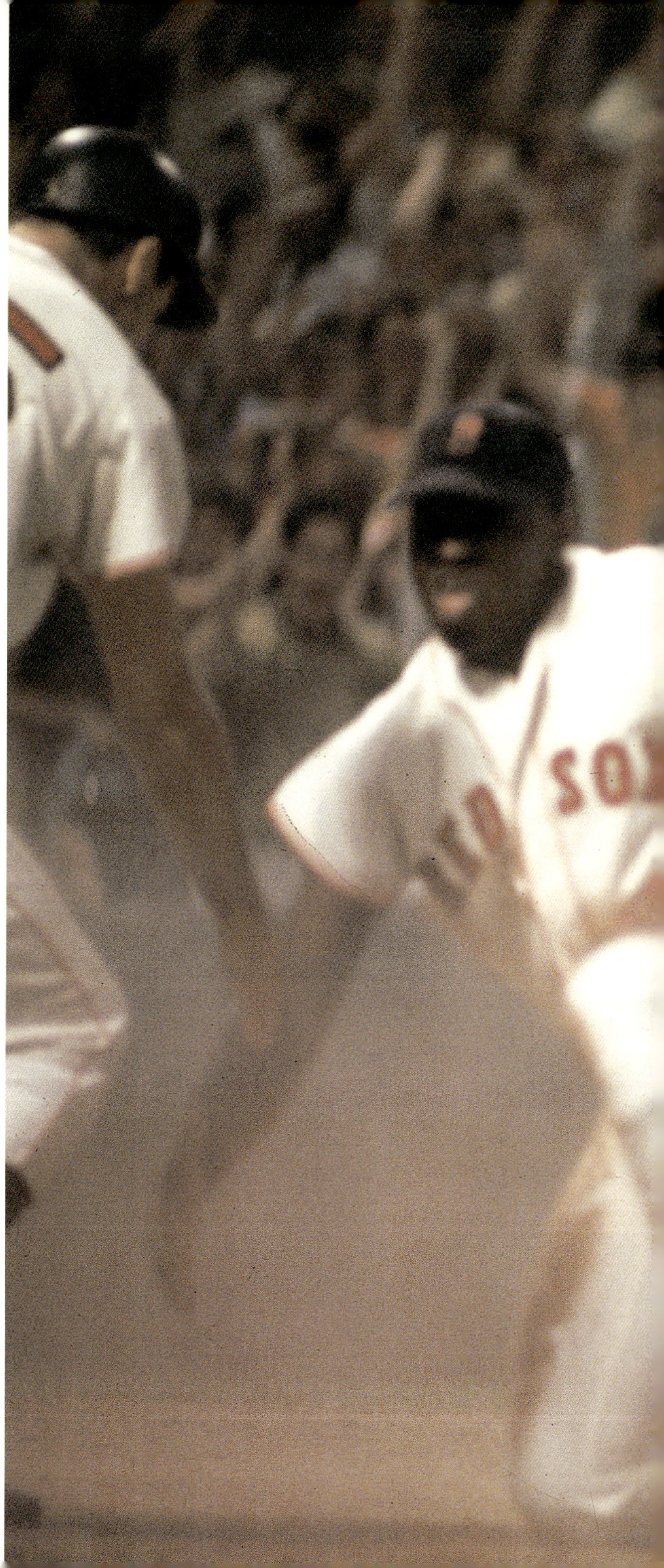

JULIAN JAVIER, Clearwater, Florida, 1964

JIM PERRY, Boston, 1967

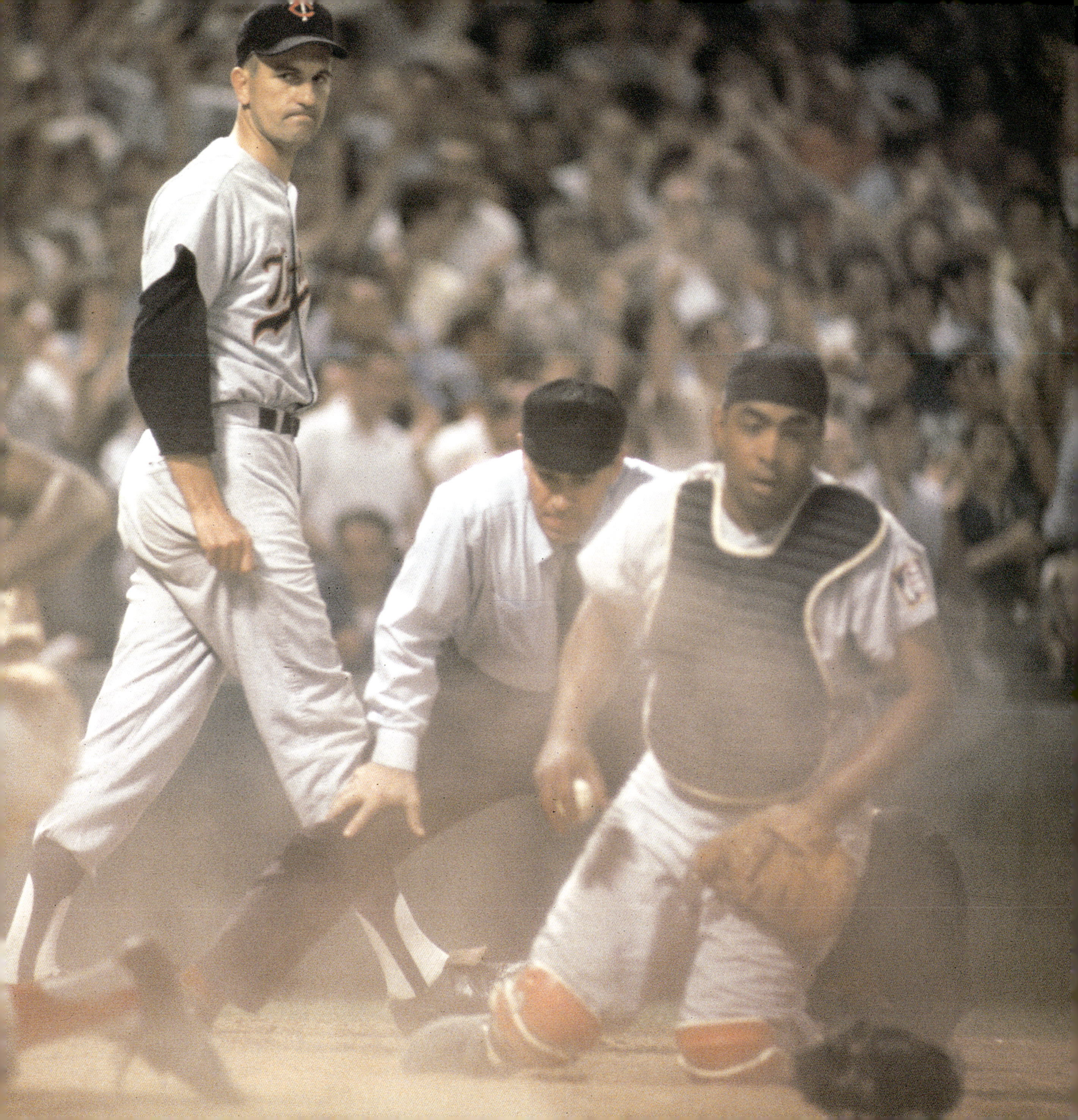

MANAGERS

CASEY STENGEL, Polo Grounds, New York, 1962

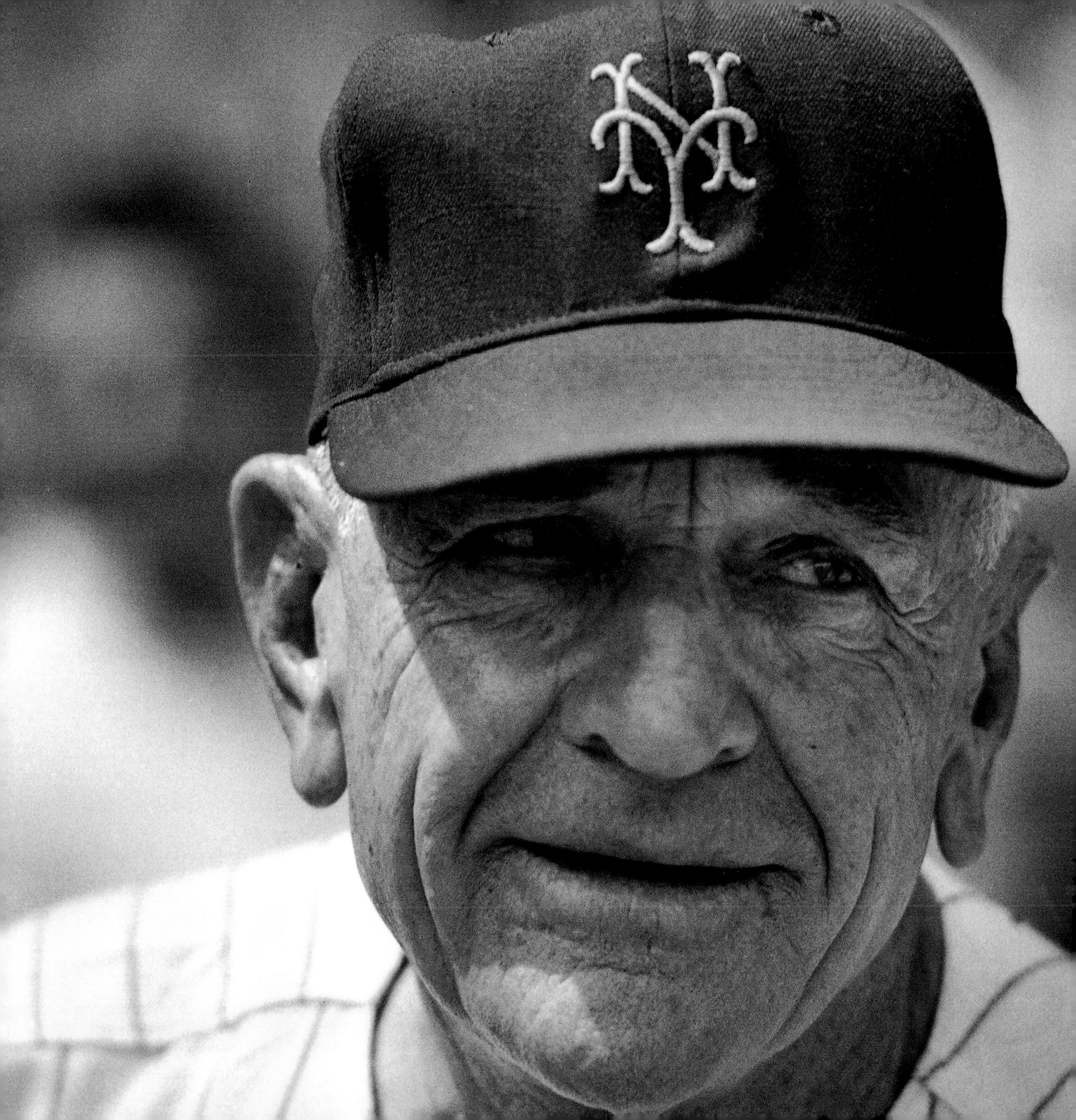
NY

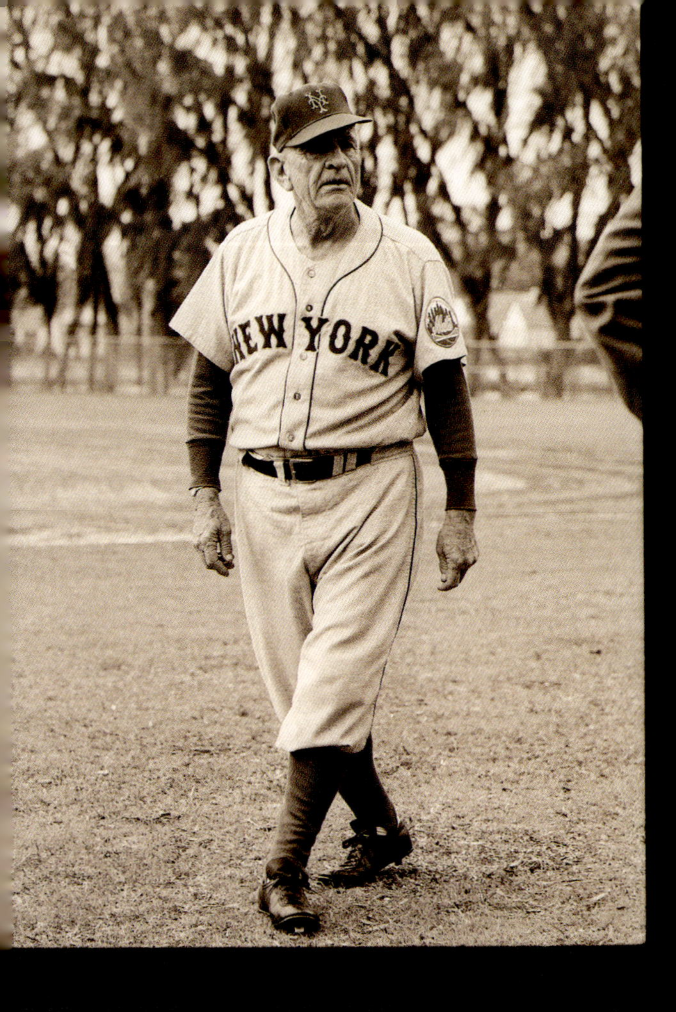
NEW YORK

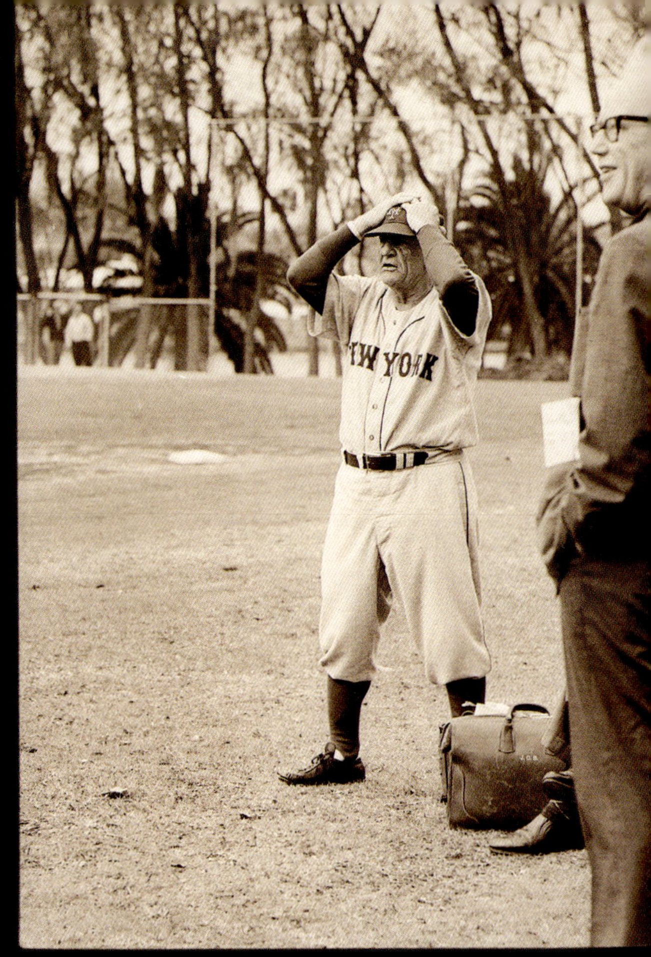

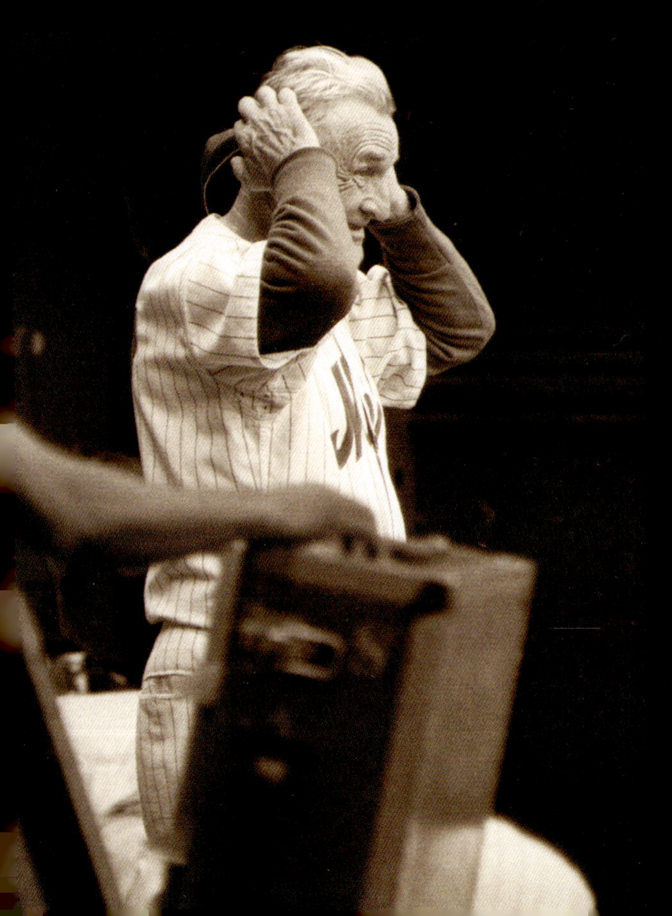

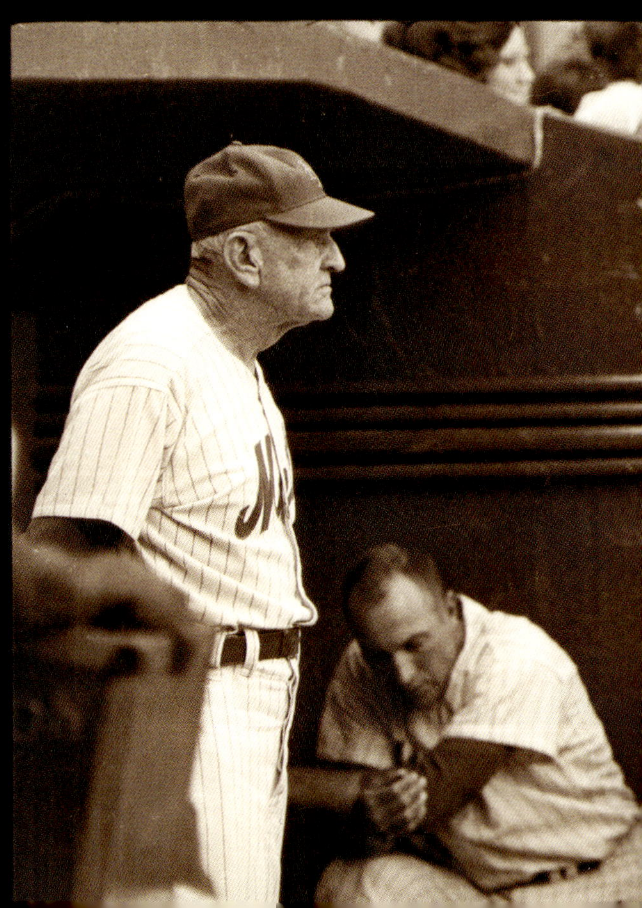

FOR MORE THAN A CENTURY, there have been big-league baseball managers—and then there was Casey Stengel. "Everything he did looked good in the camera," Iooss says. "He was like a great Hollywood actor. You couldn't take your eyes off him. And if he was talking, you couldn't take your ears away from him." As the manager of Yankees teams that won seven World Series and ten American League pennants in twelve seasons, Stengel was a genius. As the manager of the terrible early Mets teams, he was comic relief. "When the Mets were in spring training," Iooss says, "the sign outside the Colonial Inn in St. Petersburg read, 'Welcome Casey Stengel and the N.Y. Mets.' What other manager ever had top billing like that?"

One reason, of course, was that none of the Mets players, or the team as a whole, deserved any billing at all.

Over Stengel's three and a half seasons as manager, the Mets had records of 40–120 (a record in itself for most losses), 51–111, 53–109, and 31–64 before he suffered a broken hip in a fall on July 24, 1965, ending his career.

"You could listen to his stories forever," Iooss says. "He was hilarious. So was his body language, especially his legs."

And here is Stengel, walking as only he did, yakking away as only he did. To the side, sports columnist Red Smith is laughing.

Stengel, his Mets cap usually cocked to the side, was also accommodating. To photograph George Altman, a Mets outfielder, in spring training, Iooss asked Stengel for a favor: when Altman was at bat, could he shoot while crouched on the outfield grass behind second base during an exhibition game?

"Go ahead," Stengel said. "I'll tell the umpires."

When Altman was about to bat, Iooss ran out and crouched behind second base with his camera, but most of the fans thought he was one of those kooks who run onto the field.

"They were yelling for the cops to come get me," Iooss says, "but the umpires waved the cops off."

Knowing he could be conked with a line drive that he probably wouldn't see, Iooss was hoping for a quick at-bat, but both times Altman was up, his at-bat dragged out.

"Nothing happened," Iooss recalls. "The pictures were dull, but it was a good idea."

In the Polo Grounds dugout, Stengel usually wore his cap straightaway, like the old baseball soldier he was. But sometimes he got so exasperated with his Mets, he didn't wear his cap at all. Sometimes he appeared ready to tear his hair out. What hair he had.

Not all managers react as expressively or as emotionally as Casey Stengel did.

Joe Torre, whose Yankees teams won four World Series

CASEY STENGEL AND RED SMITH, St. Petersburg, Florida, 1963 (TOP PAIR) **CASEY STENGEL,** Polo Grounds, New York, 1962

in the five seasons from 1996 to 2000, seldom moves from his cushioned seat in the Yankee dugout. Others, like Mets manager Bobby Valentine, pace the dugout. Others are always perched on the top step of the dugout, peering at what's happening.

But sooner or later, all managers question the umpires. Here is Fred Hutchinson, the Reds manager in the early 1960s, staring at an umpire's explanation while two other umpires smile slyly. And here is the reverse of that scene—Johnny Keane, who led the Cardinals to a World Series triumph in 1964, explaining ground rules to the umpires before a spring-training game.

Other managers are seldom so restrained when dealing with an umpire.

"Earl Weaver," Iooss says of the Hall of Fame manager of the Orioles, "was so famous for getting into so many arguments with umpires, I asked him to get in one for me. He went out screaming and kicking dirt and on the way back to the dugout, he looked over at me and said, 'How's that, Wally?'"

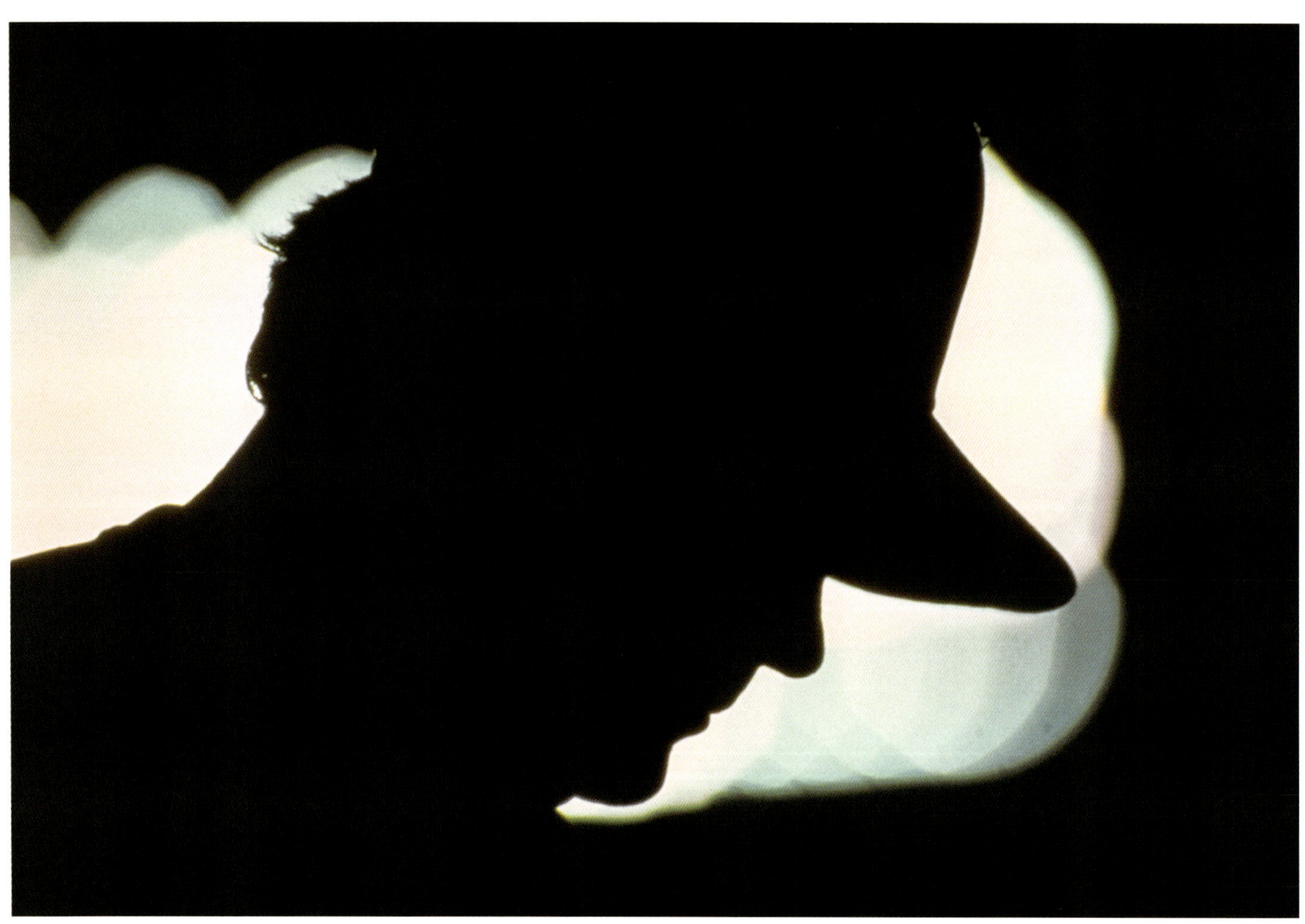

EARL WEAVER, Baltimore, 1979

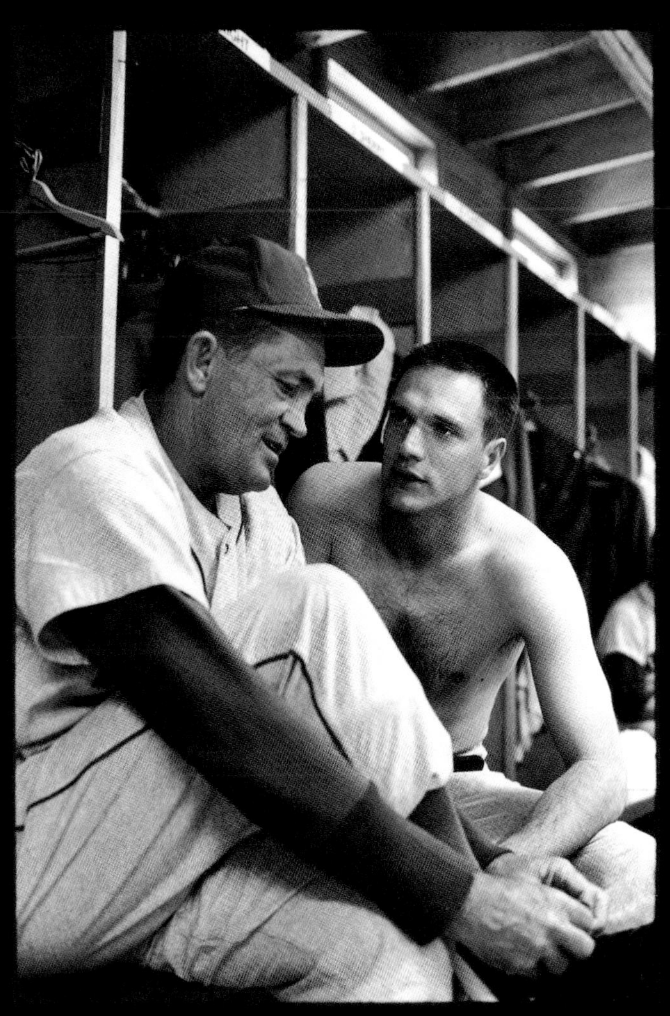

COACH DON HEFFNER AND ROD KANEHL N.Y. Mets locker room, St. Petersburg, Florida, 1963

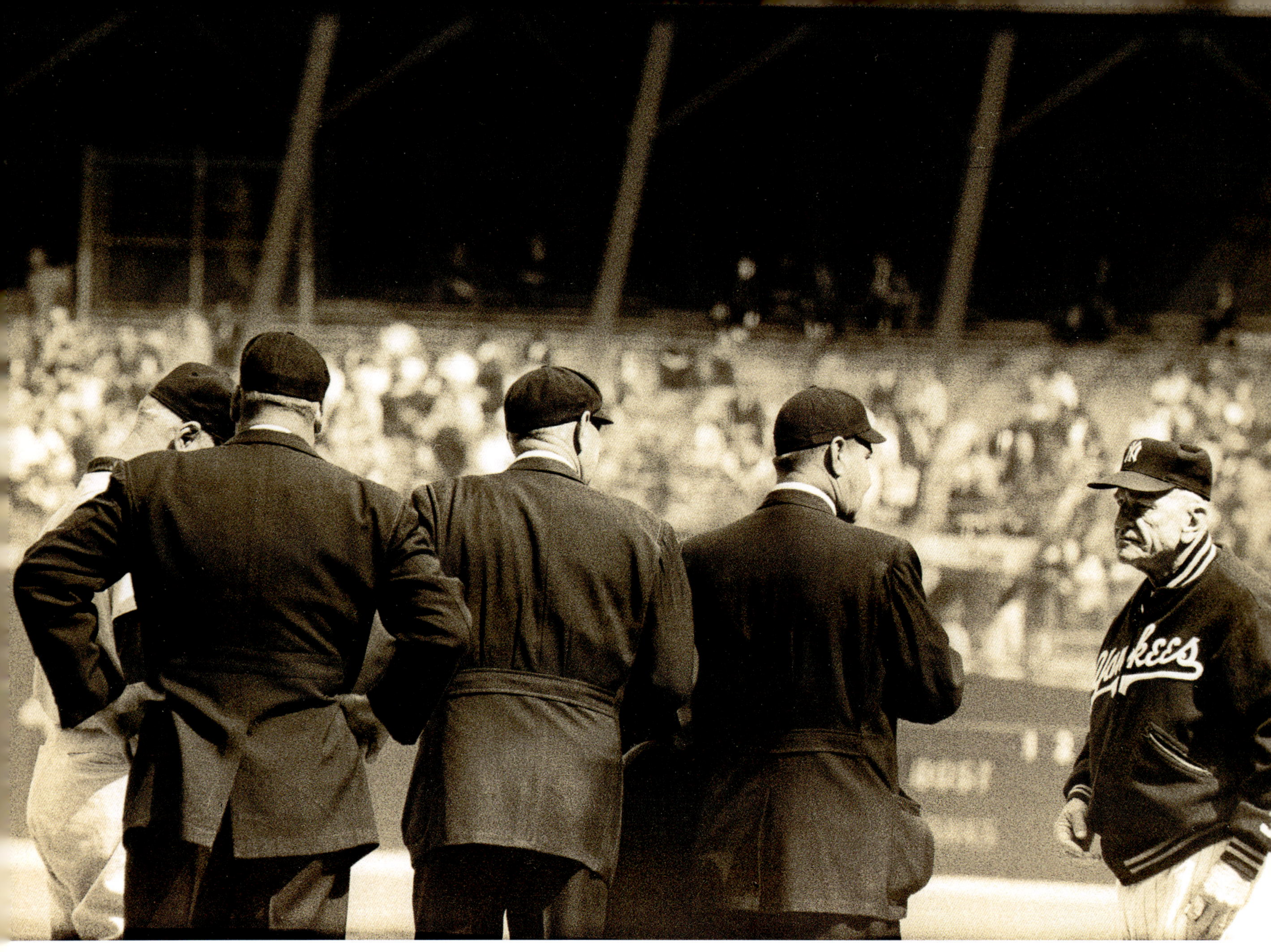

CASEY STENGEL, Yankee Stadium, 1960

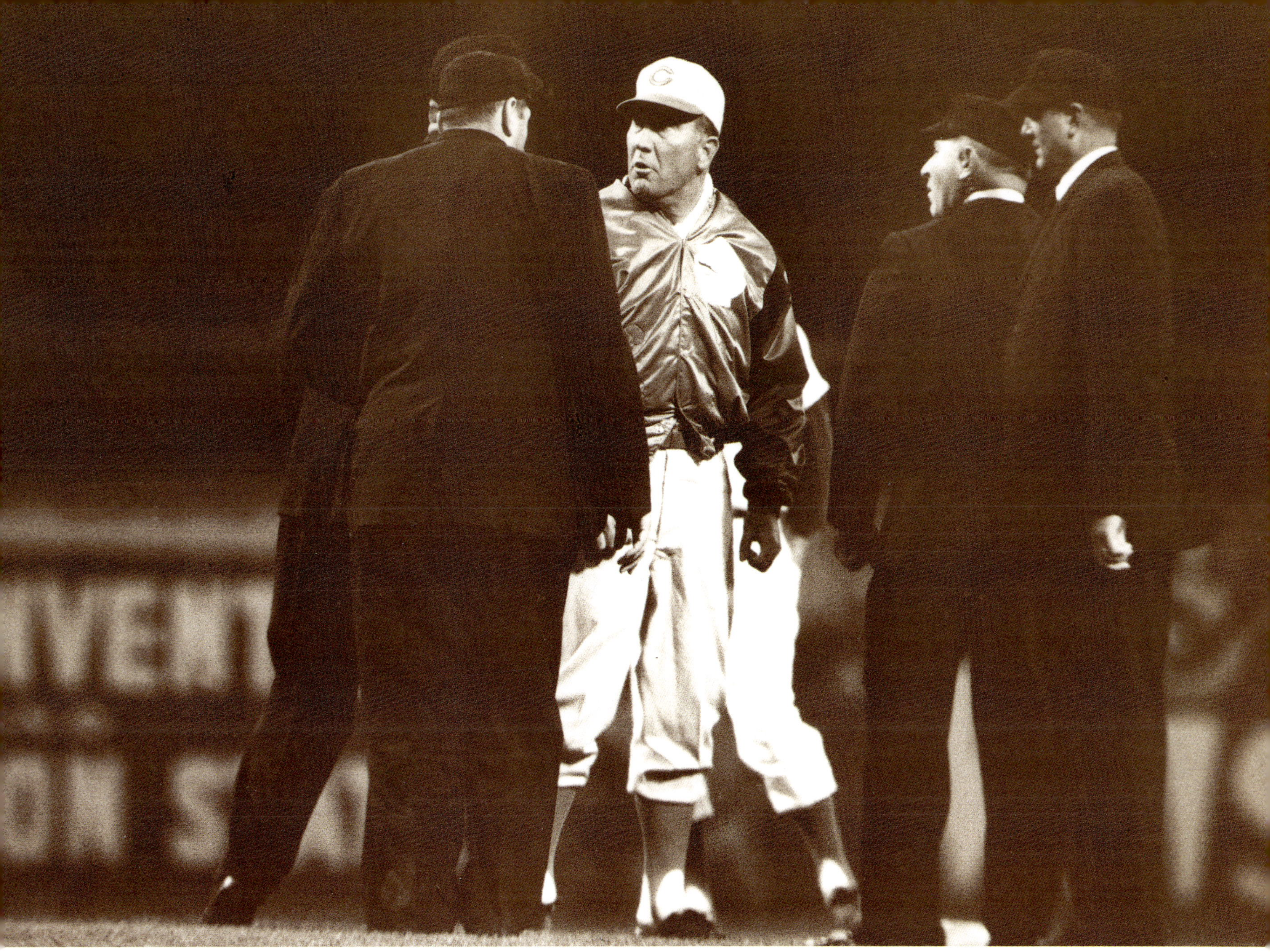

FRED HUTCHINSON, Cincinnati, 1964

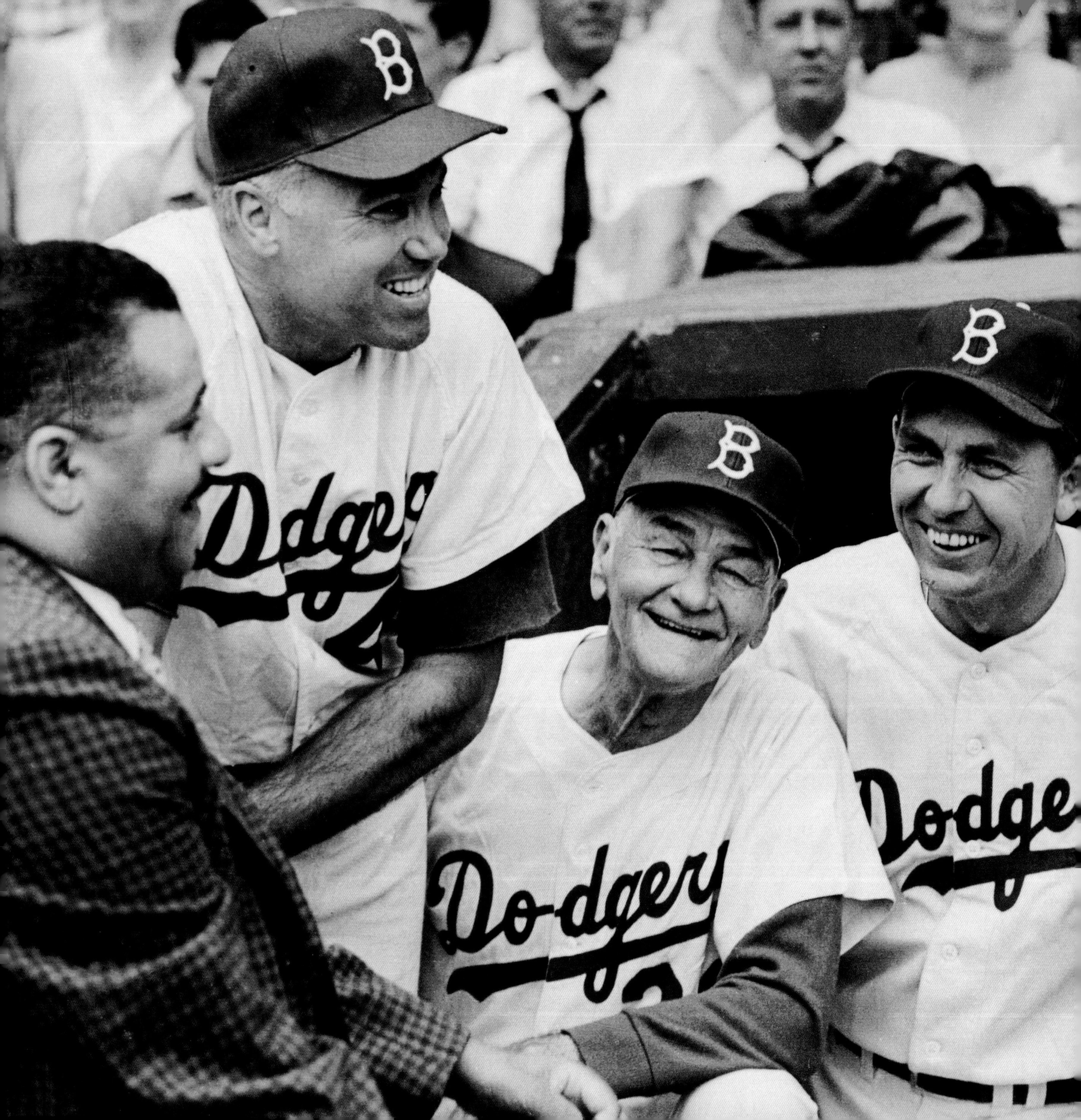
Dodgers

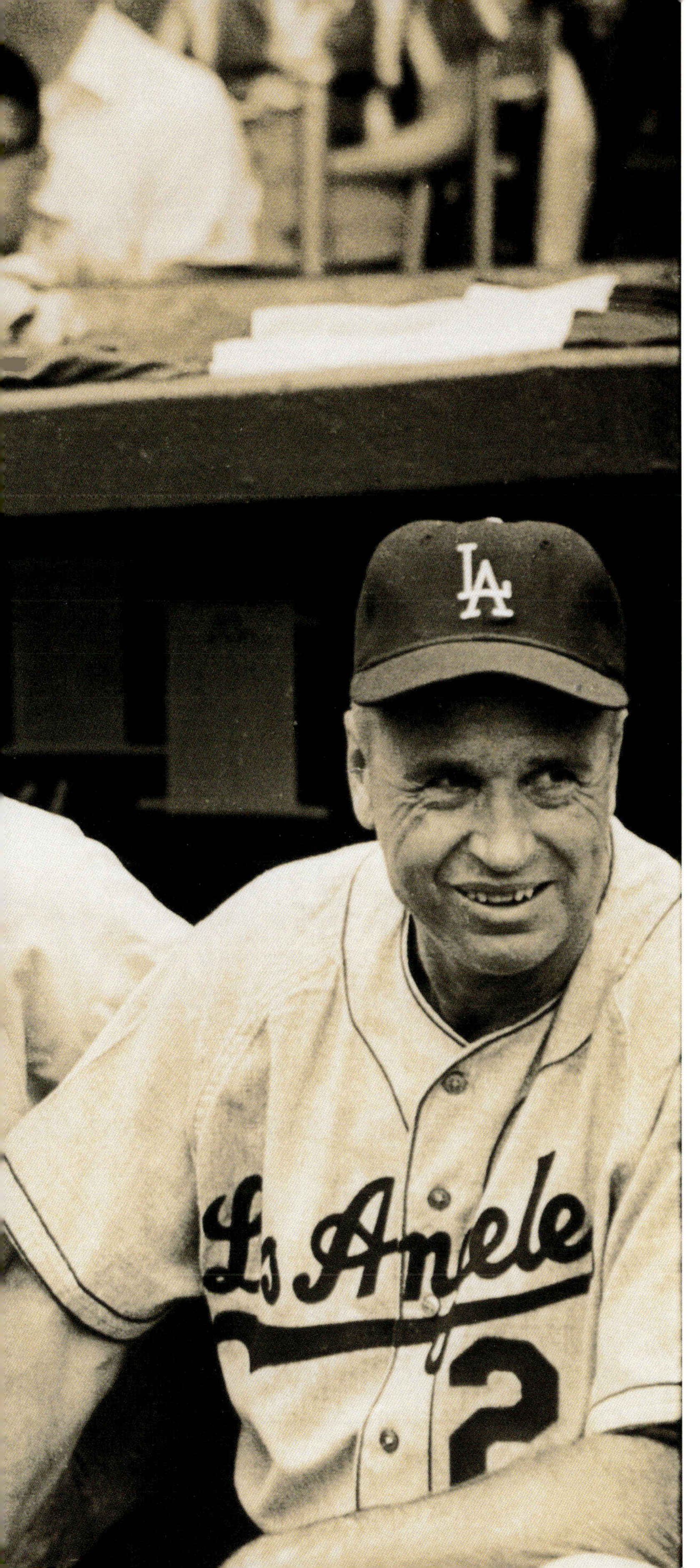

ROY CAMPANELLA, DUKE SNIDER, JAKE PITLER, GIL HODGES, WALTER ALSTON,

Brooklyn Dodgers, Old-Timers Day, Polo Grounds, 1962

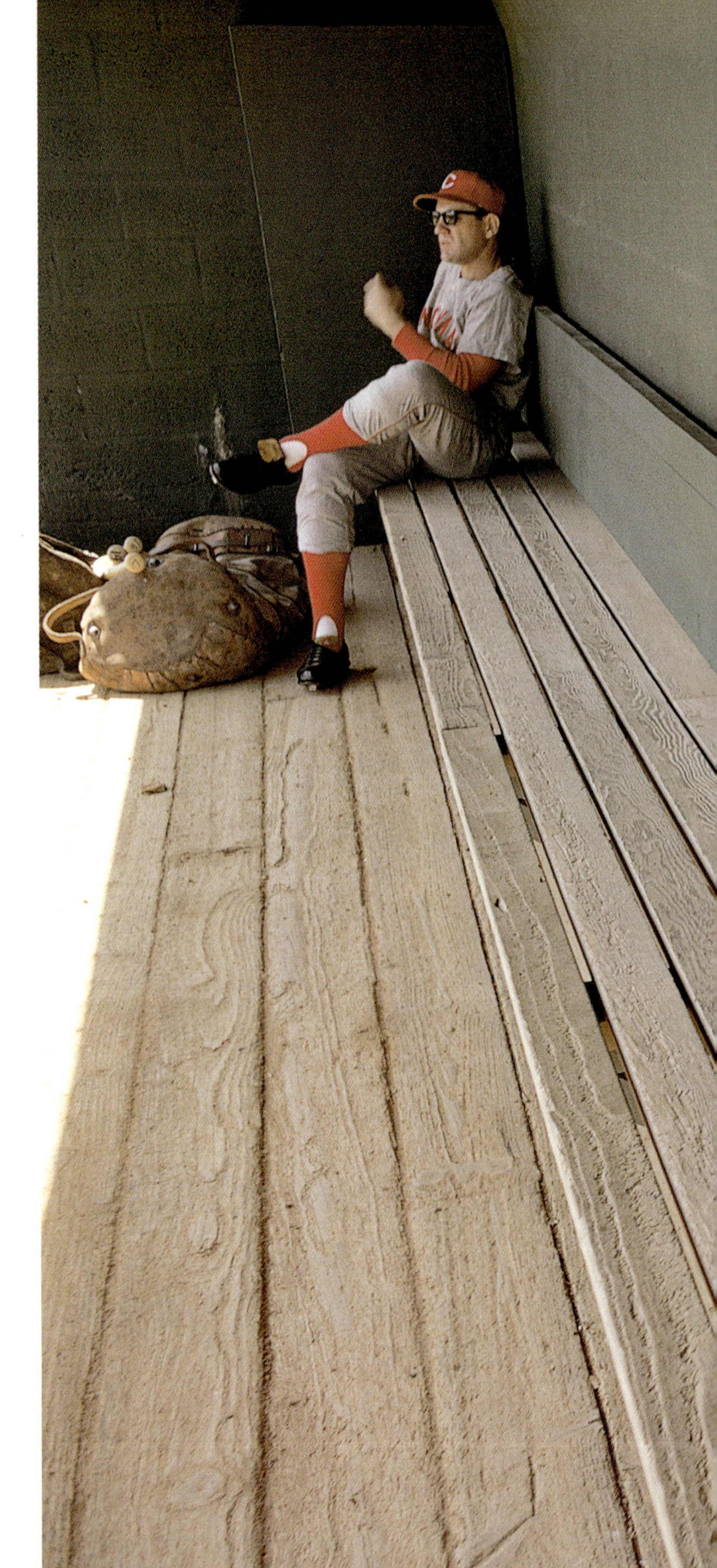

DAVE BRISTOL, Tampa, Florida, 1969

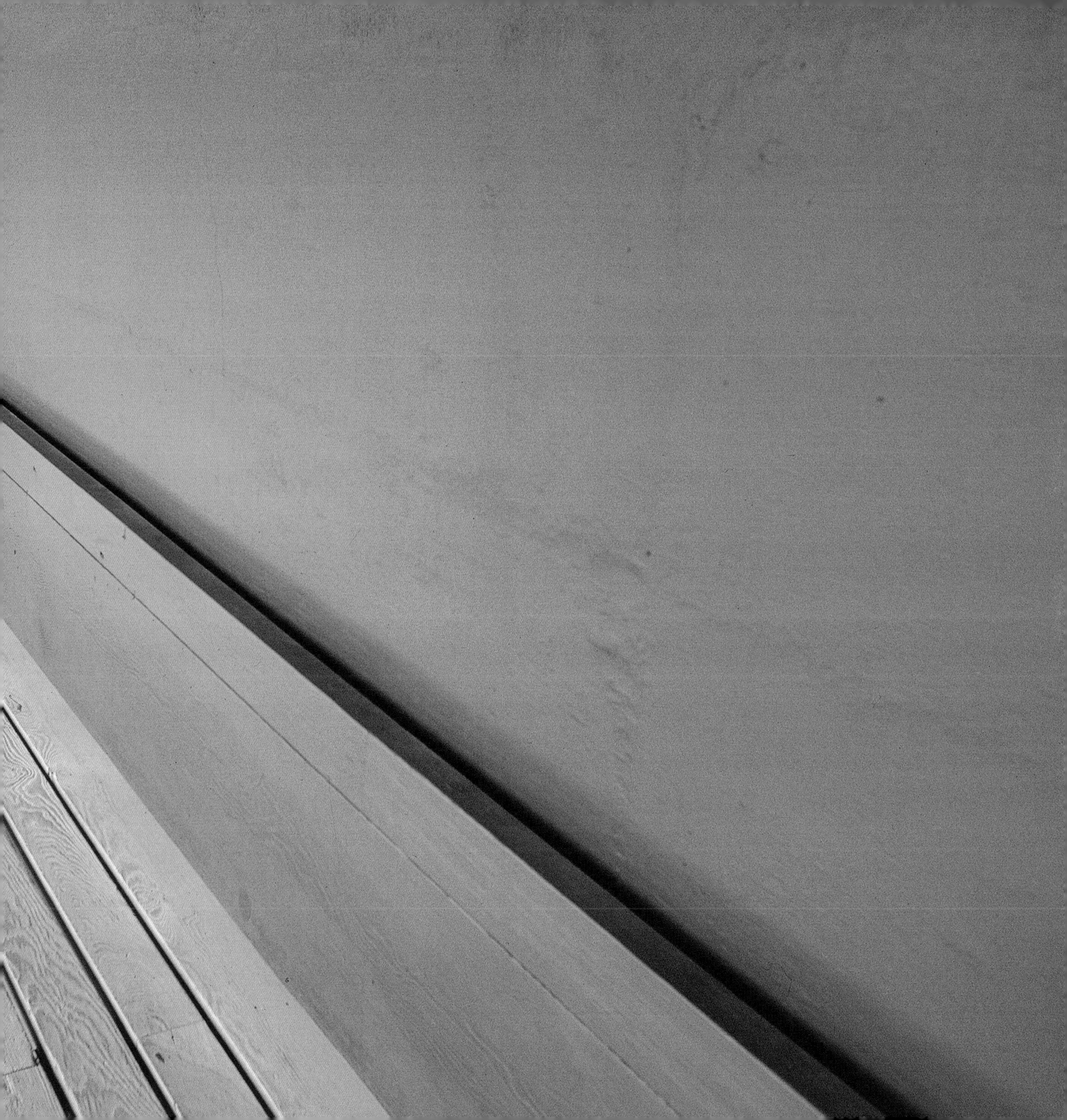

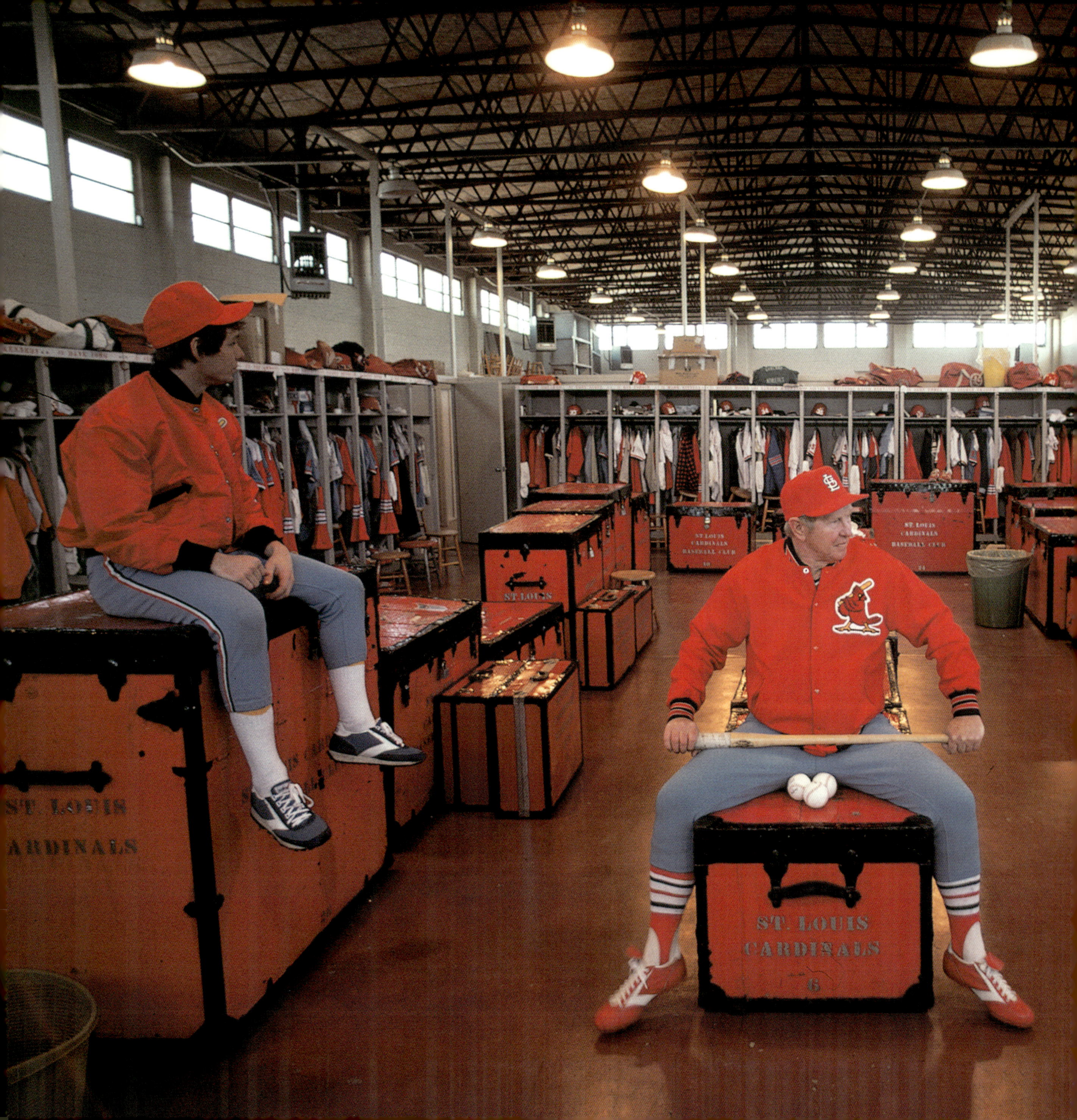
ST. LOUIS
CARDINALS
6

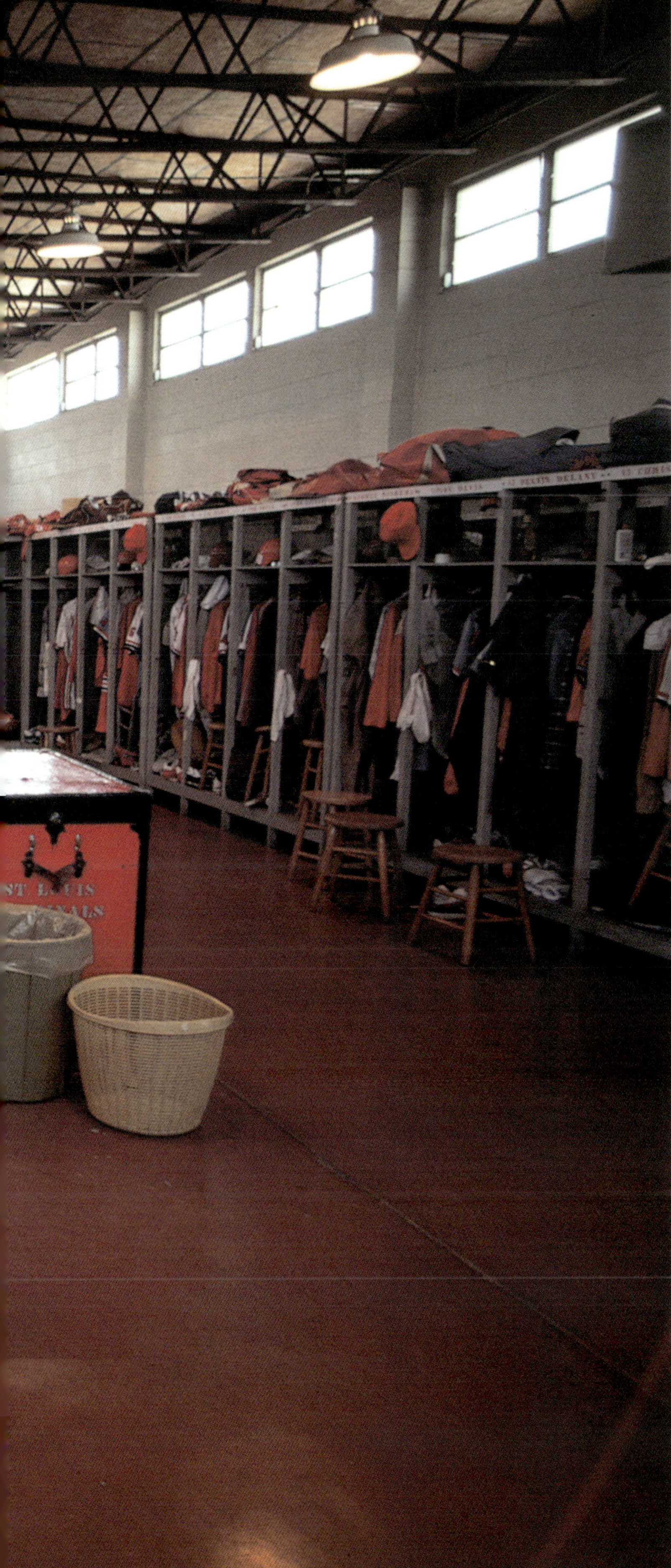

COACH RED SCHOENDIENST, St. Petersburg, Florida, 1981

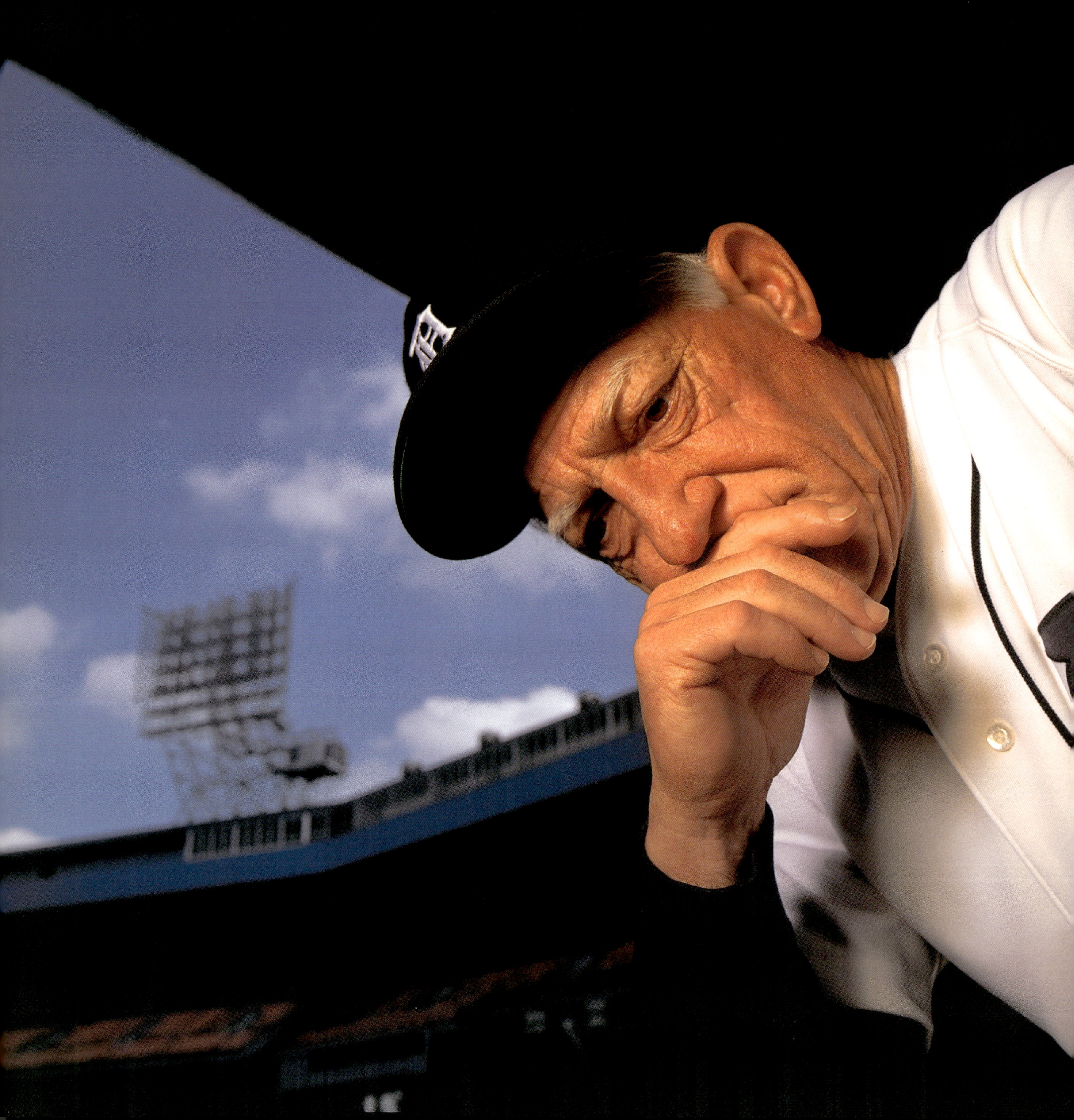

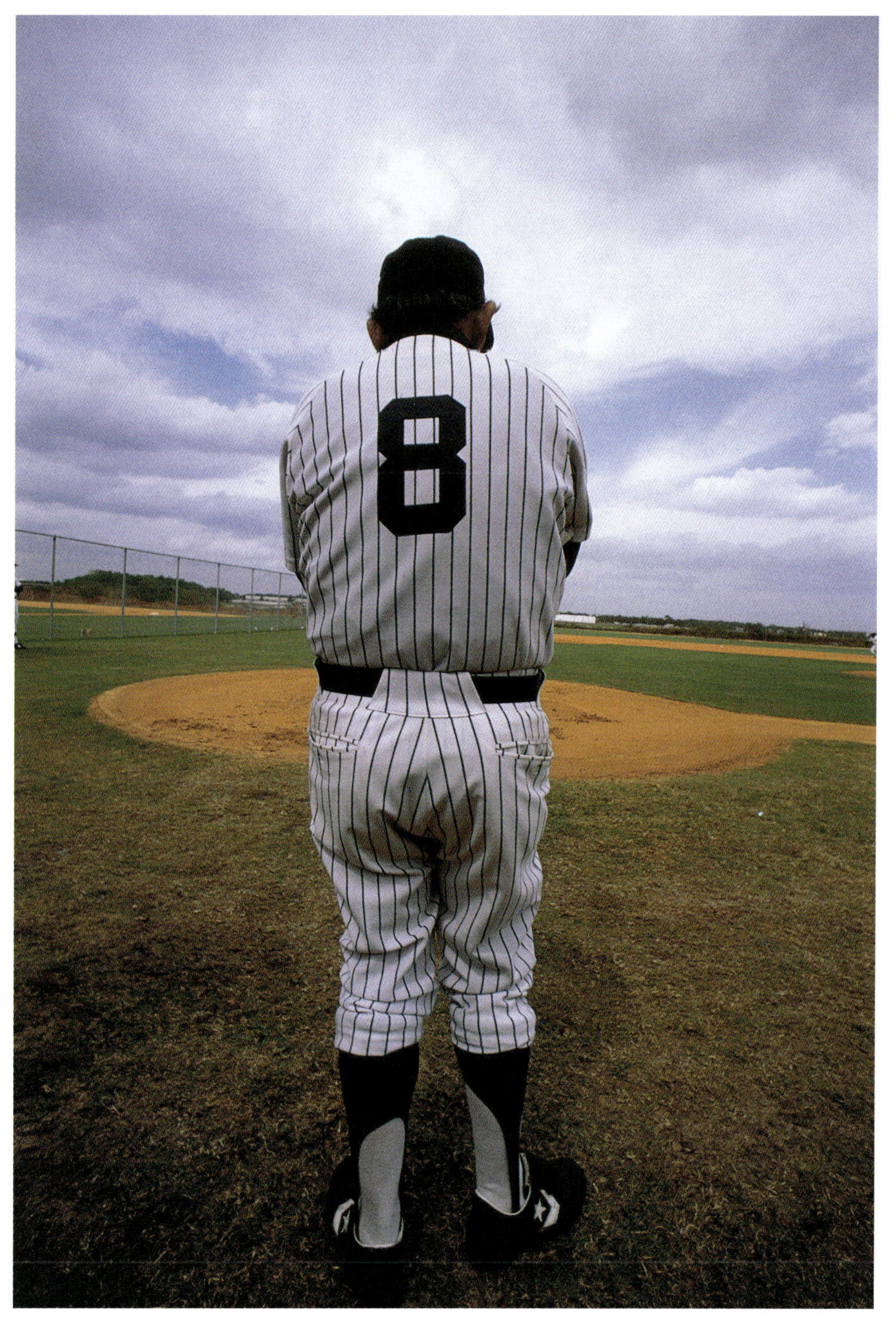

SPARKY ANDERSON, Detroit, 1993 (LEFT)

YOGI BERRA, Fort Lauderdale, Florida, 1984 (ABOVE)

CELEBRATIONS

CARL YASTRZEMSKI, Fenway Park, Boston, after Red Sox pennant victory, 1967

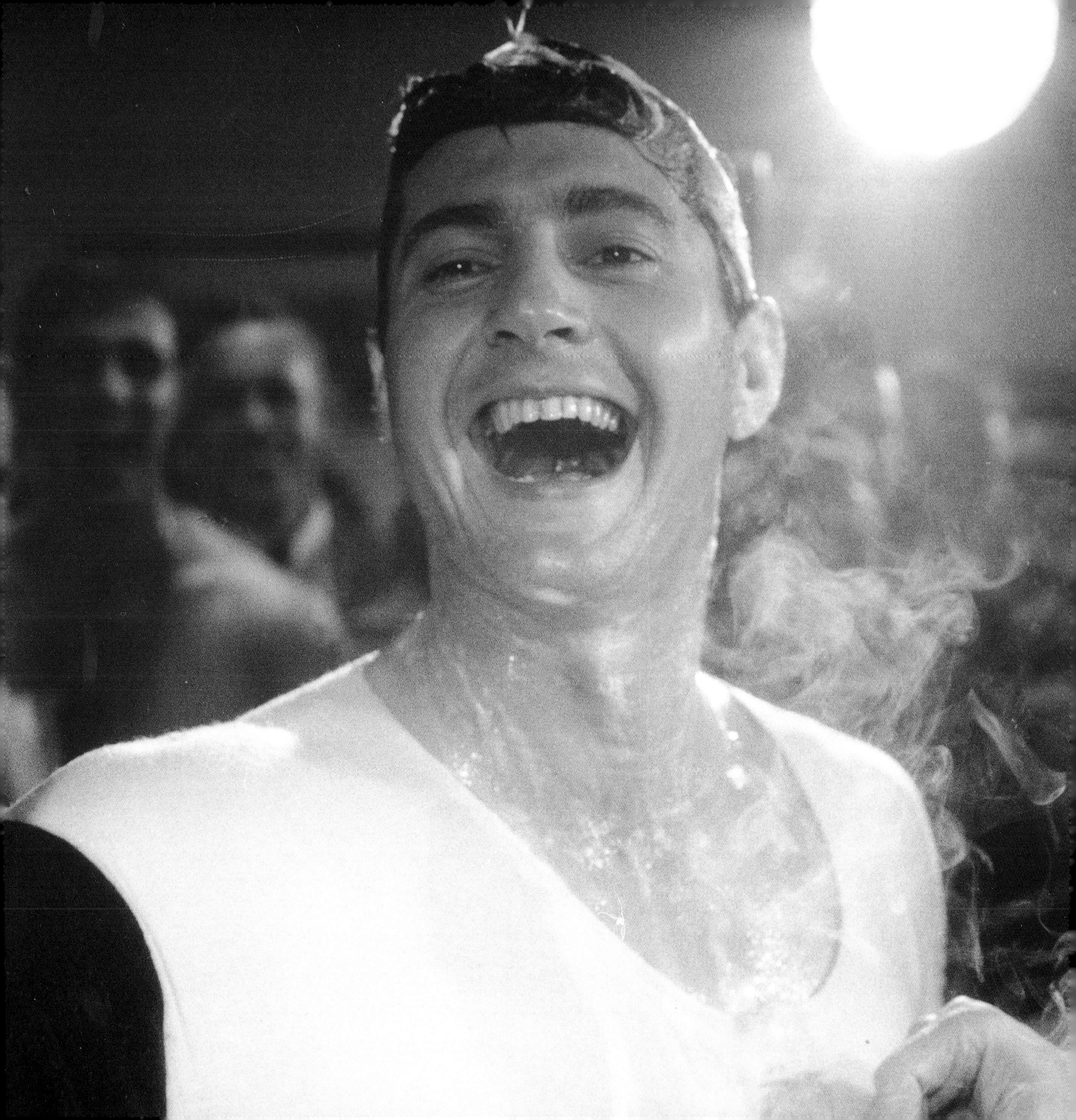

WHEN THE WORLD SERIES ENDS NOW, the winning team's pitcher pumps a fist, jumps into the air, leaps toward his catcher, and disappears under the pile of celebrating teammates that resemble swarming bees. It's become a rite of television. But once upon a time World Series celebrations were much more civilized, much more mannerly. When the Dodgers won the seventh game of the 1965 World Series on Sandy Koufax's 2–0 three-hitter in Minnesota, none of his teammates rushed the mound. Nobody did that then. Instead, as Koufax hurries toward the Dodgers dugout, his catcher, John Roseboro, has already congratulated Koufax and turned away, his mask still on. Walt Alston, the Dodgers manager, and several teammates have gathered around Koufax.

But there's no jumping, no leaping, no piling on. Not even a fist or an arm in the air.

As for Koufax, if he is looking anywhere, it's directly at Walter Iooss's camera.

Across the field, near the red-white-and-blue bunting along the box seats behind first base in Metropolitan Stadium, two Twins, their heads bowed in surrender, plod toward their dugout. It's never easy to lose the World Series in your own ballpark.

In the Dodger clubhouse, no champagne is in sight as Don Drysdale puts his Hall of Fame right arm around Koufax, who had an 0.38 earned-run average in three starts in that World Series. Over 24 innings, he allowed only 1 earned run and 13 hits while striking out 29 and walking 5.

Two years later, when Jim Lonborg assured the Red Sox of at least a tie for the American League pennant with a 5–3 victory over the Twins on the final day of the 1967 season, none of his teammates rushed the mound. But hundreds of Fenway Park fans did.

The other Red Sox ducked into their dugout as Lonborg, floating atop the fans, was swept out to right field. His uniform and sweatshirt were torn. His cap was stolen. Eventually, with two of Boston's finest rescuing him, he wobbled into the Red Sox clubhouse. When the Detroit Tigers lost to the California Angels, 8–5, later that afternoon, the Red Sox had their first pennant since 1946 and Carl Yastrzemski celebrated with a cigar and a smile. Yaz didn't smile much, but he was smiling in that clubhouse.

That season Yaz led the American League with 44 homers, 121 runs batted in and a .326 average—the last major-leaguer to win what is known as the Triple Crown.

When the World Series opened in Fenway Park three days later, Yaz, surrounded by security guards and Boston police, was the natural choice to be interviewed by NBC broadcaster Tony Kubek not far from the Red Sox dugout. But, alas, the Red Sox lost that World Series to the Cardinals in seven games. And as the twenty-first century began, they had not won a World Series since 1918 when Babe Ruth was their ace pitcher.

All that security around Lonborg and Yaz in Fenway Park would eventually evolve into Veterans Stadium's

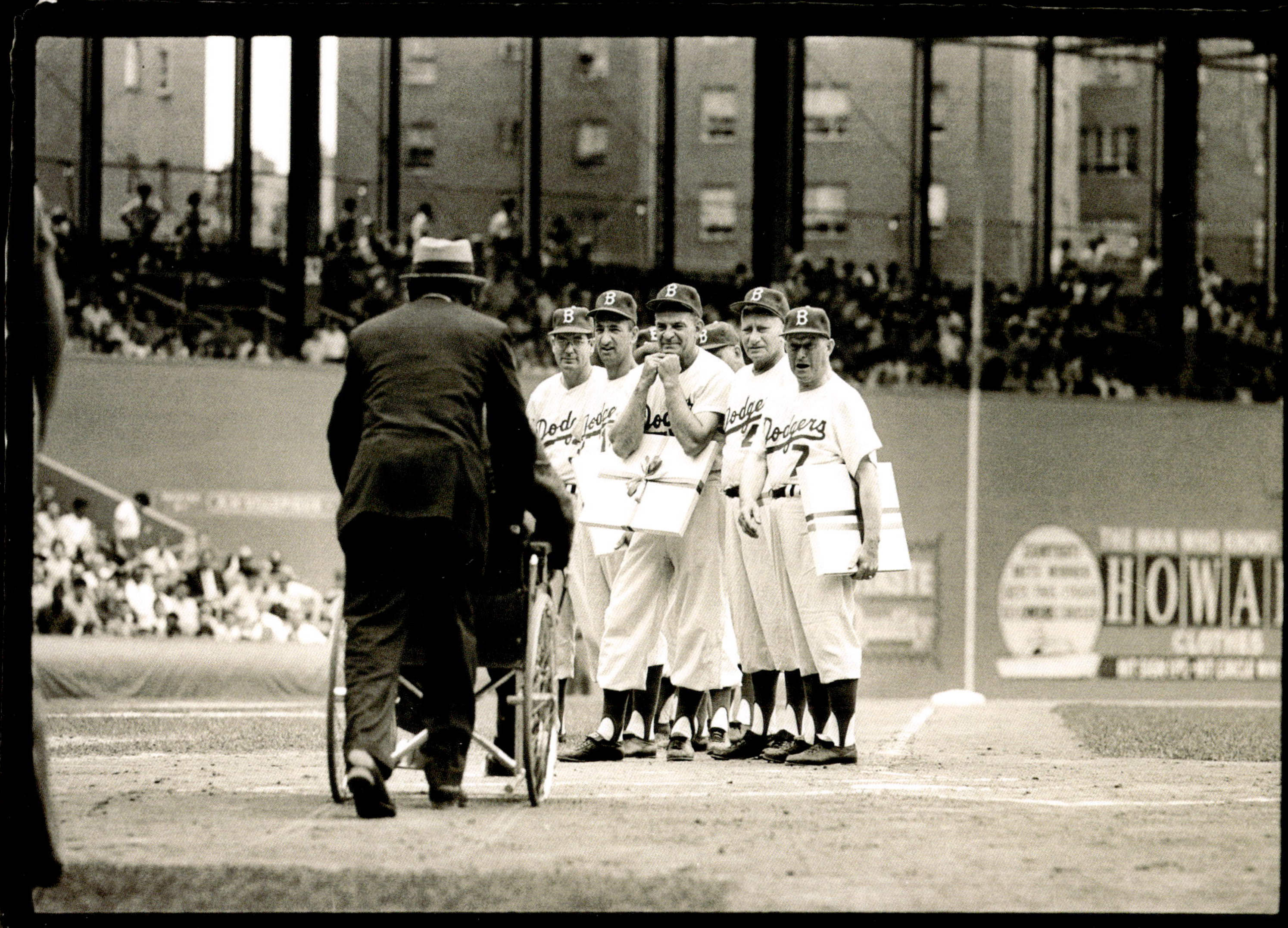
Dodgers
HOWA

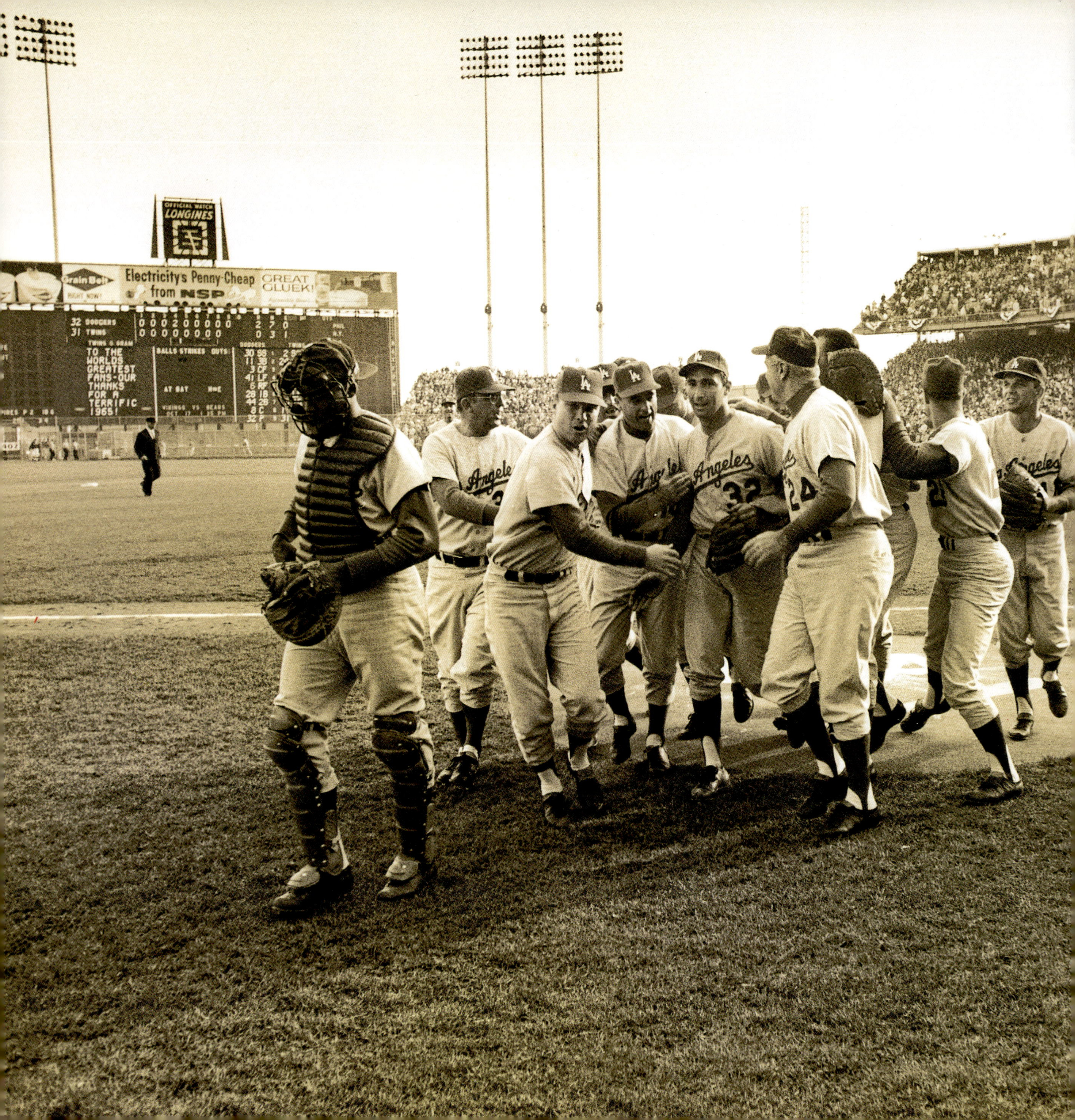
OFFICIAL WATCH
LONGINES
Grain Belt
Electricity's Penny-Cheap
from NSP
GREAT
GLUEK!
32 DODGERS
31 TWINS
0 0 0 2 0 0 0 0 0
0 0 0 0 0 0 0 0
2 7 0
0 3 1
TO THE
WORLDS
GREATEST
FANS-OUR
THANKS
FOR A
TERRIFIC
1965!
BALLS STRIKES OUTS
AT BAT
VIKINGS VS BEARS
Angeles
32
24

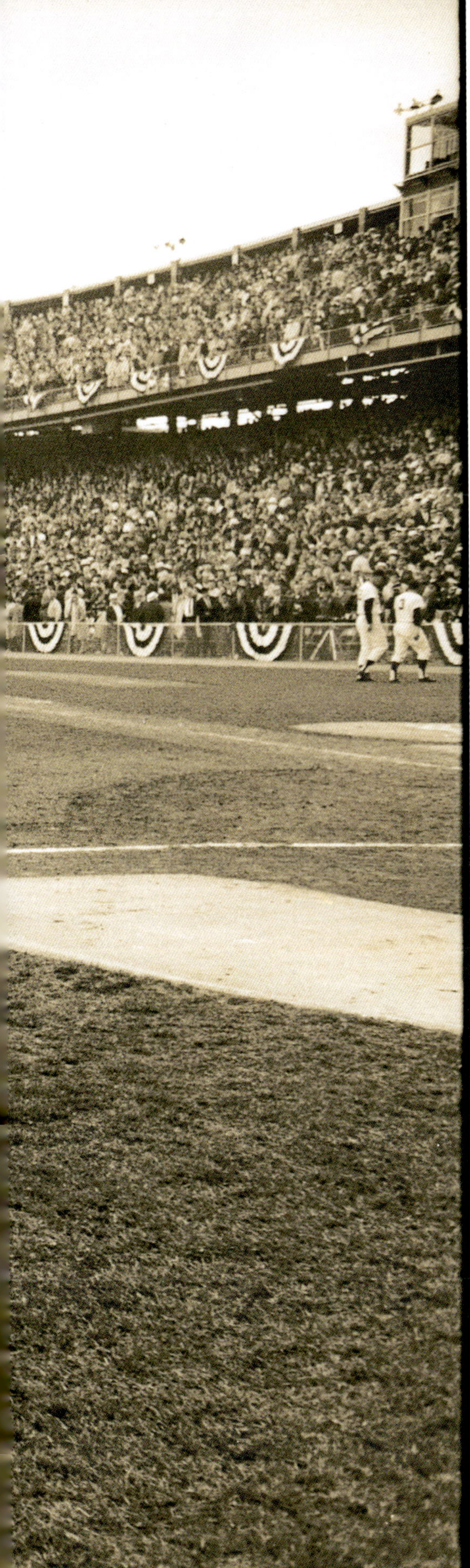

armed camp when the Phillies won the 1980 World Series in Philadelphia.

With the final out, the sudden appearance of mounted city police and police with dogs stifled whatever rowdy thoughts had occurred in the stands. More than an hour later, they were still on duty, still in their helmets, looking around for any troublemakers foolish enough to misbehave. But at least two horses and one German shepherd had relaxed.

But not every baseball celebration needs a World Series backdrop. Sometimes sentiment is enough.

When the Dodgers, who had departed Brooklyn for Los Angeles after the 1957 season, returned to New York in 1962 to play the expansion Mets at the Polo Grounds, an Old-Timers Day celebrated those Brooklyn Dodgers teams from 1947 to 1957 that won six National League pennants and the 1955 World Series. Of particular interest was the return of Roy Campanella, the Dodger catcher paralyzed in an auto accident near his Long Island home.

Here is Campy, in his wheelchair, with Duke Snider, coach Jake Pitler, and Gil Hodges (then with the Mets), each wearing that familiar "B" on their blue caps, and Walt Alston, still the Dodgers real manager, in his gray Los Angeles road uniform.

And here is Campy being wheeled out to welcoming smiles from teammates Clyde King, Cal Abrams, coach Harry (Cookie) Lavagetto, and manager Charlie Dressen. Behind them, in the distance down the left-field foul line, is the lower grandstand where Bobby Thomson's home run off Dodgers right-hander Ralph Branca landed to win the National League pennant for the Giants in the decisive third game of the 1951 playoff.

Even while enjoying an Old-Timers Day return eleven years later, those old Dodgers must have felt they were in a haunted house.

DODGERS CONGRATULATE SANDY KOUFAX after winning World Series, Minneapolis, 1965

EMMETT ASHFORD and the crew, World Series, Detroit, 1968

JIM LONBORG mobbed as Red Sox win pennant, Fenway Park, Boston, 1967

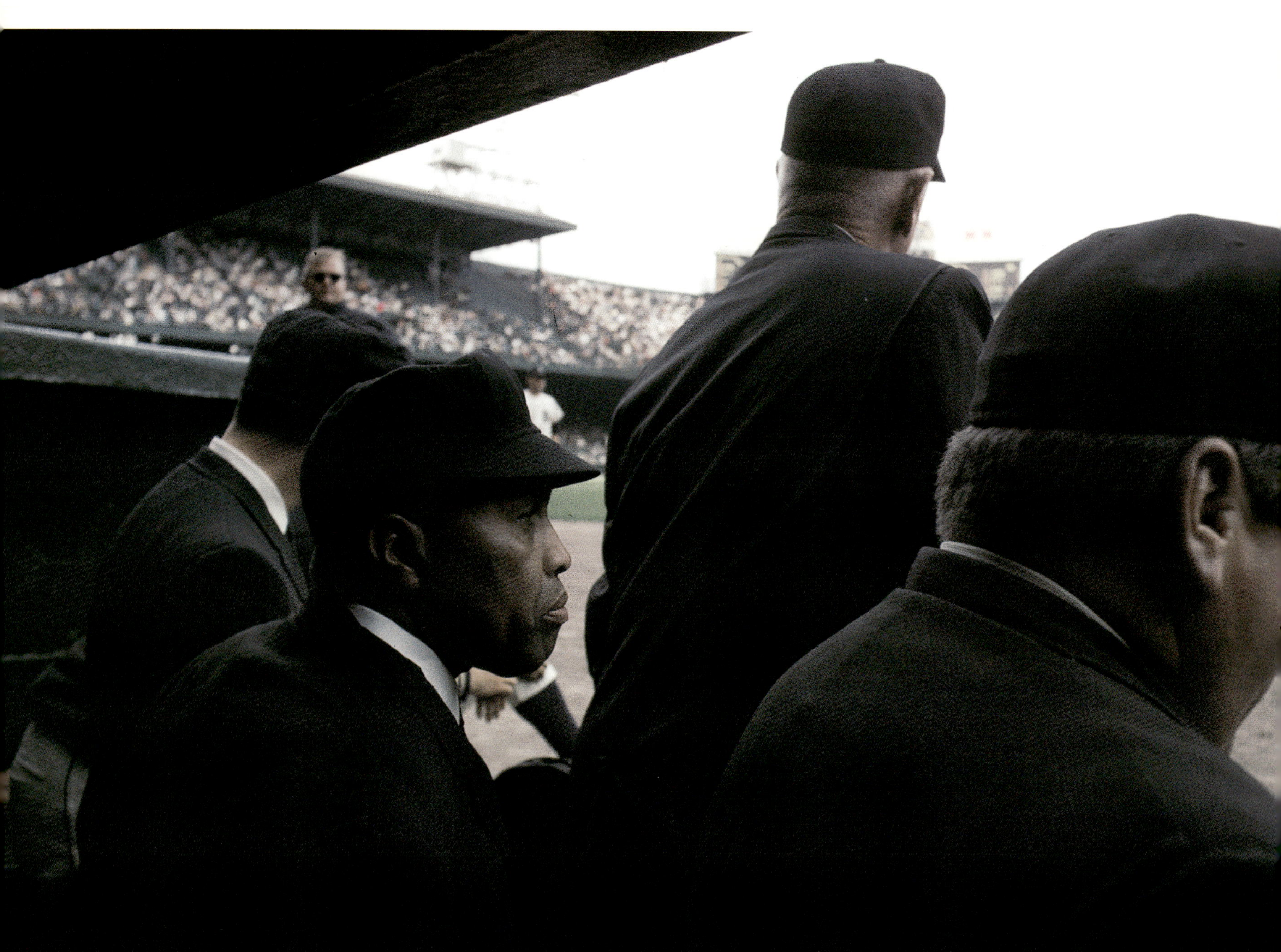

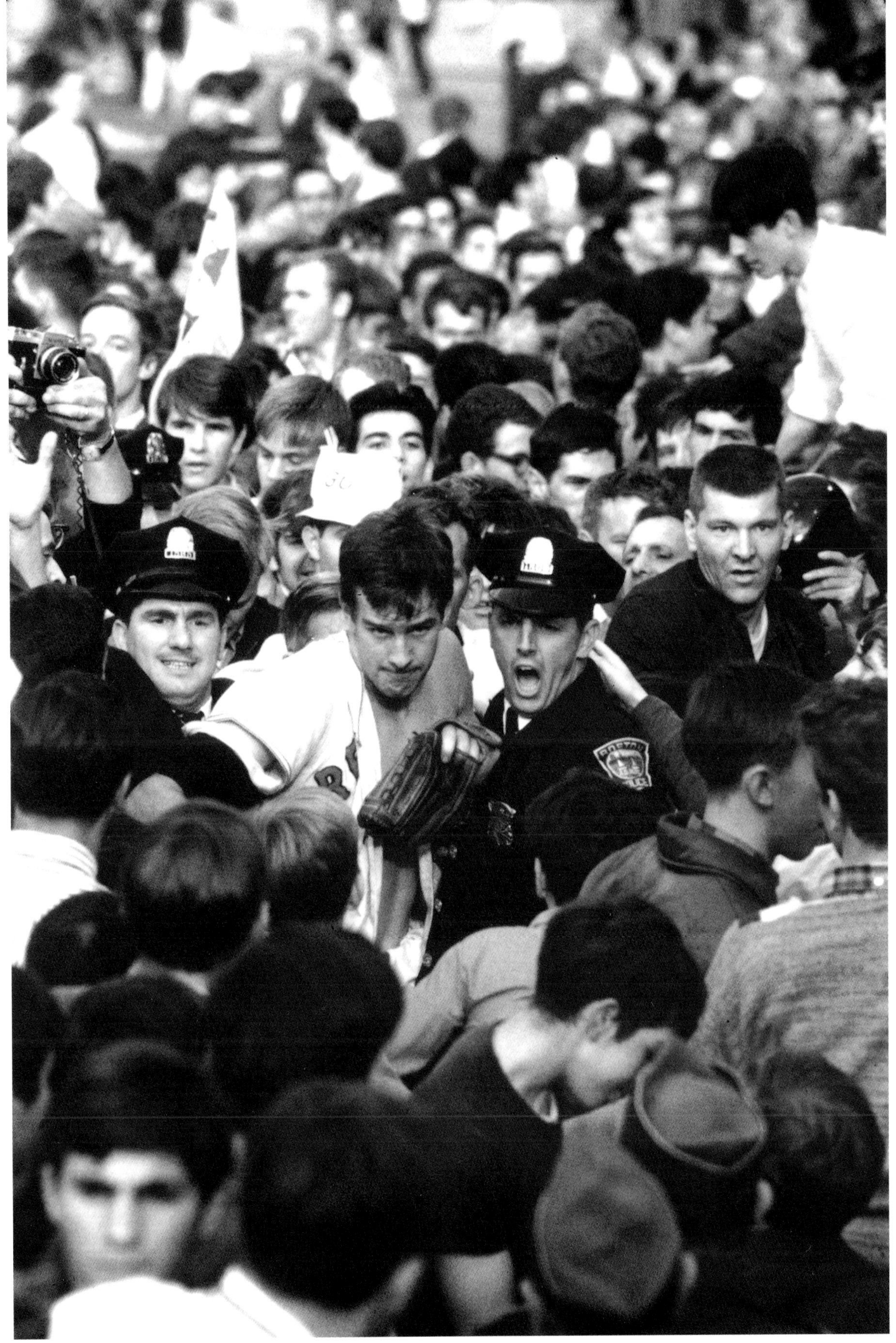

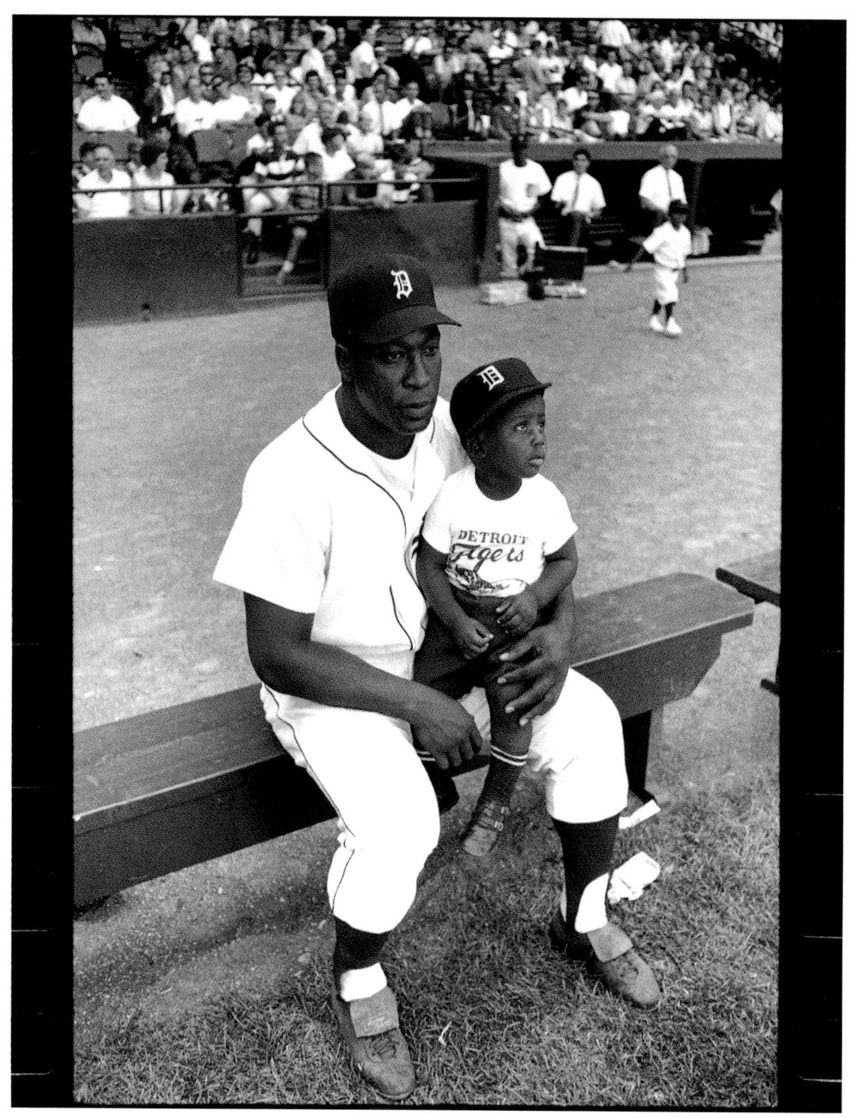

GATES BROWN and son, Tiger Stadium, Detroit, Family Day, 1966

PHILLIES WIN WORLD SERIES, Philadelphia, 1980

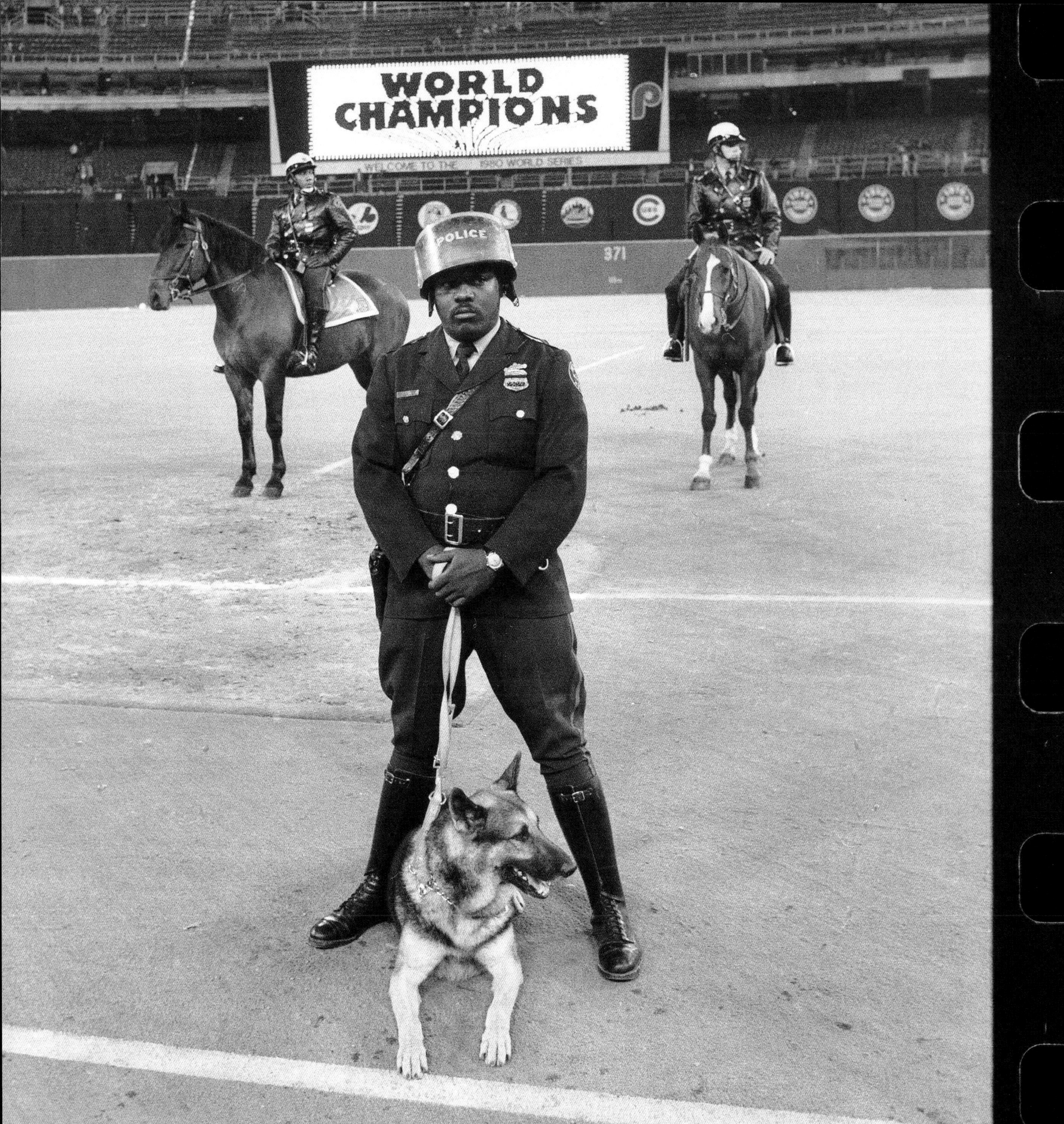
WORLD
CHAMPIONS
POLICE
371

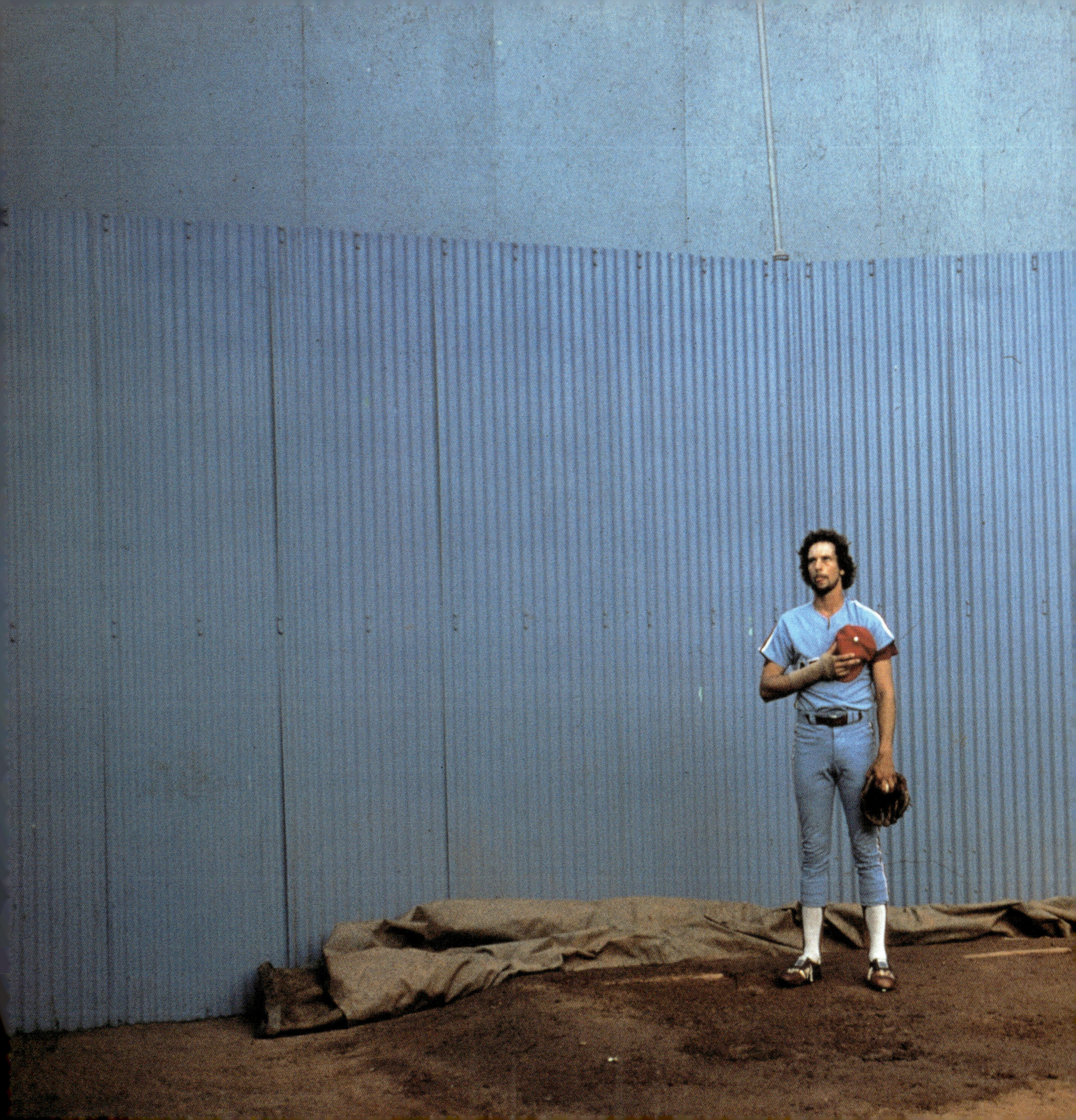

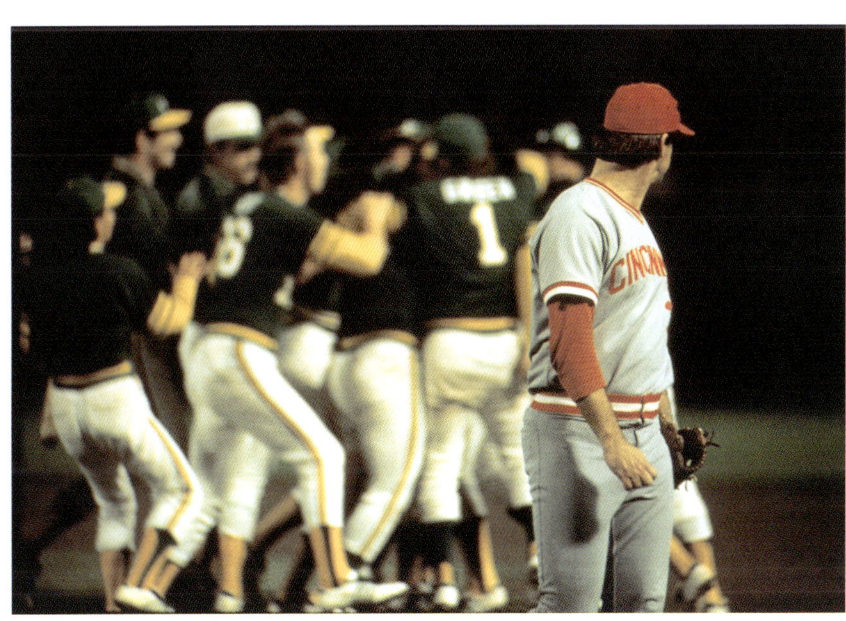

RANDY LERCH, Dodger Stadium, Los Angeles, 1979 (LEFT)

OAKLAND VS. CINCINNATI WORLD SERIES, Oakland–Alameda Stadium, Oakland, California, 1972 (ABOVE)

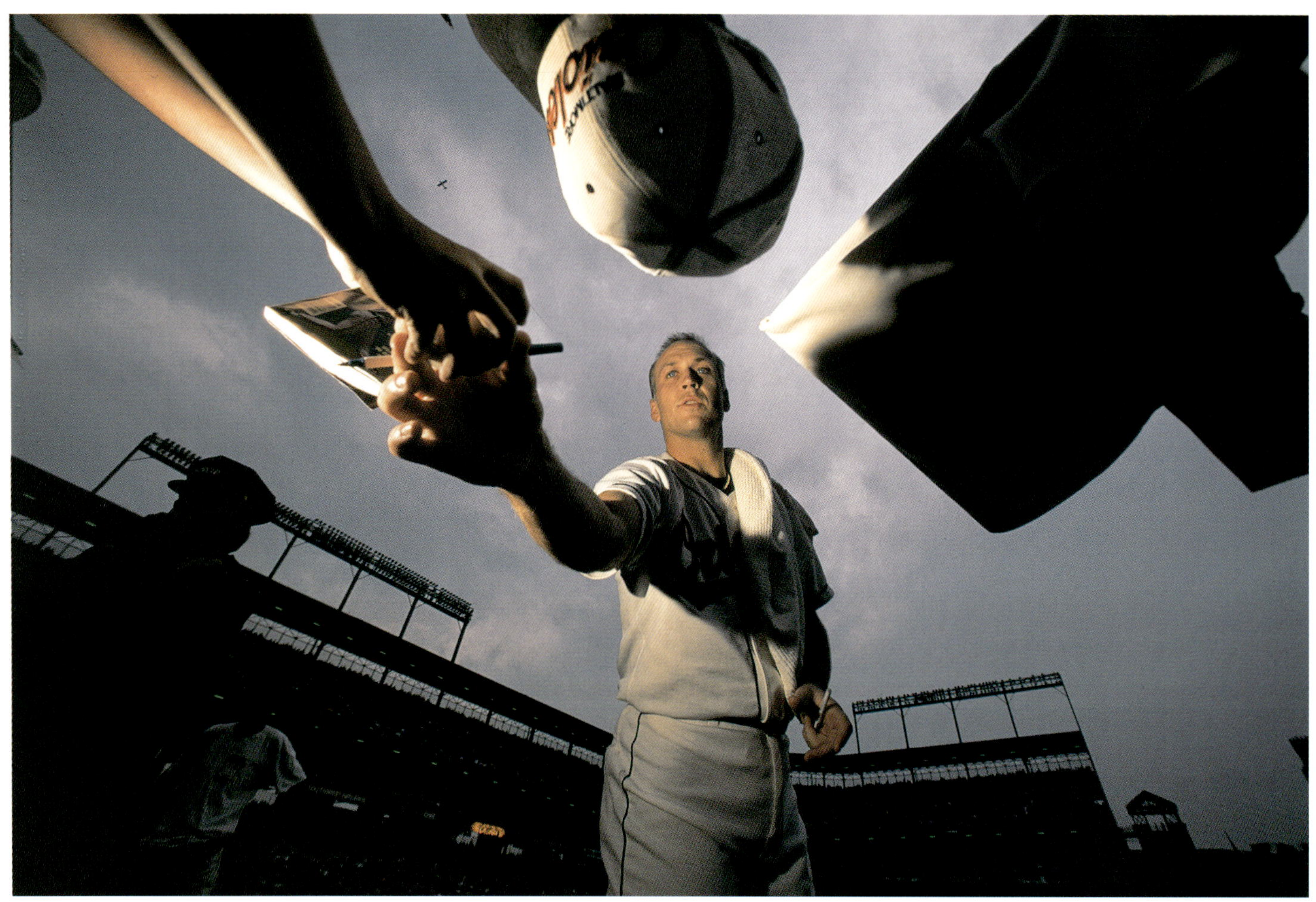

CAL RIPKEN JR., Baltimore, 1995

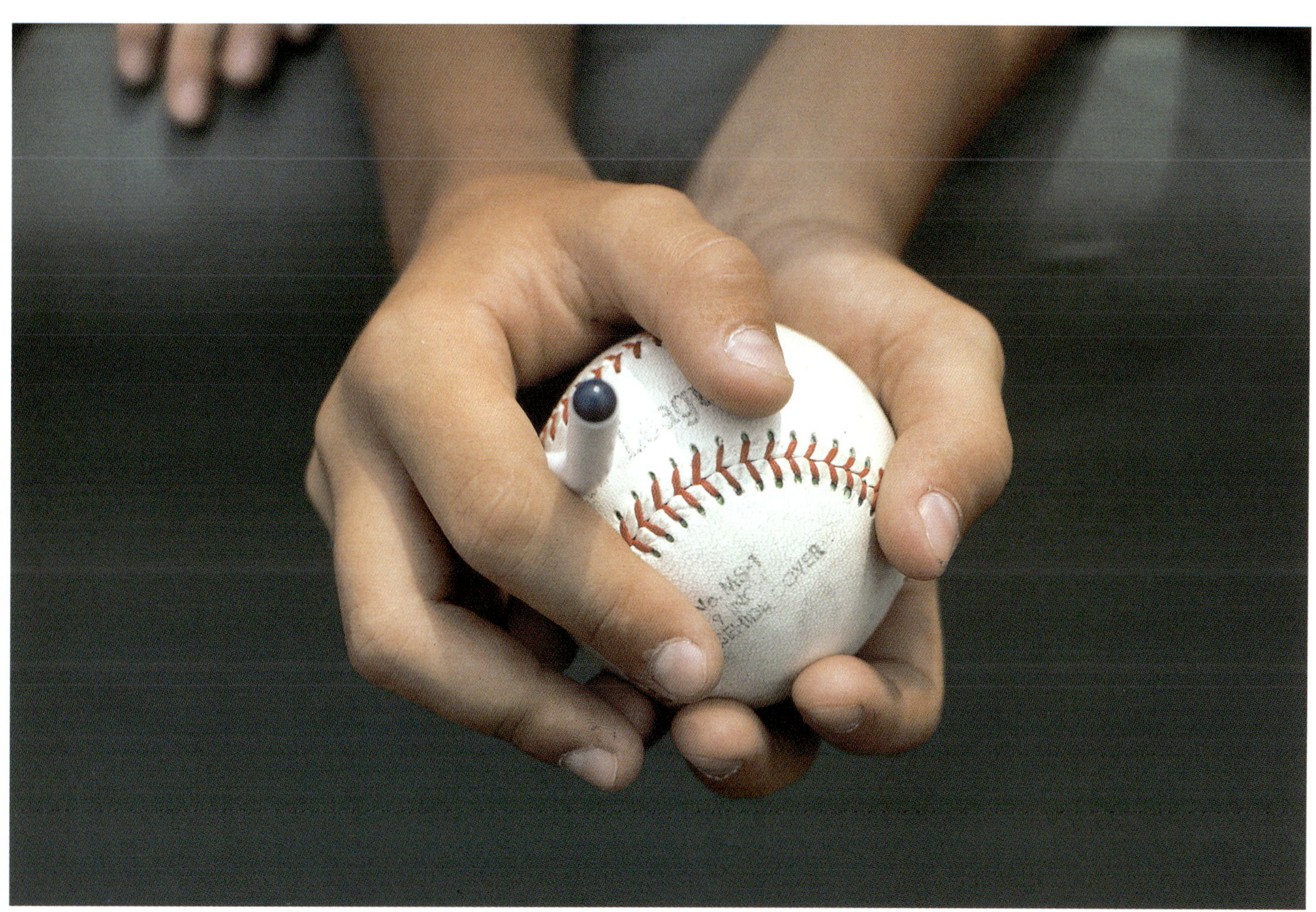

AUTOGRAPH SEEKER, Boston, 1979

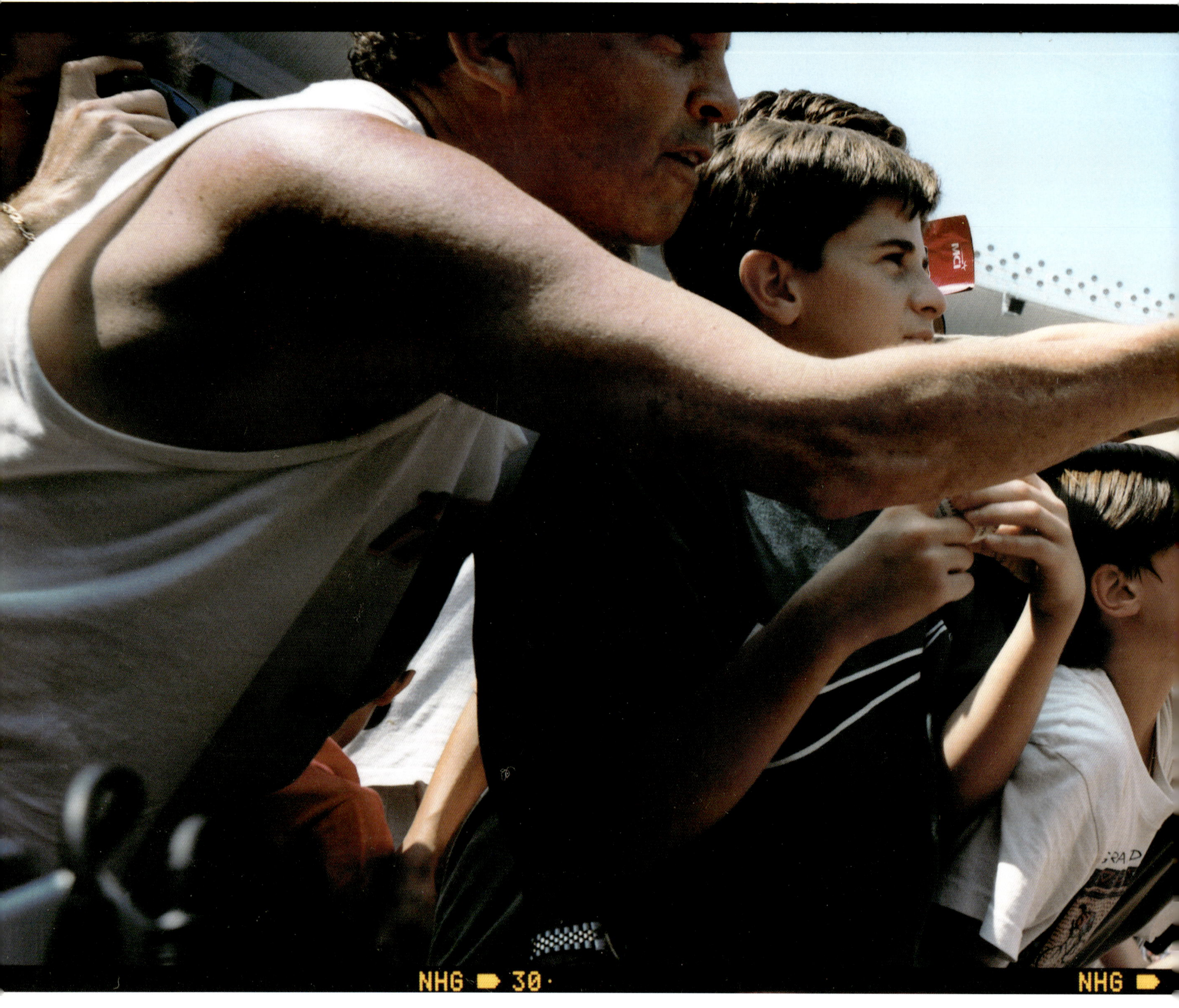
MCI
NHG 30
NHG

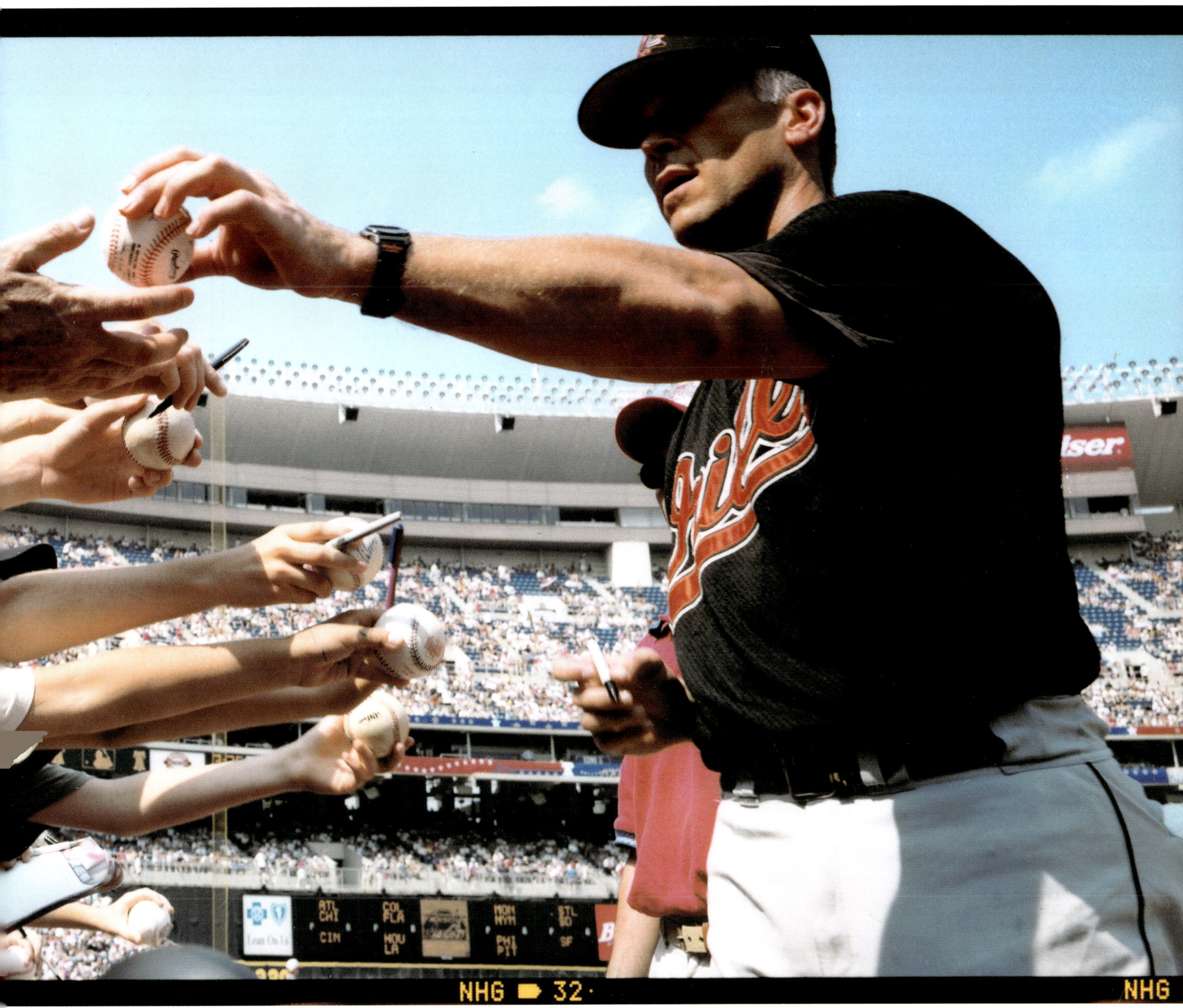

CAL RIPKEN JR., All-Star Game, Philadelphia, 1996

EDITOR: Robert Morton
DESIGNER: Michael J. Walsh Jr.
PRODUCTION MANAGER: Stanley Redfern

LIBRARY OF CONGRESS CATALOGING-IN-PUBLICATION DATA

IOOSS, WALTER.
CLASSIC BASEBALL : THE PHOTOGRAPHS OF WALTER IOOSS JR. / TEXT BY DAVE ANDERSON.
P. CM.
INCLUDES BIBLIOGRAPHICAL REFERENCES AND INDEX.
ISBN 0-8109-4258-5 (HC)
1. PHOTOGRAPHY OF SPORTS. 2. BASEBALL—PICTORIAL WORKS. 3. IOOSS, WALTER.
I. ANDERSON, DAVE. II. TITLE.
TR821 .I64 2003
779'.9796357'092—DC21
2002008850

PUBLISHED IN 2003 BY HARRY N. ABRAMS, INCORPORATED, NEW YORK

PRINTED AND BOUND IN JAPAN
10 9 8 7 6 5 4 3 2

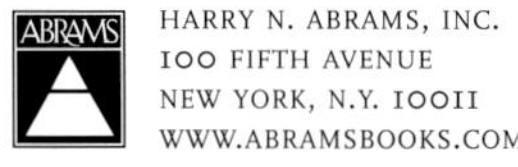

HARRY N. ABRAMS, INC.
100 FIFTH AVENUE
NEW YORK, N.Y. 10011
WWW.ABRAMSBOOKS.COM

ABRAMS IS A SUBSIDIARY OF

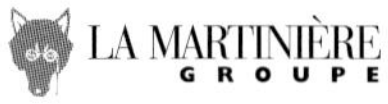

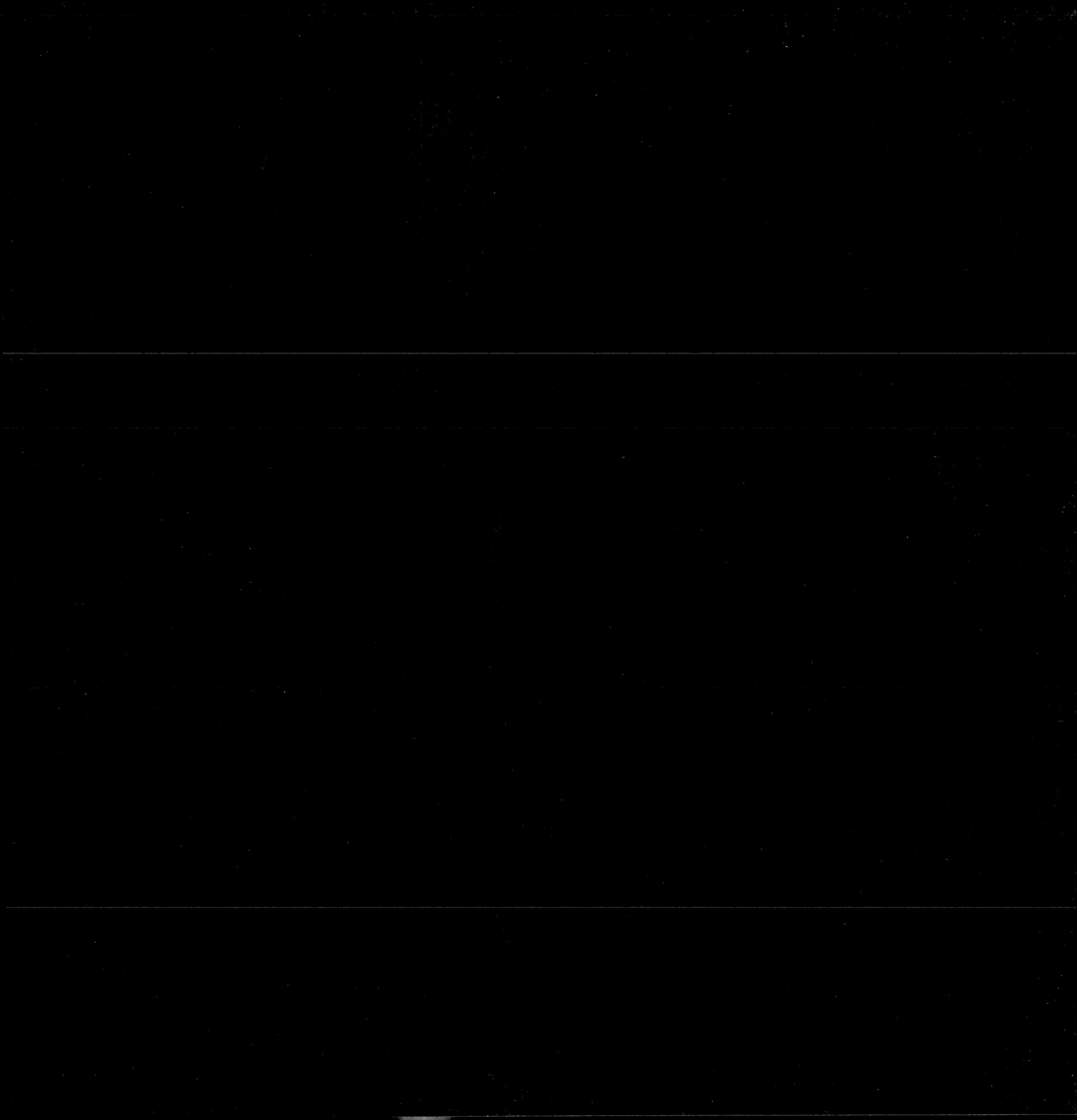

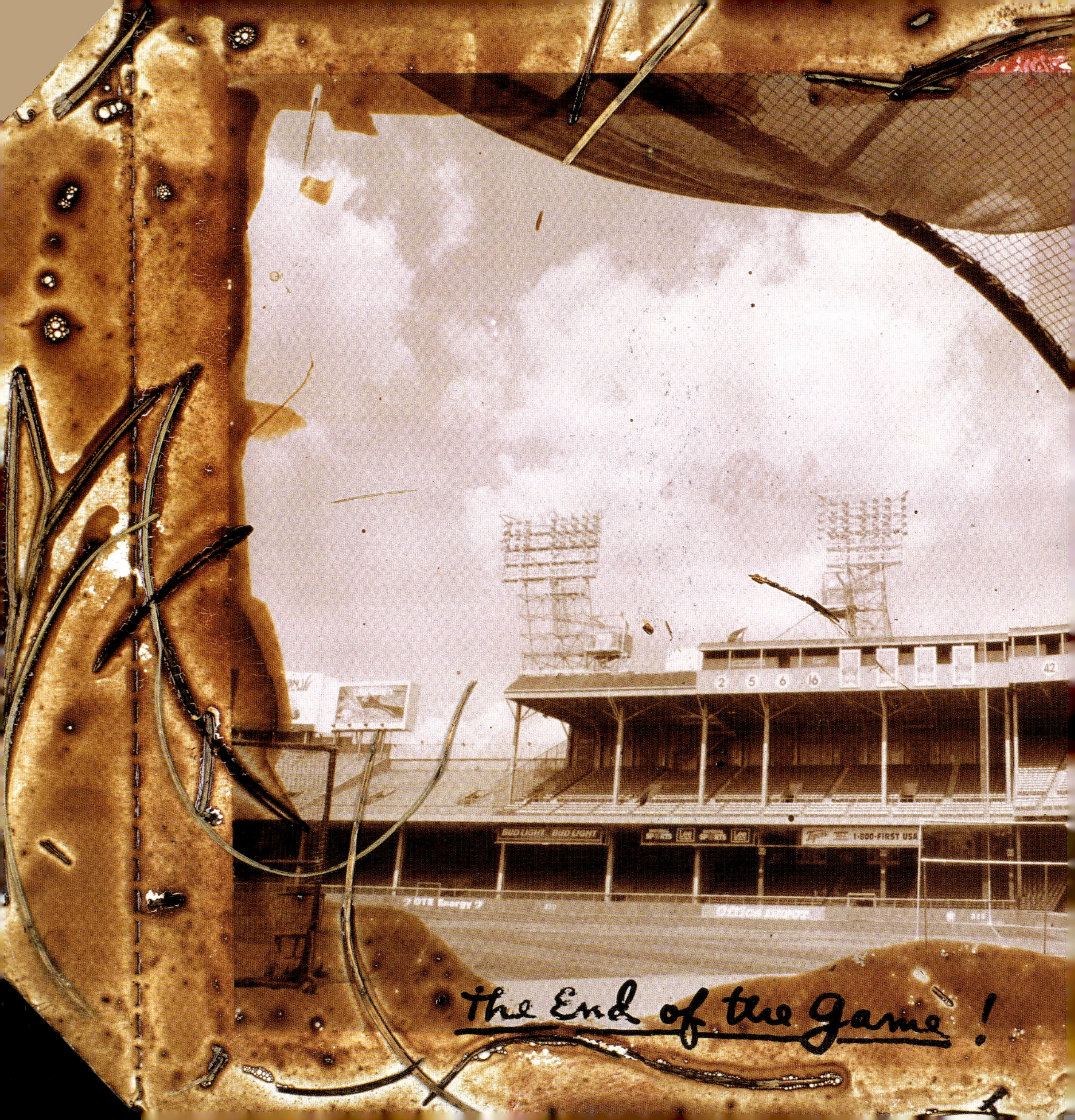
BUD LIGHT BUD LIGHT
1-800-FIRST USA
DTE Energy
The End of the Game!